Sport and Gender in Canada

Sport and Gender in Canada

Edited by Philip White and Kevin Young

OXFORD
UNIVERSITY PRESS

OXFORD
UNIVERSITY PRESS

70 Wynford Drive, Don Mills, Ontario M3C 1J9

www.oup.com/ca

Oxford New York
Auckland Bangkok Buenos Aires Cape Town Chennai
Dar es Salaam Delhi Hong Kong Istanbul Karachi Kolkata
Kuala Lumpur Madrid Melbourne Mexico City Mumbai Nairobi
São Paulo Shanghai Singapore Taipei Tokyo Toronto

Oxford is a trade mark of Oxford University Press

Canadian Cataloguing in Publication Data

Main entry under title:

Sport and gender in Canada

Includes bibliographical references and index.

ISBN 0-19-541317-2

1. Sex discrimination in sports – Canada.   2. Sports – Social aspects – Canada.
I. White, Philip, 1952– .   II. Young, Kevin Mark, 1959– .

GV706.5.S657 1999   306.4'83   C99-931337-1

Designer: Tearney McMurtry
Cover Photographs: Girls' Hockey Team, Moss Park (RG 8-52-998),
Boys' Basketball Team (RG 8-52-1369). Arthur Goss, photographer.
Courtesy of City of Toronto Archives

Copyright © Oxford University Press Canada 1999

3 4 — 05 04 03

This book is printed on permanent (acid-free) paper ∞

Printed in Canada

For Anne, Jill, Nicholas, Andy, Nicole, and Stephen

Contents

Acknowledgements

We would like to thank the contributors to *Sport and Gender in Canada* for their flexibility and patience in responding to our editorial requests and suggestions. Thanks are also due to Valerie Ahwee, Laura Macleod, Euan White, and Phyllis Wilson at Oxford University Press for guiding us through the process of putting this book together. They demonstrated professionalism, support, and humour at every turn. We are grateful to the anonymous reviewers whose fair and constructive reaction to an earlier draft improved the book considerably. Of course, the conventional caveat applies—any mistakes and shortcomings remain our own. For their help and support in our respective 'workplaces', we also gratefully acknowledge Mary Cleland, Krista Denholm, Rosalie Goodwin, Deanna Goral, and Elvia Horvath of the Department of Kinesiology at McMaster University, and the Calgary Institute for the Humanities at the University of Calgary. Finally, we would like to thank those from whom we have learned most about our own gendering. In this respect, our gratitude and love go out to Anne, Jill, Nicholas, Andy, Nicole, and Stephen, who have taught us more than any research we have done or books we have read.

The publisher would like to thank the following for permission to reproduce previously published material:

About the Authors

Anouk Bélanger is a doctoral candidate in the School of Communication at Simon Fraser University. She completed a Master's degree in sociology at the University of Montréal. Anouk is currently working on her dissertation on sport and popular culture in Montréal entitled 'Where have the Ghosts Gone? Hockey and the Remaking of Popular Memory in a Global Landscape.'

Jamie Bryshun received his undergraduate degree in sociology at the University of Saskatchewan and his MA in sociology at the University of Calgary. Entitled 'Hazing in Sport: An Exploratory Study of Veteran/Rookie Relations', Jamie's Master's thesis is one of the first in-depth examinations of hazing rituals in a range of sport in Canada. Jamie is a former football player and a qualified coach of football and basketball.

Caroline Davis is an associate professor in the Department of Kinesiology and Health Science and in the graduate program in psychology at York University. Caroline also holds an adjunct appointment as associate professor in the Department of Psychiatry at the Toronto Hospital and on the Faculty of Medicine at the University of Toronto. She has published extensively in the areas of eating disorders, diet, body image, and exercise.

Peter Donnelly is a professor in the Faculty of Physical Education and Health at the University of Toronto and director of the Centre for Canadian Sport Policy. His current research interests include various aspects of sport and social inequality, particularly the combined effects of social class, gender, age, and heritage on access to involvement in sport and physical activity. He is also interested in the problems experienced by children in high-performance sport.

M. Ann Hall is a professor emeritus at the University of Alberta and a visiting research fellow at De Montford University in England where she occasionally lectures. She has written extensively on the topic of women in sport and has presented papers at dozens of conferences internationally. Her most recent book is *Feminism and Sporting Bodies: Essays on Theory and Practice*. Ann serves on the editorial board of several academic journals, and is coeditor of the 'Sport and Culture' book series published by the University of Minnesota Press. She is presently completing a book on the history of women's sport in Canada.

Jean Harvey is a professor in the School of Human Kinetics/Ecole des Sciences de L'activité Physique at the University of Ottawa. From 1992 to 1998 he also served as associate dean of research in the Faculty of Health Sciences. Jean has written extensively on topics such as social theory applied to sport, sport and politics, sport and social inequalities, and sport and globalization. He is the principal investigator on a current research project investigating Canadian sport and leisure industries in the context of globalization.

Jennifer Hoyle is a lecturer in the Department of Women's Studies at Brock University. She received her MA in sociology at McMaster University. Her thesis examined the leisure experiences of women with disabilities.

Helen Jefferson Lenskyj is professor of education, and physical education and health at the University of Toronto. She has written three books and numerous scholarly and popular articles on women, sport, and sexuality, and on related social justice issues in sport and recreation. In her research, Helen has analysed homophobia and heterosexism in sporting practices, the sport media, and the sport sciences. She has also investigated community involvement in the Olympic bid process and is currently examining power dynamics in the organization of the Gay Games.

Margaret MacNeill is an assistant professor in the Faculty of Physical Education and Health at the University of Toronto. She teaches courses in the sociology, history, and media studies of sport and physical activity. Her research interests include gender issues in health communication, athletes' rights, and Olympic media studies.

Jim McKay teaches courses on gender, sport, and popular culture in the Department of Anthropology and Sociology at the University of Queensland, Australia. He is the editor of the *International Review for the Sociology of Sport*. His most recent books are *No Pain, No Gain? Sport and Australian Culture*, *Managing Gender: Affirmative Action and Sport*, and, with Michael Messner and Donald Sabo, *Men, Masculinities, and Sport*.

Sandra O'Brien Cousins is a professor in the Faculty of Physical Education and Recreation at the University of Alberta, and an expert on 'healthy' aging through physical activity. Since 1995 she has been research guardian of ALCOA, Canada's Active Living Coalition for Older Adults. She is associate editor for the *Journal of Aging and Physical Activity*. Sandra has two forthcoming books. The topic of the first is motivation—*Exercise, Aging and Health: Overcoming Barriers to an Active Old Age*. Her current work is a companion piece to Canada's Food Guide— *The Canadian Guide to Older Adult Physical Activity*.

Victoria Paraschak is an associate professor in the School of Human Kinetics at the University of Windsor. She spent five years in the Northwest Territories as a participant observer in community and territorial sport, which included working as a policy officer for the Government of the Northwest Territories Sport and Recreation Division. Victoria has also examined sporting practices on the Six Nations reserve in Ontario. Her research addresses the social construction of indigenous cultural practices, power relations underlying these practices, and the ability of Native peoples to be self-governing. She has recently published articles on variations in Native race relations, Native women in sport, and Native images in multisport festivals in Canada.

Brian Pronger is the author of *The Arena of Masculinity: Sports, Homosexuality and the Meaning of Sex* and is a leading expert on male homosexuality in sport and physical education. He publishes on postmodern theories of the body, desire, sexuality, gender, sport, and physical fitness, as well as the philosophy of science and technology. He is assistant professor of Physical Education at the University of Toronto, where he teaches in both undergraduate and graduate programs. He has been active in lesbian and gay politics for more than twenty years.

Patricia Vertinsky is professor and head of the Department of Educational Studies at the University of British Columbia. Author of *The Eternally Wounded Woman: Women, Doctors and Exercise in the Late Nineteenth Century*, her research interests focus upon the cultural and social construction of the gendered, aging, and racial body. She is currently president of the North American Society for Sport History.

Kevin Wamsley is an associate professor in the School of Kinesiology in the Faculty of Health Sciences at the University of Western Ontario. His research interests include leisure and the state in nineteenth-century Canada, sport and masculinity, and the Olympic Games. Along with publications in various North American and international journals, he has an edited book entitled *Method and Methodology in Sport and Cultural History*, is the co-editor of *Olympika*, and the director of the International Centre for Olympic Studies at the University of Western Ontario.

Philip White is a professor of kinesiology at McMaster University. His research interests are varied and include collaborative work with Kevin Young on gender and injury, violence, and physicality. He is also conducting research on the cultural significance of professional sport franchises for the community, the impact of recreation drop-in centres on the lives of inner-city youth, and factors that predict adult involvement in physical activity. Phil coaches the Ontario Women's Rugby team and the McMaster Varsity Men's Rugby team. In 1997 he coached the Canadian Men's Rugby team at the Maccabiah Games in Israel.

Brian Wilson is a doctoral candidate in sociology at McMaster University. His research interests include media representations of race and gender, audience studies, youth culture, and sport sociology generally. Brian is currently writing his dissertation entitled 'Sanctuaries in the City: Studies of Youth Culture in Canada', which examines the culture of 'at risk' youth in recreation/drop-in centres, and the 'rave' subculture. Brian participates on a community level in initiatives focused on youth violence and violence in amateur sport.

Kevin Young is an associate professor at the University of Calgary where he teaches and researches in such areas as sport, crime, youth, and mass media. In recent publications, he has examined topics as diverse as sport-related violence and litigation issues, female athletes and aggression, and the Canadian skinhead subculture. He and Philip White continue their collaborative work on pain and injury in sport. Kevin has served on the editorial board of the *Sociology of Sport Journal*, is currently on the editorial board of *Avante*, and has completed two terms as member-at-large for the North American Society for the Sociology of Sport.

Preface

Research on how sport is 'gendered' represents one of the fastest areas of growth in sport studies in the last few decades, with Canadian scholars often occupying a leading role. Coinciding with the broad progress of the women's movement, and also with the international successes of élite Canadian female athletes, such as ice hockey player Manon Rheaume, rower Silken Laumann, biathlete Miriam Bedard, wrestler Christine Nordhagen, and speed skaters Susan Auch and Catriona LeMay Doan, a number of gender-related issues have taken centre stage. A burgeoning literature has emerged on an array of topics such as equity issues, funding, violence, injury, drug use, abuse and harassment, health and illness, and homophobia. Scholars, journalists, sport officials, politicians, and athletes themselves have all been involved in debates on these issues, and research is being undertaken in a wide range of fields, including sociology, physical education/ kinesiology, women's studies, men's studies, cultural studies, and gay studies. This growing body of knowledge is making greater sense of how gender operates as a key factor in the way sport is played, organized, and funded.

To date, collected works on sport and gender have been primarily American (cf., Birrell and Cole 1994; Cohen 1993; Costa and Guthrie 1994; Messner and Sabo 1990). Though there are also some excellent Canadian sources available (cf., Gruneau and Whitson 1993; Hall 1996; Lenskyj 1986; Pronger 1990), research on gender conducted by Canadian sport scholars (who feature prominently among researchers worldwide) has been published disparately in a variety of journals and books. Little or no attempt has been made to generate order within the field or to take stock of recent developments in Canadian sport. As university instructors, we have been frustrated and discouraged by the lack of appropriate and, equally importantly, accessible sources available for our students and our courses, especially at the undergraduate level. This anthology goes some way towards filling this gap by publishing the work of leading Canadian researchers in one volume. In brief, given the rapid growth of the field, the increasing number of university and college courses focusing on sport and gender, and the number and quality of Canadian scholars working in the area, the time seems right for a specialized anthology that addresses the interface between sport and gender.

The main goal of this book is to show how sport in Canada has been and remains ordered in such a way that it is experienced differently by girls and boys, women and men, and gays and straights. While inquiry into sport and gender might seem relatively straightforward—after all, Canadian sport remains an area dominated by heterosexual males—we will explore perhaps less recognized facets of sport and gender, including aspects of sexuality, that expose how inequality is maintained and produced over time.

As an introduction to how the relationship between sport and gender can be complex and even paradoxical, consider first that sport experiences for Canadians, whether male or female, straight or gay, can be both liberating and constraining, even at the same time. For example, through long struggle women have torn down many barriers that previously limited their involvement. Greater numbers of girls and women are participating in sport now than ever before, and their involvement has enabled them to experience their bodies boundlessly, powerfully, and, *crucially*, in community with other girls and women. For instance, for the first time in Canadian Olympic history, most of the Canadian delegates at the 1996 Atlanta Games were female, and girls and women are increasingly participating in sports traditionally defined as 'male preserves' (such as rowing, ice hockey, rugby, soccer, and wrestling). Conversely, there are areas within sport that apparently remain closed to women, or where women's participation remains ridiculed, marginalized, and still viewed with suspicion. Here, sport is more likely experienced by females as negative, restrictive, or even hostile. Given these two outcomes or, more realistically, combinations of experiences that fit somewhere between the two, it is important to recognize the potential of sport for contributing to progressive change in the lives of all athletes, regardless of gender or sexual identity.

In assembling a collection of readings on sport and gender, we were concerned that the book should be a unified whole rather than a series of individual 'takes' on a cluster of scattered sport topics. Thus, while this particular collection of papers is varied in its adoption of a range of interdisciplinary approaches and its use of different methods, the chapters are centred around one overarching organizing principle—the position that gender is a central way in which sport is stratified.

As Ann Hall points out, there are at least three different levels of analysing the gender process in sport:

> (a) *categoric research*, with a primary focus on quantifying and empirically studying sex or race differences in athletic participation, performance, and abilities, and attempting to explain their existence in terms of biological factors and socialization; (b) *distributive research*, which examines the distribution of resources (e.g., competitive opportunities, coaching positions, administrators, income levels, sponsorship) and focuses on inequality in opportunities, access, and financial resources; and (c) *relational analyses*, which begin with the assumption that sporting practices are historically produced, socially constructed, and culturally defined to serve the interests and needs of powerful groups in society (Hall 1996:11).

While each of these approaches has its own strengths, and while they are far from mutually exclusive, the readings in this volume mostly emphasize the usefulness of distributive and relational perspectives on sport and gender. That is, they move beyond the recognition of biological differences between males and females to more significant questions of equality, power, meaning, and change *both between and within* males and females. This latter point is key because it underlines the fact that the terrain of gender is complex, contested, and historically shifting. Indeed, while several of the chapters indicate that power differences between males and females in sport have remained relatively stable over time and that the balance of power continues to privilege men's involvement and marginalize women's involvement, others are far more indicative of gender-related struggle, resistance, and change in sport. In this respect, this book demonstrates that sport has an important part to play in both the reproduction *and* transformation of social processes and social structures.

In Canada we are fortunate to have a number of scholars whose work represents the cutting edge of research on sport and gender. This book is an acknowledgement and celebration of this intellectual wealth and provides a venue for scholars to communicate the latest developments in their work. Because we are aware of the charge that academic writing can be dry and obscure, every effort has been made to make each chapter accessible both to students and to the lay reader.

The book is divided into two main sections. In Part I we place sport and gender in an historical and conceptual framework. This is important for two reasons. First, the fact that sport remains profoundly influenced by gender can only be understood by looking back to how sport came to exist in Canada, and how some social groups had more to say in both the organization and rules of the game and also the meanings of involvement. For example, Gruneau and Whitson's (1993) wonderfully rich account of the social roots of Canadian ice hockey shows how early participants were overwhelmingly males from the middle and upper classes who borrowed ideas and meanings from sports like field hockey, lacrosse, and rugby to create a 'manly' rough-and-tumble game. In other words, it is evident that ice hockey has been gendered in a masculinist direction from the beginning. Second, it is also important to consider theoretical and conceptual approaches in order to go beyond merely describing the relationship between sport and gender to *explaining* and *interpreting* this relationship. It is not enough, for example, to know that fist-fighting in hockey is closely connected to prevailing norms of manliness—it is also important to understand *why* that relationship has been and remains so culturally meaningful to many Canadians, including, interestingly enough, females as well as males.

In Part II, the largest section of the book, the contributors explore and bring evidence to bear on a number of substantive issues within sport, all of which exhibit clearly gendered underpinnings. Among other matters, these chapters show how the relationship between sport and gender is a fundamentally sociological one that interfaces with other social phenomena such as race, ethnicity, and sexuality. In the latter of these cases, for example, it is shown that as a relatively conservative area of social life, sport has to a large extent been guilty of harbouring and even promoting homophobic attitudes and practices. When examined through the lens of gender and power, we learn that homophobia in sport affects sport organizations and practices in deeply insidious ways. And we also learn that sport is filled with contradictions in, for instance, the way it may at times provide an unfriendly environment for lesbians, but at others provide a community of support.

Though dominated by what might best be characterized as sociological, feminist, and cultural studies perspectives, the anthology represents a number of social scientific disciplines including not only sociology but also history, anthropology, and psychology. Likewise, the book also promotes the adoption of diverse methodological approaches in studying gender. For example, the varied methods used by the contributors include survey and archival research, ethnography, in-depth interviews, participant observation, semiotics/content analysis, and laboratory experimentation. However, regardless of the approach taken, as sociologists we primarily endorse the use of what C. Wright Mills (1959) called a 'sociological imagination', which can be witnessed in the critical and/or reflexive orientation that most of the contributors bring to their assessment of the way sport is organized and ordered according to certain types of 'gender logic' (Coakley 1998:9). In this respect, our aim is to highlight and critically challenge dominant and prevailing assumptions about gender and sport. It is very important to us that readers do not misunderstand our position in these matters of approach. While critical in a sociological sense, this is not an anti-sport book. Neither is it 'anti-men', though it does not accept patriarchy and other social structures that prohibit, constrain, or otherwise compromise the ability of sport to play a healthy and meaningful role in the lives of participants.

Sport and Gender in Canada, then, is a state-of-the-art report by Canadian scholars on the relationship between sport and gender at the end of the twentieth century. By outlining the state of extant research in Canada, the ultimate objective of this book is not only to illuminate the complex ways in which sport and gender intersect but also to work towards progressive social change. Finally, while we acknowledge that the sport processes discussed here reflect primarily Canadian society, we suspect that these Canadian experiences may speak to gendering dynamics in other societies and cultures where girls and boys, women and men, and straights and gays play sport. With this in mind, our hope is that this book is a useful resource for those interested in sport and gender specifically, or gender more generally both within and beyond Canada.

References

Birrell, S., and C. Cole. 1994. *Women, Sport and Culture*. Champaign, IL: Human Kinetics.

Coakley, J. 1998. *Sport in Society: Issues and Controversies*, 6th edn. New York: Irwin McGraw Hill.

Cohen, G. 1993. *Women in Sport: Issues and Controversies*. Newbury Park, CA: Sage.

Costa, D., and S. Guthrie, eds. 1994. *Women and Sport: Interdisciplinary Perspectives*. Champaign, IL: Human Kinetics.

Gruneau, R., and D. Whitson. 1993. *Hockey Night in Canada: Sport, Identities and Cultural Politics*. Toronto: Garamond.

Hall, M.A. 1996. *Feminism and Sporting Bodies: Essays on Theory and Practice*. Champaign, IL: Human Kinetics.

Lenskyj, H. 1986. *Out of Bounds: Women, Sport & Sexuality*. Toronto: The Women's Press.

Messner, M., and D. Sabo, eds. 1990. *Sport, Men & the Gender Order: Critical Feminist Perspectives*. Champaign, IL: Human Kinetics.

Mills, C.W. 1959. *The Sociological Imagination*. London: Oxford University Press.

Pronger, B. 1990. *The Arena of Masculinity: Sports, Homosexuality and the Meaning of Sex*. New York: St Martin's Press.

Part I:

Historical and Conceptual Issues

Before moving on to an exploration of contemporary Canadian research on the relationship between sport and gender, we need to begin by situating this relationship historically. It is important that we do not assume that the way sport is currently organized, played, and funded along gender lines reflects the way things have always been. While there may be some relative constants across time—there is more than enough evidence to suggest that males have been privileged in Canadian sport in ways that females have not—it should not be assumed, for example, that there has never been any opposition to this fact, that females have not participated in sport in any systematic way until recently, or that sport has reached all Canadian males in exactly the same way regardless of their social background, status, or identity.

In light of the organizing principles discussed in the Preface, we are suggesting two things here: (1) that the relationship between sport and gender has not developed in a smooth, uncontested, linear way that always privileges males and discriminates against females; and (2) that the relationship between sport and gender can best be understood sociologically by tracing the intersections between sport, gender, and other ways that Canadian life has been and remains stratified such as social class, age, race, ethnicity, and sexuality. Though the first three chapters represent individual approaches to this clearly complex relationship between sport, gender, and society, they underscore the overall framework of the book by using distributive and relational perspectives. In other words, they demonstrate that sport is affected by the distribution of resources and that sport is a cultural expression of broad social relations that go beyond gender to include social class.

The book begins with a feminist and critical perspective on the gendering of Canadian sport written by one of the leading figures in the field. In 'Creators of the Lost and Perfect Game? Gender, History, and Canadian Sport', Ann Hall traces the history of women's sport in Canada. She describes this history as a long process of cultural struggle through which women, both on and off the field, have had to fight to gain and maintain control over their sporting practices. Hall's chapter highlights both the ups and downs of women's sport participation across time. We learn, for example, that among other devices used (usually by men) to restrict women's involvement were crude, common, and by now familiar arguments about the potential damage to 'frail' female bodies. On the other hand, Hall also shows that women's sport in Canada is built on far stronger foundations than is often assumed, and that Canadian women's sport has a rich history, especially when it comes to team sports such as ice hockey and baseball. A key argument Hall makes, and one we would like to emphasize more broadly, is that the relationship between sport and gender is both *dynamic* and *processual*. In this sense, the history of women's sport in Canada should indeed be understood as a form of cultural struggle that has produced a series of 'victories' and 'defeats' across time according to different historical and social conditions.

Of course, if sport is infused with power relations as Hall suggests, then we would also expect the history of men's sport in a patriarchal society to be quite different in organization and content than that of women. Using empirical examples drawn from the eighteenth and nineteenth centuries, Kevin Wamsley's chapter shows this by underlining that sport was used both to create and confirm what he calls the 'public importance of men and the importance of public men'. But, at the same time, Wamsley argues that not all men were privileged by early Canadian sport practices. For instance, he outlines the process through which sport became an arena for the construction of particular types of masculinity, notably masculinities that helped reinforce the dominance of powerful groups of men. Again, we are reminded that gender is a complex and multidimensional phenomenon that can best be understood if we trace power differences not only between different groups of men and women but also between different versions of 'masculinity' and 'femininity' associated with particular social groups, social classes, and social settings.

The final chapter in Part I extends the notion that power is played out through gender relations by examining the relational interface between gender and social class in sport. Beginning from the premise that Canadian society—and thus Canadian sport—is far from 'classless', Peter Donnelly and Jean Harvey provide numerous examples to show that there 'have been major social class and gender inequalities throughout the history of sport'. These examples of inequality range from the professional level to amateur and community sport, and from the very top ranks of Canadian sport programs (including Sport Canada itself) to more loosely organized forms of recreation and physical activity. Using well-known Canadian programs such as ParticipACTION and

Active Living, Donnelly and Harvey argue that structural barriers to involvement in sport are best understood not by looking at gender in isolation but by examining how social processes more broadly intersect to reproduce structures of privilege and disadvantage. Once again, this sociological approach to understanding the relationship between sport and gender is a theme that runs throughout the book and links many of the substantive chapters that follow in Part II.

Chapter 1

Creators of the Lost and Perfect Game?
Gender, History, and Canadian Sport

M. Ann Hall

Pro football with 250-pound guided missiles capable of running four-second forty-yard dashes on a 100-yard postage stamp of a field, has turned into a kind of meso-morphic pinball; NHL hockey, as much a game of space as speed, is too often more of the same. NBA basketball, half the time a breathtaking nightly highlight package, for the other half is a pituitary, one-dimensional jamboree, with as many field goals being released above the rim as below, with jump shots clanging off the rims, and two guys playing one-on-one the rest of the game. In men's golf, prodigal übermensches like Tiger Woods have made the notion of par fives, and even fours, obsolete with 350-yard drives, and in tennis the 120-mile serve-and-volley game has turned the sport into a live-action Super Mario game that ends every seven seconds.

—J. Teitel, 'Shorter, Slower, Weaker'

Writing in *Saturday Night*, sportswriter Jay Teitel (1997) argues that while men have literally outgrown many of their traditional sports like basketball, hockey, golf, and tennis, women have been slowly growing into them. Male professional athletes, he suggests, have 'outstripped in size and speed the confines of the stan-dard playing spaces that define their games' and their sports are no longer as exciting or as fun to watch as they once were. Male athletes today are signifi-cantly bigger and stronger than they were before the days of highly commer-cialized and commodified professional sport, and they just don't seem to fit their spaces anymore.

Teitel (1997:63) writes: 'In their rudeness, their ego, the unseemly magnitude of their contracts, and their substitution of contempt for sportsmanship, a large percentage of male pro athletes today have become emotional misfits'. Robert Lipsyte (1995:56), a long-time commentator of sport in the United States, made much the same observation in a controversial article in *The New York Times*

Magazine a few years ago: 'Sports no longer reflect the America of our dreams, and the stars of sport are no longer the idealized versions of ourselves'. Along the way, he observed, 'those manly virtues of self-discipline, responsibility, altruism, and dedication seem to have been deleted from the athletic contract with America' (1995:52). In recent years we have witnessed umpires spat on, photographers kicked, female sport reporters harassed, an opponent's ear bitten, and a coach nearly strangled to death.

Women athletes, now experiencing more competitive and professional opportunities than ever, are seen to be playing the 'pure' game as it was played many decades ago. They are, declares Teitel, 'creators of the lost and perfect game'. Their exploits on the court or rink or field are more interesting to watch, more like the games of the past, and women athletes themselves are a reflection of the sincerity, sports*man*ship, humility, and love for the game that once was. Women, he argues, are rejuvenating sports that men have become too big to play. Lipsyte is not so sure. He agrees that a sport like women's basketball has become more appealing because of its reliance on finesse and teamwork, but at the same time he asks, 'what happens when all the women now coming into the arena display the same killer instincts that we thought were exclusive to men' (Lipsyte 1995:55)? He sees a new American gladiatorial class that goes beyond gender, social standing, or race and, like men, women athletes are not immune to the stress and strain of the athletic entertainment industry. Look, says Lipsyte, at anorexic gymnasts, teenagers burned out by tennis daddies, swimmers who are sexually exploited by male coaches, and the disgraced skating star Tonya Harding.

Sport commentators like Teitel and Lipsyte may be right, but they also show a stunning lack of understanding of how women athletes today benefit from years of struggle by their sisters in the past to break free of the stranglehold of *men's* sport. While proclaiming the unprecedented explosion in the popularity of women's sport towards the end of the twentieth century, they write as if it were occurring for the first time. They simply do not know their history. There was probably *more interest* in women playing sport (although by no means as many women competed) in the decades before the advent of television and its astonishing impact on men's professional sport than is apparent today. Yet, fifty and sixty years ago, sport commentators of the day warned that creeping commercialism would corrupt both women and their sport.

There are many reasons for the ebbs and flows in women's sport participation and spectatorship over the last century, and it is not hard to explain why men's sport has always been seen as the more legitimate version of the game. For example, witness the title of Teitel's piece, which is 'Shorter, Slower, Weaker'. Women athletes do not want to be seen as substitute males, something to be watched as a last resort. Rather, they want to be treated as athletes in their own right and not constantly compared to men. History helps us to understand why this has never seemed possible.

The history of modern sport, as in all areas of popular culture, is a history of cultural struggle. There have been numerous and often bitter conflicts in Canada over which sporting practices, styles, beliefs, and bureaucratic forms should predominate. Early Canadian sporting practices like lacrosse, played principally by Aboriginal peoples, were marginalized or incorporated into more 'respectable' and 'useful' ways of playing as the colonizers (primarily the British) imposed their particular sport on the colonized. Marginalized groups, like women and racial and ethnic minorities, have struggled to preserve their values and their ways of playing. Privileged groups in our society—seemingly by consent—are able to establish their own cultural practices as the most valued and legitimate, whereas subordinate groups (like women) have to fight to gain and maintain control over their own sport experience and at the same time have their alternative practices and activities recognized as legitimate by the dominant sporting culture. Sport in our culture is still viewed by many as a 'masculinizing project', a cultural practice in which boys learn to be men and male solidarity is forged. Sport has been and remains a prime site for the maintenance of masculine hegemony, which refers to the ways in which male power shapes our view of the world. As an explanatory tool, hegemony allows us to conceptualize resistance, and how dominant power groups seek to shape, manipulate, or control that resistance mainly by incorporating elements of resistance into the existing hegemonic structures. For example, when women actively participate in the symbols, practices, and institutions of sport, what they do there is often not considered 'real' sport, nor in some cases are they viewed as real women.

What follows from this notion of sport as a site of cultural struggle is that the history of women in sport is a history of cultural resistance. In fact, the very presence of women in the male preserve of sport is evidence of 'leaky hegemony' (Birrell and Theberge 1994). How masculine hegemony in early Canadian sport was resisted by women and, in turn, how their efforts were opposed and sometimes supported by men is the focus of this chapter. Women resisted popular notions of their biologically restricted bodies through their involvement in male-defined sport, but at the same time their physical emancipation was rarely without opposition, certainly from men, and sometimes from other women (Cahn 1994; Hargreaves 1994).

The Victorian women who ignored medical warnings regarding athletic activity were challenging the primacy of the uterus, and when they rode defiantly about on their 'safety bicycles' (ones with rubber tires) in their fashionable bloomers, they broke tradition and asserted their independence. Although the school games and sports that girls began to play at the end of the nineteenth century were intended to make them healthier and more fit for academic toil and ultimately motherhood, they nonetheless challenged the notion of the 'weaker sex'. Their new-found physical freedom of the 1920s and 1930s produced great women athletes like Suzanne Lenglen, Helen Wills, 'Babe' Didrikson, Gertrude Ederle, 'Bobbie' Rosenfeld, and so many others who were publicly admired, indeed treated like 'personalities,' in the new era of women's competitive sport. Despite this admiration, many newly trained women physical educators fought to keep women's sport as unlike men's and as far removed from male control as possible by advocating separate programs, teachers, coaches, and officials. They campaigned against all championships (including the Olympics), tournaments, and interscholastic competitions, denouncing them as unsuitable for young women who eventually would become wives and mothers. Despite these concerns, women's sport in countries not devastated by the Second World War was able to flourish. However, following the war, men's professional sport and its subsequent dependence on television brought us to where we are today, with less coverage and attention paid to women's sport than was true fifty or sixty years ago. Resistance, therefore, is never wholly successful, and it often does not result in progressive change. The point is that sport is an important though often overlooked or underestimated site for understanding the reproduction of (and resistance to) gender relations.

The history of both men's and women's sport in Canada is still somewhat fragmented. We know a great deal about the history of male sports—for example, hockey, football, baseball, golf, curling, figure skating, even cricket and lacrosse. We are now starting to gain an understanding of the rich history of some team sports played by women like hockey and baseball (see, for example, Avery and Stevens 1997; Browne 1992; Etue and Williams 1996; Howell 1995; Humber 1995; McFarlane 1994). We also know much more about the lives of outstanding male and female athletes who have distinguished themselves throughout the years. Not surprisingly, there are far more biographies and auto-biographies of Canadian male athletes than there are of women (but see Ferguson 1985; Long 1995; McDonald 1981). We also know a fair amount about famous Canadian teams, and again there is much more written about men's teams than women's. For instance, there is no book yet written about the inter-nationally famous Edmonton Grads who dominated women's basketball in Canada and elsewhere for over twenty years between 1919 and 1941. The Preston Rivulettes, a women's ice hockey team that compiled an unprecedented win-loss record of 348–2 in the 1930s also deserve to have their story told. Although the All-American Girls Professional Baseball League (1943–54) has received considerable attention through books, documentaries, and the film *A League of Their Own*, it is not well known that almost 10 per cent of the players came from Canada, mostly from the Prairies. They, too, deserve special atten-tion. There are doubtless many more fascinating stories of superb women's sport teams that remain unheard.

What you will read in this chapter is not a chronology of women's sport in Canada, nor is it an historical account of gender relations in Canadian sport. Rather, my purpose is to use several examples from the early days of Canadian sport to illustrate how gender relations actually worked. In the process I want to address the following questions. How did women's sport begin in Canada given that men had such a head start? Under what conditions did it start? How did women have to negotiate with men to have *their* sport recognized as legitimate? What choices did they have? How did men respond? Under what conditions did women's sport flourish? What were the central issues around which men and women agreed and disagreed? Were women in agreement with each other as their sport grew and developed?

Early Beginnings: The 'New Woman' and Athleticism

As New Woman on a bicycle, however, she exercised power more fundamentally, changing the conventions of courtship and chaperonage, of marriage and travel. As her sphere of influence broadened and her physical stamina increased, the focus of satire and caricature that recorded her development also changed. Rather than depicting women as fragile beings to be patronized for frivolous tastes, humorists joked about the Amazonian physique exercise produced and warned in mock horror about the inevitable submission of men (Marks 1990:174).

If there is a single factor that led to more women's participation in sport, exercise, and physical activity, it would be the introduction of the 'safety' bicycle in the mid-1880s. Unlike cumbersome earlier versions, the safety bicycle had two wheels of equal size cushioned by pneumatic rubber tires and was driven by a sprocket and chain. Women in billowing skirts could ride this new contraption, although they soon adopted much shorter styles, including the controversial bloomers with tight-fitting knee-length hose, or the more acceptable split skirt. They eagerly joined bicycle clubs, took lessons at special schools, and for the first time were free to go where they wanted, when they wanted, and with whom they wanted. As one historian has observed, 'it extended her sphere across the threshold, for in loosening her stays and dividing her skirts, the New Woman also took possession of her own movements and achieved a measure of self-confidence that carried her into the twentieth century' (Marks 1990:201). The bicycle offered women, at least those who could afford one and had the time to enjoy it, a means to enjoy exercise and good health, and a source of entertainment, transportation, and, above all, freedom (from a chaperone, for instance). It also helped to redefine the relationship between the sexes, certainly in their sporting lives. Here's how it came about.

Cycling, as well as other forms of women's exercise, was the cause of much debate in the 1890s among medical practitioners, both male and female. Some of the more positive authorities argued that cycling, especially in the open air, was invigorating for women's health because it encouraged them to dispose of their restrictive, damaging corsets; it strengthened their muscles, especially for childbirth, and it refreshed their mind and body. However, many others warned of the damage to the female reproductive system, including uterine displacement, the potential for masturbation caused by friction with the saddle, and the 'pelvic mischief' that would befall the poor woman who rode during her menstrual period (see Lenskyj 1983 and Vertinsky 1990). Little of this negative advice, of course, was backed up by medical research. Rather, it reflected the prevailing gender ideology of the time, which was that women had a moral duty to foster the traits of 'true womanhood'. This meant learning how to be a good wife and preserving their vital energy for childbearing (Lenskyj 1986). Women who rode bicycles and engaged in other forms of physical exercise were challenging myths about their supposed frailty and restrictive ideas about their eventual roles as wives and mothers.

They were also challenging widely held assumptions concerning the connections between sport, morality, and manliness. These were not new ideas—the concept of muscular or manly Christianity, which originated with the British novels of Charles Kingsley (*Westward Ho*, 1855) and Thomas Hughes (*Tom Brown's Schooldays*, 1857), had long since made its way across the Atlantic and become firmly entrenched in the curricula of boys' private schools with their emphasis on producing men of character through athleticism and team sports (Brown 1988). Among the early pioneers struggling to establish and maintain British culture in a foreign land, sport and team games like cricket, rugby football, and soccer were thought to nurture the manly qualities of robustness, mental vigour, determination, discipline, fair play, and integrity, and they were easily transplanted to reproduce values of the British Empire (Mott 1980). Historian Colin Howell (1995:5) shows how baseball in the Maritimes 'defined and consolidated notions of manhood, provided a form of social bonding, and brotherhood, and served to legitimate notions of male privilege'. The winter climate also afforded the opportunity to express a distinctly Canadian form of manliness through snowshoeing, curling, and ice hockey.

In the last decades of the nineteenth century, the notion of Christian manliness broadened considerably to encompass not only physical and moral development but success in later life, particularly in business. In 1892 R. Tait McKenzie, early Canadian physical educator, sculptor, and orthopaedic surgeon, wrote that rugby football 'cultivates pluck and determination in men'. He continued, 'the *sine qua non* of a good footballer is grit, and in after life the grit cultivated by the hard knocks will stand men in good stead in the contests of business or professional life' (McKenzie 1892). Another doctrine in vogue at the time was Social Darwinism, the belief that the concepts of natural selection, the survival of the fittest, or differentiation could be applied to both the animal and human worlds. Coupled with Muscular Christianity, Social Darwinism was entrenched in the private boys' schools of this period where those who survived the Spartan conditions and physically demanding activities were best suited to become the economic and political élite (Brown 1988).

Aside from the obvious role of manly sports in promoting nationalism, rectitude, and later success, why was this doctrine addressed to males but never to females? The answer lies in the strict Victorian dichotomy between *manliness* and *womanliness*. The former involved physical virility coupled with a Christian morality, ensuring influence and success in the public and economic spheres. Womanliness, on the other hand, embodied a feminine ideal, no doubt stressing an equally impeccable rectitude but also grace and beauty leading to mutual sharing and intimacy in the domestic sphere. Without sport, argued the moralists of the time, boys will become like women—delicate and effeminate: 'Flabby muscled boys become pliant men who only talk. Well developed boys become men who will say and act and produce results,' intoned the manual for the Canadian Standard Efficiency Tests, a program designed to promote intellectual, physical, religious, and social accomplishments among young boys.

Schools, churches, and other organizations also soon began to promote sport participation among male youth in particular. The Protestant churches, increasingly concerned about losing their male youth membership to commercialized forms of recreation, began organizing athletic teams, leagues, events, and special programs to attract young men (Howell and Lindsay 1986). Organizations like the Young Men's Christian Association (YMCA), the Boy Scouts, and Boys' Clubs all began to increase their emphasis on sport by building facilities, hosting events, and developing programs. Following the private schools' inordinate emphasis on athleticism, the public school system began to attach importance to nutrition, hygiene, and physical exercise. While military drill and discipline were still preferred, more emphasis was placed on organized games and sport by instituting interclass and interschool leagues.

Therefore, when women started riding bicycles in Canada in the 1890s, not only did they challenge the medical authorities whose world view was blind to active, vigorous, healthy, fit, and unrestricted sportswomen, they also became perceived as 'masculinized' in the sense that they entered the exclusively male domain of sport (also causing much consternation about the subsequent feminization of men). If women developed masculine interests, it was argued, this would mean that men in turn must learn to cultivate 'feminine' interests like running a household and minding children. Gender transference, as one writer put it, was the 'root fear behind complaints about women's athleticism' (Marks 1990:176).

Despite these objections, more and more women, at least those who could afford the costs and who had the time, began to participate in a variety of sports from figure skating, tobogganing, snowshoeing, skiing, curling, and ice hockey in winter to swimming, tennis, golf, field hockey, lawn bowling, equestrianism, mountaineering, sculling, and canoe racing in the summer (Hall 1968; Lenskyj 1986; Smith 1988). Games and sport began to appear in Canadian girls' private schools, although athleticism never acquired the same dominance it had over the boys' schools. Aggressive nationalism was not a feature of female education, and girls' games were rarely used for instilling discipline since the maintenance of order was not a problem as it sometimes was in similar schools for boys. As

McCrone (1988:89) suggests, 'games, therefore, were part of a systematic and quasi-social Darwinistic programme of measurement, medical inspection and physical training intended to make students healthier and so fitter for academic toil and ultimately motherhood'.

Within the public school curricula, there were calisthenics, marching drills, and a limited form of gymnastics for girls. Many schools began engaging physical training instructors, who were often military men, but soon women began to teach 'physical culture'. Sport was slowly introduced into the physical education curriculum. Gymnasiums and changing rooms were built especially for girls, and girls' school athletic associations took charge of the growing intramural sport programs (Gurney 1982). A plethora of articles, reports, lectures, and demonstrations about physical culture for women generated much greater public acceptance and even enthusiasm about the value of exercise for the so-called 'weaker' sex.

It was primarily through the playground movement, which began in the major urban centres before the First World War, that girls were exposed to the same sports as their brothers—ice hockey, basketball, baseball (eventually softball for the girls), and later track and field. By 1915, the city of Toronto, for example, had eleven playgrounds providing girls (and boys too) with the opportunity to learn how to play a variety of sports outside the school environment. Organizations like the Young Women's Christian Association provided swimming, basketball, and physical culture for older, often working girls and women through facilities reserved for females and more often in the better-equipped YMCAs (Lenskyj 1982). Churches also organized leagues for girls, although their sporting facilities were limited, unlike the recreational sites purchased by large stores like Eaton's and Woodward's specifically for the use of their employees.

Parallelling the growth of the many women's organizations that came into being in the late nineteenth century, such as the National Council of Women, the Women's Institutes, and the Woman's Christian Temperance Union, were sport clubs and tournaments exclusively for women. Membership and participation, however, were still limited predominantly to the young, the middle and upper classes, and those living in the major urban centres. Although women's sport became more organized in this period, the women themselves still had limited opportunities for involvement because the facilities were completely controlled by men, and their clubs and organizations were almost always affiliated with the men's, which meant restricted hours and no organizational representation (Pitters-Caswell 1975).

Therefore, prior to the onset of the First World War in 1914, women's sport in Canada had taken hold on both a recreational and competitive basis. However, very little of this sport was run and controlled by women. The war brought about some change. Although major tournaments were cancelled and Dominion and provincial championships postponed, women often competed in local and club tournaments in order to raise funds for the Red Cross, prisoners of war, or the war effort in general. Within the private sport clubs, their participation increased often to support patriotic causes and, with men at war, they took on more organizational responsibility, which would reap benefits for them when the war ended (Pitters-Caswell 1975).

Assuming Control: Women's Sport Run [Almost] By Women

There are still a couple of tennis courts that prohibit girls from playing during certain hours. . . . The same rule applies to a great number of golf courses and the same answer is readily given re the fee with the gratis remark added that 'women clutter up the course.' . . . The tragic part of it from the business woman's point of view is that she usually cannot pick up her clubs or her tennis racquet somewhere around one or two o'clock in the afternoon and say: 'I'm out on business,' and hie to a club—usually a golf club (Gibb 1929:10).

The First World War brought many changes for women in Canada, including a taste of employment in the men's world of streetcars, railways, steel and cement, munition factories, and in banks as tellers and clerks. After the war, even with the vote won and proof that their efforts had been invaluable to the war effort, women were sent back to their homes or into domestic service or, if they were young, single, and well educated, into traditionally female occupations like teachers, secretaries, social workers, librarians, and the like. They could not compete for jobs with men, especially those returning from the war, and they were warned not to infringe on men's social and cultural space. Yet women, especially if they were young, energetic, working (and therefore had some money of their own) wanted to experience everything their brothers and boyfriends did, including sport. The issue was whether they would create their own clubs and organizations, or whether they would try to align with men, seek their advice, and slowly move forward to autonomy. As it turns out, they chose both routes.

Golf is a good example. It is likely that Canadian women began to take up the game in the late 1880s with the advent of 'Ladies' Days' at established clubs. By 1894, the Toronto Golf Club had organized a ladies' branch with over 100 members, and a club in Ottawa had twenty-five lady associate members (Hall 1968). At the Winnipeg Golf Club, the 'ladies were as numerous on the links as the men and, if possible, more enthusiastic'. In the Maritimes the club in Halifax listed only four members when it was founded in 1896. By 1901, this number had increased to 115 (Smith 1988).

In 1901 a ladies' branch of the Royal Canadian Golf Association was established and the first open Canadian women's championship was held in Montréal. Organizationally, the Canadian Ladies Golf Union, the first of the national sport governing bodies for women's sport in Canada, was formed in 1913. Two years later there were thirty-seven affiliated clubs. It was forced to disband in 1915 due to the war, but was revived again in 1919 as a 'colonial affiliate' of the Ladies Golf

Union of Great Britain. Significantly, though, it was almost totally dependent on the Royal Canadian Golf Association for financial and organizational assistance. For example, in 1922 the men's association issued an edict that the women must submit their constitutional changes and handicap rulings to them for approval (Mitchell 1976). Looking back, it is unclear whether women acquiesced to this paternalistic control. If women wanted to play golf, they had to play in clubs controlled by men and under the rules they established. During this era only one golf club was founded and run specifically for women—the Toronto Ladies Golf and Tennis Club, which was opened in 1924 by Canada's first outstanding female golfer, Ada MacKenzie. Therefore, women had no choice but to cooperate not only with the men's association but also with their sister association in Britain. They also knew that if their game was to grow, they would have to slowly take charge of their own affairs, an end they achieved by the end of the 1920s. By all accounts this autonomy seems to have been won primarily through the efforts of their leader, Ella Murray, president of the Union from 1919 to 1927, who 'exuded a special charm which she utilized in her dealings with the male executives of the clubs whom she wished to incorporate' (Mitchell 1976:51).

Another useful example is the Women's Amateur Athletic Federation of Canada, which was founded in 1926 and existed until its demise in 1953 (Kidd 1996). Organized women's track and field began to take hold in Canada after the war so much so that by 1925, a writer for *Maclean's Magazine* commented: 'The point is that Canadian girls, as never before, and in ever-increasing numbers, are storing up health, discipline, self-control and fine spirit of sportsmanship on the playing fields of the Dominion, and that the performances of many closely approximate those of the world's women leaders in track events' (Raine 1925). In other countries, especially in the United States and in Europe, women's athletics were developing quickly with international meets taking place since 1921 (see Pallett 1955 and Webster 1930 for detailed descriptions, including competitors, times, records, and photographs of these early international track and field meetings).

Who controlled women's athletics in Canada in this period? Certainly it was men, particularly the Amateur Athletic Union of Canada (AAU) who, despite repeated requests, refused to accept female registrants (Kidd 1996). Moreover, with both the International Olympic Committee and the powerful International Amateur Athletic Federation (IAAF) opposed to including women's track and field events in the summer Olympics, Canada's governing body took a 'do nothing' position. That was the case until 1922 when Alice Milliat and her newly formed Fédération Sportive Féminine Internationale (FSFI) organized a spectacular international track and field event in Paris and called it the Olympiques Féminine. The IAAF finally took notice and asked its member nations to take charge of women's track and field in their respective countries. With no official body for women's track and field in Canada, the AAU had two options: one was to encourage women to form their own association to control the sport, and the other was to take control themselves (Kidd 1996). They chose the latter option.

Canadian women did not compete in these first women's world track and field meets because the AAU had little interest in promoting the sport for women even though Canada was formally admitted to the FSFI at its Third Congress in Paris in 1924. Why were these men opposed to women competing at a high level—men like the influential Dr Arthur S. Lamb, director of physical education at McGill University who, for most of the 1920s, was president of the AAU and secretary of the Canadian Olympic Committee?

The situation is complicated because it was not simply the men in authority who were suspicious of highly competitive sport for girls and women. Some women, particularly newly trained women physical educators who advocated a minimally competitive version of sport for girls and women, were also suspicious. Central to their philosophy was the acceptance of supposed female limitations: menstruation hindered a woman; her lower weight, inferior strength, and lighter bone structure made her more accident-prone; intense physical activity displaced her womb, leaving her barren; and so on. Not only was highly competitive sport harmful to the female, they asserted, she could never do as well as a man, so it was pointless to try. These women believed and followed the creed adopted by the Women's Division of the National Amateur Athletic Federation in the United States: 'A game for every girl and a girl for every game.' On the practical level, they fought to keep women's sport as unlike men's and as far removed from male control as possible by advocating separate programs, teachers, coaches, and officials. They campaigned vigorously against all championships, tournaments, and interscholastic competitions, branding them 'unwholesome'. They modified sport to suit their philosophy, such as the six-player, limited court, two-dribble version of basketball known for many years as 'girls' rules'.[1] They sought alternatives to the competition they so despised by encouraging 'play days' or 'sports day' where girls from different schools played *with* rather than *against* each other. In sum, they championed what they saw as a more moral and democratic athletic philosophy than men's.

Men like Dr Lamb, a physical educator himself, were greatly influenced by these ideas and indeed contributed to them. His word was extremely influential. For example, he was later quoted in a *Maclean's Magazine* article as saying:

> We need more, not less, activity for our girls and women, but let these be of the type that will be suitable to their physical and mental natures. Let us have more concentration on the ninety per cent instead of spending our time and energies upon the highly specialized ten per cent. The tendency for girls to ape the activities of boys is regrettable. In most cases it is physiologically and psychologically unsound and may be definitely harmful (Ferguson 1938:32).

On the other hand, women like Alexandrine Gibb took a different stance and along with others fought hard to provide as many competitive opportunities for girls and women as possible. Gibb was a keen athlete and a graduate of Havergal

College in Toronto. When only in her twenties, she helped found the Toronto Ladies Club, which had teams in several sports exclusively for girls and women, coached and administered by them. She also helped found the Ladies Ontario Basketball Association. In 1928 Gibb joined the staff of the *Toronto Star* where soon she wrote a lively women's sport column ('In the No Man's Land of Sport: News and Views of Women's Sporting Activities'). Her experiences were also to include managing the highly successful women's track team at the 1928 Olympics in Amsterdam and the less notable one at the 1932 Olympics in Los Angeles.[2] In 1925 Gibb was invited by the AAU to conduct selection trials for a women's track and field team to compete in a 'triangular' international meet in England. She did this ably and took ten athletes to London where they received coaching assistance from British coaches Frederick Webster and Sam Mussabini (the personal coach of Harold Abrahams, immortalized in the film *Chariots of Fire*), who were both strong supporters of women's athletics. Although the Canadians finished third behind Great Britain and Czechoslovakia, Webster (1930:53) commented on their remarkable improvement in the space of a week, and that they 'spared no pains to put themselves right'.

When Alexandrine Gibb returned to Canada, having been inspired by how seriously she and her athletes had been treated in England, she immediately went to work to establish a Women's Amateur Athletic Union affiliated with the AAU. She was determined that women should run their own sports, that girls should be coached by women, and although men were encouraged as advisers, they must stay in the background. Her motives, which were different from those of Dr Lamb and the more conservative women physical educators who were concerned about the physiological and psychological harm to girls if they competed at a highly competitive level, were focused on keeping women's sport out of the control of men. Gibb and her contemporaries wanted girls to have the very best athletic experiences possible at every level, and they felt that they knew how to accomplish that better than the men who were running things. They wanted to create a national organization with branches in all the provinces to administer and control girls' and women's sport.

The first annual convention of the Women's Amateur Athletic Federation of Canada (WAAF) took place at the Mount Royal Hotel in Montréal in December 1926. Gibb and others had worked for two years to draw up a constitution and encourage the formation of branches in the provinces.[3] Affiliated organizations had been formed in Ontario, Québec, and the Maritimes, and the number of athletes registered in the federation was approximately 1,200, although most of these were from the Ontario Ladies Softball Association. The convention was attended by representatives from the newly formed WAAF branches, other women's organizations, interested women athletes and physical educators, and, not surprisingly, a large number of men, including executive members of the AAU and the Canadian Olympic Committee. Strange as it may seem to us now, it was important that the 'ladies' receive the men's blessing in their new venture, although I doubt if any were prepared for the paternalistic remarks of John DeGruchy of the AAU, who:

> . . . expressed his personal gratification and delight at the way the ladies had thrown themselves into the work of the organization. He was amazed at the energy they had shown and wished to congratulate them upon their business-like methods. . . . He wished to emphasize, however, that in all these athletics for women, the womanly side must not be lost sight of, and that the women themselves must always keep in mind that the important thing is not so much athletics for women as that they are the mothers of the coming nation (*Montreal Daily Star* 1926).

The WAAFers, as they became known, soon established branches throughout the West in British Columbia, Saskatchewan, Alberta, and Manitoba, and by 1935 boasted a membership of 3,500 athletes (Kidd 1996). Increasingly they became an autonomous body with control over women's sport, especially in track and field, basketball, ice hockey, and softball, although they never had much money for their activities. They required annual medical certificates for all athletes to counter the concerns of the more conservative physical educators discussed earlier, although they were unsuccessful in challenging the 'girls' rules' and play day movement. Men were seen as more experienced in the administration of amateur sport, and they continued to play an advisory (but non-voting) role in both the national and provincial branches, as was clearly spelled out in their constitution. As historian Bruce Kidd has commented, there was always a double-sidedness to their relationship with the men—the desire for autonomy co-existed with the need for advice and support. The WAAFers' greatest contribution is that it 'drew leaders from both the working and middle class, [and] was able to encourage Canadian women to aspire to whatever level of competition they wanted, while maintaining women's leadership in both the educational system and the community' (Kidd 1996:141). Sadly, the Second World War took its toll, and money became scarce, as did the women leaders, so that in 1953 a decision was taken, accepted by some and resented by many, to amalgamate the WAAF with the men's AAU. History has a strange way of repeating itself because several times over the next thirty years, a strong, women-centred sport organization would decide, or sometimes be forced, to join the equivalent yet more powerful men's body, again losing women's singular voice in sport.[4]

Conclusion: Contesting the Gender Order

In her superb historical study of women's sport in the United States, Susan Cahn (1994:209) noted that in the 1920s there was 'a kind of carnivalesque fascination with women's athletic feats as a symbol of the changing gender order in

American society'. 'The image of the female athlete', she added, 'signalled a total inversion of established gender relations, an indication that female dominance might eventually replace men's traditional authority'. The same was true in Canada, although the Canadian sport media were far kinder and more supportive of women athletes in this era than was true of the male-dominated media in the United States. Henry Roxborough, for example, widely known across Canada as a sportswriter and author, who contributed regularly to *MacLean's Magazine*, wrote a laudatory article in 1929 entitled 'Give the Girls a Hand.' Here he profiled the recent achievements of world-class athletes in speed skating, basketball, track and field, swimming, polo, and softball, commenting: 'Canadian women are not just knocking at the door of the world of sport, but rather they have crashed the gate, swarmed the field and, in some cases, have driven mere man to the sidelines.' It is notable that male sportswriters often used expressions like 'invaded', 'captured', 'crashed', and 'encroached' when describing women's sport so that their accomplishments were *always* compared to those of male athletes. In Canada, unlike the United States, negative criticism from the male media was usually countered by the half dozen or so women sportswriters, themselves former top athletes, who regularly wrote columns for the major newspapers.[5]

On the organizational front, women had challenged men for control of their own sports. If the men were reluctant to give up control and their words seemed paternalistic, they believed that there were good reasons to be cautious. In his 1928 presidential report to the AAU, Dr Lamb reiterated his belief that women's athletics should be governed entirely by women, yet he reasoned that the independent status of the WAAF could not be granted until they were convinced that 'the administration of their affairs will not fall into the hands of unscrupulous promoters or those whose chief interest might be self-glorification' (Lamb 1928). Henry Roxborough said much the same thing when he wrote:

> . . . it might also be suggested girls' sports would become even more effective if coaching and managing 'manpower' was replaced by the constant supervision and leadership of elder women; if executive officers discouraged all attempts to use girls for personal or industrial publicity; and if the practice of 'sports for stars' was succeeded by the ideal of developing wholesome play on a generous scale with the objective of contributing to the maintenance of a healthy, happy Canadian womanhood (Roxborough 1929:19).

Men like Lamb and Roxborough were saying that women could, even should, control their sport provided traditional gender roles went undisturbed and the gender order of society was left intact. Many men of this era, as was true for women, had an unshakeable belief in the Victorian notions of manliness and womanliness, masculinity and femininity, and the clear distinction between the two. Men were willing to allow women the right to participate in sport, even to compete at the highest levels for the good of Canada, provided they conducted themselves with proper feminine decorum. More importantly, they must not allow the tainted world of professionalism and commercialism to corrupt women's sport as was increasingly the case, they believed, with men's sport of this era. Women's sport must remain pure, and women athletes should devote themselves to the love of the game, never straying into the evil and exploited world of marketing their talents. It should be noted that most women physical educators of the day felt exactly the same way and said so.

All of this sounds eerily familiar. Sportswriters today claim that women are rejuvenating sport because they play the game differently when compared with men, the way sport used to be many decades ago in its pure and untainted form. There are some who argue that sport has lost its way. The acclaimed American sportswriter Robert Lipsyte (1995:56) argues that 'sports are over because they no longer have any moral resonance', and that women, if they are not now certainly will be, just as liable as men for sport's downfall. Pessimism aside, the point is that a strict gender order still persists in sport, as is true in society, one that has been contested by women since they first rode their bicycles at the end of the nineteenth century. Recounting even a small bit of this history helps us to understand how and why women have struggled against masculine hegemony in sport, why they succeeded and why they failed, and why they must continue to struggle for some time to come.

Notes

Some of the material in this chapter has also appeared in Hall et al. (1991), Chapter 3. I am grateful to the Social Sciences and Humanities Research Council of Canada for research monies to undertake an ambitious historical study, still in progress, of women's sport in Canada.

1. I was still playing a version of girls' rules basketball when I competed for Queen's University between 1960 and 1964, although by this time they were now called 'intercollegiate rules', which allowed each player to range over two-thirds of the court. There was considerable disparity between women's basketball in eastern and western Canada because when I played for the University of Alberta in 1966–7, we played by men's rules. The famous Edmonton Grads played by men's rules almost exclusively except when they came east to compete in a Dominion championship where they would sometimes be forced to play by girls' rules, or even both in the same tournament. By 1941, a national survey indicated that the numbers playing by the two sets of rules were about even (Kidd 1996).

2. As with most of the early pioneers in women's sport in Canada, there is very little biographical information available about Alexandrine Gibb. The best sources are

Kidd (1996), Chapter 3; the columns Gibb wrote for the *Toronto Star* between May 1928 and November 1940; her obituaries (see *Toronto Daily Star*, 16 December 1958, p. 5 and 29, as well as the *Globe* and *Toronto Telegram* of the same date).

3. Kidd (1996) notes that few WAAF of Canada records remain because they were either destroyed or stolen (see note 60, p. 290), and that it is necessary to rely on press reports, which fortunately are fairly numerous because Alexandrine Gibb and other women sport columnists of the day wrote about the organization. I also found a copy of the 1938 version of their constitution in the National Archives of Canada (MG30 C 164, Vol. 35, File 16).

4. For example, the Women's Athletic Committee of the Canadian Association for Health, Physical Education, and Recreation, founded in the late 1930s, was dissolved in 1973 due to a lack of national support and funding. The Canadian Women's Intercollegiate Athletic Union, formed in 1969, amalgamated only a few years later with the more powerful Canadian Interuniversity Athletic Union. In the United States, the influential women's organization controlling intercollegiate sport, the Association for Intercollegiate Athletics for Women, was taken over by the more powerful men's organization, the National Collegiate Athletic Association, even though they fought the takeover in court. Back in Canada, there are now no separate women's sport governing bodies at the federal level since for some time Sport Canada has had a policy of funding only one national sport governing body. Those that still existed (e.g., women's field hockey) were forced to amalgamate with the men's organization.

5. As far as I know, these were: Phyllis Griffiths (*Toronto Telegram* 1928–42); Alexandrine Gibb (*Toronto Star* 1929–40); Myrtle Cook (*Montreal Star* 1929–68); Fanny 'Bobbie' Rosenfeld (*Montreal Daily Herald* 1932–3; *Globe and Mail* 1937–59); Gladys Gigg Ross (*Capital News*, North Bay, dates unknown); Lillian 'Jimmy' Coo (*Winnipeg Free Press* 1937–42, 1946–7); Patricia Page Hollingsworth (*Edmonton Journal* 1935–40); Anne Stott (*Vancouver Sun* 1939–41); and Ruth Wilson (*Vancouver Sun* 1943–5).

References

Avery, J., and J. Stevens. 1997. *Too Many Men on the Ice: Women's Hockey in North America*. Victoria: Polestar.

Birrell, S., and N. Theberge. 1994. 'Feminist Resistance and Transformation in Sport'. In *Women and Sport: Interdisciplinary Perspectives*, edited by D.M. Costa and S.R. Guthrie, 361–76. Champaign, IL: Human Kinetics.

Brown, D.W. 1988. 'Social Darwinism, Private Schooling and Sport in Victorian and Edwardian Canada'. In *Pleasure, Profit, Proselytism: British Culture and Sport at Home and Abroad 1700–1914*, edited by J.A. Mangan, 215–30. London: Frank Cass.

Browne, L. 1992. *Girls of Summer: In Their Own League*. Toronto: HarperCollins.

Cahn, S. 1994. *Coming on Strong: Gender and Sexuality in Twentieth-Century Women's Sport*. New York: Free Press.

Etue, E., and M.K. Williams. 1996. *On the Edge: Women Making Hockey History*. Toronto: Second Story Press.

Ferguson, B. 1985. *Who's Who in Canadian Sport*, 2nd edn. Toronto: Summerhill Press.

Ferguson, E. 1938. 'I Don't Like Amazon Athletes'. *Maclean's Magazine* (1 August):32–3.

Gibb, A. 1929. 'In the No Man's Land of Sport: News and Views of Women's Sporting Activities'. *Toronto Star* (15 May):10.

Gurney, H. 1982. *A Century of Progress: Girls' Sports in Ontario High Schools*. Don Mills, ON: Ontario Federation of Schools Athletic Associations.

Hall, M.A. 1968. 'A History of Women's Sport in Canada Prior to World War I'. MA thesis, University of Alberta.

_____, T. Slack, G. Smith, and D. Whitson. 1991. *Sport in Canadian Society*. Toronto: McClelland & Stewart.

Hargreaves, J. 1994. *Sporting Females: Critical Issues in the History and Sociology of Women's Sports*. London and New York: Routledge.

Howell, C.D. 1995. *Northern Sandlots: A Social History of Maritime Baseball*. Toronto: University of Toronto Press.

Howell, D., and P. Lindsay. 1986. 'Social Gospel and the Young Boy Problem, 1895–1925'. *Canadian Journal of History of Sport* 17:75–87.

Humber, W. 1995. *Diamonds of the North: A Concise History of Baseball in Canada*. Toronto: Oxford University Press.

Kidd, B. 1996. *The Struggle for Canadian Sport*. Toronto: University of Toronto Press.

Lamb, A.S. 1928. *Report to the Amateur Athletic Union of Canada*, December. National Archives of Canada MG30 C 164, Vol. 19, File 7.

Lenskyj, H. 1982. 'Femininity First: Sport and Physical Education for Ontario Girls, 1890–1930'. *Canadian Journal of History of Sport* 13:4–17.

_____. 1983. 'The Role of Physical Education in the Socialization of Girls in Ontario, 1890–1930'. Ph.D. dissertation, University of Toronto.

_____. 1986. *Out of Bounds: Women, Sport and Sexuality*. Toronto: The Women's Press.

Lipsyte, R. 1995. 'The Emasculation of Sports'. *The New York Times Magazine* (2 April):51–7.

Long, W. 1995. *Celebrating Excellence: Canadian Women Athletes*. Vancouver: Polestar.

McCrone, K. 1988. *Playing the Game: Sport and the Physical Emancipation of English Women, 1870–1914*. Lexington: University of Kentucky Press.

McDonald, D. 1981. *For the Record: Canada's Greatest Women Athletes*. Toronto: John Wiley & Sons Canada.

McFarlane, B. 1994. *Proud Past, Bright Future: One Hundred Years of Canadian Women's Hockey*. Toronto: Stoddart Publishing.

McKenzie, R.T. 1892. 'Rugby Football in Canada'. *The Dominion Illustrated Monthly* 1:11–19.

Marks, P. 1990. *Bicycles, Bangs, and Bloomers: The New Woman in the Popular Press*. Lexington: University of Kentucky Press.

Mitchell, S.L. 1976. 'The Organizational Development of Women's Competitive Sport in Canada in the 1920's'. MHK thesis, University of Windsor.
Montreal Daily Star. 1926. (4, 6, 7, 8, 10 December).

Mott, M. 1980. 'The British Protestant Pioneers and the Establishment of Manly Sports in Manitoba, 1870–1886'. *Journal of Sport History* 7:25–36.

Pallett, G. 1955. *Women's Athletics*. London: The Normal Press.

Pitters-Caswell, M.I. 1975. 'Woman's Participation in Sporting Activities as an Indicator of Femininity and Cultural Evolution in Toronto, 1910 to 1920'. MA thesis, University of Windsor.

Raine, Norman R. 1925. 'Girls Invade Track and Diamond'. *MacLean's Magazine* (15 August):12–14.

Roxborough, H. 1929. 'Give the Girls a Hand'. *MacLean's Magazine* (15 February):16, 18–19.

Smith, M. 1988. 'Graceful Athleticism or Robust Womanhood: The Sporting Culture of Women in Victorian Nova Scotia, 1870–1914'. *Journal of Canadian Studies* 23:120–37.

Teitel, J. 1997. 'Shorter, Slower, Weaker'. *Saturday Night* (July/August):61–3.

Vertinsky, P.A. 1990. *The Eternally Wounded Woman: Women, Exercise and Doctors in the Late Nineteenth Century*. Manchester: Manchester University Press.

Webster, F.A.M. 1930. *Athletics of Today for Women: History, Development and Training*. London: Frederick Warne & Co., Ltd.

Chapter 2

The Public Importance of Men and the Importance of Public Men:

Sport and Masculinities in Nineteenth-Century Canada

Kevin B. Wamsley

This chapter outlines how sport in late nineteenth-century Canada provided for the public display of physical masculinities. While men performed sport in public, women remained for the most part excluded from active participation. In this way, sport helped construct and reinforce the idea that men were supposed to be strong, physical, and active in public affairs and that women were supposed to be weak, passive, and involved in domestic or charitable activities. It will also be argued that the domination of sporting activity by middle- and upper-class men legitimated their public status as community leaders. In exploring the issue, this chapter will also show that an important role of sport history is to develop an understanding of the meanings of sport for different groups of people over time. That men and women experienced sport in remarkably different ways in nineteenth-century Canada will be of particular concern.

Arguing that social practices, understandings, and experiences do not emerge 'naturally' or simply 'evolve', Connell (1995:30) asserts that, in the English-speaking world, the 'exemplary status of sport as a test of masculinity' was an historically produced and deliberate political strategy. While connections between sport and masculinity have been established in sociological research, historical analyses have rarely explored sport as a 'gendering' agent. Historical research has tended to explore specific rather than general topics. For example, 'Muscular Christianity' and manliness have been identified as important factors in the emergence of nineteenth-century sport (cf., Brown 1986a; Morrow 1988; Mott 1980, 1983; Redmond 1979), while Gruneau (1983) and Metcalfe (1987) have touched on the gender- and/or class-based organization of sport. More recently, Gruneau and Whitson (1993), Howell (1995), and Kidd (1996), in their analyses of hockey, baseball, and Canadian sport respectively, have identified the importance of gender (specifically masculinity) for an historical understanding of sport.

The notion of 'hegemonic masculinity' will be employed in this chapter to account for how some masculinities are valued over others and how inequalities are systematically established, sustained, and reproduced between men and women, and between men and other men (Connell 1993). Referring to commonly shared and socially valued understandings of what constitutes 'being a man', the concept of hegemonic masculinity is borrowed from Gramsci (1992) whose broader notion of hegemony explains how unequal relationships are often maintained by the consent of those subordinated to forms of domination. While this concept was aimed at explaining class relationships, it has also been useful for understanding gender relationships.

Dominant expressions of masculinity and femininity have tended to vary over time in response to shifts in the social order. Dominant groups have tended to establish and maintain what they have regarded as appropriate ways of being men and women. They have also benefited the most from the definitions of gender they established and encouraged others to embrace. At the same time, dominant gender definitions have always been *contested*. Some groups have challenged hegemonic gender relations and have celebrated other ways of being men and women.

A significant problem for historians has been to explain the process through which dominant forms of gender have been maintained and reproduced. This chapter will explore these processes, particularly in relation to how, over time, sport has contributed to the acceptance of and resistance to gender orders that have consistently subordinated women.

Physical Activity, Sport, and Colonial Masculinities

In the late nineteenth and early twentieth centuries, varying brands of sport-related masculinity can be found in popular periodicals (Brown 1986b, 1989), in the songs and proclamations of men's sporting clubs (Morrow 1988), and in the records of Canadian courtrooms (Young and Wamsley 1996) and the Canadian Parliament (Wamsley 1992). Among these varied sources, a prevalent image is that of a hardy Canadian male who lived within a competitive context of conquest, killing, survival, and the harsh physical conditions of the fur trade and early agricultural economies. Within this context, there were ample opportunities to engage in heroic feats and to create a number of 'masculine' myths and legends.

The processes of imperialism, however, changed things significantly. Along with imperialist and missionary invasions, the oppression of Native peoples, and the settlement of the French and English in North America, there was also what Connell (1993:606) refers to as the 'obliteration of gender regimes'. For example, Native gender orders were significantly altered (Devens 1997) when the bachelor cultures of the fur trader, soldier, missionary, and colonial mercenary were being established.

For the *coureurs du bois*, or independent French traders, extreme physical hardship and hard labour helped forge their now storied reputations. Epitomizing a raw and sometimes feared masculinity, to other young men of New France who lived in isolated and often impoverished circumstances, these men showed little deference to authority and lauded the freedom of the bush (Clark 1971). Their unrefined brand of masculinity remained exemplary throughout the French colonial period although it was not generally favoured by the Church or state. Like the voyageurs hired by the North West Company and later by the Hudson's Bay Company and the fur traders of York Factory (Payne 1989), the *coureurs du bois* often underscored their physical masculinity through contests of strength, paddling, and foot-races (Lappage 1984; Salter 1976).

In general, masculine identity was based in the labour process. For the voyageurs of the late eighteenth and early nineteenth centuries, manliness was associated with the ability to paddle and portage, to carry heavy loads, and to use a vast singing vocabulary to maintain paddling rhythm. As one voyageur boasted:

> No portage was too long for me; all portages were alike. My end of the canoe never touched the ground. . . . Fifty songs a day were nothing to me, I could carry, paddle, walk, and sing with any man I ever saw. . . . No water, no weather, ever stopped the paddle or the song. I have had twelve wives in the country; and was once possessed of fifty horses, and six running dogs, trimmed in the first style (Eccles cited in Lappage 1984).

Thus, labour-related skills such as paddling were construed as competitive tests of masculinity. Similarly, competitions between men became an inherent part of the labour process of the fur trade, with each task serving as a test of masculinity. However, as Connell (1995:29) argues, masculinity was not just 'an idea in the head, or a personal identity'. Bush masculinities constructed in the fur trade economy also influenced other social relations. In the popular imagination the 'masculine' feats of the *coureurs du bois*, the voyageurs, and other early settlers became a vital part of French- and English-Canadian culture and male identity throughout the nineteenth century.

British North America

In the late eighteenth and early nineteenth centuries, along with the diversification of the trade economy, the establishment of British institutions, government, gentry, and Church power in the colonies, and the settlement of Loyalists and immigrants, there was also the emergence of what might be called 'competing' masculinities, some of which were not based on physical prowess. Male-dominated British rule in the colonies was achieved through land appropriation and the establishment of networks of institutional power. Powerful political oligarchies in Québec, York, Halifax, St John's, and Fredericton were established through patronage and the assertion of social influence (Morton 1972). The significance of physical endurance and strength, which defined the 'bush masculinity' of the traders, differed markedly from the distinctions of rank, status, and the notions of honour embodied in the 'gentry masculinities' of British North America.

Men of power and influence in British North America were generally Anglican and conservative, often with military experience. For many of these men, masculinity was measured by the notion of 'honour', which was both a source of pride and a marker of status. Such was its importance that the prospect of losing honour was extremely threatening. Sometimes masculine honour was defended through the duel, a 'manly' ritual through which upper- and middle-class men upheld their reputations in public displays of violence (Morgan 1995). Fought between two men armed with pistols, the duel was positively valued as a demonstration of courage. Victors were sometimes tried in court, but if they followed the agreed-upon rules of 'fair' killing, they were usually acquitted (Morgan 1995). Within this culture, questions of honour over a personal or professional slight, or the integrity or treatment of a woman often necessitated a proper challenge and a fair duel. Fortunately for many, given the limited accuracy of firearms at that time, if both contestants missed the mark with their shots, the confrontation was considered over and appropriately resolved.

In sum, in the late eighteenth and early nineteenth centuries there were clear differences between 'bush masculinity' and 'gentry masculinity'. Bush masculinity involved displays of physical performance, such as feats of labour, fights, races, and contests of strength (Guillet 1933). By contrast, the masculinity of some of the gentry was displayed through duelling rituals based on aristocratic norms of chivalry and more refined expressions of courage.

Competing notions of masculinity were also present in other areas of social life. In most social practices, including sport, the main structures of power in British North America were highly gendered and the role of women was extremely limited (Strong-Boag and Fellman 1997). This was evident in the recruitment and promotion of men rather than women to positions of power within the state, the military, and the Church. Simply stated, men managed the economy, the military, the law, and most other public affairs in British North America. Not surprisingly, it was also ruling- and middle-class men who established segregated sport and social clubs throughout the nineteenth century (Metcalfe 1987; Wise 1974). Indeed, sport provided an important place where paternalist class- and race-based masculinities could be fashioned. Masculinity politics, then, were clearly evident during the emergence of sport in nineteenth century Canada and in the organization of sport clubs and competitions in the pre-Confederation era (Metcalfe 1987; Mott 1989; Redmond 1982).

The processes legitimizing patriarchal organization and practices during the nineteenth century originated in British imperialism, the emergence of the medical profession, the doctrine of science, and dominant ideas associating women with domesticity, dependence, and moral strength. In this era, ruling- and middle-class men rationalized their segregated sporting pursuits as neces- sary for the maintenance of British ideals of manliness and gentlemanly integrity. Thus, cricket was popularized by officers of the military garrisons in cities such as Montréal, Québec City, Halifax, Ottawa, Saint John, and Victoria (Day 1989; Metcalfe 1987) and introduced at private schools such as Upper Canada College. Elsewhere, ex-military officers in places such as Woodstock, Ontario celebrated their social distinction and their connection with other colonial élites through participation in cricket matches (Bouchier 1989). Men's curling clubs organized by the Scots in Montréal (1807), Kingston (1820), Québec City (1821), Halifax (1824–5), and Fergus (1834) (Metcalfe 1987; Redmond 1982) were also sites for the consolidation of 'appropriate' masculinities. At the same time, however, even the most modest physical exercises were considered unbecoming to 'respectable' women (Hall et al. 1991). This social distinction eventually became rationalized by popular medical opinion to suggest that exercise could be unhealthy or even dangerous for women (Vertinsky 1994).

For military men, sport and exercise were considered appropriate vehicles for the development of 'good character'. For example, in his study of Halifax, Day (1989:35) argues that the officers of the garrison, renowned for their cricket matches, regattas, horse races, and athletics, were considered to be 'men of upright character and strong moral fibre'. Often organized to alleviate boredom among the men, garrison sports were also valorized as expressions of appropriate masculinity and as demonstrations of commitment to British tradition and culture. As public displays of 'character', they also helped improve relations with the community, which were sometimes tense following occasions when drunken, profane, and brawling garrison soldiers spent their pay in the local taverns and brothels (Fingard 1989; Greer 1992).

While these physical expressions of maleness were cast in a positive light, other types of male physicality were not looked upon so favourably. The rougher physicality of working-class men was often regarded as an affront to social order by 'respectable' citizens who valued the suppression of public violence, drunk- enness, gambling, and Sabbath-breaking. For example, the drinking and fighting that often accompanied barn-raising and harvesting bees in rural areas (Hall et al. 1991), and the contests of strength and skill, boxing, and wrestling, which pitted townships against one another, were considered offensive by some but revered by others (Guillet 1933).

Such revelry was predominantly a male phenomenon. Although Bitterman (1995) found in his study of the pre-Confederation Escheat movement in Prince Edward Island that women could also be violent and capable of assault, there are few accounts of women fighting women or women fighting men in public contests during this period (Marks 1996). As is the case today, these gender distinctions were largely explained away by ideologies of 'natural' difference and notions of women as the weaker sex (Connell 1995)—this despite the fact that historically the physical strength of women who laboured alongside men on farms, in cottage industries, and later in the factories (Bradbury 1997; Noel 1997; Potter 1997) belied medical opinions about their alleged physical 'weakness' (Vertinsky 1994). In sum, then, sport came to be an important part of the ideology and practice that made the political and domestic segregation of men and women seem normal and desirable. In general, most men benefited in some way from such distinctions.

Again, however, there were constantly competing and shifting versions of masculinity among men. The declining popularity of the duel during the 1830s as a means of defending gentlemanly honour (Morgan 1995), and its prohibition by law in 1847 in the Province of Canada, posed a challenge to gentry masculinity. This cultural shift was symptomatic of the growing influence of moderate social movements in British North America within which less reactionary Tories, both businessmen and professionals, increasingly assumed prominent positions of power (Mills 1988). The older landed rights of political power, previously secured by patronage, were gradually usurped by the supposition that political rewards should be earned through professional success and merit and protected by democratically formed political policy (Johnson 1989; Noel 1990).

The formation of the Canadian state was integral to the emergence of this new historic bloc and the infrastructural foundation of a new capitalist socio-economic order. Simultaneously, ascendant notions of 'order' and 'rationality', and the setting by law of 'official' standards for public behaviour had a dampening effect on the use of the body in leisure and recreation. Temperance advocates argued that alcohol consumption was the cause of crime and poverty and were successful in lobbying for restrictive liquor legislation in all provinces during the pre-Confederation period. This legislation controlled licensing, hours of operation, and provided a mechanism for dealing with 'public nuisances' related to drunkenness. Legislation regulating gambling activities was passed in Nova Scotia, New Brunswick, and the Province of Canada, and Sabbath observance laws were passed in Canada West (Wamsley 1992). These measures were part of a broader movement to create a rational workforce and rational business practices to better serve economic interests (Clark 1971).

Despite these efforts to assert bourgeois notions of being a man, or what Rotundo (1987) called a 'Christian gentleman', approximately 4,000 tavern licenses were issued per year between 1859 and 1866 in the Province of Canada (Wamsley 1992). Discrepancies between the goals of the temperance movement and their achievements were due largely to the fact that legislation affected only public, not private, behaviour. While there was some success in controlling the use of alcohol in public places, liquor consumption, gambling (Wamsley 1998), Sabbath non-observance (Wamsley and Heine 1995), and hunting and fishing (Wamsley 1994) continued in private. Social activities in the home, club, and on private property were generally not affected by legislation.

These types of legislation were enacted as part of the broader movement of social reform whose supporters tended to categorize men as 'naturally' unable to resist the temptation to sin and women as society's moral guardians (Marks 1996). The 'nuisance' laws dealt explicitly with curbing undesirable public behaviours, providing mechanisms, for example, to deal with the tavern brawler. The legal system provided little, however, for the protection of women from practices such as domestic violence, which were most often perpetrated by men (Strong-Boag and Fellman 1997).

Acting in alliance, organized religion, education, temperance societies, mechanics' institutes, and agricultural societies each contributed to the construction of separate spheres for men and women, thus enabling ruling-class men to assume social leadership during the pre-Confederation period (Guildford and Morton 1994). By the late 1850s, business*men* in central Canada emerged as the dominant social group. Their interests and favoured positions became secured through investment legislation, private investment, political policy, and an expanded state (Baskerville 1992; Noel 1990).

Post-Confederation: Sport and Masculinity in the New Dominion

The British North America Act of 1867 centralized the control of trade and tariffs, debt, and public property in the new Dominion of Canada. It also exacted power over education, agriculture, municipalities, and justice to the provinces. This political arrangement extended the influence of the pre-Confederation historic bloc fronted by White, middle- and upper-class men. It also aided the formulation of the idea of a national political structure and economy. Many Canadian men's first experiences with the new national political structure came through the establishment of voluntary military service, which, as a publicly visible hierarchy, identified particular masculine behaviours as exemplary and patriotic (Connell 1990). Military practices such as drilling, marching, and rifle shooting were culturally significant for large numbers of Canadian men throughout the late nineteenth century.

Between 1867 and 1908, the Dominion federal government spent $1.5 million on equipment, facilities, and prizes to encourage and promote competitive rifle shooting (Wamsley 1995). Initially valued because it demonstrated British loyalty during the mid-1860s, rifle shooting was later more broadly defined as a patriotic and 'manly' exercise. Local, regional, national, and international competitions became popular as publicly valued demonstrations of masculinity measured by appearance, dedication, and performance. Military masculinity and expertise with firearms legitimated a paternalist order within which the role of men was to protect their wives, children, mothers, sisters, and other non-militia men. Ironically, such activities took men away from their homes on a regular basis because discipline, technique, and competence, it was argued, could only be achieved through practice (Wamsley 1995). Therefore, the sport of competitive rifle shooting not only physically removed men from domestic roles and obligations but further contributed to a gender order based on the public role of men and the domestic role of women, which came to seem natural and normal.

These ideas of nationalism and masculinity were also articulated through a perceived need for economic competitiveness at local and regional fairs, exhibitions, and world expositions (Wamsley and Whitson 1993) and for social competitiveness at sporting events, clubs, and carnivals. This powerful rhetoric, combining patriotism, masculinity, and sport, took a firm foothold to the extent that 'national' championships attracted spectator interest in the latter part of the period, which further legitimized organized sport as played by urban middle-class men (Gruneau and Whitson 1993; Kidd 1996; Morrow et al. 1989).

Sport clubs, based clearly on the notion of the public importance of men and the importance of public men, were highly valued by 'respectable' Canadians who viewed particular forms of exercise as expressions of orderly, emotionally controlled, Christian manliness (Mott 1980, 1983). They were also antithetical to disorderly practices associated with tavern sports (de Lottinville 1981–2; Guillet 1933) and many working-class recreations (Metcalfe 1978). The men of the exclusive Montreal Snowshoe Club, for example, met regularly for torchlit snowshoe tramps, dinners, and social functions, celebrating a kind of maleness associated with good food, wine, and the company of 'pretty lasses' (Morrow 1988:12). Influenced by cross membership with the Montreal Lacrosse Club, a summer sport popularized as Canada's 'national' game by fervent patriot W. George Beers, the Montreal Snowshoe Club organized races in the immediate post-Confederation period, which attracted as many as 5,000 spectators. The organizers of both lacrosse and snowshoeing, which were appropriated from Native custom and practice, systematically made racist distinctions between the games as played by White, middle-class men and Native men—and the meanings attached to the sport by these groups. At times, Native snowshoe racers who were used to attract spectators were ridiculed and not even allowed to compete with White racers (Morrow 1988). Native lacrosse players who accompanied White 'gentlemen' teams on international promotional tours were made to wear warpaint and costumes in order to distinguish themselves from 'civilized' men, and to attract the interest of immigrants and foreign investors to Canada (Wamsley 1997). Demonstrating that sport is often a site where meanings about gender, class, and race intersect, Morrow's (1988:23) quote from a Montreal Snowshoe Club member is illuminating: '[t]he sachems seem to have an hereditary power of running that even their natural laziness and love of fire water cannot destroy'.

The various physical versions of maleness expressed in urban sporting clubs, in contests held in taverns and at local fairs, in the sport of private schools, at boys' clubs, and at the YMCAs were all based on the idea of social power associated with men's bodies (Hall et al. 1991). Physical gender differences were emphasized in the military and in the medical community where a socially constructed distinction between the 'strong man' and 'weak woman' was endorsed, even though women working in urban factories and farm fields were a common sight (Lenskyj 1986). Christian gentlemen who organized men's sporting clubs and leagues or operated programs in private schools rationalized the exclusion of females from sport by combining the ideas of Social Darwinism and Muscular Christianity (Hall et al. 1991). Social Darwinists applied the biological concept of the 'survival of the fittest' to the human social hierarchy, which presupposed that the subjects in question were male. Muscular Christianity held that the physically developed man, tempered and guided by Christian morality, was better positioned for a successful life. The combination of these beliefs was applied both to sport and to the economic and political order by powerful men in post-Confederation Canada. And as Hall et al. (1991) have argued, these ideas about appropriate physicalities helped reproduce the Victorian distinction between manly and womanly ideals, which further reinforced the broader notions of 'public' men and 'domestic' or moral reformist women (Marks 1996).

The establishment of gender differences was also sustained by class-based notions of amateurism. Playing sport for its intrinsic values and for building character was the basis of amateurism, an ideal around which White, middle-class men organized their urban clubs (Howell 1995). Middle-class sporting ideals had little meaning for working-class men, however, who preferred to spend some of their non-working hours in taverns taking much-needed respite from physical exertion. In this regard, de Lottinville (1981–2) argues that middle-class reformers of Montréal had no understanding of working-class culture. They often associated the leisure activities of men who did not conform with the social rules of gentlemanly conduct with slothfulness and common criminality.

Nevertheless, while middle-class men ruled the organized club sports, vibrant working-class recreational cultures flourished in Montréal and small-town Ontario (Bouchier 1990; de Lottinville 1981–2; Metcalfe 1978). Pedestrian contests, dogfights, cockfights, wrestling and boxing matches, demonstrations of strength, informal games, and emerging professional spectator sports were an important part of the late nineteenth-century Canadian sporting landscape. Drinking, gambling, and Sabbath-breaking were also an integral part of some of these activities. Together, they represented a direct affront to the 'public face' of middle-class ideas about an ordered and temperate society. Privately, middle-class professionals and artisans could often be found at such events (Bouchier 1990), and drinking and gambling were common behind the closed doors of private clubs (Wamsley 1998).

Women also actively resisted the controlling influence of male, middle-class sport practices. Upper- and middle-class Canadian women established their own sporting events when refused entry into men's sporting clubs and facilities. Their activities were largely limited to sports like croquet, lawn tennis, golf, and figure skating where, it was argued, the social expectations for 'ladylike' behaviour could be better accommodated (Kidd 1996). In the last decade of the century, however, when bicycle riding became a popular activity for some women, attitudes towards women's physicality slowly began to change. Shifts also occurred in medical thinking. Physicians began to recommend light exercise for women, but only as a means of preparing for motherhood (Lenskyj 1986). Subsequently, gender norms shifted in other ways: more women began playing hockey, basketball, and baseball (Kidd 1996); middle-class women won more political power through such organizations as the National Council of Women and the Woman's Christian Temperance Union.

Despite these shifts in social attitudes, at the turn of the century sport was still viewed primarily as a means of developing character and moral restraint in young men and boys and as a strategy for 'de-feminizing' men who no longer worked in physically challenging occupations. Churches, schools, and reform organizations like the YMCA all developed sport programs for male youth (Howell and Lindsay 1986). Sport was seen as a valuable alternative to loitering on street corners, which, it was feared, might lead to other 'vices' (Marks 1996).

Around this time, in another sporting area, entrepreneurs were busy exploring ways of making money by attracting paying customers to spectator events. For example, crowds in Québec flocked to see 'strongmen' like Louis Cyr, one of the earliest Canadian spectacle performers, whose strength and physical feats nostalgically embodied the masculinities of French-Canadian pioneer farmers and voyageurs of previous eras (Wise and Fisher 1974). Commercialized sport, however, developed in an atmosphere of tension. Proponents of middle-class amateurism scorned and resented commercialized sport's emphasis on money and winning (Bouchier 1990). Such values were anathema to amateur sport enthusiasts. However, promoters, professional sportsmen, and town boosters were eager to find ways to attract 'respectable' men and women to their events as spectators. One strategy that emerged was for booster campaigns to link the exploits of local athletes and teams with the business and settlement opportunities that were supposedly available in towns and cities (Voisey 1981). In order to legitimate this association, boosters began to link sport with the rhetoric of 'science', which also underscored the logic of industrial capitalism. Formerly considered to be lower-class vices scorned by social reformers, violent sports such as boxing and wrestling were promoted instead as 'manly' demonstrations of scientific technique or as modern and more civilized versions of older sport (Wamsley and Whitson 1998). So entrenched were these manly displays of sanctioned public violence that the Canadian justice system generally turned a blind eye to brutality and injury and generally declined to convict athletes on criminal charges, even when players and participants were killed (Young and Wamsley 1996). Public displays of male sporting physicality were considered to be an important and instructive social practice in turn-of-the-century Canada.

Conclusion

The making of informal and organized sport in nineteenth-century Canada ingrained the value of competition between men and created a public testing ground for various forms of masculinity. Similar to earlier periods in Canadian history, particular brands of masculinity were defined as exemplary and others were marginalized. The establishment and reproduction of relations of power in British North America and later the Dominion of Canada created a context for the establishment of a range of socially appropriate and inappropriate gender behaviours. A dichotomy separating maleness from femaleness became institutionalized in many areas of Canadian life, including sport. Middle-class men who were strong, physical, and active in important public affairs were said to have respectable qualities, while women of the same station were expected to be weak, passive, and involved in domestic or social reform activities. In sum, sport reaffirmed and helped to construct the notion and practice of separate spheres for men and women during the Victorian period.

In the immediate pre- and post-Confederation periods, the public expression of competitiveness became valued by all classes of men, and various forms of sport and spectatorship provided venues for these expressions. Sport reaffirmed the meanings of dominance-based masculinity, providing connections between work and domestic life. Indeed, sport was enmeshed with broad societal changes, such as the Confederation process and the gradual emergence of industrial capitalism. Although predominantly aligned with powerful social groups, sport also served as a site of resistance for some men and women, providing alternatives to officially sanctioned social meanings.

In the latter part of the nineteenth century, newspapers, promoters, educational and social reform institutions, and the state contributed to a wider, more popular level of exposure to sport and the gendered meanings that it embodied. Gender, class, and race remained significant social forces following the turn of the century, and sport factored prominently in Canada's emergence as a nation. As part of a long-term process emerging from a very influential Victorian period, men and women continued to experience sport in remarkably different ways.

References

Baskerville, P. 1992. 'Transportation, Social Change and State Formation in Upper Canada, 1841–1864'. In *Colonial Leviathan: State Formation in Mid-Nineteenth-Century Canada*, edited by A. Greer and I. Radforth, 230–56. Toronto: University of Toronto Press.

Bitterman, R. 1995. 'Women and the Escheat Movement: The Politics of Everyday Life on Prince Edward Island'. In *Rethinking Canada: The Promise of Women's History*, edited by V. Strong-Boag and A. Clair Fellman, 79–92. Toronto: Oxford University Press.

Bouchier, N. 1989. 'Aristocrats and Their "Noble Sport": Woodstock Officers and Cricket During the Rebellion Era'. *Canadian Journal of History of Sport* 20, no. 1:16–33.

_____. 1990. 'For the Love of the Game and the Honour of the Town: Organized Sport, Local Culture and Middle Class Hegemony in Two Ontario Towns, 1838–1895'. Ph.D. dissertation, University of Western Ontario.

Bradbury, B. 1997. 'Women's Workplaces: The Impact of Technological Change on Working-Class Women in the Home and in the Workplace in Nineteenth-Century Montreal'. In *Rethinking Canada: The Promise of Women's History*, edited by V. Strong-Boag and A. Clair Fellman, 154–69. Toronto: Oxford University Press.

Brown, D. 1986a. 'Militarism and Canadian Private Education: Ideal and Practise, 1861–1918'. *Canadian Journal of History of Sport* 17, no. 1:46–59.

_____. 1986b. 'Prevailing Attitudes Towards Sport, Physical Exercise and Society in the 1870s: Impressions from Canadian Periodicals'. *Canadian Journal of History of Sport and Physical Education* 17, no. 2:58–70.

_____. 1989. 'The Northern Character Theme and Sport in Nineteenth Century Canada'. *Canadian Journal of History of Sport* 20:47–56.

Clark, S. 1971. *The Developing Canadian Community*. Toronto: University of Toronto Press.

Connell, R. 1990. 'The State, Gender, and Sexual Politics: Theory and Appraisal'. *Theory and Society* 19, no. 5:507–44.

_____. 1993. 'The Big Picture: Masculinities in Recent World Histories'. *Theory and Society* 22, no. 5:597–623.

_____. 1995. *Masculinities*. Los Angeles: University of California Press.

Curtis, B. 1992. 'Class Culture and Administration: Educational Inspection in Canada West'. In *Colonial Leviathan: State Formation in Mid-Nineteenth-Century Canada*, edited by A. Greer and I. Radforth, 103–33. Toronto: University of Toronto Press.

Day, R. 1989. 'The British Garrison at Halifax: Its Contribution to the Development of Sport in the Community'. In *Sports in Canada: Historical Readings*, edited by M. Mott, 28–36. Mississauga: Copp Clark Pitman.

de Lottinville, P. 1981–2. 'Joe Beef of Montreal: Working-Class Culture and the Tavern, 1869–1889'. *Labour/Le Travailleur* 8/9:9–40.

Devens, C. 1997. 'Separate Confrontations: Gender as a Factor in Indian Adaption to European Colonization in New France'. In *Rethinking Canada: The Promise of Women's History*, edited by V. Strong-Boag and A. Clair Fellman, 11–32. Toronto: Oxford University Press.

Eccles, W. 1969. *The Canadian Frontier, 1534–1760*. Toronto: Holt, Rinehart and Winston.

Fingard, J. 1989. *The Dark Side of Life in Victorian Halifax*. East Lawrencetown, NS: Pottersfield.

Gramsci, A. 1992. *Selections from the Prison Notebooks*, edited and translated by Q. Hoare and G.N. Smith. New York: International Publishers.

Greer, A. 1992. 'The Birth of the Police in Canada'. In *Colonial Leviathan: State Formation in Mid-Nineteenth-Century Canada*, edited by A. Greer and I. Radforth, 17–49. Toronto: University of Toronto Press.

Gruneau, R. 1983. *Class, Sports and Social Development*. Amherst: University of Massachusetts Press.

———. 1988. 'Modernization or Hegemony: Two Views of Sport and Social Development'. In *Not Just a Game: Essays in Canadian Sport Sociology*, edited by J. Harvey and H. Cantelon, 9–32. Ottawa: University of Ottawa Press.

———, and D. Whitson. 1993. *Hockey Night in Canada: Sport, Identities and Cultural Politics*. Toronto: Garamond Press.

Guildford, J., and S. Morton, eds. 1994. *Separate Spheres: Women's Worlds in the Nineteenth-Century Maritimes*. Fredericton: Acadiensis Press.

Guillet, E. 1933. *Early Life in Upper Canada*. Toronto: Ontario Publishing.

Hall, A., T. Slack, G. Smith, and D. Whitson. 1991. *Sport in Canadian Society*. Toronto: McClelland & Stewart.

Howell, C. 1995. *Northern Sandlots: A Social History of Maritime Baseball*. Toronto: University of Toronto Press.

Howell, D., and P. Lindsay. 1986. 'Social Gospel and the Young Boy Problem, 1895–1925'. *Canadian Journal of History of Sport* 17, no. 1:75–87.

Johnson, J. 1989. *Becoming Prominent: Regional Leadership in Upper Canada, 1791–1841*. Kingston: McGill-Queen's University Press.

Kidd, B. 1996. *The Struggle for Canadian Sport*. Toronto: University of Toronto Press.

Laclau, E., and C. Mouffe. 1985. *Hegemony and Socialist Strategy: Towards a Radical Democratic Politics*. London: Verso.

Lappage, R. 1984. 'The Physical Feats of the Voyageur'. *Canadian Journal of History of Sport* 15:30–7.

Lenskyj, H. 1986. *Out of Bounds: Women, Sport and Sexuality*. Toronto: The Women's Press.

_____. 1989. 'Femininity First: Sport and Physical Education for Ontario Girls, 1890–1930'. *Canadian Journal of History of Sport* 13:4–17.

Marks, L. 1996. *Revivals and Roller Rinks: Religion, Leisure, and Identity in Late-Nineteenth-Century Small-Town Ontario*. Toronto: University of Toronto Press.

Metcalfe, A. 1978. 'The Evolution of Organized Physical Recreation in Montreal, 1840–1895'. *Social History/Histoire Sociale* 11, no. 21:144–66.

_____. 1987. *Canada Learns to Play: The Emergence of Organized Sport, 1807–1914*. Toronto: McClelland & Stewart.

Mills, D. 1988. *The Idea of Loyalty in Upper Canada, 1784–1850*. Kingston: McGill-Queen's University Press.

Morgan, C. 1995. 'In Search of the Phantom Misnamed Honour: Duelling in Upper Canada'. *The Canadian Historical Review* 76, no. 4:529–62.

Morrow, D. 1988. 'The Knights of the Snowshoe: A Study of the Evolution of Sport in Nineteenth Century Montreal'. *Journal of Sport History* 15, no. 1:5–40.

_____, M. Keyes, W. Simpson, F. Cosentino, and R. Lappage. 1989. *A Concise History of Sport in Canada*. Toronto: Oxford University Press.

Morton, W. 1972. *The Kingdom of Canada: A General History from Earliest Times*. Toronto: McClelland & Stewart.

Mott, M. 1980. 'The British Protestant Pioneers and the Establishment of Manly Sports in Manitoba, 1870–1886'. *Journal of Sport History* 7, no. 3:25–36.

_____. 1983. 'One Solution to the Urban Crisis: Manly Sports and Winnipeggers, 1990–1914'. *Urban History Review* 12, no. 2:57–70.

_____. 1989. *Sports in Canada: Historical Readings*. Toronto: Copp Clark Pitman.

Noel, J. 1997. 'New France: Les femmes favorisées'. In *Rethinking Canada: The Promise of Women's History*, edited by V. Strong-Boag and A. Clair Fellman, 33–56. Toronto: Oxford University Press.

Noel, S. 1990. *Patrons, Clients, Brokers: Ontario Society and Politics, 1791–1896*. Toronto: University of Toronto Press.

Payne, M. 1989. 'The Sports, Games, Recreations, and Pastimes of the Fur Traders: Leisure at York Factory'. In *Sports in Canada: Historical Readings*, edited by M. Mott, 50–77. Mississauga: Copp Clark Pitman.

Potter, J. 1997. 'Patriarchy and Paternalism: The Case of the Eastern Ontario Loyalist Women'. In *Rethinking Canada: The Promise of Women's History*, edited by V. Strong-Boag and A. Clair Fellman, 57–69. Toronto: Oxford University Press.

Redmond, G. 1979. 'Some Aspects of Organized Sport and Leisure in Nineteenth Century Canada'. *Loisir et société/Society and Leisure* 2:73–100.

_____. 1982. *The Sporting Scots of Nineteenth Century Canada*. Toronto: Farleigh Dickinson University Press.

Rotundo, E. 1987. 'Body and Soul: Changing Ideals of American Middle Class Manhood'. *Journal of Social History* 16, no. 4:23–38.

Salter, M. 1976. 'L'Ordre de Bon Temps: A Functional Analysis'. *Journal of Sport History* 3, no. 2:111–19.

Strong-Boag, V., and A. Clair Fellman, eds. 1997. *Rethinking Canada: The Promise of Women's History*. Toronto: Oxford University Press.

Vertinsky, P. 1994. *The Eternally Wounded Woman: Women, Doctors, and Exercise in the Late Nineteenth Century*. Manchester: Manchester University Press.

Voisey, P. 1981. 'Boosting the Small Prairie Town, 1904–1931: An Example from Southern Alberta'. In *Town and City: Aspects of Western Canadian Urban Development*, edited by A. Artibise, 147–76. Regina: Canadian Plains Research Institute.

Wamsley, K.B. 1992. 'Legislation and Leisure in 19th Century Canada'. Ph.D. dissertation, University of Alberta.

_____. 1994. 'Good Clean Sport and a Deer Apiece: Game Legislation and State Formation in 19th Century Canada'. *Canadian Journal of History of Sport* 25:1–20.

_____. 1995. 'Cultural Signification and National Ideologies: Rifle-shooting in Late Nineteenth Century Canada'. *Social History* 20, no. 1:63–72.

_____. 1997. 'Nineteenth Century Sport Tours, State Formation, and Canadian Foreign Policy'. *Sporting Traditions* 13, no. 2:73–89.

_____. 1998. 'State Formation and Institutionalized Racism: Gambling Laws in Nineteenth and Early Twentieth Century Canada'. *Sport History Review* 29, no. 1:77–85.

_____, and M. Heine. 1995. 'Sabbath Legislation and State Formation in 19th Century Canada'. *Avante* 1, no. 2:44–57.

_____, and D. Whitson. 1993. 'Representations of Competitiveness: International Expositions and Sport Festivals in the Production of National Identity'. Paper presented at the North American Society for Sport History Annual Conference, Albuquerque, New Mexico.

_____, and D. Whitson. 1998. 'Celebrating Violent Masculinities: The Boxing Death of Luther McCarty'. *Journal of Sport History* 25, no. 3:419–31.

Wise, S. 1974. 'Sport and Class Values in Old Ontario and Quebec'. In *His Own Man: Essays in Honour of Arthur Reginald Marsden Lower*, edited by W. Heick and R. Graham, 93–117. Kingston: McGill-Queen's University Press.

_____, and D. Fisher. 1974. *Canada's Sporting Heroes*. Don Mills: General Publishing Company.

Young, K., and K. Wamsley. 1996. 'State Complicity in Sports Assault and the Gender Order in Twentieth Century Canada: Preliminary Observations'. *Avante* 2, no. 2:51–69.

Chapter 3

Class and Gender:
Intersections in Sport and Physical Activity

Peter Donnelly and Jean Harvey

> The girls are out to bingo,
> And the boys are getting stinko,
> They'll think no more of Inco,
> On a Sudbury Saturday night.
> —Stompin' Tom Connors, 'Sudbury Saturday Night'

The chorus from Stompin' Tom's song, 'Sudbury Saturday Night', reminds us of gender differences in how people experience leisure. And while the chorus reflects a stereotype (there are men who play bingo and women who get drunk), Stompin' Tom is not just singing about gender differences. His song is also about working people, people who perform manual work; people who work shifts; people who are employed by the Inco mining and smelting company, and whose job security depends on the availability of ore and the international price of nickel. These are working-class, lower-class people; people who may not have a university education (although, in a Canadian society where there is a degree of social mobility, some of their children may go to university). We do not expect them to be skiing or playing tennis. We expect that the men play softball, or pool, or bowling, and we expect that the women play . . . well, bingo.

There is a widespread myth that Canada is a classless society, that we are all middle class now. Clearly this is not the case. As Little (1997:A6) puts it: 'Even to the casual observer, Canada's contradictions show up everywhere. On one side are the homeless, the food banks and the unemployed. On the other are soaring sales of pricy sport-utility vehicles, booming ski resorts and a mad rush of consumers to buy expensive computers.' And even where class differences have been acknowledged, they are often denied in the case of sport. As Coakley (1998:290) suggests: 'It is widely believed that only performance counts in sport[s that are] open to everyone, and . . . success in sports [is] the result of individual abilities and hard work, not money and privilege'. Others have gone further to suggest that involvement in sport may help overcome social class barriers:

> Sport has often been responsible for breaking down social class lines, racial and ethnic barriers, and sex role stereotypes. Sport often is the common denominator for members of different social classes—they may use sport as a focus for conversation or may band together to participate or support a sport team. Thus, members of different social classes may unify in the cause of sport (Sage 1974:398).

Assertions such as these are difficult to substantiate with evidence. Indeed, nowadays people are finding it increasingly difficult to afford seats at professional and major sport events, and the boom in building corporate boxes is beginning to further distance the rich from the less rich in sport stadia. What is clear is that there is an inverse relationship between social class and participation in sport and physical activity. What is less clear is whether this relationship operates differently for males and for females.

There have been major social class and gender inequalities throughout the history of sport. And while gender has often distinguished those who have participated from those who have not, social class has tended to determine the sports that males (and, to a much lesser extent, females) were permitted to participate in and the form of their participation (Sugden and Tomlinson, forthcoming). Further, as Coakley (1998:291) suggests of contemporary sport, those 'with economic, political, and social power are able to organize and promote games and physical activities that fit their interests and foster their ideas about how social life should be organized'. They do this, for example, by segregating their activities in exclusive clubs, or by determining the form, values, and location of major professional and international sport events.

In this chapter we first examine definitions of social class, the consequences of living in a class-based society, and relationships between social class and gender. Second, we consider the research on social class and gender in sport and the effects of class and gender on sport and physical activity participation in Canada.

Definitions and Consequences

Social class, social status, social stratification, and socio-economic status are all related terms referring to one of the most significant topics in sociology. In simple terms, social stratification borrows from geological imagery in order to describe the structure of a society in terms of layers of social classes. Examples of terms commonly used for these layers are: upper class (ruling class, power élite); upper middle class, middle class, lower middle class; working class, lower class, and underclass. In more analytical terms, social class has been described as 'the social and cultural expression of an economic relationship. Classes are made up of people who are similarly placed in terms of the contribution they make to economic production, the command over resources this gives them, and the lifestyles which this helps to generate' (Sugden and Tomlinson, forthcoming; see also Giddens 1989). Different definitions of class form the basis of varying types of empirical research: for example, the 'classification of the total population into broad "occupational classes" or "socioeconomic status groups"' (Jary and Jary 1995:77). In this sense, class represents a measure of one's income, the prestige associated with one's occupation, and/or the level of education one has attained.

While social class is fundamental to understanding social inequality, it also overlaps with other aspects of inequality such as race and gender. In North America there are wide income and wealth 'gaps' both between those of African and European heritages, and between men and women.[1] It is generally understood, for example, that women earn approximately 70 per cent of the amount men earn, regardless of education level.

While there is little 'subsistence poverty' (individuals lacking access to basic necessities such as food, warmth, and shelter) in modern welfare states such as Canada, there is a substantial and growing gap between the rich and the poor, leading to a situation of 'relative poverty' (the difference between the standard of living of some groups and the majority of the population) (Giddens 1989).[2] These differences in material rewards, as well as social and cultural opportunities, tend to persist despite free access to state-funded education and health care, suggesting that there is a tendency for social classes to reproduce themselves across generations. Although class is not an inherited characteristic like race, sex, age, or height, children are born into their parents' social class. And despite the apparent opportunities for social mobility (moving up or down in the stratification system), there is far less social mobility than many people think (cf., Jencks et al. 1972; Sennett and Cobb 1973).

This apparent incongruity has been addressed by prominent sociologists such as Bourdieu and Passeron (1977) and Willis (1977), who have asked: 'How do working-class kids get working class jobs?' (And, of course, middle-class kids get middle-class jobs.) This question asks if everyone supposedly has equal opportunity in the educational system, why does occupational and educational achievement still reflect social class origins? In the public education system, there is a strong positive relationship between educational achievement and social class, and middle- and upper-class high school graduates attend university in far greater numbers than their lower-class counterparts (Galt and Cernetig 1997; Mitchell 1997a, 1997b; Philp 1997).[3] More conservative thinkers tend to assume that class differences are inevitable and they argue, at the most extreme, that money spent educating lower-class individuals beyond the basics is wasted. Progressive individuals are more concerned with the processes by which 'the hidden injuries of class' (Sennett and Cobb 1973) are reproduced from generation to generation so that they might intervene in those processes to ensure greater equality of opportunity.

In terms of health, the injuries of class are much more apparent. In addition to much higher rates of industrial injury:

> Working-class people have on average lower birth-weight and higher rates of infant mortality, are smaller at maturity, less healthy, and die at a younger age, than those in higher class categories. Major types of mental disorder and physical illness including heart disease, cancer, diabetes, pneumonia and bronchitis are all more common at lower levels of the class structure than towards the top (Giddens 1989:215).

These relationships have been studied in detail, particularly the findings regarding longevity. As Evans (1994:3) notes, 'Top people live longer', and the relationship stands up to all types of analyses and controls.

In Canada the National Forum on Health (1997), a group of experts brought together by Prime Minister Jean Chrétien to advise the federal government on innovative ways to improve Canada's health system, reached similar conclusions. The forum concluded that the only way to significantly improve the health of Canadians would be to invest resources where they would have the most impact—in the non-medical determinants of health such as socio-economic status: 'Higher incomes are related to better health not only because wealthier people can buy adequate food, clothing, shelter and other necessities, but also because wealthier people have more choices and control over decisions in their lives. This sense of being in control is intrinsic to good health' (National Forum on Health 1997:15). The relationship between social class and health is, of course, influenced by rates of sport and physical activity participation, as we will discuss later.

These consequences of social class remind us that class is both an economic and a cultural category. Bourdieu (1984) has developed the concept of 'economic capital'—usually used to refer to income and wealth—to also consider 'cultural' capital. Both of these concepts are particularly important when considering involvement in sport. First, economic capital has an obvious effect on determining the form and nature of our sport participation because much of our sport involvement costs money. Second, cultural capital (network of family, friends, and other contacts; knowledge base in terms of sport, music, art, literature, etc.) also has a profound impact on involvement. Those with more cultural capital are more likely to feel comfortable in many sport environments. However, before turning to sport participation, it is necessary to consider the intersections between class and gender.

Class and Gender

In the preceding discussion we treated class as if it were not gendered, as if the effects of class were the same for males and females. This was the norm for many years in sociology. Because social class research was based primarily on occupational status, and the division of labour in the twentieth century (particularly following the Second World War) tended to exclude married women from the paid labour force, sociologists employed what Crompton (1996) calls an 'employment-aggregate' approach. That is, a dominant male breadwinner was assumed, and the social class of a family unit was based on his occupation (see also Stacey 1981 and Waring 1988).

A feminist critique of this approach started in the 1970s, beginning with research documenting the increasing presence of married women in the workforce, the increasing number of women-headed households, and lack of value placed on domestic and reproductive labour. Waring (1988) identified the economic value of such labour by reminding us how much professional couples, for example, often pay to have meals cooked, houses cleaned, children cared for, and clothes laundered.

Feminist research revolutionized sociological research and thinking in other ways, however, by recognizing that class effects may operate differently by gender. As Crompton (1996:121) suggests, 'in reality, class and gender processes are inextricably entwined, rather than separate phenomena'. Thus, feminist research has exposed the distortions introduced by analysing behaviour on the basis of only a single social characteristic such as social class. Rather, the multi-dimensionality of humans has been recognized—each of us has a gender, a social class background, one or more racial/ethnic affiliations; we belong to a specific age category, we have a certain body size and shape, varying degrees of (dis)ability, and a sexual orientation (Donnelly 1996).

The importance of examining the effects of gender and class is clear, although analyses can be complex: it is not simply a matter of 'adding' gender to class. The two sets of relations combine in a multitude of ways such that, while 'men in general are advantaged through the subordination of women . . . intersections of gender relations with class and race relations yield many other situations where rich white heterosexual women, for instance, are employers of working-class men, patrons of homosexual men, or politically dominant over black men' (Carrigan, Connell, and Lee 1987:177). Thus, while arguments about 'men in general' or 'women in general' may hold, it is necessary to take into account multiple masculinities and femininities and the ways in which they intersect with various social classes and class fractions. And even this represents a more limited view of human behaviour than one that incorporates other human dimensions such as racial or ethnic heritage and age.

There is little research in the sociology of sport that deals with the intersections of class and gender or other combinations of social background characteristics. The following explores the way research on class and gender has developed in the sociology of sport, and the effects of the intersections between class and gender on sport and physical activity participation in Canada.

Class, Gender, and Sport

... class, race, age and gender are not tangential and incidental but central and fundamental influences on leisure 'choice' (Clarke and Critcher 1985:145).

The relationship between sport and social class has a long history, with evidence that élites enjoyed greater opportunities for involvement than the masses as early as ancient Greece and Rome. Class distinctions persisted through the Middle Ages, particularly in restrictions regarding military training and hunting. The most evident class distinction—the amateur/professional distinction—was introduced shortly after the development of modern sport in the mid-nineteenth century. While this distinction is now finally beginning to disappear in sport, its introduction was, in large part, an attempt to exclude working-class participants. The wealthy did not wish to participate alongside or against those they considered to be their social inferiors, or risk the humiliation of defeat (Metcalfe 1987). The distinction was adopted by female athletes, but applied mostly to males because of the virtual absence of women's professional sport and the lesser likelihood of working-class women's involvement in sport (discussed later).

Early research on sport and social class in the sociology of sport generally involved documenting the different sport preferences of different social classes by determining the social class background of the athletes (or their fathers). North American studies (e.g., Gruneau 1976; Loy 1969; Stone 1957, 1969) showed that the upper and lower classes tended to prefer individual sports, and the middle classes tended to prefer team sports. Physical contact also appeared to vary by class, with the amount of contact increasing at lower levels on the social scale. However, studies outside of North America (e.g., Collins 1972; Crawford 1977; Lüschen 1969; Renson 1976) showed some variation from the North American pattern. Attempts to explain these participation patterns (e.g., Lüschen 1969; Yiannakis 1975) appeared only to describe local situations rather than explain them. For example, the same sport represented quite different levels of social status in different societies—'gymnastics is low in Belgium . . . at the middle in Germany . . . and at the upper middle in the United States' (Loy, McPherson, and Kenyon 1978:366). Such studies were useful in terms of better understanding the relationship between sport and social class. However, they tended not to take into account the power differences between the social classes, particularly in terms of the power to choose one's form of participation.

Most of these studies focused on males, with only Gruneau (1976), Lüschen (1969), and Paivia and Jacques (1976) studying both male and female athletes. Despite the fact that their studies were conducted in Canada, Germany, and Australia respectively, all discovered something quite revealing about the class/gender relationship in sport. While athletes, especially high-performance athletes, tended to come mostly from the middle and upper classes, there was a greater proportion of female athletes than male athletes from higher social class backgrounds, even when the athletes were involved in the same sport. As Loy et al. (1978:347) note, this 'suggests that there may be greater social obstacles for lower class females than for lower class males'.

While the previous paragraphs indicate that there are some clear differences between social classes in the type of sports in which people participate, there is also a large body of research that indicates that 'the higher the class, the greater the rate of participation' in sport and physical activity (Hargreaves 1986:96). This finding is repeated at all levels of research, from market surveys to full academic surveys. For example, McCutcheon, Curtis, and White (1997), using a sample of 3,606 respondents to the Campbell's Survey on Well-being in Canada, found that for both males and females there were direct relationships between the level of education and the level of income and the amount of sport and physical activity in which people participated. In other words, the higher the education and income levels, the more the participation. Similarly, a survey of 3,783 US high school students and their parents showed very similar results. The higher the socio-economic status of the students (determined by their parents' education and income), the higher the level of their participation in high school sport (Fejgin 1994). When these findings are combined with the traditionally lower participation rate of females, they add substance to Loy et al.'s (1978) speculation that lower-class females may experience even greater obstacles to sport involvement than lower-class males.[4]

Certainly, class and gender tend to be powerful predictors of sport involvement. In fact, Fejgin (1994:220) found that, after gender, 'the single most powerful explanation for individual athletic involvement is parent education', and that that influence was even stronger for females than males. These findings are confirmed in two more recent studies from outside North America. A study of youth participation in a French city found that: 'boys participated more in sport than girls. The majority of the active girls participated in formal settings [a condition that involves more expense than informal participation]. Social class was the most dominant factor determining whether the subjects participated in sport and whether such participation was in formal or informal sport' (Waser and Passavant 1997:7). And in a large study of junior sport participation in Australia, the data also reveal that parents of the female athletes tended to come from higher social class backgrounds than those of the male athletes (Kirk et al. 1996).

Articulation of Class and Gender

Both class and gender influence the *form* (types of sport and physical activity) and *frequency* of sport and physical activity participation. These differences, at least for social class, are usually interpreted in a simplistic way as being related to economic capital. That is, what types of sport and physical activity participation can a person afford, and how often? Another simple interpretation combines the results of research: males participate more than females; upper classes participate more than lower classes; therefore, the lowest levels of participation will be found among lower-class females (a conclusion actually confirmed by research findings). However, in order to understand how class and gender intersect to influence sport and physical activity involvement, it is necessary to understand the different meanings that sport may have in the lives of men and women, and the way in which those meanings are influenced by their respective class locations.

As Bourdieu (1978:819) notes, it is necessary to go beyond a simple analysis of the statistical distribution of sport activity by class (and gender), and look at 'the meaning which the practices take on in [class and gender] relationships'. Bourdieu (1988) also argues that different kinds of sport mean different things to individuals according to their social class background (and gender). Moreover, among participants in the same sport, individuals from different social classes (and genders) will have different views about the appropriate way of playing that sport. In terms of social class, Bourdieu (1978) classified these meanings as follows: aristocratic/upper-class sports are depicted as 'disinterested' (free from self-interest) practices; middle-class sports are representative of the 'developmental' ethic; and working-class sports are expressive of an 'instrumental' relationship with the body. Disinterestedness means not being heavily invested in an activity, maintaining distance, dignity, and a keen sense that 'it is only a game'. The developmental ethic is represented in middle-class investment in self-improvement in all areas from health and the body to social mobility. An instrumental relationship implies using the body as a tool towards some end—to earn money, or to dominate an opponent—and it is represented in the greater working class involvement in contact sports noted earlier.

Bourdieu's research was conducted in France, a country with a somewhat different class structure than Canada. However, if we take ice hockey as a typical Canadian example, it is possible to develop the following hypothesis with regard to participation, and in support of Bourdieu's position on the meaning of sport in people's lives. It is likely that, given the high cost of the sport, young Canadian males involved in ice hockey are mostly from the wealthier fractions of the working class and from specific segments of the middle class. Among the parents of these players, the higher the level of economic and cultural capital, the greater the interest in skill development (the 'developmental' ethic), and the lesser the interest in body checking and other forms of 'violence'. Working-class parents will have less problem with aggressive physicality, arguing that body checking is a part of the game ('instrumental' relationship with the body) and helps to make their children stronger players. While Bourdieu has not addressed gender specifically, drawing from the work of Laberge (1995) and Laberge and Sankoff (1988), it is possible to hypothesize that girls who are involved in hockey would have parents in higher social classes than the boys because only those with higher levels of cultural capital would entertain the modern 'developmental' ideal that all opportunities open to their sons should also be open to their daughters, and also possess the status security to permit their daughters to step outside traditional gender boundaries. This reasoning is consistent with the findings noted previously that high-performance female athletes tend to come from a higher social class background than the males.

The research evidence, while not dealing with hockey specifically, appears to support Bourdieu's ideas about how meaning is implicated in the articulation of class and gender relationships in sport. Even before adolescence, different meanings have been established regarding sport participation, and the most distinct gender differences appear to be at the level of the working class. For example, Coakley and White (1992) have shown how adolescent, mostly working-class youth in England make decisions about participation. They found that decisions about sport participation:

- Were based on concerns about becoming adults: 'Young women were more likely than young men to conclude that sport participation had little or nothing to do with adulthood for them' (1992:25).
- Were based on concerns about personal competence: 'The young women in our sample were not as likely as young men to define themselves as sportspersons, even when they were physically active' (1992:26);
- Reflected constraints related to money, parents, and opposite-sex friends: 'Fairness did not seem to be an issue when parental protectiveness constrained the sport participation of [females, but not males]; the basis of the constraints were either accepted or associated with parental concern for their safety and well-being' (1992:29). In addition, while financial constraints affected both males and females, girlfriends tended to give priority to their boyfriends' activity preferences rather than vice versa.
- Reflected support and encouragement from significant others: 'Young women were more likely than young men to mention the influence of same-sex friends' (1992:30) in increasing the likelihood of their participation, but both males and females were dependent on parental support and/or the support of adult mentors.
- Reflected past experiences in school sport and physical education classes: 'It seemed that the physical education and sport activities were organized in ways that fit more closely with [the] interests and skills [of young men] than was the case for young women' (1992:31).

When these constraints are combined with the fact that working-class teenage girls are frequently expected to look after younger siblings after school (Coakley 1998), it is easier to understand why sport in general seems to be less significant and less meaningful in the lives of working-class girls and young women.

For middle- and lower-income women, there are similar constraints, particularly in a family setting. A great deal of research shows that working women also take on the lion's share of 'the second shift'—household work and parenting in addition to paid labour (e.g., Hochschild 1989)—and that women's 'second shift' is often involved in increasing men's and children's participation (e.g., Coakley 1998; Thompson 1992; Woodward, Green, and Hebron 1989). As Coakley notes:

> Without money to pay for child care, domestic help, and sport participation expenses, these women simply don't have many opportunities to play sports. Nor do they have time to spare, or a car to get them to where sports are played, or access to gyms and playing fields in their neighborhoods, or the sense of physical safety they need to leave home and travel to where they can play sports (Coakley 1998:300).

In addition, these women often do not have other females with whom they can participate (Gems 1993). And yet, as noted earlier, they often make sacrifices in terms of time, money, or access to the family vehicle(s) to facilitate the participation of their husbands and children.

While financial concerns also constrain sport participation for young lower-class males, two additional gender differences are evident. First, sport is far more meaningful in male lives because of perceived opportunities to become professional athletes. Second, sport is key for establishing a masculine identity. In the first case, because of the visibility and high status of professional athletes, sport may be seen as a realistic and desirable means of social mobility for ambitious and athletically talented lower-class boys. Other avenues to success are often viewed by working-class boys as offering much less opportunity. Thus, for the élite hockey player from a single-industry town in northern Manitoba, or the talented basketball player from a Toronto tenement, there is a great deal at stake and a real possibility that he will 'put all his eggs in one basket' (cf., Messner 1992). That is, he will focus all of his efforts on his athletic skills rather than attempt to succeed in school or develop other talents.

While athletic talent demands respect in lower-class male culture, toughness in sport and other aspects of life is also highly valued. And though we are now beginning to see evidence of girls, especially middle-class girls, using sport to establish their feminine identities (e.g., Miller and Penz 1991; Young 1997), the practice is long established for boys (Messner 1992). In line with Bourdieu's characterization of (male) working-class sport as involving an 'instrumental' relationship with the body, McCutcheon et al. (1997:58) suggested that the sport injury rate might be higher among lower-class males because 'there is a tendency for the lower class to be overrepresented in sports associated with physical risks'. They cite a number of studies showing how working-class males use sport as a means of developing and demonstrating stereotypical masculine characteristics (e.g., toughness, aggression, dominance, risk taking, pain tolerance). Even as such men mature and become established in the workforce, the role of sport for the maintenance of masculine identity remains important. Dunk's (1991) study of working-class men in Thunder Bay shows how masculinism in the work-place—homophobia, toughness, male camaraderie—carries over into their social and sporting lives.

Apart from a continuing lower level of participation by females, gender differences in the meaning of sport and physical activity involvement are becoming less pronounced in the middle and upper classes. Traditional constraints on women's participation are less evident at the upper income level: 'They have resources to pay for child care, domestic help, carryout dinners, and sport participation. They often participate in sport activities by themselves, with friends, or with other family members. They have social networks made up of other women who also have the resources to maintain high levels of sport parti-cipation' (Coakley 1998:300). For the upper/upper middle classes, sport is often about healthy exercise, social contacts, and demonstrating one's class location (and, of course, excluding others). It is not usually taken too seriously (cf., Bourdieu's 'disinterestedness'), and is rarely thought of in terms of gaining 'respect' or as a means to achieve success:

> . . . young people from upper-income backgrounds often have so many opportu-nities to do different things that they may not focus attention on one sport to the exclusion of other sports and other activities. For someone who has a car, nice clothes, money for college tuition, and good career contacts for the future, playing sports may be good for bolstering popularity among peers, but it is not perceived as a necessary foundation for an entire identity (Coakley 1998:301; see also Messner 1992).

However, this does not mean that sport participation is not considered important. Upper-income children are taught to ski and play tennis, to swim and sail. The ability to participate is considered such an important social and developmental skill that participation is often mandatory at many of the better private schools.

For the middle class, the most diverse of the class categories, participation seems to emphasize achievement (cf., Bourdieu's 'developmental' ethic). Moreover, gender differences around the issue of achievement seem to be dimin-ishing over time. Achievement may be expressed in three specific ways in rela-tion to sport: (1) success in sport itself; (2) the development of career skills through sport participation; and (3) the achievement of an 'ideal' body type.

The middle class is the most socially mobile class, and success in sport is now sometimes viewed as a viable career option. This is mainly because the large salaries that are now available have made sport an attractive middle-class ambi-tion. While middle-class athletes are less likely to be allowed by their parents to 'put all of their eggs in one basket', highly talented individuals from (upper) mid-dle-income families, such as Eric Lindros, are now more likely to consider it appropriate to put their education on hold (by following the junior hockey route) in order to pursue a professional hockey contract. Other talented middle-class players may hedge their bets by following the athletic scholarship route to a career as a professional hockey player. However, involvement in other professional and non-professional sports—ranging from golf to track, and figure skating to tennis—is also considered appropriate for both males and females in order to pursue 'success', not only because of potential income from prizes and endorsements but also because of the fame, networks of contacts, and even the full scholarship to an American university that might result from such athletic success.

Even when middle-class children show less athletic talent, participation is often encouraged in the belief that they will learn achievement skills that are considered valuable in the work world. The idea that 'the road to the boardroom leads through the locker room' is very evident here, especially for males. In Seeley, Sim, and Loosley's (1956, 1976) classic study of 'Crestwood Heights', the fictional name given to an upper-middle class community in Toronto, 'even in recreational activity, the youth of the community do not engage in sport or games as activities to be participated in for enjoyment only. Sport provides an enculturative milieux that prepares boys to become executives, or more broadly, upwardly mobile *career competitors*' (Gruneau and Beamish 1976:298). Although it is obvious that 'the youth' referred to above were boys, nowadays the meaning of female participation appears to be increasingly similar to that of male participation. The point is now being made widely by feminist advocates (e.g., Nelson 1991) and by organizations (such as the Women's Sport Foundation) that women's success in the career world is related to the skills of teamwork, competitiveness, and motivation, which have traditionally been available only to men through their sport participation. In one of the recent studies of women's values in sport participation, Young and White (1995) found that middle-class female participants in risky sports shared values about risk, injury, pain tolerance, and success that were very similar to those held by males (cf., Young, White, and McTeer 1994).

Meanings of achievement are also constructed by male and female middle-class participants in the area of exercise and diet, where achievement involves the sculpting of an 'ideal' body type. Long a characteristic of middle-class women's physical activity, there is growing evidence that males are increasingly becoming 'victims of fashion' in their attempts to control their body shapes (cf., MacNeill 1988; Markula 1995; White and Gillett 1994). Of course, there are different 'ideals' for males and females, and some different motivations involved in their attempts to sculpt their bodies, but the use of physical activity not as an end in itself but as an attempt to achieve some goal is characteristic of the middle-class 'developmental' ethic. Interestingly, in this case, there is sometimes a link between male working-class and middle-class meanings. Bodybuilding implies an 'instrumental' relationship with the body and is also associated with some ideals of masculine identity and toughness. Social mobility is blurring the boundaries between the middle and working classes.

The meanings outlined here are not static. One of the effects of the women's movement in the past twenty-five years has been to change the meanings around gender and participation in sport. The movement has had the most impact on middle- and upper-income women who are rapidly establishing woman-centred meanings around participation. These changes have also led to paradoxical meanings whereby, for example, fitness clubs may be seen by women on the one hand as places to engage in weight loss and body sculpting, and on the other hand as women's spaces where they can meet in the absence of men. Middle-class notions of achievement and the development of achievement skills through sport are also increasingly linked as middle-class female participation in both sport and the workforce increases dramatically. The unintended consequences of such changes are outlined in the following section.

Democratization

Democratization refers to the process of change towards greater social equality. The term has generally been applied to social class, but, to the extent that class articulates with other aspects of social inequality (gender, racial/ethnic heritage, age, etc.), democratization can be taken to refer to any movement towards greater social equality. In terms of sport and leisure: 'A fully democratized sport and leisure environment would include both the right to participate, regardless of one's particular set of social characteristics, and the right to be involved in determination of the forms, circumstances and meanings of participation' (Donnelly 1993:417).

Democratization can be initiated by those seeking greater equality (e.g., the women's movement), by enlightened governments, or by governments responding to a perceived public demand. In the late twentieth century in Western neoliberal societies, however, governments and corporations are rarely persuaded by arguments for the rightness and justice of democratization. They tend to be more interested in democratization only if it involves economic (or cost-saving) outcomes. In Canada there have been two major attempts by the federal government to promote the democratization of sport and physical activity. In both cases class and gender have figured prominently. The first came about because of concerns about a perceived lack of Canadian success in international sport. The second concerns the health of Canadians and the way in which physical activity is involved in health promotion (and a reduction in health care costs).

As success in international sport gained political importance for nation-states during the Cold War, it also became evident that, in order to produce more competitive athletes, a rational sport delivery system would ideally involve larger segments of the population—male and female, from all social classes—in sport. This would provide a broader base of athletes from which potential medal-winning athletes could emerge.[5] In Canada, and even before many of the research findings previously noted were publicized, it was evident that a great deal of social inequality existed in Canada's amateur sport system:

> We must face the fact that the opportunity for involvement in sports and recreation is extremely unequal between the socio-economic classes within our population. . . . It's only fair, just as a dash [sprint] in a track meet is only fair, that everyone has the same starting line, and the same distance to run. Unfortunately, in terms of facilities, coaching, promotion and programming, the sports scene today resembles a track on which some people have twenty-five yards to run, some fifty, some one-hundred, and some as much as a mile or more (Munro 1970:4–5).

John Munro was the federal minister for health and welfare in the early 1970s and, in the climate leading up to the 1976 Montréal Olympics, his policy document entitled *A Proposed Sports Policy for Canadians* (1970) led to a number of changes aimed at democratizing access to competitive sport and thus improving Canada's performance in international sport. These included establishing a system of paying high-performance ('carded') athletes, building sports facilities in underserviced areas of Canada, and setting up the National Sport and Recreation Centre in Ottawa.

Two studies—Gruneau's (1976) study of 1971 Canada Winter Games athletes and Beamish's (1990) study of 1986 Canadian national team athletes—provide clear evidence that Munro's policies failed to broaden the social class base of Canadian athletes. The first study, conducted around the time the policy was introduced, and the second conducted fifteen years later, provided a clear period of time in which to assess the effects of the policy. Gruneau found that 42 per cent of the athletes' fathers came from the highest occupational categories (compared with 17 per cent of the Canadian male labour force). By 1986, Beamish found that 68 per cent of the athletes' fathers ranked in the highest occupational categories. Thus, rather than having a democratizing effect, the *Proposed Sports Policy* appears to have had an opposite effect. (It should be noted, however, that various gender equity policies have been much more successful to the extent that they have provided greater access to sport for middle-class females.)

Beginning in the period around 1980, fiscally conservative governments in Canada, the United States, and the United Kingdom began to express concerns about public expenditure. One of the areas that came under scrutiny was spending on health care. Subsequently, a major shift in public policy resulted in a greater focus on preventive issues such as diet and lifestyle. Exercise promotion became a key component of this policy, and public service campaigns (e.g., Life, Be In It [Australia] and ParticipACTION [Canada], see MacNeill 1999, this volume) were created and became part of what we now refer to as 'the fitness industry'. Medical and physical education professions determined optimum levels of exercise for 'good health', and physicians and physical education teachers began to prescribe ideal 'doses' of activity (e.g., twenty minutes of aerobic exercise, at least three times per week, at 70 per cent maximum heart rate).

Since the inception of ParticipACTION twenty-five years ago, the proportion of active Canadians has increased from 25 per cent to 33 per cent (McIlroy 1998). However, the campaign has failed to democratize leisure physical activity involvement beyond some sectors of the middle and upper middle classes. Quite obviously, people with fewer resources at their disposal are less able to change their levels of physical activity. As Ingham (1985) suggested:

> The fusion of new right ideology and right-thinking common sense . . . promotes a lifestyle which exhorts us to save our hearts by jogging in the arsenic filled air of Tacoma. If jogging is not for you, then there are other routes to fitness—routes which conveniently ignore the fact that millions of people who hover around and below the poverty line cannot afford ten-speeds, tennis racquets, and memberships in health fitness centers. And, as an active rather than passive lifestyle, it exhorts us to burn off calories while denying State dependents the food they need to survive (Ingham 1985:50).

Subsequently it was recognized that individuals tend not to follow government- or even physician-mandated exercise prescriptions. As a result, there was a shift in Canada towards Active Living, a program that takes into account all the activities of daily life while not imposing activity thresholds.[6]

After approximately seventeen years of policies and programs encouraging Canadians to be more active, there has been only a small increase in the activity level of the population. Females are shown consistently to be less active than males, and people with lower education, income, and occupational status are less active than those with higher income, education, and occupational status:

> Ontarians who are inactive in their leisure time are more likely to be females. They are more likely to be older as well. The inactive population is more likely to be concentrated among lower education and income levels. Inactive people are more likely to live in communities with fewer than 75,000 residents. They are more likely to be found among the sales and clerical workforce and among home-makers. A sizable number are also blue collar workers (Craig, Russell, and Cameron 1995:97).

The combination of class and gender is more evident in the following:

> Whether it is measured by income, education levels or occupation, low socioeco- nomic status (SES) has long been associated with lower levels of participation in activity and an increased likelihood of illness, disability and early death. Low-SES families are more likely to have low birth weight babies who are at high risk for the development of physical, social, emotional and behavioural problems while

growing up. [More than] one million Canadian children . . . live in low income families. About 50 per cent of these families are headed by female single parents (*Focus on Active Living* 1994:6).

In order to understand the failure of these two important attempts to democratize participation in sport and physical activity in Canada, we conclude by considering these failures in the light of the meanings produced in the articulation of class and gender noted in the previous section.

Conclusion

Evidence of the connections between class and gender, and participation in sport and physical activity, are all around us. Recent examples range from interpretations of the Tonya Harding-Nancy Kerrigan incident in 1993,[7] which were strongly connected to North American images of gender and social class (Stoloff 1995), to the recent revelations about Alan Eagleson,[8] a tough and formerly working-class lawyer who was jailed for exploiting and defrauding young, naive, and uneducated hockey players. In a broader sense, social class issues remain evident in the relative absence of working-class athletes on Canadian teams, and gender issues are evident in the relative absence of media coverage of women's sports.

If we work from the assumption that voluntary participation in sport and physical activity can be a pleasurable social experience that brings physical and mental health benefits, or that participation can be materially rewarding for physically talented individuals and entertaining to watch for the less talented, then there are powerful reasons for wanting to overcome class and gender barriers to participation. It makes sense that there should be equal opportunities to participate. Any democratization that has occurred has been the result of various social movements devoted to social equality, human rights, and health issues. However, many of the attempts to promote changes have been imposed from the 'top down' without consultation with those targeted, and without involving those who are about to be 'given' the opportunities in deciding 'the forms, circumstances, and meanings of participation' (Donnelly 1993:417).

For example, in the early 1970s Sport Canada too often funded programs aimed at middle-class individuals for whom such participation was already a meaningful activity. And gender equity programs have also increased the number of athletes in the sport development and high-performance systems without breaking down class barriers. Similarly, the ParticipACTION, Active Living, and other exercise prescription programs have increased the numbers of middle-class participants both male and female, but they have also failed to breach the class barriers. In each of these cases, the programs were designed by middle-class bureaucrats and 'experts', and consequently rooted in middle-class meanings and values. Little attempt has been made to understand working-class culture, or to involve working-class people in the planning of such programs.

Two recent studies argue the value of this 'bottom up' approach. Donnelly and Harvey (1996), in a wide-ranging examination of structural barriers to involvement in Active Living programs, emphasized the following:

- The importance of empowering individuals from disadvantaged populations. Potential participants in active living initiatives must be empowered to determine their own forms of activity, as well as to have some control over the provision of services. This may be achieved only through the development of community action at the local level (1996:42).
- Initiatives that attempt to increase access to active living without taking into account the overall living and working conditions of the target populations are unlikely to be successful in terms of improving health (1996:43).

Recently, Frisby, Crawford, and Dorer (1997:19) were involved in precisely the type of project we are advocating, a modified 'bottom up' project in British Columbia that targeted 'women living below the poverty line who were interested in increasing their opportunities for participation in physical activity'. We say 'modified' because the target population were in partnership with a large group of middle-class individuals and agencies (e.g., university researchers, parks and recreation department, family services, health unit, etc.). The target group members, who identified themselves as 'low income women', immediately expanded the activity group to include their children. They 'did not separate their needs from those of their immediate families [and] stated that "their children came first," and they would sacrifice their own involvement to ensure their children's needs were met' (Frisby, Crawford, and Dorer 1997:19). These women were empowered to not only name themselves but also to change the project itself to meet their own needs and those of their children. Without the participants' intervention, the provision of the program only for the women (i.e., one that did not take into account their whole living circumstances, which included children) would have been a failure. The researchers and program providers would probably have blamed the victims for not taking the opportunities provided. Even with their involvement, the researchers realized that the women were already self-selecting—they 'were White, had preschool children, and were ready to reduce the social isolation they were experiencing' (Frisby, Crawford, and Dorer 1997:20). Among other 'women living below the poverty line', they had failed 'to reach the most marginalized low-income women in the community (e.g., visible minority women, women isolated by abuse, and older low-income women)' (Frisby, Crawford, and Dorer 1997:20). The project took steps to overcome the barriers to involvement identified by the women involved, and approximately seventy women and 150 children attended regularly. As Frisby et al. (1997:20) note, 'the women felt ownership for the programs because they had the freedom to choose whether to get involved and their voices were taken into account during the project'.

When individuals are involved in creating and transforming the meaning of their physical activities, the transformative effects could reach beyond health and quality of life issues: 'It is possible that the struggle to achieve a fully democratized sport and leisure might result in the capacity to transform communities. People could learn initiative, community endeavour, collective rather than individual values, self determination, etc., that could permit them to begin to take charge of their own lives and communities' (Donnelly 1993:428). Frisby et al. (1997:8) found that the Women's Action Project took steps in this direction: '[the project] demonstrated how the process can result in a more inclusive local sport system and, at the same time, provide a rich setting for examining organizational dynamics including collaborative decision-making, community partnerships, power imbalances, resource control, resistance to change, and nonhierarchical structures'. In the intersections of class and gender, upper- and middle-class women's sport and physical activity involvement are increasing and changing. While it may not be changing in the most healthy of directions (i.e., an apparent modelling of men's risk taking/injury-prone behaviour), increased empowerment and involvement could take it in other directions. The models for increased lower-class involvement and empowerment are only now being worked out for women and for men. When they are, it will be interesting to re-examine the Canadian sport system to see the changes that result.

Notes

1. '"Wealth" refers to all the assets an individual owns (stocks and shares, savings and property such as homes or land; items which can be sold)' (Giddens 1989:216; see also Oliver and Shapiro 1996). It differs from 'income' (wages and salaries, interest and dividends), which is the usual basis of statistics and frequently used as a measure of social class.

2. a. In order to assess the distribution of reported income (rather than wealth), Statistics Canada divides the population into fifths (quintiles). The following indicates the proportion of total income received by each quintile in 1995:

Quintile	0–20%	21–40%	41–60%	61–80%	81–100%
% Income	3%	9%	16%	25%	47%

The median income was $20,134, while the mean income was $25,518, a clear indication of the top-heavy income distribution (Little 1997). Despite economic growth in 1996, income for the lowest quintile fell by 3.1 per cent while that for the highest quintile increased by 1.8 per cent (Statscan 1997).

b. Since the 1980s, government policies in Canada, the United States, and Britain, referred to by John Kenneth Galbraith (1997) as 'the war on the poor', have resulted in an increase in poverty and an increasing gap between the rich and the poor (Campbell 1996; Frean 1997).

3. Recent studies by Statistics Canada and the Organization for Economic Cooperation and Development reaffirm the relationship between poverty and lack of school success in Canada (Dwyer 1997:70).
4. In Fejgin's (1994) sample of US high school students, 59.7 per cent of the males participated in sports compared to 47.5 per cent of the females. Canadian data indicate the decline in participation among adolescent females: 'In the 10–14 age group, 49% of the female population are involved in sport, versus 72% of the male population. Beginning at age 12, involvement in girls declines steadily until only 11% are involved by grade 11' (Best, Blackhurst, and Makosky 1992:149).

5. This is the model that was purportedly in place in the highly successful athletic nations of eastern Europe and Cuba. However, it is now apparent that there were parallel systems—a 'sport for all' system to maintain an active and healthy population, and a system of early talent identification and élite training.

6. There are serious problems with much of the research, which only takes into account leisure physical activity. 'Housework, child care, manual labour, work that involves being on your feet, and the . . . activities [that some define as leisure and others as a chore, e.g., gardening] . . . account for the majority of energy expenditure of Canadians; and yet, this source of energy expenditure remains unrecorded in most surveys' (Donnelly and Harvey 1996:39).

7. Friends of Harding attacked and injured Kerrigan in an attempt to prevent her from participating in the 1994 Lillehammer Olympics.

8. Alan Eagleson served a prison term for misuse of funds in his multiple roles as player agent, head of the National Hockey League Players' Association, and organizer of the Canada Cup hockey series.

References

Beamish, R. 1990. 'The Persistence of Inequality: An Analysis of Participation Patterns among Canada's High Performance Athletes'. *International Review for the Sociology of Sport* 25, no. 2:143–53.

Best, J.C., M. Blackhurst, and L. Malosky. 1992. *Sport: The Way Ahead*. Report of the Minister's Task Force on Canadian Sport Policy. Ottawa: Sport Canada.

Bourdieu, P. 1978. 'Sport and Social Class'. *Social Science Information* 7, no. 6:819–40.

_____. 1984. *Distinction: A Social Critique of the Judgement of Taste*. London: Routledge & Kegan Paul.

_____. 1988. 'Program for a Sociology of Sport'. *Sociology of Sport Journal* 5, no. 2:153–61.

_____, and J.-C. Passeron. 1977. *Reproduction in Education, Society and Culture*, translated by R. Nice. London: Sage.

Campbell, M. 1996. 'Poverty in Canada: The Shifting Line Between the Haves and Have-Nots'. *The Globe and Mail* (12 October):D5.

Canadian Council on Social Development. 1996. *The Progress of Canada's Children: 1996*. Ottawa: Canadian Council on Social Development.

Carrigan, T., B. Connell, and J. Lee. 1987. 'Hard and Heavy: Toward a New Sociology of Masculinity'. In *Beyond Patriarchy: Essays by Men on Pleasure, Power and Change*, edited by M. Kaufman, 139–92. Toronto: Oxford University Press.

Clarke, J., and C. Critcher. 1985. *The Devil Makes Work: Leisure in Capitalist Britain*. London: Macmillan.

Coakley, J. 1998. *Sport in Society: Issues and Controversies,* 6th edn. Boston: McGraw Hill.

_____, and A. White. 1992. 'Making Decisions: Gender and Sport Participation Among British Adolescents'. *Sociology of Sport Journal* 9, no. 1:20–35.

Collins, L. 1972. 'Social Class and Olympic Athletes'. *British Journal of Physical Education* 3 (July):25–7.

Craig, C., S. Russell, and C. Cameron. 1995. *Benefits of Physical Activity for Ontario: Executive Summary and Implications for the Development of a Physical Activity Framework*. Toronto: Queen's Printer for Ontario.

Crawford, S. 1977. 'Occupational Prestige Rankings and the New Zealand Olympic Athlete'. *International Review of Sport Sociology* 12:5–15.

Crompton, R. 1996. 'Gender and Class Analysis'. In *Conflicts About Class: Debating Inequality in Late Industrialism*, edited by D. Lee and B. Turner, 115–26. London: Longman.

Donnelly, P. 1993. 'Democratization Revisited: Seven Theses on the Democratization of Sport and Active Leisure'. *Loisir et societé/Society and Leisure* 16, no. 2:413–34.

_____. 1996. 'Approaches to Social Inequality in the Sociology of Sport'. *Quest* 48, no. 2:221–42.

_____, and J. Harvey. 1996. 'Overcoming Systemic Barriers to Access in Active Living'. Report presented to Fitness Branch, Health Canada and Active Living Canada.

Dunk, T. 1991. *It's a Working Man's Town: Male Working-Class Culture in Northwestern Ontario*. Montréal and Kingston: McGill-Queen's University Press.

Dwyer, V. 1997. 'The Roots of Failure'. *Maclean's* (22 September):70.

Evans, R.G. 1994. 'Introduction'. In *Why Are Some People Healthy and Others Not? The Determinants of Population Health*, edited by R.G. Evans, M. Barer, and T. Marmor, 3–26. New York: Aldine de Gruyter.

Fejgin, N. 1994. 'Participation in High School Competitive Sports: A Subversion of School Mission or Contribution to Academic Goals?' *Sociology of Sport Journal* 11, no. 3:211–30.

Focus on Active Living. 1994. 'Equity Ideas and Action'. *Focus on Active Living* 1, no. 4:4–6.

Frean, A. 1997. 'Poverty Gap Widens For Class of 1970: Poorest of a Generation Are Trapped in Deprivation While Privileged Prosper Even More'. *Times* (25 June):8.

Frisby, W., S. Crawford, and T. Dorer. 1997. 'Reflections on Participatory Action Research: The Case of Low-Income Women Accessing Local Physical Activity Services'. *Journal of Sport Management* 11, no. 1:8–28.

Galbraith, J.K. 1997. 'A Message for the Socially Concerned'. *The Globe and Mail* (17 January):A15.

Galt, V., and M. Cernetig. 1997. 'Two Schools Worlds Apart: Poverty a Barrier to Student Opportunity'. *The Globe and Mail* (26 April):A1, A12.

Gerns, G. 1993. 'Working Class Women and Sport'. *Women in Sport and Physical Activity* 2, no. 1:17–30.

Giddens, A. 1989. *Sociology*. Cambridge: Polity Press.

Gruneau, R. 1976. 'Class or Mass: Notes on the Democratization of Canadian Amateur Sport'. In *Canadian Sport: Sociological Perspectives*, edited by R. Gruneau and J. Albinson, 461–519. Don Mills: Addison-Wesley.

_____, and R. Beamish. 1976. 'Introduction: Sports and Recreation in the Canadian Community'. In *Canadian Sport: Sociological Perspectives*, edited by R. Gruneau and J. Albinson, 295–301. Don Mills: Addison-Wesley.

Hargreaves, J. 1986. *Sport, Power, and Culture*. Cambridge: Polity Press.

Health Canada. 1996. *Report on the Health of Canadians*. Ottawa: Health Canada.

Hochschild, A. 1989. *The Second Shift*. New York: Avon.

Ingham, A. 1985. 'From Public Issue to Personal Trouble: Well-being and the Fiscal Crisis of the State'. *Sociology of Sport Journal* 2, no. 1:43–55.

Jary, D., and J. Jary. 1995. *Collins Dictionary of Sociology*, 2nd edn. Glasgow: HarperCollins.

Jencks, C., et al. 1972. *Inequality: A Reassessment of the Effects of Family and School in America*. New York: Basic Books.

Kirk, D., P. Burke, T. Carlson, K. Davis, S. Glover, and A. O'Connor. 1996. *The Social and Economic Impact on Family Life of Children's Participation in Junior Sport*. Canberra: Australian Sports Commission.

Laberge, S. 1995. 'Toward an Integration of Gender into Bourdieu's Concept of Cultural Capital'. *Sociology of Sport Journal* 12, no. 2:132–46.

_____, and D. Sankoff. 1988. 'Physical Activities, Body Habitus, and Lifestyles'. In *Not Just a Game: Essays in Canadian Sport Sociology*, edited by J. Harvey and H. Cantelon, 267–86. Ottawa: University of Ottawa Press.

Little, B. 1997. 'Income Game Won in the Final Quarter'. *The Globe and Mail* (13 January):A6.

Loy, J. 1969. 'The Study of Sport and Social Mobility'. In *Aspects of Contemporary Sport Sociology*, edited by G. Kenyon, 101–19. Chicago: The Athletic Institute.

_____, B. McPherson, and G. Kenyon. 1978. *Sport and Social Systems*. Don Mills: Addison-Wesley.

Lüschen, G. 1969. 'Social Stratification and Social Mobility Among Young Sportsmen'. In *Sport, Culture and Society*, edited by J. Loy and G. Kenyon, 258–76. New York: Macmillan.

McCutcheon, T., J. Curtis, and P. White. 1997. 'The Socioeconomic Distribution of Sports Injuries: Multivariate Analyses Using Canadian National Data'. *Sociology of Sport Journal* 14, no. 1:57–72.

McIllroy, A. 1998. 'Sloth Truly a Deadly Sin, Study Finds'. *The Globe and Mail* (22 January):A1, A11.

MacNeill, M. 1988. 'Active Women, Media Representations, and Ideology'. In *Not Just a Game: Essays in Canadian Sport Sociology*, edited by J. Harvey and H. Cantelon, 195–211. Ottawa: University of Ottawa Press.

Markula, P. 1995. 'Firm But Shapely, Fit But Sexy, Strong But Thin: The Postmodern Aerobicizing Female Bodies'. *Sociology of Sport Journal* 12, no. 4:424–53.

Messner, M. 1992. *Power at Play: Sports and the Problem of Masculinity*. Boston: Beacon Press.

Metcalfe, A. 1987. *Canada Learns to Play: The Emergence of Organized Sport, 1807–1914*. Toronto: McClelland and Stewart.

Miller, L., and O. Penz. 1991. 'Talking Bodies: Female Bodybuilders Colonize a Male Preserve'. *Quest* 43, no. 2:148–63.

Mitchell, A. 1997a. 'The Poor Fare Worse in Schools: Study Underlines Need for Early Intervention'. *The Globe and Mail* (18 April):A1, A9.

_____. 1997b. 'The Affluent Use Tutors, Camp in Race to Give Children an Edge'. *The Globe and Mail* (28 April:A1, A8.

Munro, J. 1970. *A Proposed Sports Policy for Canadians*. Ottawa: Department of Health and Welfare.

National Council of Welfare. 1996. *Poverty Profile 1994*. Ottawa: National Council of Welfare.

National Forum on Health. 1997. *Canada Health Action: Building on the Legacy,* 2 vols. Ottawa: Public Works and Government Services.

Nelson, M.B. 1991. *Are We Winning Yet?* New York: Random House.

Oliver, M., and T. Shapiro. 1996. *Black Wealth White Wealth: A New Perspective on Racial Inequality*. London: Routledge.

Paivia, G., and T. Jacques. 1976. 'The Socioeconomic Origin, Academic Attainment, Occupational Mobility, and Parental Background of Selected Australian Athletes'. Paper presented at the International Congress of Physical Activity Sciences, Québec City.

Philp, M. 1997. 'Poor Already Behind by Time They Reach School'. *The Globe and Mail* (29 April):A1, A14.

Renson, R. 1976. 'Status Symbolism of Sport Stratification'. Paper presented at the International Congress of Physical Activity Sciences, Quebéc City.

Sage, G., ed. 1974. *Sport and American Society: Selected Readings*. Reading, MA: Addison-Wesley.

Seeley, J., R.A. Sim, and E. Loosley. 1956. *Crestwood Heights*. Toronto: University of Toronto Press.

_____, R.A. Sim, and E. Loosley. 1976. 'Sports and the Career in Crestwood Heights'. In *Canadian Sport: Sociological Perspectives*, edited by R. Gruneau and J. Albinson, 354–62. Don Mills: Addison-Wesley.

Sennett, R., and J. Cobb. 1973. *The Hidden Injuries of Class*. New York: Vintage Books.

Stacey, M. 1981. 'The Division of Labour Revisited or Overcoming the Two Adams'. In *Practice and Progress: British Sociology 1950–1980*, edited by P. Abrams, R. Deem, J. Finch, and P. Rock, 172–90. London: Allen & Unwin.

Statscan. 1997. *Income Distributions by Size in Canada*. Ottawa: Statistics Canada.

Stoloff, S. 1995. 'Tonya, Nancy, and the Bodily Figurations of Social Class'. In *Women on Ice: Feminist Spectacles on the Tonya Harding/Nancy Kerrigan Spectacle*, edited by C. Baughman, 225–40. New York: Routledge.

Stone, G. 1957. 'Some Meanings of American Sport'. In *Proceedings of the National College Physical Education Association for Men, 60th Annual Meeting*, 6–29. Washington, DC: CPEA.

_____. 1969. 'Some Meanings of American Sport: An Extended View'. In *Aspects of Contemporary Sport Sociology*, edited by G. Kenyon, 5–16. Chicago: The Athletic Institute.

Sugden, J., and A. Tomlinson. Forthcoming. 'Theorizing Sport, Social Class and Status'. In *Handbook of Sport and Society*, edited by J. Coakley and E. Dunning. London: Sage.

Thompson, S. 1992. 'Sport for Others, Work for Women'. Paper presented at the Olympic Scientific Congress, Malaga, Spain.

Waring, M. 1988. *Counting for Nothing: What Men Value and What Women Are Worth*. Wellington, NZ: Allen & Unwin.

Waser, A.-M., and E. Passavant. 1997. 'Sport as a Leisure Time Pursuit Among the Youth of Caen, France'. *International Review for the Sociology of Sport* 32, no. 1:7–17.

White, P., and J. Gillett. 1994. 'Reading the Muscular Body: A Critical Decoding of Advertisements in *Flex* Magazine'. *Sociology of Sport Journal* 11, no. 1:18–39.

Willis, P. 1977. *Learning to Labour: How Working Class Kids Get Working Class Jobs*. Farnborough, UK: Saxon House.

Woodward, D., E. Green, and S. Hebron. 1989. 'The Sociology of Women's Leisure and Physical Recreation: Constraints and Opportunities'. In *Proceedings of the Jyväskylä Congress on Movement and Sport in Women's Life*, vol. 1, 512–24. Jyväskylä: Press of the University of Jyväskylä.

Yiannakis, A. 1975. 'A Theory of Sport Stratification'. *Sport Sociology Bulletin* 4 (Spring):22–32.

Young, K. 1997. 'Women, Sport and Physicality: Preliminary Findings from a Canadian Study'. *International Review for the Sociology of Sport* 32, no. 3:297–305.

_____, and P. White. 1995. 'Sport, Physical Danger, and Injury: The Experiences of Elite Women Athletes'. *Journal of Sport and Social Issues* 19, no. 1:45–61.

_____, P. White, and W. McTeer. 1994. 'Body Talk: Male Athletes Reflect on Sport, Injury, and Pain'. *Sociology of Sport Journal* 11, no. 2:175–94.

Part II:

Contemporary Issues and Research

We now turn to the contemporary scholarship on sport and gender in Canada. This growing body of work is indicative of the diversity that exists among Canadian sportswomen and sportsmen in terms of factors such as age, race, heritage, sexuality, and social class. It also underscores the fact that the experiences of young, White, middle-class, heterosexual, non-disabled sports participants are not representative of all Canadians. Taken as a whole, the chapters show that the privileging of men relative to women, and of straights relative to gays in Canadian sport has also been influenced by other relations of dominance and subordination. They go some way in expanding current levels of understanding of the complex relationship between sport and gender and raise questions that need to be addressed in future research.

In concert with the historical and conceptual issues examined in Part I of this book, the research reported in this section demonstrates that there are multiplicities of gender identities in sport and that sport practices in Canada are characterized by struggles over their meaning. To speak of a 'generic' sporting masculinity or femininity simply does not do justice to the complexity of Canadian sporting life. Whether through substantive research or through new ways of conceptualizing sport and gender in Canada, the chapters that follow make a significant contribution towards documenting the diversity of relations of power in Canadian sport.

The idea that there is no singular masculinity and femininity operating within Canadian sport is developed in Chapter 4 in which Philip White and Kevin Young review research findings on gender and rates and types of sport injury. Their findings show marked differences in sport injury both between males and females and within male sport and female sport. Similarly, Caroline Davis's discussion of biological, sociological, and psychological factors acting on the relationship between sport, physical activity, and eating disorders recognizes that some femininities are more closely associated with body image disorders than others. Her chapter revisits the thorny debate on the extent to which human behaviour is influenced by biological factors or environmental factors, or an interaction between the two, and her discussion points to the important role that multidisciplinary approaches can play in making sense of exercise-related eating disorders such as anorexia and bulimia.

This collection of chapters includes research on the experiences of both women and men in sport. If, as we suggest, sport is infused with power relations between and within the genders, it is again important to understand the sport experiences of both males and females in *relational* terms. As Ann Hall (1996:45) has argued elsewhere: 'The explication of women's oppression and subordina-tion *in* and *through* sport is totally bound up with the analysis of men and masculinity.' That is, one is better able to analyse unequal gender relations and the oppression of women (and some men) if one understands male privilege and power.

Clearly, the chapter entitled 'Who's Fair Game? Sport, Sexual Harassment, and Abuse' by Peter Donnelly addresses this issue head on by identifying how power differences tend to underlie abusive and exploitive sport-based relation-ships. Victoria Paraschak's chapter on sport and Canada's First Nations peoples, and Jim McKay's analysis of gender relations within Canada's federal sport bureaucracy, provide vivid examples of how unequal gender relations are created and reproduced over time, albeit in different areas of Canadian sport. That power relations can be acted out *within* male and female sport groups is demon-strated by Jamie Bryshun and Kevin Young. Their chapter, which provides perhaps for the first time substantial evidence for the routine involvement of female athletes in hazing rituals, points less to differences between male and female hazing practices and more to the similar adoption of hierarchical power relations on male and female sport teams. Bryshun and Young's evidence suggests that female involvement in sport does not in and of itself imply processes of social transformation. In this particular case, it is shown that power relations between neophyte and veteran female players may be just as aggressive, coercive, and dangerous as those occurring on male teams.

Notions of power relations are also central to the chapter written by Sandy O'Brien Cousins and Patricia Vertinsky on the effects of gender on participation in sport among older Canadians. Specifically, their paper demonstrates how older women are disadvantaged relative to men when it comes to involvement in sport and physical activity. Power differences between racial groups is the subject of a chapter written by Brian Wilson. His findings suggest that some young and dis-enchanted African Canadians use a macho 'cool pose' in their sport behaviour as a way of compensating for their perceived lack of power elsewhere in society.

Similarly, Anouk Bélanger argues that the intertwining of hockey and a hetero-sexual, homophobic masculinity in Québec has its roots in what she sees as the alienating effects of membership in a subordinated ethnic history in Canada.

Two chapters in Part II directly examine the issue of sexuality in Canadian sport. Among other matters, the chapters by Helen Lenskyj and Brian Pronger address the role played by sport in keeping lesbian and gay athletes invisible and in reinforcing and reproducing homophobia. Both authors make the case that Canadian sport remains predominantly an arena of 'compulsory heterosexuality', and that the terms 'masculinity' and 'femininity' in our culture are thinly dis-guised codewords for 'heterosexuality'. In these respects, it is argued that an understanding of sexuality issues is key to any meaningful analysis of sport and gender.

Finally, the fact that gender is a complex and multidimensional phenomenon is illustrated by two chapters that focus on the central role played by the body in sport. Jennifer Hoyle and Philip White, for example, examine how gendered power differences affect the lives and physical activity experiences of disabled women. As their findings suggest, disabled women experience a 'double bind' because they do not fit well into a sport world dominated by 'masculinist' and non-disabled values and norms. In the chapter written by Margaret MacNeill, the notion that power is played out through gendered bodies is demonstrated through an analysis of the federal government's ParticipACTION campaigns. MacNeill shows how these campaigns have tended to feature White, middle-class participants, stereotyped gender characteristics, and have failed to portray the diversity of the Canadian population.

In sum, Part II of this book focuses on the work currently being done by leading researchers in the area of sport and gender in Canada on a broad spec-trum of sport-related topics. The chapters reflect a variety of theoretical stand-points and methodological procedures, but are also at one in emphasizing the need to study gender in a way that is not only non-categorical but perhaps moves beyond the distributive level towards understanding how sport assumes partic-ular forms at particular historical junctures and grows out of relations of power that are determined culturally and reinforced ideologically.

Reference

Hall, M.A. 1996. *Feminism and Sporting Bodies: Essays on Theory and Practice*. Champaign, IL: Human Kinetics.

Chapter 4

Is Sport Injury Gendered?

Philip White and Kevin Young

In the first few days of 1998 there were several skiing tragedies in North America. In addition to the high-profile deaths of Americans Michael Kennedy and Sonny Bono, both of whom struck trees while downhill skiing, eight Canadians perished in snowy graves in southeastern British Columbia after three deadly avalanches roared through the Kootenays (Canadian Press 1998; *The Globe and Mail* 1998). At the time of their deaths, these eight recreational back-country skiers had all been warned of unstable snow conditions that posed a serious avalanche danger.

Of the eight Canadian skiers who died, six were men and two were women. They died because they took risks pursuing their sport. In Michael Kennedy's case, the family clan was playing a modified game of football on the slopes of Aspen despite warnings of danger from the ski patrol. Sonny Bono died after striking a tree while skiing in Utah. He was skiing alone, a practice widely discouraged in the interests of safety. His body wasn't found until three hours after the tow lifts had closed for the day. In all of these cases, most of which involved male participants, it wasn't the activity itself that was unduly hazardous; it was the manner of their participation that led to their demise.

The growth of research on sport injury from a sociological perspective is a relatively recent development. In a few short years, though, more and more researchers have turned their attention to issues of pain and injury (see, for example, Curry and Strauss 1994; Kotarba 1983; Messner 1992; Nixon 1994a, 1994b, 1996; Sabo and Panepinto 1990). In Canada there has also been research conducted on violence, pain, and injury, but only by a relatively small group of scholars (see, for example, Ellison and Mackenzie 1993; McCutcheon, Curtis, and White 1997; Rail 1990; Smith 1987, 1991; Tator and Edmonds 1984; Young and White 1995; Young, White, and McTeer 1994). While some of the earlier work in Canada was primarily epidemiological and did not question the nature of sport itself in accounting for injury, sociological approaches were pioneered by the late Michael D. Smith (see, for example, Smith 1991). It is on the foundation of his work that the social and legal implications of injury have been further examined.

In this chapter, using information from a variety of sources as evidence, we will argue that sport injury may be 'gendered'. As will become evident, it is not enough to say that catastrophic injuries to the spine are caused by poor equipment or poor technique. It is also vital to recognize and deal with the fact that much of the blame for how young (and some older) athletes become maimed, disabled, and killed lies in macho values, which are at the very core of much of our sport. That is, most injuries to Canadian athletes are suffered by boys and men, and a large proportion of those injuries seem to occur because of *ways of playing* sport that are extremely dangerous—but that also have come to be regarded as natural, normal, even desirable.

We became involved in research into pain and injury in sport, at least in part, through direct experience. We mention this because when we have raised issues about violence, aggression, and sport, a common illogical response by some people (predominantly men) who seem to be threatened by such challenges are questions such as 'Oh yeah, have *you* ever played contact sport. Have *you* ever been injured?' Fortunately (and unfortunately) for both of us, the answer to both of these questions is 'Yes' and 'Yes'. Both of us had prolonged and active careers in soccer and rugby, and we have both been hospitalized with serious injuries suffered when younger. We are also both male.

Having said that, of course, our personal biographies hardly count as scientific evidence that males suffer sport injuries more than females, nor do they identify sport injury as a particularly serious social problem. But in addition to letting us know how it *feels* to be injured (both physically and mentally), what our experiences indicate is how sport injury and masculinity codes may intersect. This chapter will examine evidence for this claim. In particular, we will examine how the effects of dominant forms of masculinity and taken-for-granted ways of playing sport combine to exact a considerable toll on the physical and emotional well-being of many Canadians.

We begin our analysis with a brief review of what has been written about masculinity, masculinities, and hierarchies of masculinity. The focus of this review will be to establish that masculinity codes are best understood as *social constructions*. From this basis we then develop the idea of 'dangerous masculinities', suggesting that dominant forms of masculinity are often consistent with learned behaviours that involve risk taking, violence, and a disregard for health. We introduce evidence from various sources that support the proposition that macho sport norms tend to restrict the options available to young boys both in terms of sports available and in the ways in which sport is played.

Masculinity and Masculinities

People think about masculinity in different ways ranging from social psychological versions of sex-role theory to 'rediscovered' ideas of 'traditional' masculinity typified by the writings of Robert Bly and others in the mythopoetic movement, and to feminist models of gender identity, which argue that in patriarchal societies some masculinities are dominant over femininities and other forms of masculinity. Certainly, as Kimmel (1992:166) has suggested, masculinity is defined as a multilayered entity that shifts and changes: '(1) from one culture to another, (2) within any one culture over time, (3) over the course of any individual man's life, and (4) between and among different groups of men depending on class, race, ethnicity, and sexuality'. This process of gender construction, it must be emphasized, is hugely influenced by power differences between men and women (and also, incidentally, between men and other men, and women and other women).

The idea of hierarchical masculinities has been subject to rich debate in recent theorizing in gender studies (Connell 1987, 1995; Hearn 1992; Morgan 1992; Rutherford 1992; Segal 1990). Much effort has been devoted to understanding the processes through which power and privilege are differentially allocated within and between groups of men. However, processes occurring within intermale dominance hierarchies themselves operate within other systems of social stratification. As Sabo and Gordon (1995:13) observe, 'Some critical feminist approaches are attempting to fill the need for a conceptual scheme that theorizes the varied and shifting dimensions of male domination as they interact with other forms of social domination. The term *multiple systems of domination analysis* has been used to describe these efforts.'

While it has become common to acknowledge the existence of multiple masculinities, it is also important to understand relations among them. In his analysis of the social organization of masculinity, Connell (1995) identifies the principal patterns of masculinity as 'hegemonic', 'subordinate', 'complicit', and 'marginal'. The relations among these broad categories form a cultural dynamic that tends to reproduce a gender order that subordinates women and less dominant masculinities.

Connell's (1987) concept of 'hegemonic masculinity' is key because it refers to an ideological construction that serves and maintains the interests of dominant male groups. A key aspect to understanding the idea of hegemonic masculinity is to recognize that societies such as Canada encompass a range or hierarchy of masculinities. Some men embrace hegemonic masculinity, others protest it, and others feel more or less (un)comfortable with certain aspects of it. Within a particular set of historical and social conditions, though, some types of masculinity are clearly ascendant over others. Some men enjoy more access to power and influence than others, while other men suffer from levels of exploitation, marginalization, and abuse that are also similarly experienced by women. What most men in patriarchal societies share in common, however, is the ability to benefit from 'patriarchal dividends' or rewards derived from their privileged position.

The Rewards of Privilege

Although hegemonic masculinity codes tend by definition to be dominant, many men do not exhibit characteristics such as physical toughness or emotional stoicism, which are commonly understood to typify masculinity. It is the legitimacy of domination that is important, and while these men may not conform to the blueprint of hegemonic masculinity, they may still benefit from it. As Connell has argued:

> The number of men rigorously practising the hegemonic pattern in its entirety may be quite small. Yet the majority of men benefit from its hegemony, since they benefit from the patriarchal dividend, the advantage men in general gain from the overall subordination of women (Connell 1995:79).

For example, patriarchal dividends are visible in men's domination of corporations, the media, and the state. Men also have greater access to privileges of wealth and income, and a gender ideology that subordinates women in a broad sense.

Patriarchal dividends extend not only to social inequalities in status, prestige, and material rewards. As Jackson suggests, hegemonic gender relations also affect how men think of their physical selves:

> Learning that you were naturally entitled to social, legal and financial power over women was translated into learning to hold power over your body—tautening your muscles, holding yourself firm and upright, striding with a cocky strut, throwing out your chest and walking from the shoulders (Jackson 1990:54).

But, for all of this, the alliance between men, hegemonic masculinity, and social privilege also has its drawbacks. As students of men's health have observed, claims of patriarchal dividends should be made cautiously. In the words of one anti-sexist male collective, 'Our power in society as men not only oppresses women but also imprisons us in a deadening masculinity which cripples our relationships—with each other, with women, with ourselves' (Segal 1990:287).

The Costs of Privilege

In 1992 Michael Kimmel (1992:vii) succinctly explained how men pay a price for the 'privileged' positions they occupy and enjoy: 'Most of the leading causes of death among men are the results of men's behaviors—gendered behaviors that leave men more vulnerable to certain illnesses and not others. Masculinity is one of the more significant risk factors associated with men's illness.' What Kimmel is suggesting here is that to be socialized into most dominant forms of masculinity involves not only learning and celebrating emotional denial and neutrality but also the cultural value of risk, danger, pain, and even injury (Jackson 1990). Male prowess is often based on types of physicality that are potentially destructive (Rutherford 1992). Relatively spartan approaches to physical health often desensitize many men to the importance of maintaining bodily well-being. Matters of preventive health in general tend to be viewed as feminizing and the jurisdiction of women and 'ambiguous' men. In sum, health care interests tend to be conspicuously absent in the lives of many men, the consequences of which are described below.

Men die at greater rates than women at almost every age, and more often from preventable causes (Stillion 1995). In the 1990s the leading causes of death among North American males between the ages of fifteen and nineteen are car accidents, suicide, and AIDS, all at rates far higher than for females. Among Canadian men ages twenty to forty-four, twenty-eight per 100,000 die from suicide, followed by car accidents (twenty-one per 100,000) and AIDS (eighteen per 100,000). The corresponding rates for women are seven suicide deaths, seven deaths from car accidents, and one AIDS death per 100,000. In the fifteen to nineteen age group, the death rate from suicide is almost four times higher for males than females, while the death rate from car accidents is almost twice as high. Gender differences in both death rates from external causes start to widen following early childhood (Government of Canada 1995). By the early teens, accidents become a leading cause of death, but more so for males than females.

In Canada Reasons (1985) and Reasons, Ross, and Patterson (1981) have also documented the hazardous nature of a number of workplaces dominated by men, including the asbestos, mining, paper milling, construction, electrical, and chemical industries. Males have much higher rates of workplace injury than females, a trend that is at least partly attributable to gender. As Young has argued:

> Although this differential may be explained in part by the often uneven numbers of men and women involved in dangerous work, it would be a mistake to overlook the explanatory potential of a culture of 'masculinism' which tends to accompany male preserves, vocationally and elsewhere (Young 1993:379).

In sum, data from the literature on gender and occupational health highlights problematic male health and injury issues, and an association between the 'culture of masculinism', risk taking, and the avoidance of thoughtful preventive measures.

Sport, Men, and Injury

In this section we suggest that men are more susceptible than women to sport injury. This is *not* to suggest that: (1) sport injuries are unique to men, especially with regard to high-performance sport (cf., Young and White 1995); (2) that specific codes of masculinity are alone responsible for injury; or (3) that participants in highly intense and/or competitive types of involvement are vulnerable to injury regardless of gender. In presenting data on gender differences in injury, we should also caution that gender is not an exclusive predictor of injury in all sport/exercise arenas. Sports that celebrate the testing of personal body limits—for example, running an ultramarathon, pursuing excellence in dance, or exploring physicality through yoga—may harbour norms that make injury highly likely but have relatively little to do with gender. Having said this, there are numerous ways that men, more so than women, take risks, endure pain, and suffer ill health through sport and play.

Much of the research conducted to date has focused on male participants and has explored the role of violent contact or high-risk sport in the process of masculinization (Curry and Strauss 1994; Sabo and Panepinto 1990; Young, White, and McTeer 1994). At school the violent physicality of sport is one of the cornerstones of a type of masculinity that 'not only defines itself positively through assertiveness, virility, toughness, and independence, but also negatively by defining itself in opposition of what it is not—feminine or homosexual' (Jackson 1990:123–4; see also Bryson 1987; Connell 1983; Messner 1990; Sabo and Panepinto 1990; White and Gillett 1994; Young 1993). However, while toughness, aggression, and even violence in sport are still admired by many, there is also growing unease and concern about serious sport injury.

A recent example of the paradoxical situation in which violence and injury are thought of both in positive and negative ways is that while many rules in ice hockey have been changed to avoid serious injuries, the violent images and meanings of the sport remain entrenched. For example, two advertisements (one in a magazine and one on television) have recently valorized and naturalized fist-fighting. In a magazine advertisement for ESPNEWS network (*Sports Illustrated*, 26 October 1996:60–1), Cam Neely, a former player for the Boston Bruins, suggests that he is so frustrated that a twenty-four hour sport news channel would start broadcasting after his retirement that he might 'kick your face in'. In a television advertisement associating sport violence with Budweiser beer, a player is championed, not for any demonstrated talent or contribution to his team but for the number of penalty minutes he has amassed as a professional 'enforcer' (i.e., a player who makes his living largely by fighting other players). The paradox here lies in how the advertisements financially and subculturally privilege the men involved, yet ignore the injurious outcomes of fighting in professional hockey, which, it has recently been argued, are a leading cause of games lost in the NHL (Dryden 1997). In the past few years, fighting resulted in Rob Ray of the Buffalo Sabres having his orbital bones crushed, Bill Berg (then of the Toronto Maple Leafs) breaking his leg, and Nick Kypreos of the Toronto Maple Leafs suffering a severe concussion. Kypreos subsequently missed all of the 1997–8 season with postconcussion syndrome.

In our arguments we have suggested that there is something about the ways in which boys and men experience and play sport that exposes them to greater risk of injury than their female counterparts. As we will see later, the greater incidence of injury among males is explained by a number of factors, including the fact that more boys and men play sport than women and girls, that males play sports that are more conducive to injury, and that males play in ways that pay insufficient attention to physical self-preservation. In what follows, we present evidence from a variety of sources to help identify the injurious outcomes of the 'gendering' processes we describe—processes through which physical risk among boys and men are naturalized, promoted, and even celebrated. In doing this, we show how this relationship has become so entrenched and internalized that it is difficult to see beyond; that alternative, less physical and forceful versions of masculinity seem at face value to be irrational and inappropriate, especially in such a macho setting as sport. In examining these processes, we also point to their insidious consequences for men's health. The insidiousness of this pursuit lies in the degree to which the inevitability of injury, and the physical and emotional pain it implies, go largely unchallenged in the world of sport. As Young (1993) argued in his study of masculinist work cultures that include that of professional male athletes, there is currently a significant silence in the culture of male sport about the physical toll exacted upon players in the process of sport-related masculinization.

In the following section we review the research documenting gender differences in sport injury in general and ice hockey in particular. This review is not definitive in terms of establishing the exact extent of the problem posed by catastrophic injury. It is not the purpose of this chapter to suggest that sport injuries are rampant or that all men fall prey to injury-inducing sport norms. To put our evidence in perspective, we would caution that survey data show that injury rates in the general population are substantial but not epidemic (cf., McCutcheon, Curtis, and White 1997). We offer instead a preliminary understanding of how serious sport injuries are socially structured. On the basis of these patterns, we will argue that there is need for a better understanding of the gendering of sport injury and for progressive intervention to make future sport practices safer and, arguably, more humane.

Gender Differences in Sport Injury

A recent Canadian study of sport injury (Tator et al. 1993) reported on 556 incidents that caused either death or long-term disability in 1992 (see Table 4.1). Among those injured or killed, 84.7 per cent were male and approximately 33 per cent were thirty years old or younger. While another study conducted by Statistics Canada (*Accidents in Canada* 1995) reported an increase in sport accidents from 1988 to 1993, serious injuries in hockey declined from seventy-nine in 1986 to twenty-six in 1992. Nevertheless, hockey accounted for 4.6 per cent of catastrophic injuries in Ontario in 1992, of which 92.3 per cent were incurred by males.

Water sports such as boating, canoeing, and fishing were the major contributors to catastrophic sport injuries in Ontario—they were presumably, to some

Table 4.1

Sport and Recreational Injuries by Sport Type and Gender in 1992

Sport Type	Male N	Male Per cent	Female N	Female Per cent
Water sports (boating, diving, fishing, water skiing, etc.)	135	86.5	21	13.5
Motor sports (ATV, snowmobiling, etc.)	114	89.7	13	10.3
Bicycling	73	81.1	17	18.9
Winter sports				
Hockey	24	92.3	2	7.7
Alpine skiing	12	80.0	3	20.0
Other	11	44.0	14	56.0
Field sports				
Football	5	100.0	0	0.0
Rugby	3	100.0	0	0.0
Soccer	5	100.0	0	0.0
Track and field	2	100.0	0	0.0
Baseball	18	94.7	1	5.3
Miscellaneous (seventeen activities, e.g., rollerblading, skydiving, hiking)	35	81.0	8	19.0

Source: C.H. Tator, V.E. Edmonds, and L. Lapczak, 'Ontario Catastrophic Sport-Recreation Injuries Survey', 1993 report by SportSmart Canada for Ontario Ministry of Tourism and Recreation.

extent, caused by crashes and drowning rather than by inherent dangers in the activities themselves. Males accounted for 86.5 per cent of those injured in water sports. Motor sports, such as snowmobiling, were also hazardous (22.4 per cent of all injuries), again overwhelmingly for males who comprised 89.7 per cent of those injured. Field sports, including football, rugby, soccer, and track and field, accounted for only 2.6 per cent of all serious injuries in

Ontario, almost all of them sustained by male athletes. While not reported in Table 4.1, there were 226 sport- and recreation-related fatalities in Ontario in 1992, disproportionately among males. Males accounted for 62.5 per cent of fatalities in winter sports, 89.5 per cent of fatalities in water sports, and 91.5 per cent of fatalities in motor sports. Similar gender differences in sport injury are evident among children and youth. In a study of sport injuries among Canadians ages five to nineteen, males accounted for 68 per cent of the 37,169 recorded treatments in hospital emergency rooms in 1990 and 1991 (Ellison and Mackenzie 1993). By comparison, only 57.8 per cent of patients treated for non-sport injuries were male. Injured boys outnumbered injured girls at all age levels. For males, ice hockey accounted for the highest proportion of injuries in each age group, although this might be accounted for by the overall popularity of the game rather than the nature of the game itself. For females, basketball injuries were the most frequent of those reported.

Ellison and Mackenzie (1993) also reported that males tend to suffer more severe injuries than females. At each age, males were more often admitted to hospital or held for observation as a result of their injuries. This difference might be explained, in part, by variations in the nature of injuries experienced by males and females. For respondents over the age of ten, boys were more likely than girls to have been treated for a bone fracture, a cut or laceration, a concussion, or an abrasion. Females were more commonly treated for sprains and strains (particularly of the lower extremities), inflammation, or swelling. These differences possibly reflect boys' propensities to be more often involved in high-risk sport or physical contact sport and for them to play sport more aggressively than girls (Messner 1990; Nicholl et al. 1993; Zaricznyj et al. 1980).

These aggregate data provide strong support for the proposition that gender is a key determinant of sport injury in Canada. To further elucidate how and where males are particularly susceptible to sport injury, the following case-study provides more detail on a 'Canadian' sport that has historically operated as a male preserve.

Injuries in Ice Hockey

Recent Cases of Injury
- In February 1990 seventeen-year-old John Davies of the Orillia midget hockey team was checked into the boards from behind by an opponent. His face mask snapped off and his face was severely lacerated, requiring more than 280 stitches. The tip of his nose was also lost in the accident, necessitating a skin graft.
- In December 1995 Windsor Spitfire defenceman Chris Van Dyk suffered a detached retina when a player 'high sticked' him from behind.
- In March 1996 twenty-two-year-old Mark Goodkey, a player with the Edmonton Young Offenders' Centre, was killed when he blocked a 'slapshot'.

The shot struck him in the neck from a distance of 1.5 m, breaking his neck and crushing a major artery to his brain.

- During a pre-game brawl between players of the Cobourg Cougars and the Ajax Axemen of the Ontario Provincial Junior A Hockey League on 22 December 1997, twenty-year-old Markus Quinn was knocked unconscious and fell to the ice. He suffered a fractured skull, a bruised brain, and permanent brain damage.

- During an NHL pre-season game in 1997, Nick Kypreos of the Toronto Maple Leafs was punched to the ice by Ryan Vandenbussche of the New York Rangers. For some minutes, Kypreos lay semiconscious on the ice in a pool of his own blood, a sight so grotesque that it alarmed even the most fervent supporters of fighting in hockey. By mid-season 1998 Kypreos had not returned to action because of postconcussion syndrome.

Review of Evidence

A number of studies on injury rates in ice hockey have been undertaken in Canada (McLaren 1996; Pashby 1989; Regnier et al. 1989; Smith 1991; Tator 1987). While the findings can convey the impression that hockey is the leading producer of sport injury, this conclusion should be regarded with caution because it is often difficult to tell from most sets of findings whether the high overall number of hockey injuries was attributable to high levels of hockey participation in Canada or to the nature of the game itself. Similarly problematic, relatively low levels (albeit rapidly growing) of involvement among females and a lack of research on gender and injuries in ice hockey make gender comparisons difficult.

In terms of overall rates of hockey injuries in Canada, a study commissioned by the Ontario Sport Medicine and Safety Advisory Board (Tator 1987) provided data on the annual incidence of hockey injuries among the general population and among players in organized leagues in Canada. Among the general population, 31 per cent of adult males, and 18 per cent of children (seventeen years or younger) of both sexes who participated in hockey at least once in 1986, had sustained at least one hockey injury. In the same study, among a subsample of competitive hockey players, 54 per cent of adult players and 66 per cent of minor hockey players reported an injury in 1986. This suggests a higher prevalence of injuries in more competitive and organized environments, a plausible interpretation given the finding that competitive players were also likely to have been injured more than once.

Another study commissioned by the same board paid attention to the relative risk of receiving a 'significant' injury (one involving musculoskeletal trauma requiring treatment in a medical facility) while playing different sport (Pelletier 1987). Results showed that hockey was the leading source of significant injury (more than 40 per cent of all injuries reported), and that basketball was the second highest with 9 per cent of significant injuries. Again, though, without comparative data on rates of participation, it is not possible to conclude from these findings that hockey *per se* is more hazardous than other sports. It is plausible that higher numbers of injuries in hockey are accounted for by higher participation rates. Similarly, the finding that males were three times more likely to be injured than females also probably reflects gender differences in rates of involvement. Participation rates in hockey are far higher among males than females.

In a third Canadian study on catastrophic sport injury (Tator 1987), almost 15 per cent of injuries in 1986 occurred in hockey (there were no hockey deaths). Ninety-six per cent of these victims were male. Rates of catastrophic injury were much lower in other sports, but again they might be explained by differing rates of involvement. Sports including rugby, soccer, football, lacrosse, and field hockey accounted for 7 per cent of catastrophic deaths in Ontario in 1986, of which 84 per cent of participants were male.

Catastrophic spinal injuries also seem to have been overrepresented among hockey players, although progress has been made since the mid-1980s when rule changes were introduced to make checking from behind illegal. Earlier studies (cf., Tator and Edmonds 1984) showed that forty-eight spinal injuries occurred in hockey in Canada between 1976 and 1983, eighteen of which were caused by a check from behind into the boards. Following rule changes banning checking from behind, rates of spinal injury have declined, although young hockey players still suffer catastrophic cervical injuries each year.

In a recent study comparing injuries incurred in Pee Wee leagues (twelve and thirteen year olds) in Québec that allow body checking versus leagues that do not allow body checking, Marcotte et al. (1986) found a much higher injury rate in the former than the latter. The study showed not only that injuries occurred more often in the body-checking leagues but that almost all 'major' injuries (such as fractures, dislocations, and concussions) also occurred in these leagues and resulted almost entirely from body checks. Bone fractures were twelve times more common in the body-checking leagues than in the leagues with no body checking.

Eye injuries have also been problematic in ice hockey, although incidents have dropped to almost nil in leagues that require the use of face protectors approved by the Canadian Standards Association. Eye injuries continue to occur in hockey (1,095 incidents between 1976 and 1988, with 186 blinded eyes) when players do not wear approved masks (Pashby 1989).

Discussion

The evidence that we have reported here and in our earlier work on the suppression of sport-related pain suggests an ongoing complementarity between dominant codes of masculinity and the sport-related injury process. If we reflect on the football lineman who revels in the pain he inflicts on his opponents (Young 1993), the ice hockey player, coach, administrator, or commentator who insists that fist-fighting remain an essential and 'honourable' part of the game (Faulkner 1973; Gillett, White, and Young 1996), or the downhill skier who remains unconcerned about the implications of his injury-jinxed sport for his long-term health (Young, White, and McTeer 1994), we think it is clear that conventional forms of masculinity are still highly valued by many Canadian males.

There remains a fundamental association between sport involvement in boyhood and socialization to dominant (and, we might add, heterosexual) masculinity in adulthood. As Pronger argues elsewhere in this volume, playing sport, particularly those sport connected with aggression and toughness, distances the participant from the possibility of being labelled a 'sissy' or a homosexual. To give up the opportunity to participate in the sporting rite of passage, or at the very least to identify with sport heroes or teams, is to risk estrangement from other boys.

In saying this, we do not mean to argue that hegemonic modes of masculine body expression are embraced by all males involved in sport. Across Canada, for example, young hockey players are finding non-contact versions of their favoured pastime more enjoyable and less hazardous (White, Young, and Gillett 1995). Nevertheless, our research suggests that men's use of sport and athletic bodies as key sites for 'masculinity verification' (Dubbert 1979) remains extremely important, even when the outcomes may be debilitating.

The theoretical links we have drawn between masculinity and injury and risk in sport and our use of sundry data sources only provide, of course, preliminary groundwork in this area of research. The nature of the evidence available to us make gender comparisons between sports difficult. While our overview of existing data suggests a relationship where sport injury seems strongly predicted by gender, further research is required to determine more accurately whether 'masculinizing' processes within sport contribute to a disproportionate level of damage to male athletic bodies.

With firmer evidence at hand, it is a realistic goal that sport could be made safer. For the moment, however, we conclude from the existing research that sport is often played in ways that put participants at undue risk of physical harm. In this regard, it seems clear that males are more likely than females to be socialized into ways of playing that are potentially injurious. If this pattern were challenged, the sparing of only one victim of a catastrophic sport injury would be a resounding step forward.

References

Bryson, L. 1987. 'Sport and the Maintenance of Hegemonic Masculinity'. *Women's Studies International Forum* 10:349–60.

Canadian Press. 1998. 'B.C. Avalanche Peril Remains After 8 Die'. (5 January):A1.

Connell, R. 1983. *Which Way Is Up? Essays on Sex, Class, and Culture*. Sydney: Allen & Unwin.

———. 1987. *Gender and Power*. Cambridge: Polity Press.

———. 1995. *Masculinities*. Los Angeles: University of California Press.

Curry, T., and R. Strauss. 1994. 'A Little Pain Never Hurt Anybody: A Photo-essay on the Normalization of Sport'. *Sociology of Sport Journal* 11:195–208.

Dryden, S. 1997. *The Hockey News* (28 February):2.

Dubbert, J. 1979. *A Man's Place: Masculinity in Transition*. Englewood Cliffs: Prentice-Hall.

Ellison, L., and S. Mackenzie. 1993. 'Sports Injuries in the Database of the Canadian Hospitals Injury Reporting and Prevention Program—an Overview'. *Chronic Diseases in Canada* 14:96–104.

Faulker, R. 1973. 'On Respect and Retribution: Toward an Ethnography of Violence'. *Sociological Symposium* 9:17–36.

Gillett, J., P. White, and K. Young. 1996. 'The Prime Minister of Saturday Night: Don Cherry, the CBC, and the Cultural Production of Intolerance'. In *Seeing Ourselves: Media Power and Policy in Canada*, edited by H. Holmes and D. Taras, 59–72. Toronto: Harcourt Brace.

The Globe and Mail. 1998. 'The Risks in the Snow'. (7 January):A14.

Hearn, J. 1992. *Men in the Public Eye: The Construction and Deconstruction of Public Men and Public Patriarchies*. New York: Routledge.

Jackson, D. 1990. *Unmasking Masculinity: A Critical Autobiography*. London: Unwyn Hyman.

Kimmel, M. 1992. 'Reading Men: Men, Masculinity, and Publishing'. *Contemporary Sociology* 21:162–71.

Kotarba, J.A. 1983. *Chronic Pain: Its Social Dimensions*. Beverly Hills: Sage.

McCutcheon, T., J. Curtis, and P. White. 1997. 'The Socio-economic Distribution of Sport: Multivariate Analyses for the General Canadian Population'. *Sociology of Sport Journal* 14:57–73.

McLaren, R. 1996. *A Study of Injuries Sustained in Sport and Recreation in Ontario*. Ottawa: Report to the Ontario Ministry of Citizenship, Culture, and Recreation.

Marcotte, G., D. Bernard, D. Belangerk, and R. Larouche. 1986. 'Incidence des blessures chez les hockeyeurs d'âge pee wee avec ou sans misen échec'. In *Rapport d'étude sur la mise en échec au hockey pee wee*, edited by R. Boileau, 126–51. Régie de la securité dan les sports. Trois-Rivières: Governement du Québec.

Messner, M. 1990. 'When Bodies Are Weapons: Masculinity and Violence in Sport'. *International Review for the Sociology of Sport* 25:203–18.

_____. 1992. *Power at Play: Sports and the Problem of Masculinity*. Boston: Beacon Press.

Morgan, D. 1992. *Discovering Men*. New York: Routledge.

Nicholl, J., P. Coleman, and B. Williams. 1993. *Injuries in Sport and Exercise*. London: The Sports Council.

Nixon, H.L.1994a. 'Coaches' Views of Risk, Pain, and Injury in Sport with Special Reference to Gender Differences'. *Sociology of Sport Journal* 11:79–87.

_____. 1994b. 'Social Pressure, Social Support, and Help Seeking for Pain and Injuries in College Sports Networks'. *Journal of Sport and Social Issues* 13:340–55.

_____. 1996. 'The Relationship of Friendship Networks, Sports Experiences, and Gender to Expressed Pain Thresholds'. *Sociology of Sport Journal* 13:78–87.

Pashby, T. 1989. 'Epidemiology of Eye Injuries in Hockey'. In *Safety in Ice Hockey*, edited by C. Castaldi and E. Hoerner, 29–31. Philadelphia: American Society for Testing and Materials.

Pelletier, R. 1987. 'Significant Sport/Leisure Injuries in Ontario'. In *Report of the Ontario Sports Medicine and Drug Safety Board*, vol. 2:179–207.

Rail, G. 1990. 'Physical Contact in Women's Basketball: A First Interpretation'. *International Review for the Sociology of Sport* 25:269–85.

Reasons, C. 1985. 'Ideology, Law, Public Opinion, and Worker's Health'. In *Law in a Cynical Society*, edited by D. Gibson and J. Baldwin, 42–61. Calgary: Carswell.

_____, I. Ross, and C. Patterson. 1981. *Assault on the Worker: Occupational Health and Safety in Canada*. Toronto: Butterworths.

Regnier, G., R. Boileau, and G. Marcotte. 1989. 'Effects of Body-checking in the Pee Wee (12 and 13 Year-Old) Division in the Province of Quebec'. In *Safety in Ice Hockey*, edited by C. Castaldi and E. Hoeruer, 85–103. Philadelphia: American Society for Testing and Materials.

Rutherford, J. 1992. *Men's Silences: Predicaments in Masculinity*. New York: Routledge.

Sabo, D., and D. Gordon. 1995. 'Re-thinking Men's Health and Illness'. In *Men's Health and Illness: Gender, Power, and the Body*, edited by D. Sabo and D. Gordon, 1–22. Thousand Oaks, CA: Sage.

_____, and J. Panepinto. 1990. 'Football Ritual and the Social Reproduction of Masculinity'. In *Sport, Men, and the Gender Order: Critical Feminist Perspectives*, edited by M. Messner and D. Sabo, 115–27. Champaign, IL: Human Kinetics.

Segal, L. 1990. *Slow Motion: Changing Masculinities, Changing Men*. New Brunswick, NJ: Rutgers University Press.

Smith, M. 1987. 'Violence in Canadian Amateur Sport: A Review of Literature'. *Report for the Commission for Fair Play*. Ottawa: Government of Canada.

_____. 1991. 'Violence and Injuries in Ice Hockey'. *Clinical Journal of Sports Medicine* 1:104–9.

Statistics Canada. 1995. *Accidents in Canada*. Ottawa: Government of Canada.

Stillion, J.M. 1995. 'Premature Death Among Males'. In *Men's Health and Illness: Gender, Power, and the Body*, edited by D. Sabo and D.F. Gordon, 46–68. Thousand Oaks, CA: Sage.

Tator, G. 1987. 'Catastrophic Sports and Recreational Injuries in Ontario During 1986'. *Report of the Ontario Sport Medicine and Safety Advisory Board*, vol. 2:5–77. Toronto: Ministry of Tourism and Recreation.

_____, and V. Edmonds. 1984. 'National Survey of Spinal Injuries in Hockey Players'. *Canadian Medical Association Journal* 130:878–80.

_____, V. Edmonds, and L. Lapczak. 1993. 'Ontario Catastrophic Sport-Recreation Injuries Survey'. Report by SportSmart Canada for Ontario Ministry of Tourism and Recreation.

White, P., and J. Gillett. 1994. 'Reading the Muscular Body: A Critical Decoding of Advertisements in *Flex* Magazine'. *Sociology of Sport Journal* 11:18–39.

_____, K. Young, and J. Gillett. 1995. 'Bodywork as a Moral Imperative: Some Critical Notes on Health and Fitness'. *Loisir et Société* 18:159–82.

Young, K. 1993. 'Violence, Risk, and Liability in Male Sports Culture'. *Sociology of Sport Journal* 19:373–96.

_____, and P. White 1995. 'Sport, Physical Danger and Injury: The Experiences of Elite Women Athletes'. *Journal of Sport and Social Issues* 19:45–61.

_____, P. White, and W. McTeer. 1994. 'Body Talk: Male Athletes Reflect on Sport, Injury, and Pain'. *Sociology of Sport Journal* 11:175–94.

Zaricznyj, B., L. Shattuck, T. Mast, R. Robertson, and G. D'elia. 1980. 'Sports-Related Injury in School-Aged Children'. *American Journal of Sports Medicine* 8:318–34.

Chapter 5

Eating Disorders, Physical Activity, and Sport:

Biological, Psychological, and Sociological Factors

Caroline Davis

Introductory Remarks

Over the past several years there have been many press reports of an increasing incidence of eating-related disorders. In fact—and with little in the way of clear evidence—this idea has progressed from a mere *impression* in the 1960s to a *conviction* in the 1970s—and finally to a *certainty* in the 1980s. Although the epidemiology supporting this viewpoint is actually very complex, uncertain, and difficult to interpret, many people, even among the medical community, have tended to accept as conventional wisdom that eating disorders are rapidly becoming more prevalent (see van't Hof and Nicolson 1996).

At this point, all we can safely say from the available evidence is that eating disorders are more common than previously recognized, and that in some regions their incidence may have risen three- to fourfold since the 1960s, but only among adolescents and young women (Eagles et al. 1995; Lucas et al. 1991). It is also clear that some of the apparent increase reflects the fact that more of the less severely ill patients are now being referred for treatment than in previous years (Eagles et al. 1995). Current estimates suggest that about 0.5–1.0 per cent of young women meet the strict diagnostic criteria for anorexia nervosa (AN), and an additional 2–3 per cent for bulimia nervosa (BN), while another 5–10 per cent may suffer from partial forms of either disorder (Fairburn and Beglin 1990; Lucas et al. 1991; Moller-Madsen and Nystrup 1992). Typically, only about 5 per cent of cases are male.

The diagnostic criteria for AN, as defined by the *American Psychiatric Association Diagnostic and Statistical Manual* (4th edn, 1994), are: (1) weight loss below 85 per cent of average body weight; (2) at least three months of amenorrhea associated with an uncompromising pursuit of thinness in women who have reached menarche; and (3) a disturbance in the self-perception of the body. The BN syndrome may occur at average, or even above average, weight, and in all cases is associated with strong body dissatisfaction. Diagnostic criteria for BN require at least two binge-eating episodes a week for at least three months, accompanied by some attempt to reverse the effects of the caloric intake. This generally takes the form of self-induced vomiting, laxative and/or diuretic abuse, fasting, or intense exercising.

Over the years, some have argued that it is more appropriate to consider eating disorders as differing in degree of pathology rather than as discrete disease entities. Fries (1974) was the first to propose a 'continuum hypothesis' for conceptualizing the aetiology of AN. He considered the disorder as the final stage in a progression from normal dieting (often for justifiable cosmetic reasons) to a neurotic fixation on weight and food intake, followed by the emergence of some anorexic symptoms, leading finally to the full-blown syndrome. The symptomatic changes, he believed, reflected a psychological transition from volitional, conscious, and goal-directed behaviour to a state of dissociation and denial, and an increasing loss of insight. In other words, differences between milder forms of weight preoccupation and clinical eating disorders are essentially a matter of degree (e.g., Fairburn and Beglin 1990; Kendler et al. 1991; Nylander 1971). While there is some empirical support for this viewpoint (Beebe et al. 1995; Button and Whitehouse 1981; Scarano and Kalodner-Martin 1994), others have disputed the notion of a simple continuum, arguing that it is more valid to view clinical eating disorders as the end-point of a multifactorial dimension that incorporates a number of characteristics including both symptoms (those relating to eating habits and appearance concerns), as well as specific maladaptive personality traits.

Aetiological Considerations

Although the psychological and biological *consequences* of starvation and malnutrition are well understood (de Zwann and Mitchell 1993; Kaplan and Katz 1993; Keys 1950), we are much further from understanding the factors that *predispose* people to eating pathologies. Moreover, few disorders in medicine have attracted as diverse a range of causal theories. What we do at least recognize is that the aetiology is intricate, and that the study of simple relationships among variables offers little insight into the complexities of these disorders. Indeed, it is most probable that a number of factors combine and interact in forming a risk profile. Furthermore, it is important to recognize that eating disorders are dynamic pathologies rather than static illnesses. Therefore, different sets of factors are likely to be differentially influential as the disorders progress from onset to a more protracted form. For example, there is no doubt that sociocultural factors play a key role in understanding the initial development of eating disorders—and less severe forms of dieting. Once the disorders have become chronic, however, physiological factors seems to be of greater relevance in the maintenance of the disorders, and probably provide the best means for understanding their resistance to treatment.

One aim of this chapter is to review the sociocultural and gender-political factors that have been implicated in the high level of body-image disparagement and disordered eating currently found among women in Western societies. Illustrative of the discontent that women feel about their bodies are the results of two recent North American surveys (Horm and Anderson 1993; Serdula et al. 1993). These studies found that about 40 per cent of adult women were on a weight-loss diet at any given time, a disconcerting finding given other evidence that only about one-third of women who report 'feeling too fat' are actually overweight by objective standards (Streigel-Moore et al. 1986). Even more alarming, this dissatisfaction with weight and body shape is not restricted to adult women. Several studies have found that a substantial number of adolescents—even children as young as nine years old—rate their own bodies as larger than their ideal body (Grogan and Wainwright 1996). Reports also estimate that 50–60 per cent of teenage girls consider themselves overweight and that up to 20 per cent score in the abnormal range on standardized tests of disordered-eating attitudes (Fisher et al. 1995).

In what follows, I suggest that there are at least four sociocultural influences that have contributed in an instrumental way to eating-related pathologies over the past several decades. I will also address the manner in which they may have been exacerbated among those involved in competitive athletics. While there is evidence that concerns about weight are not exclusively a female problem—currently men have moved further along a continuum of 'bodily concern' than ever before this century (Mishkind et al. 1986)—there is no doubt that this is primarily a women's issue. Although people have disagreed on the reason, it is clear that women, more so than men, have followed the dictates of fashion in their attempts to achieve the cultural standards of female beauty and sexual attractiveness (Mazur 1986). This may be because men, to a greater extent than women, place a premium on physical appearance and attractiveness in their mate selection. This has been demonstrated frequently and mostly interpreted in terms of its evolutionary significance (Buss 1994).

The Body-Image Ideal

The first issue concerns cultural norms defining ultraslenderness as the ideal of female sexual attractiveness. This standard is most explicitly reflected in the images of women that proliferate in the media. For instance, a number of recent studies have surveyed popular women's and teen's magazines and found an increasing trend over the past few decades to display leaner, less curvaceous, and more androgenous female bodies—those with narrow hips, thin ankles, and a high waist-to-hip ratio (see Guillen and Barr 1994 for a review). The physical dimensions of a sample of New York fashion models also underscore the unrealistically thin standard exemplified by these icons of beauty; an alarming 73 per cent of them were below the lower limit of recommended age-matched weight (Brenner and Cunningham 1992). In addition, data from *Playboy* centrefolds and Miss America pageant contestants from the late 1950s to 1990 revealed a significant trend towards a thinner standard, and these changes occurred within the context of increasing standard weight norms for young women in North America (Garner et al. 1980; Wiseman et al. 1992).

A further testimony to our admiration of thinness is the fact that although AN has the highest mortality rate (about 6 per cent of those diagnosed) of any psychiatric disorder including depression and alcoholism (Sullivan 1995), there is a cultural fascination with eating disorders that is overtly conveyed by the extent to which they are associated with images of glamour and success (Malson and Ussher 1996). All too frequently, highly paid fashion models, or accomplished female athletes in sport like distance running and gymnastics, are described in the media—almost reverently—as 'anorexic' in appearance.

Several interesting, albeit rather speculative, theories have been proposed to account for the shrinking of the ideal North American woman over the past few decades. First, it has been noted that a non-curvaceous and slender body emerged as the body-image ideal at times during this century (e.g., the 1920s and the 1960s) when the proportion of professional women in the population was relatively high and rapidly increasing (Silverstein et al. 1986). Since a curvaceous body reflects a particular kind of femininity, and femininity has sometimes mistakenly been associated with low intellect, Silverstein and colleagues suggest that these cultural associations have led women who are concerned about how others assess their intelligence and competence to aspire to a slim and non-voluptuous body shape.

Second, others have argued that the current female body-ideal reflects the historically conservative thread in North American values where self-determination and Puritanism (in the form of internal control and the work ethic) are deeply rooted social principles (Crandall and Martinez 1996). Inherent in this ideology is the admiration of temperance and moderation, and the distaste for excess and indulgence. In the decades following the Second World War, the economy flourished, the deprivation of the war years ended, and ours became a society of plenty. Food as well as other commodities were freely available. During this period, the North American woman visibly fattened. In contrast, the female body-ideal thinned and came to personify the virtues of restraint and self-control. Social distinction gradually became embodied in slenderness as material constraints eased and as this body shape became less common (Becker and Hamburg 1996).

It has also been suggested that the sexual revolution of the 1960s played a role in the developing preference for a slimmer female shape. A hallmark of the liberal social attitudes of that era was the 'undressing' of the female body. Bras, corsets, and girdles were shed, and hemlines were raised to provocative heights. With more of the unfettered body on view, it is arguable that minimalism of form had a greater appeal than the more fleshy alternative. In fact, it is interesting to note that at that time the female body-ideal emulated many of the elements of contemporary architecture. 'Less is more', as Mies van der Rohe once said, was as apt a slogan for the new ideal of the female body as it was the description of the vogue in building design at that time.

Some have also drawn parallels between the sexual morality of the 1950s and fatness in the decades that followed (Nichter and Nichter 1991). In the earlier period, virginity was a prime source of symbolic capital possessed by women to be exchanged for marital security. Once sex was more freely available and divorce rates increased substantially, women's bodies as capital took a different form. Then sexual attractiveness substituted for virginity and women worked hard not only to achieve this goal but to maintain it. A valued commodity to exchange for marital security was a slim body and youthful looks.

Although this discussion has focused exclusively on the issue of body-image ideals in Western cultures like North America and Europe, it is important to keep in mind that these standards are not universal. For example, in many developing countries plumpness or moderate fatness is actually valued and idealized (Sobal and Stunkard 1989). Some have argued that is because natural selection has favoured those individuals who are efficient at storing fat during times of food shortages, which historically were frequent and unpredictable (Probast and Lieberman 1992). It has also been argued, from an evolutionary perspective, that substantial fat on women was an external indication of good health; it also tends to confer reproductive advantage to women. For that reason, extreme thinness was not a desirable characteristic from the point of view of mate selection (Singh 1993). We can see, then, that the sanctity that our societies place on ultraslenderness is both culturally derived and a cultural anomaly.

Cultural Narcissism

The second important influence concerns the dramatic shift over the last half of this century towards what Lasch (1979) has described as a 'culture of narcissism'. In a convincing treatise on the evolution of North American social values, Lasch points out that after the devastation of the Second World War, the political turmoil of the 1960s, and the increasing threat of a nuclear holocaust, people began to turn to the pursuit of purely personal goals and aspirations:

> To live for the moment is the prevailing passion—to live for yourself, not for your predecessors or posterity. We are fast losing the sense of historical continuity, the sense of belonging to a succession of generations originating in the past and stretching into the future (Lasch 1979:5).

One aspect of this self-absorption is our obsession with the pursuit of bodily per-fection at almost any cost. Symptomatic of this preoccupation is the increasing emphasis on ways to improve one's body shape in order to conform to the cultur-ally prescribed ideal (Guillen and Barr 1994). Among women, money spent on diet books, calorie-reduced food, and weight-loss programs almost doubled in the 1980s from previous decades, and in 1988 the estimated cost of these products and services in America was almost equal to that spent by the government on educa-tion and social services (Garner and Wooley 1991). Little has changed since then.

In a related argument, it has been suggested that the seeds of our egocentrism are sown early in life. In a commentary on early childhood education practices in North America, Katz (1993) has argued that school curricula, in an attempt to counteract the earlier traditions of eschewing compliments to children for fear of making them conceited, are now erring in the other direction. The domi-nating principle in education today is to bolster the self-esteem of children through praise, which has resulted in a greater overemphasis on self-congratu-lation and a more inward focus of children's attention than before. In a word, education is 'all about me'.

Lasch (1979) also explains that our current glorification of youth is a further reflection of a society that has lost interest in the future. He argues that an irra-tional fear of old age and death is strongly associated with the emergence of the widespread narcissistic personality structure that is representative of contempo-rary society. Because the narcissist has so few inner sources of self-esteem she or he looks to others for validation and admiration. Evidence of the overvaluation of youth is seen most explicitly in our dramatic and expensive attempts to coun-teract the physical signs of aging. One example is the sharp increase in the number of people seeking cosmetic plastic surgery in the form of blepharoplasty (eyelid surgery), rhytidectomy (face-lift surgery), and liposuction (Pruzinsky and Edgerton 1990).

Fitness and Health

The third influence is society's current obsession with matters of fitness and health. This has probably stemmed from the growing awareness from medical and epidemiological research that lifestyle greatly increases the risk for morbid diseases such as cardiovascular problems and many forms of cancer. Con-sequently, there has been an increasing emphasis by government agencies and the medical community on the adoption of healthy behaviours as a form of disease prevention. The primary themes focus on the virtues of weight control, active living, and a balanced diet. It is ironic that at the present time, adult obesity rates in North America are about 33 per cent and the fast food industry is rapidly expanding. On any given day it is estimated that about 20 per cent of North Americans take at least one meal from a fast food outlet (Nichter and Nichter 1991). At the same time we are bombarded with dietary advice to reduce our intake of animal fat (Hartley 1996). These messages are directed mostly towards women. One study reported that women's magazines contained over ten times as many articles and advertisements promoting weight loss and dieting than were found in men's magazines (Andersen and DiDomenico 1992). It is also notable that at the same time as the benefits of physical activity are being strongly promoted, physical activity levels, particularly among women, have been declining (Schoenborn 1993).

One side-effect of this hype about health has been the emergence of what psychologists have referred to as a 'collective hypochondriasis'. Since we are inundated with messages about the health risks and benefits of many aspects of daily life, our energies have become increasingly consumed by these concerns. Capitalist interests have been only too ready to exploit this neurosis. The fitness industry is now a multimillion-dollar enterprise, and the marketing of healthy living—much of it in the form of blatant quackery—proliferates at an astounding rate. For example, in a recent survey of fitness and nutrition messages in a magazine for teenage women, it was found that while the nutrition coverage had not changed substantially between the years 1970–90, the fitness coverage had increased significantly (Guillen and Barr 1994). In fact, the ratio of nutrition:fitness coverage changed from 10:1 in 1970 to 0.75:1 in 1990. What is particularly insidious about this shift in orientation is that fitness/health messages are frequently overlaid by messages about physical attractiveness. It is often implied that thin is beautiful and therefore healthy.

The Impact of the Mass Media

Contributing to the force of these sociocultural influences in altering our attitudes towards the body is the unprecedented and ubiquitous influence of the mass media. The guiding strategic principle of the advertising industry is to create an atmosphere of envy and dissatisfaction. We are constantly being encouraged to incorporate both control and release into our lives (Nichter and Nichter 1991). On the one hand, youth and slenderness are glamorized, exercise and physical fitness are aggressively marketed as a means to attaining a beautiful and healthy body, and dietary advice and miracle weight-loss programs abound. On the other hand, consumer excesses are also encouraged, and 'the good life' is largely reflected in commodity fetishism and the temptation to overindulge. A poignant example of these contradictory messages is the typical food advertisement. Ultraslender female models, who implicitly celebrate restraint, offer encouragement to consume highly caloric, non-essential foods like chocolate and rich desserts (Dittmar and Blayney 1996). Clearly, the impact of these mixed messages is more potent for some than for others. A recent study found that advertisements featuring food, especially 'forbidden foods', arouse more negative emotions than non-food ads, but only among those who already suffer from eating problems and disturbed attitudes towards body and weight (Dittmar and

Blayney 1996). Research has also indicated that eating-disordered women tended to overestimate their body size after viewing images of thin young women (compared to neutral photographs), while women with no eating problems were unaffected by the images (Hamilton and Waller 1993).

Magazines, television, and other media are powerful sources of information that can alter our behaviours and influence the way we think about ourselves. This is particularly so for adolescents who are vulnerable to lifestyle advertising because they desperately want to fit into adult culture and have not yet formed a core identity that is stable enough to resist the image-making of the media (Becker and Hamburg 1996). In an attempt to examine relationships among television viewing and body-image concerns, one study found that adolescent females typically watch an enormous amount of television—in excess of twenty hours a week. The *type* of programming was also significant in predicting body dissatisfaction. In particular, the time the subjects reported watching programs showing women in stereotypically 'feminine' roles (like music videos, soaps, and movies) was positively correlated with body dissatisfaction (Tiggemann and Pickering 1996). Moreover, and supporting earlier research with similar findings, although the subjects in the sample had a relatively low mean body mass index, the group of subjects as a whole perceived themselves as somewhat overweight, were dissatisfied with their weight, and had high levels of weight preoccupation. It is clearly not a coincidence that adolescence is the most common age of the onset of eating disorders.

Physical Activity and Eating Disorders

A second purpose of this chapter is to examine the psychobiology of eating disorders, particularly as it affects their progression and maintenance. From the first accounts of AN, and since that time, clinicians have observed that excessive exercising and/or generalized hyperactivity is a common characteristic among patients, even during periods of extreme emaciation (Bruch 1965; Crisp 1967; Dally 1969; Gull 1874; Inches 1895; Yates 1991). Despite the counterintuitive nature of this association—or perhaps because of it—the most common approach has been to treat the patient's physical activity as a relatively unimportant symptom; in other words, as nothing more than a conscious and wilful attempt to expend unwanted calories. Recently, however, there has been a shift in this viewpoint as a result of evidence, both from animal experimentation and from clinical field studies indicating that exercise is not simply a benign adjunct to dieting but a behaviour that can play a central and significant role in the development, progression, and maintenance of many eating disorders.

We have known for at least thirty years of animal research that when rodents are put on a restricted food intake, they begin to increase their physical activity and, in turn, eat less (Routtenberg and Kuznesof 1967). Over time there is an exponential increase in activity and a similar decrease in food intake and body weight. Some have drawn parallels between this phenomenon and the behaviour observed in AN (Epling and Pierce 1984, 1992; Russell et al. 1987). In the latter case, dieting and exercise, either together or separately, can result in weight loss, which, in a culture such as ours, has numerous social as well as biological rein-forcers. A typical mindset among women who want to lose weight is that 'if a little is good, a lot is better' and so there may be an increase in both dieting and exercise, with further weight loss and more reinforcement. For some a vicious cycle begins and is increasingly difficult to break (Epling and Pierce 1992).

In a recent study we investigated, for the first time in a systematic way, whether this animal syndrome was actually a valid model of AN in the human condition (Davis et al. 1994). A number of interesting findings emerged. For example, we found that AN patients were more physically active than a compar-ison group of age-matched healthy control subjects from childhood onwards and before the onset of their disorder. We also found that 75 per cent of the patients reported an inverse relationship between food intake and exercising during an acute weight-loss phase of their disorder. That is, the more they restricted their food intake, the more they exercised!

Prevalence Estimates

Although a few earlier studies have estimated the prevalence of excessive exer-cising among eating-disordered patients, none of the estimates are entirely satis-factory or indeed consistent (Crisp et al. 1980; Davis et al. 1994; Kron et al. 1978). The principal reason for the lack of consensus is the absence in the literature of a coherent definition of the term 'excessive'. There has also been a lack of speci-ficity concerning whether estimates were based on exercise status at the time of assessment for the study or on lifetime exercise histories. Other problems concern the frequently small sample sizes, which have compromised the representative-ness of the data upon which the estimates were based. A recent study that has addressed some of these problems found that about 80 per cent of both adult and young adolescent AN patients had exercised excessively during an acute phase of their disorder, and that these rates were significantly lower (56 per cent) among BN patients (Davis et al. 1997). In addition, 50 per cent of AN patients described their childhood activity levels (i.e., before the onset of their disorder) as greater than those of other girls their age. Rates were again significantly lower among BN patients.

Perhaps the most interesting finding in this study was that a significantly greater proportion of those who were highly physically active during childhood became excessive exercisers during their eating disorder, compared to their less active counterparts. Although these findings support the significance of sport/exercise as a predisposing factor in the development of eating disorders, one can only speculate on causation. Traditionally, dance, figure skating, and gymnastics have been the most common physical activities in which young girls participate. They are also activities that are highly body focused, and which place a strong emphasis on a slender shape for aesthetic and performance reasons. There is, therefore, the possibility that these activities can directly foster a desire for weight loss, or at least provide reinforcement when it occurs. It is also probable that those for whom physical activity has been an integral part of their childhood lifestyle are more likely to use exercise as means of expending calories should they, at some later point in their life, wish to lose weight.

Exercise, Starvation, and Obsessionality

It is becoming clear that the links between dieting and exercise operate at sociological, psychological, and biological levels. Regarding the latter, animal research has indicated that neurochemical changes that are generally associated with compulsive behaviours occur more often in exercising, semistarved rats than in their sedentary weight-matched counterparts (Broocks et al. 1991). In fact, some have proposed that the syndrome described above whereby food-restricted rodents will run excessively is a valid model for obsessive-compulsive disorder as well as for AN (Altemus et al. 1993). The former is a debilitating psychiatric condition characterized by intrusive and unwanted impulses, and time-consuming rituals (like frequent checking and hand washing), which are designed to neutralize the obsessional thoughts. With this evidence in mind, we speculated that obsessional symptomatology should be greater in exercising AN patients than in those who were non-exercisers.

In the first test of this hypothesis, we found that obessionality was positively correlated with frequency of exercise in a group of emaciated AN patients as well as among a group of high-level female exercisers (Davis et al. 1995). In other words, the higher the frequency of exercise, the higher the tendency to be obsessional. Furthermore, in the AN patient group, exercise frequency was also related to degree of weight preoccupation and to maladaptive attitudes to exercising, such as exercising despite illness and injury. In a subsequent study investigating differences in the psychological profile of excessively exercising and non-excessively exercising AN patients, we found that exercisers were more obsessive-compulsive both with respect to their symptomatology and their personality characteristics (Davis et al., forthcoming). Excessive exercisers also reported a greater degree of perfectionism and a more pathological commitment to exercise.

These studies raise the possibility that obsessionality may function at two different levels in the pathogenesis of eating disorders. On the one hand, it may function as an antecedent in the tendency to become hyperactive. On the other hand, extensive exercise may exacerbate obsessive symptomatology once the disorder has developed, thereby making it more resistant to treatment. At this point, however, we can only speculate about these associations, and about the interacting effects of culture, psychology, and biology.

Compulsive Exercising

When a seemingly healthy activity like exercising is carried on despite injury, illness, and fatigue, it suggests that something is amiss. Over the past fifteen to twenty years, there has been a growing awareness that some individuals take their training regimens to unreasonable and even unhealthy levels. During this time, anecdotes and case histories began to surface about individuals whose lives were effectively controlled by their need to exercise. Among other terms, this has been called 'compulsive exercise' (Yates 1991), 'negative addiction' (Morgan 1979), and 'exercise dependence' (De Coverley Veale 1987). In fact, the nature of this behaviour became the subject of considerable popular and academic debate when claims were made that overexercising is a variant of AN (Yates et al. 1983; Yates 1991). Based on a wealth of clinical data, Yates and her colleagues concluded that exercise and dieting are in fact 'sister activities', and that a strong investment in one is likely to be accompanied by a preoccupation with the other (Yates 1991; Yates et al. 1992).

As we discussed earlier, the prevalence of excessive exercising among eating-disordered patients, particularly those with AN, is extremely high. However, among women in the general population there is also some evidence that strong links exist between exercise and dieting (Davis et al. 1993; Estok and Rudy 1996; Krejci et al. 1992; McDonald and Thompson 1992). For example, one study found that high-intensity female runners scored higher on measures of eating-disorder attitudes/behaviours and addiction to running, and had a lower percentage of body fat than their less intense counterparts (Estok and Rudy 1996). In other words, even at lower body weights, the high-intensity runners were more preoccupied with weight than those who ran with less intensity. Interestingly, Davis et al. (1993) found similar results among both male and female exercisers across a variety of physical activities.

Despite this evidence, a handful of studies have found no relationship between exercise and weight preoccupation/dieting. However, a careful review of their methodologies indicates unequivocally that issues of measurement and classification cast doubt on their validity. In general, those studies that have simply looked at frequency of exercise have failed to find a relationship (e.g., Goldfarb and Plante 1984; Nudelman, Rosen, and Leitenberg 1988; Weight and Noakes 1987), while more recent studies that have taken account of the individual's commitment to exercise, as well as its frequency, have found significant relationships between exercise and weight and diet concerns (e.g., Davis et al. 1993; Krejci et al. 1992; Yates et al. 1992).

A matter of theoretical and practical interest in this area is the issue of whether exercise, in its extreme, is associated with features of addiction or whether it is a compulsive process. Traditionally, they have been treated as quite separate and distinct entities in psychiatry, despite their obvious similarities. This orientation reflects, in large part, the fact that addictive behaviours (like drug taking) have commonly been viewed as giving pleasure while compulsive behaviours are generally consciously experienced as distressing to the individual. Several investigators have supported the first point of view (e.g., De Coverley Veale 1987; Morgan 1979; Morris, Steinberg, Sykes, and Salmon 1990). The main impetus behind the addiction hypothesis has come from a theory that proposes that both exercise and severe food restriction increase beta-endorphins, which are highly addictive hormones produced by the body, and that both excessive exercisers and anorexics have become dependent on the mood-enhancing properties of these substances (Heubner 1993; Marrazzi and Luby 1986; Marrazzi et al. 1990). The few studies that have looked at the associations among exercise frequency and personality measures of addictiveness have obtained conflicting results that are probably attributable to differences in the way exercising was defined (Davis et al. 1993; Estok and Rudy 1996; Kagan 1987; Kagan and Squires 1985).

Yates (1991), on the other hand, claims that excessive exercising is a type of compulsion because, in the manner of compulsive behaviours, the individuals involved do not necessarily enjoy what they are doing but feel compelled to do it. Research evidence has provided some support for this point of view. Davis et al. (1993) found that exercise commitment and frequency among male exercisers was positively associated with obsessive-compulsive personality characteristics, which include perfectionism, perseverance, and rigidity. This meshes with findings that males who run excessively are differentiated from their recreational counterparts primarily by their competitiveness and achievement motives, and their need for recognition (Ogles et al. 1995).

The addiction-compulsion debate has probably occurred because the two perspectives have traditionally been treated as quite separate and distinct disease entities within psychiatry. In terms of comprehending the nature of excessive exercising, the question arises about whether it is possible to reconcile these apparently opposing viewpoints. In fact, some have recognized that compulsive behaviour is a critical component of addictive behaviours in the sense that the individual's ability to choose to discontinue the behaviour is pathologically diminished (Jaffe 1990; Marrazzi and Luby 1986). Dodes (1996) has also argued that there is a great deal to be gained in understanding both types of disorders by recognizing the *compulsive* nature of all addictions, and the *addictive* nature of some compulsions.

The combined influence of these two personality styles in relation to excessive exercising was recently demonstrated among a group of eating-disordered patients (Davis and Claridge 1998). Results indicated that addictive and obsessional personality characteristics were more pronounced among excessive exercisers than among those were not. While one can only speculate on the dynamics of these associations, it may be that addictiveness and obsessionality coexist in the pathogenesis of excessive exercising. In other words, the characteristics that comprise addictiveness may provide the constitutional vulnerability to developing an addiction, while obsessive-compulsiveness provides the personality infrastructure—rigidity, perseverance, and perfectionism—necessary to initiate and sustain the process of self-starvation and strenuous physical activity.

Eating Disorders and Competitive Sport

Female athletes have frequently been identified as a population at higher-than-normal risk for developing an eating disorder (Brownell et al. 1992; Davis 1992; Petrie 1996). The rationale is straightforward. There are a number of sports in which success is not only determined by technical skill but also by a graceful and slender body shape. Therefore, institutional pressures, beyond the normal socio-cultural ones, are imposed on women who want to compete and excel at these activities. Among the sports most often cited are gymnastics, figure skating, and distance running. It has been argued, however, that the demand for thinness and the pressure to diet is greater among dancers, particularly ballet dancers, than among any other group of athletes in our society (Garner and Garfinkel 1980). Indeed, an accumulating body of evidence over the past few decades supports this idea (Abraham 1996; le Grange et al. 1994). Studies have found as much as a sevenfold increase in the risk of eating disorders among this group compared to that found in the age-matched female population.

In general, the evidence supporting an increased risk among female athletes is compelling. While a few studies have found no differences between athletes and non-athletes in measures of body dissatisfaction and weight preoccupation (e.g., Skowron and Friedlander 1994; Taub and Blinde 1992), methodological problems with these studies seriously compromise the conclusions that one can draw. For example, in the first study, the authors claimed that a group of élite female swimmers did not differ from a group of college students on subscale scores of the *Eating Disorder Inventory* (Garner and Olmsted 1984). However, they failed to control for body weight in their analyses. In the second study, it is not clear how the investigators defined 'athletes' and 'non-athletes'. In all probability, the subjects were students who were classified simply on the basis of whether or not they participated in school sports.

Much more frequent in the literature are studies that have found increased eating-disorder symptoms among female athletes, including evidence that they often employ extreme methods such as fasting, self-induced vomiting, use of laxatives, and excessive exercising beyond training requirements to try and reduce body fat (e.g., Black and Burckes-Miller 1988; Petrie 1993; Rosen and Hough 1988; Rosen et al. 1986). Davis (1992) also found a considerably greater degree of weight and body-image concerns among high-performance female athletes than among their age and sex-matched counterparts. A substantial number who were already underweight, by objective standards, wanted to be thinner and dieted frequently. Furthermore, a significantly greater proportion of the high-performance athletes were classified as 'excessively weight preoccupied' according to established norms (see Garner et al. 1984). Although this occurred most frequently among gymnasts and synchronized swimmers, the results indicated, as others have found (e.g., Borgen and Corbin 1987; Rosen et al. 1986; Sykora et al. 1993), that these attitudes are not restricted only to athletes in sports characterized by ultraslenderness.

Additional evidence supporting links between sport and eating disorders comes from the clinical literature. In a recent study, we found that between 55–60 per cent of AN patients from two separate samples (a group of adolescent patients and a second group of adult patients) were involved in regular sport/exercise activities before they ever began to diet and before the onset of their disorder (Davis et al. 1997). We also have evidence from a sample of hospitalized AN patients that 60 per cent had been involved in high-level sport or dance before the onset of their disorder (Davis et al. 1994). What was particularly interesting in the latter study was the fact that a large proportion of these women indicated that their disorder really began *after* they stopped training and competing, reasoning that few calories should be ingested if little energy was being expended. A pattern of serious food restriction often began at this time.

Concluding Remarks

In an attempt to examine the factors that impinge on the relationship between physical activity and eating disorders, this chapter has focused primarily on a review of pertinent sociocultural influences. However, to view this as a complete picture would be a mistake. This perspective presents only one part of an intricate network of factors that may have causal associations with eating disorders. We must not lose sight of the fact that although all women in our society are exposed to very similar body-image standards, media influences, and social values and biases, only a relatively few of them develop a serious eating problem or engage in exercise excessively. Clearly, then, individual vulnerabilities play a key role in determining who among the population find more extreme solutions to the well-recognized social pressures on women to conform to culturally imposed ideals. Other personal characteristics, such as the impact of family dynamics and childhood trauma, have also been implicated. It is fair to say that no single explanation or theory has ever sufficed to describe these complex disorders. Only by taking account of factors at a number of different levels can we become more enlightened about their aetiology and prognosis.

References

Abraham, S. 1996. 'Characteristics of Eating Disorders Among Young Ballet Dancers'. *Psychopathology* 29:223–9.

Altemus, M. J.R. Glowa, and D.L. Murphy. 1993. 'Attenuation of Food-Restriction-Induced Running by Chronic Fluoxetine Treatment'. *Psychopharmacology Bulletin* 29:397–400.

Anderson, A.E., and L. DiDomenico. 1992. 'Diet vs. Shape Content of Popular Male and Female Magazines: A Dose-Response Relationship to the Incidence of Eating Disorders?' *International Journal of Eating Disorders* 3:283–7.

Becker, A.E., and P. Hamburg. 1996. 'Culture, the Media, and Eating Disorders'. *Harvard Review of Psychiatry* 4:163–7.

Beebe, D.W., G. Holmbeck, J.S. Albright, K. Noga, and B. Decastro. 1995. 'Identification of "Binge-Prone" Women: An Experimentally and Psychometrically Validated Cluster Analysis in a College Population'. *Addictive Behaviors* 20:451–62.

Black, D.R., and M.E. Burckes-Miller. 1988. 'Male and Female College Athletes: Use of Anorexia Nervosa and Bulimia Nervosa Weight Loss Methods'. *Research Quarterly for Exercise and Sport* 59:252–6.

Borgen, J.S., and C.B. Corbin. 1987. 'Eating Disorders Among Female Athletes'. *The Physician and Sportsmedicine* 15:89–95.

Brenner, J.B., and J.G. Cunningham. 1992. 'Gender Differences in Eating Attitudes, Body Concept, and Self-Esteem Among Models'. *Sex Roles* 27, no. 7/8:413–37.

Broocks, A., U. Schweiger, and K.M. Pirke. 1991. 'The Influence of Semistarvation-Induced Hyperactivity on Hypothalamic Serotonin Metabolism'. *Physiology & Behavior* 50:385–8.

Brownell, K.D., J. Rodin, and J.H. Wilmore, eds. 1992. *Eating, Body Weight and Performance in Athletes*. Philadelphia: Lea & Febiger.

Bruch, H. 1965. 'Anorexia Nervosa—Its Differential Diagnosis'. *Journal of Mental and Nervous Disorders* 141:555–66.

Buss, D.M. 1994. *The Evolution of Human Desire*. New York: Basic Books.

Button, E.J., and A. Whitehouse. 1981. 'Subclinical Anorexia Nervosa'. *Psychological Medicine* 11:509–16.

Crandall, C.S., and R. Martinez. 1996.'Culture, Ideology, and Antifat Attitudes'. *Personality and Social Psychology Bulletin* 11:1165–76.

Crisp, A.H. 1967. 'The Possible Significance of Some Behavioral Correlates of Weight and Carbohydrate Intake'. *Journal of Psychomatic Research* 11:117–31.

_____, L.K.G. Hsu, B. Harding, and J. Hartshorn. 1980. 'Clinical Features of Anorexia Nervosa: A Study of a Consecutive Series of 102 Female Patients'. *Journal of Psychomatic Research* 24:179–91.

Dally, P.J. 1969. *Anorexia Nervosa*. New York: Grune & Stratton.

Davis, C. 1992. 'Body Image, Dieting Behaviours, and Personality Factors: A Study of High-Performance Female Athletes'. *International Journal of Sport Psychology* 23:179–92.

_____, H. Brewer, and D. Ratusny. 1993. 'Behavioral Frequency and Psychological Commitment: Necessary Concepts in the Study of Excessive Exercising'. *Journal of Behavioral Medicine* 16:611–28.

_____, and G. Claridge. 1998. 'The Eating Disorders as Addiction: A Psychobiological Perspective'. *Addictive Behaviors* 23:463–75.

_____, S.A. Kaptein, A.S. Kaplan, M.P. Olmsted, and B. Woodside. Forthcoming. 'Obsessionality in Anorexia Nervosa: The Moderating Influence of Exercise'. *Psychomatic Medicine* 60:192–7.

_____, D.K. Katzman, S. Kaptein, C. Kirsh, H. Brewer, K. Kalmbach, M.P. Olmsted, D.B. Woodside, and A.S. Kaplan. 1997. 'The Prevalence of High-Level Exercise in the Eating Disorders: Aetiological Implications'. *Comprehensive Psychiatry* 38:321–6.

_____, S.H. Kennedy, E. Ralevski, and M. Dionne. 1994. 'The Role of Physical Activity in the Development and Maintenance of Eating Disorders'. *Psychological Medicine* 24:957–67.

_____, S.H. Kennedy, E. Ralevski, M. Dionne, H. Brewer, C. Neitzert, and D. Ratusny. 1995. 'Obsessive Compulsiveness and Physical Activity in Anorexia Nervosa and High-Level Exercising'. *Journal of Psychosomatic Research* 39:967–76.

De Coverley Veale, E. 1987. 'Exercise Dependence'. *British Journal of Addiction* 82:735–40.

de Zwann, M., and J.E. Mitchell. 1993. 'Medical Complications of Anorexia Nervosa and Bulimia Nervosa'. In *Medical Issues and the Eating Disorders: The Interface*, edited by A.S. Kaplan and P.E. Garfinkel, 60–100. New York: Brunner/Mazel Publishers.

Dittmar, H., and M. Blayney. 1996. 'Women's Self-Reported Eating Behaviours and Their Responses to Food and Non-Food Television Advertisements'. *European Eating Disorders Review* 4:217–30.

Dodes, L.M. 1996. 'Compulsion and Addiction'. *Journal of the American Psychoanalytic Association* 44:815–35.

Eagles, J.M., M.I. Johnston, D. Hunter, M. Lobban, and H.R. Millar. 1995. 'Increasing Incidence of Anorexia Nervosa in the Female Population of Northeast Scotland'. *American Journal of Psychiatry* 152:1266–71.

Epling, W.F., and W.D. Pierce. 1984. 'Activity-based Anorexia in Rats as a Function of Opportunity to Run on an Activity Wheel'. *Nutrition and Behavior* 2:37–49.

_____, and W.D. Pierce. 1992. *Solving the Anorexia Puzzle*. Toronto: Hogrefe & Huber Publishers.

Estok, P.J., and E.B. Ruby. 1996. 'The Relationship Between Eating Disorders and Running in Women'. *Research in Nursing* 19::377–87.

Fairburn, C.G., and S.J. Beglin. 1990. 'Studies of the Epidemiology of Bulimia Nervosa'. *American Journal of Psychiatry* 147:401–8.

Fisher, M., N.H. Golden, D.K. Katzman, R.E. Kreipe, J. Rees, J. Schebendach, G. Sigman, S. Ammerman, and H.M. Hoberman. 1995. 'Eating Disorders in Adolescents: A Background Paper'. *Journal of Adolescent Health* 16:420–37.

Fries, H. 1974. 'Secondary Amenorrhoea, Self-induced Weight Reduction and Anorexia Nervosa'. *Acta Psychiatrica Scandinavica* [Suppl] 248:5–65.

Garner, D.M., and P.E. Garfinkel. 1980. 'Socio-cultural Factors in the Development of Anorexia Nervosa'. *Psychological Medicine* 10:647–56.

_____, P.E. Garfinkel, D. Schwartz, and M. Thompson. 1980. 'Cultural Expectations of Thinness in Women'. *Psychological Reports* 47:483–91.

_____, and M.A. Olmsted. 1984. *Eating Disorder Inventory Manual*. Lutz, FL: Psychological Assessment Resources.

_____, M.P. Olmsted, J. Polivy, and P.E. Garfinkel. 1984. 'Comparison Between Weight-Preoccupied Women and Anorexia Nervosa'. *Psychomatic Medicine* 46:255–66.

_____, and S.C. Wooley. 1991. 'Confronting the Failure of Behavioral and Dietary Treatments for Obesity'. *Clinical Psychology Review* 11:729–80.

Goldfarb, L.A., and T.G. Plante. 1984. 'Fear of Fat in Runners: An Examination of the Connection Between Anorexia Nervosa and Distance Running'. *Psychological Reports* 55:296.

Grogan, S., and N. Wainwright. 1996. 'Growing Up in the Culture of Slenderness'. *Women's Studies International Forum* 19:665–73.

Guillen, E.O., and S.I. Barr. 1994. 'Nutrition, Dieting, and Fitness Messages in a Magazine for Adolescent Women, 1970–1990'. *Journal of Adolescent Health* 15:464–72.

Gull, W.W. 1874. 'Anorexia Nervosa'. Trans Clin. Soc. (London), 7:22–8, cited by A. Warah (1993) 'Overactivity and Boundary Setting in Anorexia Nervosa: An Existential Perspective'. *Journal of Adolescence* 16:93–100.

Hamilton, K., and G. Waller. 1993. 'Media Influences on Body Size Estimation in Anorexia and Bulimia: An Experimental Study'. *British Journal of Psychiatry* 162:837–40.

Hartley, P. 1996. 'Does Health Education Promote Eating Disorders?' *European Eating Disorders Review* 4:3–11.

Heubner, H.F. 1993. *Endorphins, Eating Disorders and Other Addictive Behaviors*. New York: W.W. Norton & Co.

Horm, J., and K. Anderson. 1993. 'Who in America Is Trying to Lose Weight?' *Annals of Internal Medicine* 119:672–6.

Inches, P. 1895. 'Anorexia Nervosa'. *The Maritime Medical News* 7:73–5.

Jaffe, J.H. 1990. 'Trivialising Dependence'. *British Journal of Addiction* 85:1425–7.

Kagan, D.M. 1987. 'Addictive Personality Factors'. *Journal of Psychology* 121:533–8.

_____, and R.L. Squires. 1985. 'Addictive Aspects of Physical Exercise'. *Journal of Sports Medicine* 25:227–37.

Kaplan, A.S., and M. Katz. 1993. 'Medical Illnesses Associated with Weight Loss and Binge Eating'. In *Medical Issues and the Eating Disorders: The Interface*, edited by A.S. Kaplan and P.E. Garfinkel, 17–38. New York: Brunner/Mazel.

Katz, L.G. 1993. 'All About Me'. *American Educator* (Summer):18–23.

Kendler, K.S., C. MacLean, M. Neale, R. Kessler, A. Health, and L. Eaves. 1991. 'The Genetic Epidemiology of Bulimia Nervosa'. *American Journal of Psychiatry* 148:1627–37.

Keys, A. 1950. *The Biology of Human Starvation*. Minneapolis: University of Minnesota Press.

Kreij, R.C., R. Sargnet, K.J. Forand, J.R. Ureda, R.P. Saunders, and J.L. Durstine. 1992. 'Psychological and Behavioral Differences Among Females Classified as Bulimic, Obligatory Exerciser and Normal Control'. *Psychiatry* 55:185–93.

Kron, K., J.L. Katz, G. Gorzynski, and H. Weiner. 1978. 'Hyperactivity in Anorexia Nervosa: A Fundamental Clinical Feature'. *Comprehensive Psychiatry* 19:433–40.

Lasch, C. 1979. *The Culture of Narcissism*. New York: Norton.

le Grange, D., J. Tibbs, and T.D. Noakes. 1994. 'Implications of a Diagnosis of Anorexia Nervosa in a Ballet School'. *International Journal of Eating Disorders* 15:369–76.

Lucas, A.R., C.M. Beard, W.M. O'Fallon, and L.T. Kurland. 1991. '50-year Trends in the Incidence of Anorexia Nervosa in Rochester, Minn.: A Population-Based Study'. *American Journal of Psychiatry* 148:917–22.

McDonald, K., and J.K. Thompson. 1992. 'Eating Disturbance, Body Image Dissatisfaction, and Reasons for Exercising'. *International Journal of Eating Disorders* 11:289–92.

Malson, H., and J.M. Ussher. 1996. 'Body Poly-texts: Discourses of the Anorexic Body'. *Journal of Community & Applied Social Psychology* 6:267–80.

Marazzi, M.A., and E.D. Luby. 1986. 'An Auto-addiction Opoid Model of Chronic Anorexia Nervosa'. *International Journal of Eating Disorders* 5:191–208.

———, J. Mullings-Britton, L. Stack, R.J. Powers, J. Lawhorn, V. Graham, T. Eccles, and S. Gunter. 1990. 'Atypical Endogenous Opoid Systems in Mice in Relation to an Auto-addiction Opoid Model of Anorexia Nervosa'. *Life Sciences* 47:1427–35.

Mazur, A. 1986. 'U.S. Trends in Feminine Beauty and Overadaption'. *The Journal of Sex Research* 22:281–303.

Mishkind, M., J. Rodin, L. Silberstein, and R. Streigel-Moore. 1986. 'The Embodiment of Masculinity'. *The American Behavioural Scientist* 29:545–62.

Moller-Madsen, S., and J. Nystrup. 1992. 'Incidence of Anorexia Nervosa in Denmark'. *Acta Psychiatrica Scandinavica* 86:197–200.

Morgan, W.P. 1979. 'Negative Addiction in Runners'. *The Physician and Sportsmedicine* 7:57–68.

Morris, M., H. Steinberg, E.A. Sykes, and P. Salmon. 1990. 'Effects of Temporary Withdrawal from Regular Running'. *Journal of Psychosomatic Research* 34:493–500.

Nichter, M., and M. Nichter. 1991. 'Hype and Weight'. *Medical Anthropology* 13:249–84.

Nudelman, S. J.C. Rosen, and H. Leitenberg. 1988. 'Dissimilarities in Eating Attitudes, Body Image Distortion, Depression, and Self-esteem Between High-Intensity Male Runners and Women with Bulimia Nervosa'. *International Journal of Eating Disorders* 7:625–34.

Nylander, I. 1971. 'The Feeling of Being Fat and Dieting in a School Population'. *Acta Socio-Medica Scandinavica* 1:17–26.

Ogles, B.A., K.S. Masters, and S.A. Richardson. 1995. 'Obligatory Running and Gender: An Analysis of Participative Motives and Training Habits'. *International Journal of Sport Psychology* 26:233–48.

Petrie, T.A. 1993. 'Disordered Eating in Female Collegiate Gymnasts: Prevalence and Personality/Attitudinal Correlates'. *Journal of Sport and Exercise Psychology* 15:424–36.

———. 1996. 'Differences Between Male and Female College Lean Sport Athletes, Nonlean Sport Athletes, and Nonathletes on Behavioral and Psychological Indices of Eating Disorders'. *Journal of Applied Sport Psychology* 8:218–30.

Probast, C.K., and L.S. Lieberman. 1992. 'Cultural Influences on Normal and Idealized Female Body Size'. *Collegium Antropologium* 16:151–6.

Pruzinsky, T., and M.T. Edgerton. 1990. 'Body-Image Change in Cosmetic Plastic Surgery'. In *Body Images Development, Deviance, and Change*, edited by T.F. Cash and T. Pruzinsky, 217–36. New York: The Guildford Press.

Rosen, L.W., and D.O. Hough. 1988. 'Pathogenic Weight-Control Behaviors of Female College Gymnasts'. *The Physician and Sportsmedicine* 16:141–4.

———, D.B. McKeag, D.O. Hough, and V. Curley. 1986. 'Pathogenic Weight Control Behavior in Female Athletes'. *The Physician and Sportsmedicine* 14:79–86.

Routtenberg, A., and A.W. Kuznesof. 1967. 'Self-starvation in Rats Living in Activity Wheels on a Restricted Feeding Schedule'. *Journal of Comparative Physiological Psychology* 64:414–21.

Russell, J.C., W.F. Epling, W.D. Pierce, R.M. Amy, and D.P. Boer. 1987. 'Induction of Voluntary Prolonged Running in Rats'. *Journal of Applied Psychology* 63:2549–53.

Scarano, G.M., and C.R. Kalodner-Martin. 1994. 'A Description of the Continuum of Eating Disorders: Implications for Intervention and Research'. *Journal of Counseling and Development* 72:356–61.

Schoenborn, C. 1993. *Health Practices in Canada and the United States, 1985 and 1990*. Canada's Health Promotion Survey, 1990. Ottawa: Health and Welfare Canada.

Serdula, M.K., M.E. Collins, D.F. Williamson, R.F. Anda, E.F. Pamuk, and T.E. Byers. 1993. 'Weight Control Practices of U.S. Adolescents and Adults'. *Annals of Internal Medicine* 119:667–71.

Silverstein, B., L. Perdue, B. Peterson, L. Vogel, and D.A. Fantini. 1986. 'Possible Causes of the Thin Standard of Bodily Attractiveness for Women'. *International Journal of Eating Disorders* 5:907–16.

Singh, D. 1993. 'Adaptive Significance of Female Physical Attractiveness: Role of Waist-to-Hip Ratio'. *Journal of Personality and Social Psychology* 65:293–307.

Skowron, E.A., and M.L. Friedlander. 1994. 'Psychological Separation, Self-control, and Weight Preoccupation Among Elite Women Athletes'. *Journal of Counselling & Development* 72:310–15.

Sobal, J., and A.J. Stunkard. 1989. 'Socioeconomic Status and Obesity: A Review of the Literature'. *Psychological Bulletin* 105:260–75.

Striegel-Moore, R., G. McAvay, and J. Rodin. 1986. 'Psychological and Behavioral Correlates of Feeling Fat in Women'. *International Journal of Eating Disorders* 5:935–47.

Sullivan, P.F. 1995. 'Mortality in Anorexia Nervosa'. *American Journal of Psychiatry* 152:1073–4.

Sykora, C., C.M. Grilo, D.E. Wilfley, and K.D. Brownell. 1993. 'Eating, Weight, and Dieting Disturbances in Male and Female Lightweight and Heavyweight Rowers'. *International Journal of Eating Disorders* 14:203–11.

Taub, D.E., and E.M. Blinde. 1992. 'Eating Disorders Among Adolescent Female Athletes: Influence of Athletic Participation and Sport Team Membership'. *Adolescence* 27:833–48.

Tiggemann, M., and A.S. Pickering. 1996. 'Role of Television in Adolescent Women's Body Dissatisfaction and Drive for Thinness'. *International Journal of Eating Disorders* 20:199–203.

van't Hof, S., and M. Nicolson. 1996. 'The Rise and Fall of Fact: The Increase in Anorexia Nervosa'. *Sociology of Health & Illness* 18:581–608.

Weight, L.M., and T.K. Noakes. 1987. 'Is Running an Analog of Anorexia? A Survey of the Incidence of Eating Disorders in Female Distance Runners'. *Medicine and Science in Sports and Exercise* 19, no. 3:213–17.

Wiseman, C.V., J.J. Gray, J.E. Mosimann, and A.H. Ahrens. 1992. 'Cultural Expectations of Thinness in Women: An Update'. *International Journal of Eating Disorders* 11:85–9.

Yates, A. 1991. *Compulsive Exercise and the Eating Disorders*. New York: Brunner/Mazel.

_____, K. Leehey, and C. Shisslak. 1983. 'Running—an Analogue of Anorexia?' *New England Journal of Medicine* 308, no. 5:251–5.

_____, C.M. Shisslak, J. Allender, M. Crago, and K. Leehey. 1992. 'Comparing Obligatory and Nonobligatory Runners'. *Psychosomatics* 33:180–9.

Chapter 6

Who's Fair Game?
Sport, Sexual Harassment, and Abuse

Peter Donnelly

Three days after one of his tormentors was sentenced to two years less a day, Martin succumbed.
—J. Macgowan, 'Lives Lived: Obituary of Arnold Martin Kruze', writing after the suicide of Martin Kruze, a victim of the Maple Leaf Gardens sex ring

In 1997 it seems that almost every Canadian became aware of the issue of sexual harassment in sport. On 3 January 1997 Graham James pleaded guilty in a court-room in Calgary. This former coach of the Swift Current Broncos was sentenced to three-and-a-half years in prison for sexually abusing one of his hockey players 300 times and another fifty times between 1984 and 1990. Because of a court-ordered ban on publication of the names of the victims, there was a great deal of public speculation about their identities, including rumours that one of the victims was a current NHL player and that other high-profile players had been victims. Several days later, Sheldon Kennedy, then a player with the NHL Boston Bruins, held a press conference to announce that he was the victim of the 300 cases of abuse.

In February 1997, after the arrest of Gordon Stuckless, a former equipment manager at Toronto's Maple Leaf Gardens, Maple Leafs' President Cliff Fletcher announced to the media that a 'pedophile ring' had operated at the Gardens from the mid-1970s to the early 1980s. Boys had been lured with tickets to games, visits to the locker-rooms and introductions to players, and were then coerced into sexual acts by at least three of the Gardens' employees.

In May 1997 Liam Donnelly, the swim coach at Simon Fraser University, was fired after being charged with the sexual harassment of a former swimmer, Rachel Marsden. He was reinstated three months later after further evidence indicated that Donnelly himself seemed to have been the victim of harassment by Marsden.

Although 1997 was a year in which all three cases attracted widespread media coverage, awareness and concern about sexual abuse and harassment has increased generally in the last twenty-five years, in part as a response to the women's and subsequently the children's rights movements. This has led to growing concerns and revelations about various types of sexual abuse in a wide range of settings. Schools and day care centres have been more closely monitored for sexual harassment, and there has been increased encouragement (including legislation making it mandatory) to report such incidents. Youth groups such as the Big Brothers organization and the Boy Scouts have instituted policies to guard against those seeking sexual access to children. In the workplace there has been a greater awareness of sexual harassment issues, with some corporations developing policies, and universities and colleges across Canada appointing sexual harassment officers in full- or part-time positions.

The world of sport and recreation has been very slow to respond to these changes. Generally, sport organizations have, until recently, acted as if such things could not possibly occur in the pristine world of sport and, as in the case of sport violence, behaved as if the laws of society were suspended in sport. In part, this may be because adults touching children and adults touching each other is a necessary part of the training and practice of many sports. The potentially erotic and abusive elements of such touching have invariably not been attended to until recently, and sport authorities have generally failed to recognize the opportunities for private encounters and coercion that readily exist in sport.

The result of the public revelations about sexual abuse in sport in Canada in 1997 has been the laying of a series of new charges and a variety of reports, policy changes, and other actions in an attempt to prevent future occurrences. While such initiatives are progressive, there has also been some criticism about the fact that it took the abuse of a high-profile male hockey player to finally achieve some more general action on the issue. Reports of the harassment and abuse of female athletes surfaced regularly during the 1990s, but led only to the first consideration of policy changes in 1995–6. So the outpouring of support for Kennedy led to a number of comments such as the following from an education coordinator at a rape crisis centre: 'I know of no woman, despite how credible she may be, who has been met with the kind of support which has been bestowed upon Sheldon. Most often the women have been met with denial, called liars and been subjected to the credits of their abusers that lift them above suspicion' (Schlatman 1997:N1). While responses of this type are understandable, it is not the purpose of this chapter to examine the gender politics underlying the public and official reaction to Sheldon Kennedy's revelations. Rather, the chapter is concerned with exploring the issue of sexual harassment and abuse in sport, and bringing together the best of the policies and recommendations that have been put forward to prevent the victimization of athletes.[1] Before that, the chapter will consider definitions of harassment and abuse, and attempt to determine the frequency with which they occur in sport.

Defining Harassment and Abuse

Apart from the most obvious instances, the terms sexual harassment and sexual abuse, and the differences between the two, prove to be quite difficult to define. This is particularly the case with marginal incidents of harassment, the interpretation of which varies on the basis of cultural and individual circumstances. As Tomlinson and Yorganci point out:

> . . . there are variations in the perceptions of women concerning different types of behavior regarded as sexual harassment . . . , and perceptions may depend not only on the age or gender of the perceiver but also on the type of social situation in which the interactions in question occur. [Because of the inevitable physical contact between coaches and athletes] the unwanted and unwelcome nature of the act . . . confirms the behavior as harassment (Tomlinson and Yorganci 1997:134–5; see also Reilly, Carpenter, Dull, and Bartlett 1982; Terpstra and Douglas 1987).

Brackenridge (1997:116–17) has tackled this difficult definitional problem by placing harassment and abuse on a continuum (Figure 6.1). Brackenridge (1997:117) views sexual harassment as a combination of personal and institutional issues including (but not limited to):

- written or verbal abuse or threats
- sexually oriented comments
- ridiculing of performance
- sexual or homophobic graffiti
- practical jokes based on sex
- vandalism on the basis of sex
- offensive phone calls or photos
- bullying based on sex
- jokes, lewd comments, or sexual innuendoes
- taunts about body, dress, marital status, or sexuality
- intimidating sexual remarks, propositions, invitations, or familiarity
- domination of meetings, play space, or equipment
- condescending or patronizing behaviour undermining self-respect or performance
- physical contact, fondling, pinching, or kissing

Brackenridge (1997:117) notes that harassment 'may be defined simply as "invasion without consent"'. However, there are clearly examples where consent is given, e.g., genuine affection, infatuation, just wanting to play along and/or perceiving worse consequences (such as loss of job for failing to play along), which may still be considered harassment, especially when there is a significant power and/or age difference (e.g., coach-athlete, teacher/professor-student, employer-employee, clinician-patient). Because of the complications with consent, legal

Figure 6.1

Brackenridge's Definitional Model of Sexual Harassment

SEX DISCRIMINATION	⟵⟶	SEXUAL HARASSMENT	⟵⟶	SEXUAL ABUSE
'the chilly climate'		'unwanted attention'		'groomed or coerced'
MAINLY INSTITUTIONAL	⟵⟶		MAINLY PERSONAL	

Source: C. Brackenridge, "'He Owned Me Basically. . .": Women's Experiences of Sexual Abuse in Sport'. *International Review for the Sociology of Sport* 32, no. 2 (1997):116–17.

definitions of harassment use the term 'unwelcome' rather than 'non-consensual'.[2]

The term sexual abuse tends to be reserved for the more severe, ongoing and/or coercive cases of sexual harassment. Brackenridge (1997:117) characterizes sexual abuse as involving (but not limited to):

- forced sexual activity
- physical/sexual violence
- indecent exposure
- rape
- sexual assault
- groping
- incest
- exchange of reward or privilege for sexual favours
- anal or vaginal penetration by penis, fingers, or objects

Because of this continuum (i.e., from relatively mild to very severe behaviour), and because of the difficulty of determining where harassment ends and abuse starts, sexual harassment is now more often being used as a collective term to describe both harassment and abuse. For example: 'For ease of reference, all prohibited conduct under this Policy will be referred to as "harassment", which will include harassing, discriminatory and abusive behaviour' (Kirke 1997:25). The Canadian Association for the Advancement of Women in Sport and Physical Activity (CAAWS) combines harassment and abuse to define sexual harassment as:

> . . . unwelcome sexual advances, requests for sexual favours, or other verbal or physical contact of a sexual nature when:
> - submitting to or rejecting this conduct is used as the basis for making decisions which affect the individual; or

- such conduct has the purpose or effect of interfering with an individual's performance; or
- such conduct creates an intimidating, hostile, or offensive environment (CAAWS 1994b:8).

The usual victims of sexual harassment are women and children (including youth). This is not to imply that men are not sexually harassed. Clearly some men are stalked or are subjected to unwanted sexual advances, as subsequent data indicate. Most of the evidence to date seems to suggest that this is a relatively infrequent occurrence in comparison with the harassment of women and children. However, there are some recent reports (e.g., Appleby 1998) pointing out that the harassment of males by females may be more widespread than has been suspected, but that it is underreported because of the dynamics of gender relations in Western society (e.g., men are supposed to be flattered by sexual attention from women).

The naming of behaviours as 'sexual harassment' began in the United States in the late 1970s.[3] Until that time, women had no legal recourse against the sexually offensive behaviour of some men. In an obvious outgrowth of the women's movement in the United States, 'courts incorporated the concept of sexual harassment into Title VII of the Civil Rights Act of 1964's protections against employment discrimination on the basis of sex, making it a legal cause of action' (Masteralexis 1995:143). In Canada, similar protections were introduced by the 1982 Canadian Charter of Rights and Freedoms, and were incorporated into each province's human rights act (CAAWS 1994a). More serious cases of sexual abuse are covered under the Criminal Code.

Frequency of Harassment and Abuse

Estimates and surveys indicate that a significant percentage of women in the workplace have experienced some form of sexual harassment from male employees or employers. Specific data, for example, are available for the frequency of sexual harassment on university campuses in the United States:

> Reliable estimates of sexual harassment of female students by male faculty on campuses approximate that between 20% and 30% of undergraduate women [some 1,300,000 students] and between 30% and 40% of graduate women experience some form of it during their academic lives. . . . Female students have also reported that 70% to 90% have experienced sexual harassment by male peers (Masteralexis 1995:146).

And while there may be some question about the reliability of such figures, it should be noted that, even on self-report and victimization surveys, those embellishing or exaggerating their experiences are likely to balance out those who do not report their experiences. As Lenskyj (1992b:21) notes with regard to underreporting: 'Researchers of women's experiences of male violence show that silence is used by many women as a coping strategy to deal with the shame and self-blame that often accompany these experiences.'

With regard to sexual harassment in sport, there has been mounting anecdotal evidence and reports of court cases for the last ten years. The best systematic research on the issue is Canadian. Kirby and Greaves (1996) conducted the most comprehensive survey to date, sending questionnaires to 1,200 members of Athletes CAN, a national team athletes' association in Canada. Of the 266 athletes who replied (22.2 per cent response rate; approximately 55 per cent female), 21.8 per cent had had sexual intercourse with a person in a position of authority in sport, and 'one-quarter of those say they were "insulted, ridiculed, made to feel like a bad person, slapped or hit, beaten or punched" by the aggressor' (Smith 1996a:A11). Some 8.6 per cent, including five athletes who were under the age of sixteen, experienced forced sexual intercourse in a sport context, and three male athletes also reported that they had been sexually assaulted in a sport context while under the age of sixteen. Some 3.2 per cent of the respondents stated that they had had upsetting experiences in a sporting context with a 'flasher' when they were under the age of sixteen; and 2.6 per cent had experienced unwanted sexual touching when they were under age sixteen. Seventeen of the athletes (thirteen of them females) reported that they had been stalked by a fan, coach, another athlete, or the parent of another athlete, always of the opposite sex.

Another survey (accurate to +/- 2.9 per cent, nineteen times out of twenty) involving an opportunity sample of 1995 Canada Winter Games athletes (N = 1,174) in Grande Prairie, Alberta, found that of these young athletes representing the provinces of Canada, '16 per cent had experienced sexual harassment, 11 per cent racial harassment, 18 per cent verbal abuse and 11 per cent physical abuse' (Christie 1997b:A14; McGregor 1997).

In yet another Canadian survey, Holman (1994, 1995) sent questionnaires to 1,024 Canadian Interuniversity Athletic Union (CIAU) athletes and received 457 replies (44.6 per cent response rate; approximately 66 per cent female). Holman's survey focused more on the sexual discrimination ('chilly climate') end of Brackenridge's continuum, showing that 17.7 per cent of male athletes consider sport to be an 'inappropriate activity' for women, and that in a time of declining economic resources many male athletes do not believe that those resources should be available to female athletes. She also found that 57 per cent of the female respondents reported that male athletes made sexist jokes or comments, while 31.9 per cent of the male athletes stated that female athletes had made sexist comments. The study also showed:

. . . far more evidence of harassment from peer athletes than from coaches, but when coaches became involved, 'it was more severe'. . . . [I]ntrusive behaviours such as seduction, coercion (which may involve reward for sexual favours or punishment for refusing them) and physical assault [were reported]. More than 8% said a male athlete 'made forceful attempts to touch, fondle, kiss or grab me.' More than 5% [of male athletes] said female athletes had tried force, while only [0.5%] said male coaches had done the same (Smith 1996b:A12).[4]

Despite these results, there are several strong indicators that sexual harassment in sport is underreported. For example, Lenskyj (1992b:21) notes that: 'Like women working in other traditionally male-dominated fields, many female athletes appear to grow resigned to the frequent acts of verbal and physical harassment in sport contexts.' Similarly, my in-depth interviews with retired high-performance athletes (Donnelly 1993a), which took place mostly in the late 1980s with athletes who had generally competed in the 1970s and 1980s, revealed confusion about what could be considered appropriate behaviour in sports where physical contact between coaches and athletes was the norm:

> Was the motion that a coach used to encourage or psych up the athlete a gentle punch or was it a hit? Could we consider abusive the slap a coach used to get an athlete's attention or to demonstrate how 'fat' a particular body part was? Was the slap to a particular out-of-position body part (by a spotter during the practice of a 'trick') punitive rather than educational? How excessive were some particularly punitive drills? How many rubdowns, massages, or inappropriate touches (that apparently occurred 'accidentally' during spotting) were sexually motivated? In all of these types of cases many athletes thought that many coaches and assistant coaches had gone too far, and this was a topic of discussion among athletes. But many had built up a resistance to this issue and accepted it as part of the sport. Power differences made it extremely difficult to confront the coach with such behavior (Donnelly 1993a:100).

It also became apparent that, in a number of interviews, female athletes were beginning to 'name' their experiences for the first time—to realize that they had been sexually harassed.

However, active athletes are less likely to 'name' and more likely to underreport their experiences. Studies by Tomlinson and Yorganci (1997) and Volkwein et al. (1997) both show female athletes failing to negatively characterize behaviour by coaches that is now considered harassment. For example, Tomlinson and Yorganci (1997) found that: (1) 15 per cent of their sample (of 143 female track and field athletes in the UK) had experienced 'language demeaning to the athlete (e.g., embarrassing, derogatory remarks; sexual innuendoes; dirty jokes)', but only 6 per cent saw the behaviour as harassment; and (2) 17 per cent had experienced 'Intrusive physical contacts (e.g., slapping on the bottom, tickling, putting arms around athlete)', but only 9 per cent saw the behaviour as harassment. Similarly, Volkwein et al. (1997:291) found that while their sample (of 210 US female university athletes in ten sports) generally had no problem in identifying behaviours that constituted sexual harassment, of the 18.7 per cent who had experienced 'sexist comments', 'about 25% were either untroubled, happy or even flattered about such' sexist jokes or derogatory remarks.

Tomlinson and Yorganci's (1997) study provides insights into the way athletes think when they refuse to report harassing behaviour, or to characterize certain behaviours as harassing. One athlete recalled how upset and embarrassed she had been when, at age thirteen, a coach had poked her in her genital area with an umbrella. Although she and most of the others in her group eventually left this coach, they never reported his behaviour, which also included other forms of inappropriate touching:

> It is very hard when you are very young and you get someone very old. I don't know, most of the kids, they find it very hard to speak their minds when they are younger. When you are 12, 13, you don't want to hurt people, do you? You just want to keep the peace. That's why no one speaks out to him (cited by Tomlinson and Yorganci 1997:150).

Other behaviours by male coaches were described as 'horrible', 'embarrassing', 'offensive', and 'annoying'. For example:

> He also does things like pinch your bum or something. You know. He doesn't mean to be offensive or anything. But, I find it offensive. But he is just like that . . . it is stupid, I don't know. I don't like him doing it. I don't know. But you know what he is like, so . . . but I don't think he should (cited by Tomlinson and Yorganci 1997:150).

As Tomlinson and Yorganci (1997:150) note, 'Remarkably, this athlete, actually offended by the coach's actions, could still deny that it was a form of harassment.'

This body of research leaves open the question of whether sexual harassment in sport is more or less prevalent than in other areas of life. However, unresolved as that issue might be, the particular social dynamics and culture of sport suggest that there are real reasons to be concerned that harassment may not only be more widespread in sport but also more severe. Coaches' verbal abuse of athletes is so widespread in sport that it is commonplace, accepted, and even celebrated. Such behaviour would rarely be tolerated in other areas of life—try to imagine the reactions to a schoolteacher who gave a student the type of 'in-your-face' bawling out, frequently involving humiliating and offensive language, that is seen so often in sport. Coaches' physical abuse of athletes is also frequently accepted as a part of 'the game'. For example, as a punishment or as a means of imposing discipline, coaches often use punitive drills, some of which even have names ('shit drills' or 'puke drills') and which involve intense running, push-ups, tackling drills, or other activities to be carried out until exhaustion. Again, such behaviour would rarely be tolerated in other areas of life—try to imagine the reactions to the manager of a fast food restaurant who made employees exercise to exhaustion each time they were perceived to have broken some rule.

Given this culture, and the fact that athletes (almost) never complain publicly or officially about verbally and physically abusive coaches, it is not a big step to imagine how sexually abusive behaviour also exists in the closed world of sport. A report on the Kirby and Greaves (1996) study noted:

> [They] conclude that sport is a particular 'subculture', with what they call 'a dome of violence' that allows violence to occur in ways that it could not in ordinary society. 'It also silences anyone who challenges that,' Prof. Kirby said. In a sense, for the athlete, that violence is normalized. They think that's just the way sport is.' When athletes are on the path to the Olympics and someone along that path is abusing them, 'then they have a really bad dilemma,' she said. 'Do they go forward with their career and put up with the abuse or do they leave sport? We haven't up to this point offered them any credible option (Smith 1996a:A11).

Tomlinson and Yorganci develop these points about the culture of sport, specifically locating sexual harassment in the controlling relationship that male coaches often have with female athletes. They (1997:151) note 'how those female athletes who seek out dominating male coaches may become vulnerable, in their dependent relation, to forms of exploitation, harassment, and abuse' and conclude that:

1. . . . the female athlete/male coach relation is typically based on a patriarchal, autocratic model of authority.
2. Sexist assumptions and practices in the coach/athlete relation can provide a basis for forms of control over aspects of individual personal life and private matters such as the body.
3. Sexual harassment, when it occurs in sport, is often left unrevealed, so that the perpetrator is rarely challenged (Tomlinson and Yorganci 1997:152).

Thus, the issue of whether there is more sexual harassment in sport than in other aspects of life remains unresolved. However, given the voluntary and generally unregulated nature of most sport, the conventions of internal policing, and the codes of secrecy and silence that govern everything from training techniques and tactics to inappropriate behaviour, it is appropriate to be concerned about any level of sexual harassment. Unfortunately, there are good reasons to believe that it is far more widespread in the particular culture of sport than has previously been believed.

Child Sexual Abuse

It is clear that some of the data and incidents noted earlier involved children, whether we use the United Nations' definition of 'every human being below the

age of 18 years' or some less rigorous criteria. Kirby and Greaves (1996) specifically noted athletes below age sixteen as a category, and Tomlinson and Yorganci
(1997:152), although dealing with an adult sample, note that: 'Many of the acts
of harassment and abuse . . . took place when the athlete was younger . . . when
she was 13 or 14.' There are good reasons for treating child sexual abuse as a
separate category. Children are clearly in the most vulnerable position when it
comes to predatory coaches or others in authority positions in sport, and in the
last twenty-five years we have seen the increasing involvement of children in
intensive and specialized training in specific sports. This applies even more so to
girls who, in a number of individual sport (involving a great deal of one-to-one
work with a coach) have been encouraged to achieve the highest levels of performance at very young ages (Donnelly 1993a). There are grounds for using the
term sexual abuse only when referring to the sexual harassment of, or sexual
relations with, children. In Canada such behaviour goes beyond being a human
rights issue and is governed by the Criminal Code. This is somewhat complicated by the fact that there is a disturbingly low age limit for consensual sexual
relations in Canada (age fourteen). However, this is mitigated by a growing
recognition that sexual relations with authority figures are now being perceived
as grounds for harassment, and by the emergence of guidelines for age differences—Brackenridge (1997:116) notes that 'many social work studies . . . define a
five-year age gap between the perpetrator and the victim for the incident to be
defined as abuse' (see also Finkelhor and Williams 1988).

The most comprehensive study on the prevalence of child sexual abuse in
Canada (MacMillan et al. 1997) surveyed almost 10,000 residents of Ontario.
Respondents were asked if an adult ever did any of the following things to them
while they were growing up:

- Exposed themselves to you more than once? [A positive response was categorized as 'sexual abuse'.]
- Threatened to have sex with you? [A positive response to this, and the
  following two items, was categorized as 'severe sexual abuse'.]
- Touched the sex parts of your body?
- Tried to have sex with you or sexually attacked you? (MacMillan et al.
  1997:132)

The results indicated that 12.8 per cent of the females and 4.3 per cent of the
males reported childhood sexual abuse; 11.9 per cent of the females reported
severe sexual abuse compared to 3.9 per cent of the males.[5] The results were not
affected by the socio-economic status of the participants—children from all social
classes were victims of abuse. The results also indicate that the sexual abuse of
children was most often perpetrated by non-relatives (e.g., neighbour, babysitter,
coach), and the authors make a very strong case for the likelihood that adults
were underreporting their experiences of childhood abuse.[6]

There are no equivalent data from sport, but the high incidence of non-relative abuse reported in the Ontario survey should act as a warning of the likelihood of child sexual abuse in sport.[7] A great deal of anecdotal evidence and court reports seem to indicate that there is a disturbing level of child sexual abuse in sport, and that it may be exacerbated by the fact that parents have been so unsuspecting and trusting about leaving their children in the care of coaches and other authority figures in sport. Parents who are known to interview their babysitters, and to act with suspicion about affectionate behaviour by schoolteachers, frequently leave their children with complete strangers in a sport environment. And while most child care agencies, schools, and youth organizations (e.g., Boy Scouts, Girl Guides, Big Brothers) have taken steps in recent years to make sure that children are protected from abuse, sport organizations have been more than willing to act as if they did not have a problem—that any reported incidents were isolated cases only. This separation of sport from the 'real world' has come to a rapid halt in the last two years as it has become apparent that pedophiles might actually 'be attracted to sport because of the opportunities it provides to be in close, unsupervised contact with children. . . . an Internet site exists directing perpetrators towards hockey as a venue where pedophiles could gain easy access to children' (Christie 1997b:A14).

The consequences of abuse can be devastating to adults, and even more so to children. McGregor (1997) reports on a Parks and Recreation Ontario study, which found that even mild harassment (e.g., regular verbal taunts) may have a profound effect on children. Whether harassment results simply in an individual's withdrawal from sport, or in the whole range of feelings reported by Brackenridge (1997:123) ranging from an inability to trust others to becoming suicidal, those in the sporting community must address this issue.

Responses to Sexual Harassment and Abuse in Sport

Until 1986 there were occasional newspaper reports of sexual harassment in sport. These usually involved cases where the coach of a children's team was convicted of sexually molesting one or more of the athletes. Academics, sport organizations, and policy makers for the most part paid no attention to these occasional reports, and it is only now becoming apparent how naive they were about the extent of sexual harassment in sport. In 1986, however, Todd Crosset first reported research findings on abusive relationships between male swimming coaches and female swimmers in the United States. Crosset found that there were recurrent features of coach-athlete abuse in sport, likening the strategies of abusive coaches to those of incestuous fathers, abusive husbands, and child molesters, and identifying the ways in which young athletes were disempowered by, for example, the coach's friendship with their parents. Crosset's work was not widely disseminated and responses to it were slow. Around the same time, Donnelly's interviews with retired high-performance athletes were also beginning to uncover incidents of physical, emotional, and sexual abuse (Donnelly and Sergeant 1986; Donnelly 1987, summarized in Donnelly 1993a). Subsequently, greater attention was given to the issue in the academic community (e.g., Lenskyj 1990). However, much of the research noted earlier has been published since the growth of public concern about sexual harassment in sport, beginning in 1993.

Brackenridge's (1992) paper and two articles by Lenskyj (1992a, 1992b) set the scene for the first wave of public interest in the issue in 1993:[8]

1. In April 1993 several retired Canadian female rowers appeared in disguise on CTV's 'The Shirley Show' to talk about the issue of sexual harassment in their sport. In July a *Toronto Star* reporter who heard a conference paper I gave (Donnelly 1993b) ran the topic as a front-page story the next day, causing a small flurry of media attention to the issue (e.g., 'Canada am', and several radio call-in programs).
2. An incident at the Canada Summer Games in Kamloops, BC—a group of young First Nations performers were harassed by racist and sexist comments made by some athletes, but no attempt was made to stop the behaviour or discipline the offenders—caused the Canada Games Council to begin to pay attention to the issue.
3. The Coaching Association of Canada and the Canadian Professional Coaches Association developed a coaching code of ethics, although they are only guidelines for coaches' behaviour and have no legal standing.
4. Sport Canada contracted Sandra Kirby, a former Olympic rower at the University of Winnipeg, to conduct some preliminary research on the topic.

However, the defining moment on the topic in 1993, and the event that caused the greatest response, was a CBC broadcast of 'The Fifth Estate' in November. The program, called 'Crossing the Line', documented examples of sexual harassment on two university volleyball teams, a swim club, and a rowing team. The athletes who agreed to appear on the program took an extremely courageous step towards raising public awareness of this problem in sport—many other athletes spoke to the producers, but refused to go on camera. In an interview with reporter Hana Gartner, Nancy Sears, then president of the New Brunswick Swimming Association, spoke about the lack of controls in sport: 'Clifford Olson could come out of jail, and coach your kid tomorrow.' Gartner also summarized the status quo in 1993 in terms of the options athletes had with regard to reporting that they were being abused:

Sport Canada says, if you are being sexually harassed by your coach, don't go to them, go to your national sports association. But the national sports associations say, if you play on a university team you should go to the interuniversity athletic union—but they can't really help you with your complaint because they don't have a policy dealing with sexual harassment. [The CIAU finally developed a harassment policy in 1997.] They say you should go to the coach's employer, the university; or you can go to the Canadian Coach's Association—they do have a policy on sexual harassment, but they don't have a complaint and disciplines committee so they can't help you either. But if you play on a local team, the best advice is tell your parents.

The sport community was finally forced to act. Following the program, the assistant deputy minister responsible for Sport Canada, Roger Collet, called together a representative group of officials from various sport bodies in Canada to form a harassment in sport working group. The most immediate result was a document produced by CAAWS (1994b), *Harassment in Sport: A Guide to Policies, Procedures and Resources*, which was widely distributed in the sporting community in Canada and internationally.

In other developments, in 1994 the Victoria Commonwealth Games Society became the first major multisport Games to develop a policy on sexual harassment and abuse, and by 1995 the Women's Institute on Sport and Education in the United States had developed a workshop for coaches and administrators (Oglesby and Sabo 1995). The CAAWS working group continued to be active and by the end of 1995, twenty-two national sport organizations in Canada reported that, although they had adopted a harassment policy, their greatest need was to have a trained harassment officer. In September 1996 Sport Canada produced a set of guidelines linking the receipt of federal funding by Canadian sport organizations to having harassment policies and officers in place (Christie 1996). The first workshop for training harassment officers—individuals to whom athletes could report without fear of reprisals—was held in November 1996; the revelations about the abuse of Sheldon Kennedy by Graham James reached the media at the beginning of January 1997.

The revelations had been anticipated in another program of CBC's 'The Fifth Estate', 'Thin Ice', broadcast in October 1996. While the program focused mostly on athletes as abusers, sometimes the victims were other athletes who were being abused by athletes, and by coaches and others in positions of authority during 'hazing' (initiation) ceremonies. Television personality Don Cherry, as reported by Salutin (1997), ridiculed the suggestion that such things could occur in hockey:

> He referred to reporter Linden MacIntyre as 'Linda' and called the programme 'garbage'. Then he said, 'Moms and Dads. I know what you're thinking. Should we let him go to the OHL and things like that.' He said they could trust their kids to junior hockey because it's 'a hundred per cent. They don't do that stuff any more' (Salutin 1997:C1).

By January, Cherry was calling Graham James 'a son of a bitch' on 'Coach's Corner', and suggesting far worse punishments than the three-and-a-half-year prison sentence James received.

The Canadian Hockey League (CHL), though, was taking far more conse-
quential and positive steps, contracting lawyer Gordon Kirke to develop a set of
recommendations to prevent any recurrence. The revelations also galvanized the
broader amateur sport community, and by late January the CAAWS working
group expanded from fourteen organizations (Christie 1997a) to twenty-five
organizations (Christie 1997b). The chairperson, Marg McGregor, was quoted
as saying: 'I've never seen the sport community work together quite this way. No
one's bickering over "ownership." It's everyone's problem to solve' (cited by
Christie 1997b:A14).

Players First (Kirke 1997), which was limited to junior hockey (CHL), recommended:

- a widespread education program for athletes, coaches, and other officials to
  provide awareness of issues of harassment and to promote tolerance
- a screening policy (police checks) for all those who would be officially in contact
  with players
- a toll-free help line for players
- independent harassment officers for each of the league's forty-eight clubs
- a formal complaint system to ensure due process

These recommendations are currently being implemented and picked up at lower
levels of hockey. For example, the Burlington Lions-Optimist Minor Hockey
Association in Ontario started Project Score to implement some of the Kirke recommendations (Moko 1997). The Canadian Hockey Association (CHA) has now
pulled these initiatives together in a national campaign called 'Speak Out'
(www.canadianhockey.ca). Meanwhile, in 1997 the CAAWS working group, now
called the Harassment and Abuse in Sport Collective, helped sport organizations
to develop policy on a sport-by-sport basis (because of the great differences
between sports in terms of, for example, the amount of touching between coaches
and athletes); promoted provincial initiatives (e.g., Sport BC's harassment in sport
initiatives—http://web20.mindlink.net/SportBC/ harass.htm); negotiated the
availability of the Kids Help Phone for young athletes; and promoted publications
such as the Coaching Association of Canada's *Straight Talk About Children and
Sport* (LeBlanc and Dickson 1997), *Power and Ethics in Coaching* (Tomlinson and
Strachan 1997), and CAAWS (1997) *What Parents Can Do About Harassment in
Sport*. In January 1998, as part of a major announcement of new funding for amateur sport, federal Heritage Minister Sheila Copps also confirmed the importance
of the Harassment and Abuse in Sport Collective's work for safer sport environments for children (Fraser 1998a, 1998b). In addition to announcing the publication for parents (CAAWS 1997), the minister introduced another aimed at young
athletes (*Speak Out! Abuse and Harassment Can Be Stopped*), and others to be aimed
at athletes and sport organizations (see also: www.harassmentinsport.com;
www.kidshelp.sympatico.ca; www.pch.gc.ca/sportscanada).

Conclusion

Sexual harassment and abuse must be considered in the specific context of gender relations as they exist in a certain place at a certain time. In the past, men's sexually aggressive behaviour towards women was in many ways considered normal and even admired within some male groups. Abuse victims were expected to accept it without complaint, which they usually did—in fact, they rarely had any other options. But now in the late twentieth century in North America, rapidly changing gender relations have created a great deal of confusion about appropriate relations between males and females. In a dominant male culture, sexually aggressive behaviour is still often admired—to be a 'stud' is high praise in some circles such as team contact sports (e.g., Curry 1991, 1998). However, at the same time that many men are rejecting that form of masculinity, many women are also beginning to speak out about their experiences with sexually aggressive men. Changes to the law in Canada and the United States have made illegal behaviour that was formerly accepted as one of the rewards of being a male in a position of authority (e.g., supervisor, coach) or as part of the costs of being a female who wished to work or participate in high-performance sport. Nevertheless, women are well aware that the law still often victimizes the victims—that there are often costs to 'blowing the whistle' on sexually aggressive males. Consequently, the rate of reporting abuse is still considered low. We should also note that the state of flux in current gender relations also tends to silence men who are being sexually harassed by women. Not only is this harassment considered flattering to men, but it is also often not taken seriously—even treated as a joke—by those to whom the complaints are made. Thus, men are often too embarrassed to report the behaviour of sexually aggressive females, and it is only in the climate of changing gender relations that men are now being empowered to report their experiences.

Gender relations take on a different tone in the sexual abuse of children. While the care of children has become a major human rights issue, it has done so at a time when children (particularly girls) are often sexualized in the media and in activities such as figure skating, gymnastics, dance, and beauty contests. Child prostitution, sex tourism, and child pornography have also been increasing, giving further messages about the sexual availability of children. Guilt (children often feel that they are responsible for what is happening to them) and fear (of the power of the abuser and the consequences of reporting his/her behaviour) are widespread and linked to underreporting, although the higher rate of reporting of abuse by females suggests that another gender dynamic may be at work. Boys, especially those in tough contact sports, may feel that they should have been able to physically prevent what happened to them. And there is another increment of shame associated with homosexual abuse—in the homophobic world of macho sport it is easy to feel that one's peers would believe that one should have been able to prevent it, and that failure to prevent it must mean that it was consensual.

The changing dynamics of gender relations and greater awareness of sexual harassment should encourage sociological research in this area. Feminist and critical cultural studies theories have sensitized researchers to issues of power and gender relations in contexts such as sport. Survey research is now more likely to result in more accurate reporting of the rates of harassment in various environments, particularly as victims begin to identify and label their experiences and are encouraged to report them. Research on the particular dynamics of coach-athlete relations in sport, especially qualitative research involving participant observation and interviewing, is likely to lead to a greater understanding of what is now being seen as a relationship rooted in control with all kinds of potential for abuse to occur. And the new life history methods, involving a series of in-depth interviews with a single subject, are likely to provide rich data about the circumstances, dynamics, and consequences of sexual harassment and abuse in sport.

Such research and greater understanding of the issue are needed in order to develop sound policy to prevent sexual harassment and abuse in sport. Beginning in 1993, but particularly since January 1997, we have seen a moral panic (Cohen 1972) around the issue of pedophilia and sexual harassment in sport. Moral panics create a great deal of heat and righteous moral indignation, and they attract a great deal of media and public interest, but they rarely result in the establishment of sound long-term policies. Rather, they often result in repressive measures such as the recent proposals for suspending bail and parole for convicted pedophiles, attempts to extend the 'dangerous offenders' provisions (for the indefinite extension of sentences), and proposals to publish lists and the whereabouts of 'known' pedophiles and to institute police checks for coaches.

The most obvious and perhaps overly hasty policy recommendation to emerge so far has been to implement police screening checks for all coaches of children's, youth, and even adult sports. While this is, unfortunately, a policy that must be put in place—no sporting organization could now afford the problems that would result from hiring a coach with a record for sexual harassment or abuse in their own or another jurisdiction—it is too often seen as all that is necessary to curb the problem. More cautious voices have pointed out that the task will overwhelm police forces, particularly in large urban centres, and that such a policy would not have revealed Graham James because he did not have a criminal record. A more reasonable and less panic-driven approach to policy would be to examine the culture of sport in general, and youth sport in particular, to determine the circumstances that have led to the present moral panic.

Among the most obvious issues of concern are:

- The controlling relationships between coaches and athletes that are so evident in the world of sport. Calls have been made for the reconstitution of the coach-athlete relationship as a 'dialogue' rather than a one-way communication process. For example, Coakley (1993) identifies three styles of coaching—

'dictator', 'role model', and 'advocate'—with the latter being preferred for children. Of course, many excellent coaches already practise this form of coaching.

- The fact that children and young people must often leave home to participate. Whether it is the 'midget' draft for junior hockey, or other highly talented young athletes moving to work with the best coach available, the procedures and circumstances surrounding such moves need careful consideration.
- The circumstances in which athletes travel for training or competition also need to be considered carefully. Coaches and administrators have tended to ignore, or even become involved in, postcompetition or postintensive training session excesses, including those involving underage drinking. It is under these circumstances that many cases of abuse have occurred.
- While it is clear that the moral panic will sensitize many parents and athletes to be more vigilant, there is a real need for more parent and athlete education and empowerment. Athletes and parents need to be empowered to ask any questions they feel necessary concerning their or their child's participation in sport. Parents must be permitted to observe practices and competitions, and to be assured that the sport organization has the best interests of the whole child in mind (rather than just the issue of successful athletic performance).
- Athletes of any age and parents of young athletes need to know that they can 'blow the whistle' on any behaviours that they feel are inappropriate without fear of reprisals that may jeopardize their or their child's future in the sport.
- Private meetings and private training or therapy sessions have been common in sport. Coaches and administrators have closed their office doors in order to offer support or criticism to athletes. They have visited athletes' rooms when travelling, spent time in locker-rooms and showers, given athletes a lift home, and had them over to visit their houses. Such private time has been important in sport, and most athletes will recount positive stories of nurturing and mentoring coaches who provided support in a variety of ways at vulnerable times in athletes' lives. However, such time is clearly open to abuse. Perhaps the culture of coaches could learn from the culture of schoolteachers where there has been a no-touching, no private meetings policy in place for some ten years. It became quite clear to teachers, particularly in primary schools, that a no-touching policy was inhuman—a small child who is hurt or upset clearly needs some human contact. So teachers have developed an informal policy whereby they look out for each other, do not put themselves in private one-on-one situations with students, leave office and classroom doors open, and have clear guidelines for extracurricular activities and trips. Such a culture has some costs—both teachers and coaches recognize, for example, the problem of having an upset student or athlete in their office with the door open when others are walking past outside. But such a culture is also more likely to encourage coaches and others in positions of authority in sport to intervene and report problems rather than engage in the type of cover-up that has clearly been the norm in sport.

The policies introduced by the CHL, the CHA, and the Harassment and Abuse in Sport Collective clearly take some steps in the directions outlined here, particularly with regard to the education of all involved and implementing reporting procedures. But sport in general maintains an extremely conservative and tradition-bound culture. Changes to 'the way things have always been done' do not come easily, and attempts to create a more open and safe environment will continually come up against those aspects of the culture that are believed to be necessary in order to ensure 'success'. The trick will also be to initiate the policies and cultural changes outlined here while still maintaining the positive aspects of the coach-athlete relationship.

Notes

1. There is a growing body of anecdotal evidence and research dealing with the issue of abusive athletes. However, it is not yet clear whether athletes engage in abusive behaviour at a greater rate than the non-athletic population, or whether there is a causal link between violent sport and abusive behaviour by athletes. The topic warrants a great deal more research, but it is beyond the scope of this chapter.

2. The Liam Donnelly case, noted previously, raises a further complication, that of false accusation (cf., CAUT *Bulletin* 1997).

3. However, as noted subsequently, the naming of such behaviours in the workplace took a long time to become widespread, and took even longer to be identified in 'amateur' sport contexts.

4. Some of the statistics in the Kirby and Greaves (1996) and Holman (1995) studies raise the issue of homosexual harassment and abuse in sport. However, the data are limited and a great deal more research is needed on this issue.

5. These results are somewhat lower than the results from other surveys of childhood sexual abuse, which tend to cluster around 20 per cent for females, and between 3 per cent and 11 per cent for males (fewer studies). The authors believe that the specification 'while you were growing up' and the restriction to adult abusers caused the lower reporting rate in the Ontario survey (MacMillan et al. 1997:134).

6. Critiques of the study also suggest that the rate of abuse by relatives is underreported (e.g., Culbert 1997:N3).

7. Celia Brackenridge in the UK has paid the most academic attention to the issue of child sexual abuse in sport (e.g., Brackenridge 1992, 1994, 1996; Brackenridge and Kirby 1997; Brackenridge, Summers, and Woodward 1995). However, Brackenridge's

work tends to focus on the risk factors involving athletes, coaches, sport organizations, parents, and the sports themselves. For a variety of reasons, ranging from ethical issues to the reluctance of sport organizations to provide research access, there is almost no systematic data available on the frequency of child sexual abuse in sport.

8. The following chronology is taken, in part, from McGregor (1997).

References

Appleby, T. 1998. 'Attitudes, Statistics Shroud Sexual Assaults by Women'. *The Globe and Mail* (9 March):A6.

Brackenridge, C. 1992. 'Sexual Abuse of Children in Sport: A Comparative Exploration of Research Methodologies and Professional Practice.' Paper presented at the Olympic Scientific Congress, Malaga, Spain.

_____. 1994. 'Fair Play or Fair Game? Child Sexual Abuse in Sport Organizations'. *International Review for the Sociology of Sport* 29, no. 3:287–99.

_____. 1996. 'Health Sport for Healthy Girls: The Role of Parents in Preventing Sexual Abuse of Girls'. Paper presented at the Olympic Scientific Congress, Dallas.

_____. 1997. '"He Owned Me Basically . . .": Women's Experiences of Sexual Abuse in Sport'. *International Review for the Sociology of Sport* 32, no. 2:115–30.

_____, and S. Kirby. 1997. 'Playing Safe: Assessing the Risk of Sexual abuse to Elite Child Athletes'. *International Review for the Sociology of Sport* 32, no. 4:407–18.

_____, D. Summers, and D. Woodward. 1995. 'Educating for Child Protection in Sport'. Paper presented at the Leisure Studies Association Conference, Eastbourne, UK.

CAAWS (Canadian Association for the Advancement of Women and Sport and Physical Activity). 1994a. *An Introduction to the Law, Sport and Gender Equity in Canada*. Ottawa: CAAWS.

_____. 1994b. *Harassment in Sport: A Guide to Policies, Procedures and Resources*. Ottawa: CAAWS.

_____. 1997. *What Parents Can Do About Harassment in Sport*. Ottawa: CAAWS.

CAUT Bulletin. 1997. 'Simon Fraser Swim Coach Reinstated'. (6 September):1, 6–7.

Christie, J. 1996. 'Amateur Sport Told to Fight Harassment'. *The Globe and Mail* (21 September):A1, A17.

_____. 1997a. 'Sport Groups Tackle Problem of Sexual Abuse'. *The Globe and Mail* (23 January):C14.

_____. 1997b. 'Amateur Sport Co-operate to Deal with Sexual Abuse'. *The Globe and Mail* (31 January):A13, A14.

Coakley, J. 1993. 'Social Dimensions of Intensive Training and Participation in Youth Sports'. In *Intensive Participation in Children's Sports*, edited by B. Cahill and A. Pearl, 77–94. Champaign, IL: Human Kinetics.

Cohen, S. 1972. *Folk Devils and Moral Panics: The Creation of the Mods and Rockers*. St Albans, UK: Paladin.

Crosset, T. 1986. 'Male Coach/Female Athlete Relationships'. Paper presented at the 1st International Conference for Sport Sciences, Söle, Norway.

Culbert, L. 1997. 'Abuse Study Questioned: Local Statistics Don't Reflect Survey Results; Rape Centre'. *Hamilton Spectator* (26 July):N3.

Curry, T. 1991. 'Fraternal Bonding in the Locker Room: A Profeminist Analysis of Talk About Competition and Women'. *Sociology of Sport Journal* 8, no. 2:119–35.

_____. 1998. 'Beyond the Locker Room: Campus Bars and Athletes'. *Sociology of Sport Journal* 15, no. 3:205–15.

Donnelly, P. 1987. 'Problems of Elite Participation for Children and Adolescents: The Case of Female Athletes'. Paper presented at the Conference on Movement and Sport in Women's Life, Jyväskylä, Finland.

_____, with the assistance of E. Caspersen, L. Sergeant, and B. Steenhof. 1993a. 'Problems Associated with Youth Involvement in High Performance Sport'. In *Intensive Participation in Children's Sports*, edited by B. Cahill and A. Pearl, 95–126. Champaign, IL: Human Kinetics.

_____. 1993b. 'The Good, the Bad, and the Ugly in Children's Sport'. Paper presented at the 10th World Congress on Gifted and Talented Education, Toronto.

_____, and L. Sergeant. 1986. 'Adolescents and Athletic Labour: A Preliminary Study of Elite Canadian Athletes'. Paper presented at the North American Society for the Sociology of Sport Conference, Las Vegas.

_____, and R. Sparks. 1997. 'Child Sexual Abuse in Sport'. *Policy Options* 18, no. 3:3–6.

Finkelhor, D., and L.M. Williams. 1988. *Nursery Crimes: Sexual Abuse in Day Care.* London: Sage.

Fraser, G. 1998a. 'More Funding Forecast for Amateur Sport'. *The Globe and Mail* (22 January):S1, S11.

_____. 1998b. 'Funding Delights Amateur Sport World'. *The Globe and Mail* (23 January):S2.

Holman, M. 1994. 'Sexual Harassment in Athletics: Listening to the Athletes for Solutions'. Paper presented at the North American Society for the Sociology of Sport Conference, Savannah.

_____. 1995.'Female and Male Athletes' Accounts and Meanings of Sexual Harassment in Canadian Interuniversity Athletics'. Ph.D. thesis, University of Windsor.

_____. 1997. 'In the Name of Tradition: Hazing Practices in Athletics'. Paper presented at the North American Society for the Sociology of Sport Conference, Toronto, Canada.

Kirby, S., and L. Greaves. 1996. 'Foul Play: Sexual Harassment in Sport'. Paper presented at the Olympic Scientific Congress, Dallas.

Kirke, G. 1997. *Players First: A Report Prepared for the Canadian Hockey League.* Toronto: Canadian Hockey League.

LeBlanc, J., and L. Dickson. 1997. *Straight Talk About Children and Sport: Advice for Parents, Coaches, and Teachers.* Ottawa: Coaching Association of Canada.

Lenskyj, H. 1990. 'Sexual Harassment and Sexual Abuse: An Issue for Women in Sport'. *Action Newsmagazine* 8, no. 2:16.

_____. 1992a. 'Sexual Harassment: Female Athletes' Experiences and Coaches' Responsibilities'. *Sports Science Periodical on Research and Technology in Sport* (Coaching Association of Canada) 12, no. 6, Special Topics B-1.

_____. 1992b. 'Unsafe at Home Base: Women's Experiences of Sexual Harassment in University Sport and Physical Education'. *Women in Sport and Physical Activity Journal* 1:19–33.

Macgowan, J. 1997. 'Lives Lived: Obituary of Arnold Martin Kruze'. *The Globe and Mail* (13 November):A28.

McGregor, M. 1997. 'Harassment in Sport—Discussion Paper'. Draft #3, unpublished. Ottawa: CAAWS.

MacMillan, H., J. Fleming, N. Trocmé, M. Boyle, M. Wong, Y. Racine, W. Beardslee, and D. Offord. 1997. 'Prevalence of Child Physical and Sexual Abuse in the Community: Results from the Ontario Health Supplement'. *Journal of the American Medical Association* 278, no. 2:131–5.

Masteralexis, L. 1995. 'Sexual Harassment and Athletics: Legal and Policy Implications for Athletic Departments'. *Journal of Sport and Social Issues* 19, no.2:141–56.

Moko, L. 1997. 'Hockey Campaign's Goal to Safeguard Young Players'. *Hamilton Spectator* (18 October):N1.

Oglesby, C., and D. Sabo. 1995. 'Clearing the Air: A Workshop for Coaches and Administrators on Sexual Harassment Policy in Athletics'. Presented at the National Girls and Women in Sport Symposium, Baltimore, US.

Reilly, T., S. Carpenter, V. Dull, and K. Bartlett. 1982. 'The Factorial Survey Technique: An Approach to Defining Sexual Harassment on Campus'. *Journal of Social Issues* 38, no. 4:99–110.

Salutin, R. 1997. 'Journalists Fall Over Themselves to Don Hair Shirts'. *The Globe and Mail* (17 January):C1.

Schlatman, J. 1997. 'Quotes of the Year'. *Burlington News* (26 December):N1.

Smith, B. 1996a. 'Abuse Prevalent in Sport, Survey Indicates'. *The Globe and Mail* (17 July):A1, A11.

_____. 1996b. 'Female Athletes in School Study at Disadvantage'. *The Globe and Mail* (24 July):A11, A12.

Terpstra, D., and D. Douglas. 1987. 'A Hierarchy of Sexual Harassment'. *Journal of Psychology* 121, 599–606

Tomlinson, A., and I. Yorganci. 1997. 'Male Coach/Female Athlete Relations: Gender and Power Relations in Competitive Sport'. *Journal of Sport and Social Issues* 21, no. 2:134–55.

Tomlinson, P., and D. Strachan. 1997. *Power and Ethics in Coaching*. Ottawa: Coaching Association of Canada.

Volkwein, K., F. Schnell, D. Sherwood, and A. Livezey. 1997. 'Sexual Harassment in Sport: Perceptions and Experiences of American Female Student-Athletes'. *International Review for the Sociology of Sport* 32, no. 3:283–95.

Chapter 7

Aging, Gender, and Physical Activity

Sandra O'Brien Cousins and Patricia Vertinsky

On 21 April 1997 the *Vancouver Sun* reported that nearly 38,000 people had participated in the 10-km annual Vancouver Sun Run the day before. Among the top finishers in the various categories of Canada's largest run was Ivy Granstron, second in the category of women eighty and over, with a time of 1:35:57, a full twelve minutes ahead of Harry Swinburne, who was second in the over-eighty male category. Ivy Granstron of Vancouver is one of Canada's outstanding Master's athletes, a world record holder in the over-seventy category who runs everything from 100 to 10 000 m. Now over eighty and legally blind, she epitomizes the possibilities of the aging body in action. Her achievement embodies much of what is known about gender, aging, and physical activity: that gender differences can blur over the life course; that motivation for sport matters as much as age; and that individual variability from day to day means that older athletes do better to measure themselves, not to others, but to their own standards. We see some elderly women outperforming men, older athletes outperforming younger ones, and rare stellar performances interspersed among everyday performances of all abilities (O'Brien Cousins and Burgess 1992). For aging Canadians, the goal of the elderly athlete is to be the best that one can be without letting age be a barrier. There is no definitive finish line to lifelong fitness (O'Brien and Conger 1991).

Such portrayals of fitness, vigour, and sportive behaviour shown by female and male elders alike contradict the persistent and all too common belief that aging is essentially an unavoidable process of physical decline requiring withdrawal into sedentary habits, passivity, and dependence.[1] New studies are demonstrating that adults in their eighth and ninth decades can achieve significant and clinically relevant gains from exercise program interventions and resistance strength training (Fiatarone et al. 1990; Rippe and Ward 1992; Spirduso 1995). Current research also suggests that even modestly increased physical activity levels in older adults may generate major personal and public health benefits (Blair et al. 1992; US Department of Health 1996). Moderate exercise, for example, has been reported to be a much more powerful predictor of health in the elderly than in younger people (Khaw 1990). As well, in controlled laboratory settings, hitherto unexpected positive changes in the strength of older people are being obtained, suggesting that while aerobic activities are primary choices for weight control and disease prevention, muscle strengthening has a very particular relevance to wheelchair and housebound elderly (Fiatarone et al. 1990, 1994).

In their desire to become more active, Canadian elders are placing new demands on educational systems, community recreation facilities, and public health arrangements, thereby creating new requirements for community support. Times are changing in Alberta, for example, where severe fiscal constraints and unprecedented cuts in available hospital beds compel new approaches to health promotion, which encourage the elderly to stay mobile longer. Programs to promote functional independence are increasingly being embraced by health clinics, seniors' centres, and wellness outreach groups. Maria Fiatarone, geriatrician and medical researcher at Harvard University, has created a basic, slow moving, and highly successful progressive strength training program called 'Fit for Your Life', which is fast becoming popular among elders in Edmonton (Fiatarone et al. 1996). In less than six months, 'Fit for Your Life' workshops have become popular among exercise leaders, nursing home staff, recreational and lodge programmers, and home support professionals in northern Alberta. The message is that if you are an older adult and hope to live independently, you need to lift light weights regularly and be fit for your life. Looking at aging and physical activity in Canada, McPherson (1994:329) comments that 'the lifestyles of older adults have changed dramatically in the last decade. No longer is physical activity, social isolation or physical and cognitive frailty inevitable, nor do these conditions represent the expected or common lifestyles in later life'. Most older Canadians, he concludes, have the potential to live physically, socially, and cognitively active lives well into their later years if they have the appropriate support and opportunities.

This optimistic view, of course, belies the evidence that as people age there is a trend to ever-decreasing physical activity. Only about 10 to 15 per cent of the total adult Canadian population report that they engage in regular physical activity and these figures decline for adults over sixty-five (and continue declining as they age) (McPherson 1994). In the US one in three men and one in two women over seventy-four are inactive, while those who do participate commonly list everyday tasks like walking and gardening as their main activities (US Department of Health and Human Services 1996). The same is true for elderly Canadians who cite walking, gardening, home exercise, swimming, and social dancing as their five favoured activities (Russell 1997). However, study after study show that the majority of those over sixty-five do not exercise regularly or systematically, and that vigorously active elders are the exception rather than the rule (O'Brien and Vertinsky 1991). Moreover, older women are vastly underrepresented among Canada's physically active elderly, even though it is acknowledged that elderly women can benefit from exercise to much the same degree as men (Lee 1991). Furthermore, despite the difficulty of measuring physical activity among elderly populations, it is well recognized that the elderly themselves tend to underestimate their ability to exercise, and that the lack of willingness by many older people to engage in activities requiring strength and power is related to their perceptions of aging as a time of inevitable decline and weakness.[2] They fail to see that the risks of sedentary living are as serious, for example, as being a regular smoker (Heart and Stroke Foundation 1995; Keeler et al. 1989). Nor do they hold strong values about the need for active living during their retirement years (O'Brien Cousins 1998).

This gap between perception and reality among the elderly with respect to physical activity (Buskirk 1988) is both more marked among the female elderly than among aging males, and more dramatic, since a higher proportion of women are reaching old age and living longer than men. The prominence of women in the rapidly rising proportion of the Canadian population over sixty-five (now 12.5 per cent), and the increasing longevity of the elderly population (life expectancy is seventy-six years for males, eighty-two years for females), means that aging has become, in many respects, a woman's issue. Older women over sixty-five outnumber men by three to two. Of those who survive to eighty-five, women outnumber men almost three to one. It is likely that as longevity increases, women will continue to outnumber older men. Such demographic shifts have major consequences for public health and approaches to medical care as well as health and physical activity promotion for the elderly.[3] They underline the critical role of gender in considering issues of aging, sport, and physical activity in Canada and indeed in other Western countries with similar demographic and economic profiles.

Gender, Stereotypes, and Aging

Canadians have very ambivalent attitudes towards the elderly—an ambivalence apparent in the professions, popular culture, and among the elderly themselves. This ambivalence extends to attitudes towards exercise and sport for the elderly, with more negative than positive stereotypes and images about physically active and sportive elders, at least until recently. Negative stereotypes about aging have persisted over the centuries in Western society and can be understood best in light of the social and historical circumstances in which they developed and have been sustained. As Cole (1992) points out, aging and age are certainly real, but they do not exist in some natural realm independently of the ideals, images, and social practices that conceptualize and represent them. Hence aging must not be viewed as exclusively biological or pathological, but can be seen as a socially constructed and historically specific process (Arber and Ginn 1991; Featherstone and Wernick 1995; McPherson 1994). Gender is an especially important variable since definitions of what it means to be an aging man or aging woman have been constructed in different ways at different times in Western society and have had a profound effect upon societal expectations about how aging men and women should behave, and of course about their physicality. Class, race, and ethnicity (as well as the stage of old age) are also important variables to be considered in the social construction of aging, the formation and perpetuation of stereotypes, and their perceived effects on physical ability, health, sport, and exercise.

While historians generally agree that there has been no golden era of aging for either men or women, older women arguably comprise the most denigrated and vulnerable strata of modern society. A combination of ageism and sexism can doubly and triply (in the case of racial and ethnic prejudice) emphasize negative images of aging women. In many respects the story of women and aging is a forgotten history. Until recently, the issue of aging in women's lives has been largely overlooked, and those who have examined the subject have tended to see it as a history of unrelieved oppression and dehumanization. Under patriarchy, aging women have been personified as witches and crones, or have remained invisible as persons, so far removed from a socially desired youthful beauty that their beings have become transparent and non-existent. These stigma have not been universal, of course, and there are many examples of powerful, active aging women both now and in the past. However, long-lasting cultural stereotypes have tended to reiterate the view that women peak in late adolescence when they are most attractive to men, and perhaps when their fertility is highest. The youthful, fertile, sensual female body is thus the 'real' woman: once past reproductive age, she becomes the 'Other', bound for decrepitude, her life split in two by the presence or absence of menstrual cycles, from normality to abnormality, and from a healthy to a diseased body.

In North America we worship at the altar of youth and beauty. This is reflected in popular concern with aging female bodies and their supposed loss of attractiveness. Trivialized because they are no longer young and derided because they stand outside of standard conventions of beauty (Banner 1993), aging women seldom appear in fitness magazines. It is evident, says Markula (1995:442) that 'the flabless, firm muscles do not cover an old, wrinkly, bent, gray haired body'. While everyone ages, the natural signs of aging are shown in the media to be opposite to the requirements of the beautiful body, which, in today's consumer society, is defined through health and appearance, making the owner more marketable (Featherstone 1991). Even though women have a better survival rate than men, the very fact that they live longer seems to count as a stroke against them. Contributing neither to the continuity of the species nor to the pleasure of men, elderly women are often seen simply as a problem for society.

Menopause and the Aging Female Body

The 'problem' is seen to begin at menopause. Throughout history women have been considered old after menopause, useless to society as soon as they could no longer do their special work of bearing and rearing children (Roebuck and Slaughter 1979). A century ago, the medical profession promoted its own expectations about aging women. Regardless of their current health status or expected life span, women at menopause were told to expect their normal physiological condition to become pathological (Smith-Rosenberg 1985). Physical decline, bodily and mental disorders, and diminished functions were emphasized as the general characteristics of menopausal development (Currier 1897). A woman's body had run its course and begun its final decline. Her usefulness ended, she was described as 'less of the woman she was than a man is a man at the same time of life' (Hicks 1877:473). Those who survived the 'disease' of menopause were declared candidates for very cautious exercise therapies during senescence. In this sense, any notion of a healthy and vigorous old age was a contradiction in terms. Athletic games were seen as quite unsuitable for the elderly who might overexert themselves in this last stage of life.

While it was generally thought that both old men and women needed to conserve their remaining energy and were subject to the dangers of exertion, overfatigue was considered worse for women than men, who were supposedly adapted to a more strenuous muscular life. More significant was the application and acceptance of conservative prescriptions for exercise at a much earlier age for women than men, socializing the former in their forties and fifties to take on the sedentary characteristics of aging by disengaging from active pursuits. Aging women were typically expected to be invalids in need of professional care, lacking the energy to participate in active daily living (Vertinsky 1994, 1995).

Lock (1993) confirms that in North America today, a potent fear of aging at menopause, coupled with the quest for immortal youthfulness, seems to be driving this continued medicalization of menopause and the way in which society stereotypes aging women. The biomedical model defining menopause in hormonal terms can be traced to developments in sex endocrinology in the 1920s and 1930s when estrogen supplied by the ovaries was established as the quintessential hormone (Leng 1996). Menopause was, therefore, the result of diminishing ovarian production of estrogen, which could be biologically interpreted as a deficiency disease treatable by hormone replacement. Current efforts to persuade perimenopausal women that they should embark upon a lifelong regimen of hormone replacement therapy underlines the continued medicalization of menopause in the twentieth century and the ways in which drug prescriptions have become tied to a theory of deficit and loss (Friedan 1993). Influenced by stereotyped menopausal images and biased information about menopausal changes, which are a widespread and persistent part of our culture, most women possess little accurate information about the benefits of exercise at this time of life (Callahan 1993). Brittle bones and sagging breasts, loss of femininity, and loss of sanity are common ways in which the media describe menopause (Chrisler, Torrey, and Matthes 1991). To a large extent, clinical and epidemiological research saturates the discourse on menopause and ignores first-hand accounts by women themselves about how they experience their own physicality.

While interest is mounting over the potential future health bounties for today's middle-aged women—a huge cohort that is experiencing declining hormonal levels as they approach their menopausal years—the response to date among the health professions has been largely a medical one. The available evidence for the benefits of physical activity has been somewhat lost in the vigorous debate over the pros and cons of estrogen replacement therapy (ERT), which is advocated for petite Caucasian menopausal women who are most at risk of severe osteoporosis. A closer examination of the available data on women's health could lead one to believe that the benefits to be derived from ERT could just as readily be obtained in a non-clinical setting by maintaining or resuming a physically active lifestyle to restore vitality to women and improve their bone health. Dozens of studies show that regular participation in moderate forms of exercise and sport will increase estrogen production, reduce serum lipid levels (cholesterol, triglycerides), provide a cardio-protective effect for heart disease and stroke (Heart and Stroke Foundation 1995), maintain and even increase bone mineral density (Carpenter 1987; Martin and Notelovitz 1993; Nelson et al. 1991; Stillman et al. 1986), as well as reduce or eliminate numerous unfavourable symptoms such as hot flashes, insomnia, depression, anxiety, and general aches and pains (Wilbur et al. 1990). These are the same symptoms for which ERT is prescribed, and yet daily exercise can reduce cancer risk rather than increase it, as is the case with ERT. Moreover, exercise and sport participation as therapy can also affect a host of other health problems, such as improving muscle strength (Heislein, Harris, and Jette 1994), maintaining healthier body weight by reducing fat (Schaberg et al. 1990), and managing diabetes, arthritis, and constipation. With concerns among many women about their future health prospects and the use of artificial hormones, it is interesting to speculate why so few medical researchers fail to pursue this obvious direction for healthy aging among women.

Instead, at a time in which the body is increasingly understood as the outward sign of internal self-discipline, the aging body is often seen as a potent symbol both of the failure of self-care and the imminence of death (Lupton 1996). Physical decay is easily taken as a sign of bodily neglect where lack of regulation and loss of function become a great anxiety. Popular (mis)understandings about the aging body and the erratic effects on the body of fluctuating hormone levels perpetuate the traditional view that women's behaviour might indeed be driven by their hormones and reproductive organs. Women often note that being seen as 'menopausal' means that they are old, expected to be irrational and emotionally distraught, and no longer able to mask their age and social inutility. Despite how young and energetic they may feel, to acknowledge their menopausal status is to define themselves in society's eyes as old and useless even though most of them can expect to live up to thirty years or more after menopause. Men as a collective have no comparable benchmark or set of stereotypes that marks them, at so young an age, as old and physically useless (unless, perhaps, one looks at mandatory retirement at age sixty-five) (Rips 1993).

Among women themselves, menopause has increasingly become discussed as a feminist issue since the second wave of feminism in the 1970s, provoking new questions about the actual evidence of impairment and depression supposedly ushered in by menopause and the end of childbearing. The dissemination of new evidence about the relationship of exercise to osteoporosis and other conditions has seen a number of women breaking out of the feminine mystique and attempting to empower themselves through women's groups, collective activities, and the deliberate pursuit of health and recreation through more vigorous exercise. Yet even as new sporting opportunities are pursued, new problems are uncovered. A recent report sponsored by WomenSport International raised some important points about how society views the vigorously active female Master's athlete. Touting hormone replacement therapy as an important treatment with wide-ranging benefits for aging female athletes, the report warned that sex steroid hormones are banned in international competition even though taken by many postmenopausal women to preserve their health, not enhance performance. Drug-testing regulations, the report continues, simply ignore aging female athletes as irrelevant to the world of competitive sport (Burger et al. 1996).

Health, Aging Women, and Images of Frailty

It is a paradox that while elderly women cite their declining health and their perception that they are too old as explanations for inactivity, at the same time preventive medicine research and elderly role models themselves are demonstrating that among the certain benefits of physical activity are health improvement and a better quality of life. For example, increasing women's physical activity and calcium intake by a modest amount can reduce the risk of osteoporosis at age seventy by almost one-third. Older women, including the very old, are considered to be the one social group most likely to receive significant health benefits from increased participation in physical activity (O'Brien and Vertinsky 1991).

Yet the traditional stereotypic view of female old age as a time for accepting natural declines in health and vigour and embracing inactivity seems to persist in shaping the exercise and sporting patterns of many elderly women who are falling far short of health-promoting levels of regular exercise. While the cumulative effects of time, disease, and disuse are bound to have a direct bearing on physical activity patterns, many women reaching their sixties, seventies, and eighties are free of a specific life-threatening disease. Instead, they may be suffering the consequences of years of physical inactivity and the toll of various chronic diseases, many of which further contribute to a reduction in physical activity. By age eighty-five, 50 per cent of all women have some degree of preventable chronic disability with mobility (walking, moving, carrying) and agility (bending, dressing, grooming) among the most prevalent forms (Norland 1994).

Though performance of moderate-intensity physical activity on a regular basis appears to be an important ingredient in the recipe for growing older successfully (Paffenbarger and Lee 1996), strongly held beliefs about the potential risks of physical exertion and vigorous exercise persist in preventing participation (O'Brien Cousins 1995a; Spirduso and MacRae 1991). Worrying about 'wearing out' their bodies and incurring serious injuries, many aging women tend to overestimate the health risks of exercise while underrating its health-promoting potential. Their fear of falling, for example, can constitute a severe cognitive restraint upon physical activity as does the belief that running wears out the joints—a notion all too often reinforced by the medical and health professions and one perpetuated by such editorials as 'jogging for a healthy heart and worn out hips' in the *Journal of Internal Medicine* (Ernst 1990).

Even though traditional stereotypes about the aging female body simply do not fit the typical experience of many older women today, the myths persist in a variety of ways. No other stereotype matches the power of illness and frailty, perpetuating images of physical decline and social marginality among the aging that are extremely disempowering (Minkler and Estes 1991). Accustomed to an age-calibrated social clock, older women far too readily accept the view of their families, peers, and doctors, as well as media portrayals, that certain sporting or vigorous exercise experiences can be enjoyed only at certain times of life, regardless of individual physical or psychological condition. Despite their ability to survive longer than men, old age for them has long been officially sanctioned as both a heavier burden and an earlier one (Drevenstedt 1976; Kogan 1979; Lipka 1987; Roebuck and Slaughter 1979).

On the other hand, with scientific and medical advances, disease rather than age has become the larger villain as the nature of aging is being gradually transformed with a new emphasis upon health span rather than life span, or what has variously been termed 'active life-expectancy' (Katz et al. 1983) or 'compression of morbidity' (Fries 1989). Some diminution of function and decreased strength and stamina may be unavoidable, but the slope of biological decline is changing through better health and a more supportive environment. Cutting age declines in half by achieving better health and fitness for longer, however, requires continued alertness to false assumptions about old age, especially among elderly women who have for so long been blinded by others' scripts about how they should experience their final season.

Aging Men and the Impact of Retirement

While more life course and life event studies are needed to clarify why and how physical activity behaviour often changes at key points in the life cycle, an important benchmark of aging is mandatory retirement at age sixty-five, when men (and, of course, women as well) are officially labelled as less useful to society. As with menopause, retirement is met with a good deal of social attention. While not all of it is negative, research on retirees shows that the event can be experienced as a personal assault and a forced disengagement, leading to depression, mental blocks, lowered self-esteem, and a lack of interest in health and physical activity (O'Brien Cousins 1998). Disengagement research has shown that the more disengaged one is from social networks and regular daily work and leisure routines, the less one tends to be satisfied with life (Smith, Patterson, and Grant 1992). The stress caused by the discontinuity of retirement (especially to those actively resisting the event) rarely encourages older adults to invest their time in sport or exerting activity.

At the same time, the age of retirement of professional workers is dropping with many people choosing to retire early. According to a recent Statistics Canada report, long-term retirement trends in Canada show that Canadians are retiring two-and-a-half years earlier than they did fifteen years ago, and that the percentage of Canadians retiring before age sixty has more than doubled (McArthur 1997). Some of these individuals re-employ themselves in paid work, such as consulting or private business, but many also embrace a full and active retirement lifestyle, at least for a while. In 1990 active older male participants in Canada outnumbered older female participants 42 per cent to 23 per cent. Highlights of the 1988 Campbell's Survey (Stephens and Craig 1990) showed that at age sixty-five, participation levels actually increased slightly in coached, competitive, and casual physical activities (though this rebound in active recreation is not evident in retiring women to the same degree). It is important to point out that physical activity in retirement is not a newly acquired habit for most. Seventy per cent of active retirees, especially those with a higher education, have already been active for at least seven years, while only 6 to 8 per cent are actual newcomers to later life exercise and active recreation. Corporate fitness and wellness centres have been useful in promoting good health habits before retirement and fostering lifelong social networks at the workplace (Cunningham et al. 1987). Employment settings seem to be crucial in developing friendship ties and enhancing social networks useful for future physical activity patterns (Mor-Barak et al. 1992).

Studies show that many men seem to feel that freedom earned at retirement is at risk of being lost by 'getting into a routine'. While many plan to take a 'well-deserved rest', only a few aspire to pursue a more athletic life in their leisure time. Few men care to strictly schedule themselves, nor do they like the idea of being organized by a fitness professional who might set too brisk a pace (O'Brien Cousins 1998). Some (not having grown up in an era where fitness activities and aerobics classes were commonplace) believe they may feel silly in formal exercise classes and cannot see the point of moving arms and legs 'without purpose' to music. In spite of an infinitesimal risk, many believe they could drop dead during vigorous exercise. Ironically, while dreading the prospects of having a stroke or heart attack, exercise is sometimes seen as the worst of all evils, forced upon an unwilling body requiring rest rather than exertion. Furthermore, it seems that even when interest in physical activity is present at retirement, it may not last very long since a steady gradient of reduced physical activity is the typical finding after age seventy (Shephard 1994). Retirees increasingly begin to 'take it easy' in their remaining years, sustaining the self-fulfilling prophecy of acting out old age the way society has normatively defined it.

Conceptions of Health and Healthy Aging

Conceptions of health and healthy aging are slow to change and are often confused by popular discourse around gender and exercise. Media campaigns, at least until recently, have tended to mislead the public into believing that exercise must be sweat inducing and high exertion to be health promoting (Blair et al. 1992). With an all-or-nothing view about the intensity of exercise necessary for health benefits, older adults think there is little point in engaging in brief and low-intensity activities, and simply do not feel capable of and safe with longer or more intense exercise. Taking up an athletic lifestyle in one's older years may feel like the antithesis of health—a dangerous and life-threatening task for those who have little mastery of skills or direct sporting experience. Indeed, a raft of contradictory studies about how much exercise is enough has left many people confused about how long, how intense, and how frequently one needs to exercise to stay fit and healthy (Chisolm 1996). Older Canadians report that information from professionals and organizations regarding physical activity has been contradictory and often too complex for them to understand or remember.

This confusion about what keeps an older person healthy or indeed what 'healthy' means is exacerbated by the fact that many seniors judge their health to be fine without much activity. To a point, age declines go unnoticed. A sedentary spouse, inactive friends, and a non-committal physician may all support this belief. Furthermore, the fact that women are generally less active than men in their leisure time and less inclined to exerting activity seems to run counter to scientific opinion that people who are more active are healthier and live longer. Virtually all of the participation evidence supports the fact that men spend more leisure time than women in physical activity (Stephens and Craig 1990). The reality that women live longer, on average than men, despite years of minimal vigorous activity, seems to cause consternation among men as to the real value of their own activity levels. They see that men die sooner despite playing more sport and having more vigorous pursuits throughout their lives. Women live longer despite their more passive roles. Less well known is the fact that heart disease is an equally serious issue for women as it is for men. Actuarial data show that while men die sooner, more women die on an annual basis of heart disease. The women who die each year are simply older. Moreover, women (who are already functionally weaker than men at every age) need resistance type exercise if they hope to maintain bone and muscle strength to withstand their extra longevity. Men need mainly to be active to keep their cardiovascular system in good shape and delay the onset of cardiovascular disease. Stereotypes about who gets heart disease suggest that health issues disseminated through the media reflect a strong gender and age bias towards middle-aged male health issues.

Rather than physical activity, older Canadians will often mention sleep, rest, and a good diet as the actions they are most likely to pursue for health (Stephens and Craig 1990). They seem to think that maintaining their health means conserving energy and consuming food rather than expending energy through daily exercise. Wellness fairs for seniors continue to focus on 'eating one's way to good health' even while most Canadians are overeating rather than undereating. In *Promoting Active Living and Healthy Eating Among Older Canadians*, O'Brien Cousins (1997) suggests that undernourishment in the elderly should be addressed as a serious outcome of insufficient daily activity, and that an increase in activity leading to more appropriate food intake could be the best strategy for reducing the risk of malnutrition in ambulatory healthy people. If physical activity was to be placed on an equal footing with nutrition information, the public might come to see that almost half of all older people are starving for any kind of exercise.

Gender, Aging, and Personal Experiences of Exercise and Sport

It is a truism to say that aging is about the body, yet in the study of aging we often lose sight of the lived body (Featherstone and Wernick 1995). Rarely are studies about exercise and aging designed to listen and respond to the expressed experiences of the elderly themselves whose later life exercise patterns are rooted in a variety of different ways to their past (O'Brien Cousins and Vertinsky 1995). As well, notions that aging women are more sensitive to bodily discomfort and exercise effort than men need revisiting as scholars increasingly claim that the whole topic of gender differences in health warrants re-examination with more attention to social and historical context and life histories (MacIntyre, Hunt, and Sweeting 1996). It is hardly surprising that those designing exercise promotion strategies have a formidable task in trying to better the quality of life of aging men and women without addressing the deeper issues of gender stereotyping and powerlessness on the one hand and listening more attentively to personal stories and experiences on the other.

In order to learn more about the actual experiences of being old and active, O'Brien Cousins and Janzen (1998) recently collected physical activity data on a volunteer group of 125 Alberta seniors followed by an in-depth study with thirteen of the least active men and women. Their findings reflect a wide range of continuing negative attitudes to aging and exercise. Participants feared experiencing negative social consequences from being sportive. They believed that overexertion would bring physical harm. They said they lacked the ability and confidence to participate in a number of activities and they held conventional attitudes about being too old for exercise to have any value. The women in the study cited disapproval by family and friends, and the problem of finding companionship for physical activity. Married women complained that their spouses often had their own sporting interests or were reluctant to join them in activities. Being widowed brought further problems since in getting out to join a group activity, having 'someone to go with' was often seen as a key requirement. The stereotype that women should always be partnered in their social activities is strong. For example, women who tried to maintain their involvement in social dancing after their husbands died found that, with men at a premium, they were often not welcomed at public gatherings and were perceived as being 'on the hunt' for men in physical activity settings.

Elderly sport participants worry that public participation can lead to social embarrassment and a lessening of self-esteem. Spirduso (1995), for example, points out that while it is hard to tell exactly how much better one person is than another at reading or understanding a political issue, it is not difficult to see who is still moving at the end of an exercise workout or to determine winners and losers in physical games. Fear of ridicule and negative self-perceptions can thus undermine efforts to establish or continue an active lifestyle, and again gender plays a significant role. Older women (and some men) often remember having negative experiences decades earlier with sport and childhood games, while many older men who had military preparation continue to see sport as a test of male power and strength. Perhaps because they are afraid to be seen as less masculine, older men select their physical activities carefully and avoid being placed in settings where their stamina can be directly compared to women. It is also the case that activity choices can be severely limited for gay and lesbian elders. As MacNeill (1995) points out, ParticipACTION's visions of an active lifestyle for the elderly are very much grounded in dominant biophysical definitions of what it means to be fit framed through middle-class, heterosexual images. In *Look Me in the Eye: Old Women, Aging and Ageism*, Barbara Macdonald (Macdonald and Rich 1995) talks about the compounding problem of being old and lesbian in a homophobic society and reflects upon her desire to join a feminist march, only to be told she might not be able to keep up.

There are, of course, more optimistic voices about physicality and aging, such as those reported by a group of Australian women seeking to disrupt familiar prescriptions for the aging body to which they felt they had been bound. In a writing workshop, one sixty-nine-year-old's response to the task of imagining new and more liberating ways of being old was entitled 'She let herself go' (Kamler et al. 1995):

> Boy, did she let herself go in her 69th year. She left family, friends, husband, hobbies, house and mindless domesticity. . . . Removing the mask of wife and

mother, she danced in the streets to the jazzed up music of Bach. Along with the broom, she threw out the morality makers' restrictions on women's sexual behavior. With regret for past missed joys she made love to every sensuous, clean, intelligent . . . man who crossed her path. She noted there were not too many of them. . . . She left behind her watch, her proper behavior . . . laughed, drank, ate only mangoes, home made bread and lemon curd, and talked with anyone nourishing who came her way. She had surely let herself go. And for the first time in her life, her age collided with her youth and she felt truly free (Kamler et al. 1995:22).

Challenging the limiting stereotypes of the aging body and constructing alternatives in this way can allow women to disrupt the cultural storylines of loss and decline that define and constrain them.

Master's Sport

Elders who are competitive and sport-involved exemplify tenacity, courage, and an active approach to late life. Master's athletes are more than just fit—they are also late life learners and are prepared to condition their bodies through training regimes similar to younger athletes—not for health alone—but rather for the pleasure of developing skilful performance. Spirduso (1995) calls older athletes 'the physically elite elderly', noting that although older athletes are not as powerful as younger athletes, they are still more capable in their eighties and nineties than many individuals decades younger.

While Master's sport does have its risky elements, for some people it is a route to finding (or sustaining) life meaning. In a study on Seniors' Games athletes, more men than women seemed to derive satisfaction from their personal sport achievements and physical skill (O'Brien and Conger 1991). For older men in particular, it is possible that sport and recreation may provide an important coping strategy that provides meaningful interaction with other adults and is a measure of personal achievement in late life. Being athletic in one's older years is still an atypical life choice, yet most would agree that it is a sign of 'successful aging'. However, we know very little about the actual motives of high-performance elderly men or women in sport. Do they consider themselves as 'beating the aging odds'? Does success in sport 'masculinize' older men, as it is thought to do with younger men? Further research is needed to determine if physical prowess and superior skill are seen as more important among Master's athletes than the simple pleasure of participating, and how men and women may differ in this regard. Furthermore, we still know very little about the relationship of a sporting youth to lifelong involvement in exercise and sport.[4]

The fact that Master's athletes engage in some sports more than others suggests that in Canada (as elsewhere), some sports are seen as more 'age-appropriate' as well as 'gender-appropriate'. Older people tend to avoid body contact and 'open-skilled' sports such as wrestling and football. In sports that require vigour, speed, and skill such as tennis, basketball, diving, or apparatus gymnastics, Master's athletes are rare in number. In sports that have minimal power requirements such as golf, bowling, and horseshoes, participation levels are much higher. There are, of course, some major exceptions; old-timer's hockey is very popular among men, and this is a game that has all the demands of power, speed, and body contact (O'Brien and Conger 1991).

Gender issues arise in the sport setting where few women are visible in athletics, although aging women are taking up golf in increasing numbers. Women over eighty are especially rare in Master's events, even though there are more than twice as many women as men at this age. Because of the infrequent participation of aged women, Master's world record performances for women are highly variable and drop off more rapidly after age eighty than male records. But women's peak performances at all other decades are parallel to the men's, denying the stereotype that women actually age faster than men (Spirduso 1994).

New Strategies for Increasing Physical Activity

Current theoretical understandings suggest that older adult sport and physical activity levels will increase when: (1) the benefits of participation in late life are known and appreciated more widely; (2) these benefits of being active are highly valued or are socially rewarded (incentives); (3) active recreational pursuits are judged to be easy and enjoyable for most elderly people to do; and (4) the costs, risks, and liabilities are deemed to be minimal. In short, widespread participation of the elderly in exerting physical activity requires positive public expectations that there is much to be gained in making an effort to use leisure time for physical pursuits, that it will be affordable, fun, and not difficult to do, that there will be encouragement from family members, friends, and health professionals, and that the negative physical and social outcomes will be minimal.

Even now, with health and fitness a popular topic in the mass media, the scope and magnitude of the benefits of being an active older adult are not well known among non-athletic individuals. While most physically inactive people agree that 'keeping active is good for you', few sedentary people can explain just what those benefits are—they lack direct experience with feeling better, sleeping better, and moving better. Media information has tended to magnify rather than alleviate concerns. The glorification of professional sport male models has alienated women of all ages, and prevented a good deal of the male population too from feeling worthy of participating. Since the 1980s, too many overzealous fitness professionals have fostered an image that a requirement to participate is the ability to keep up a sweat-inducing routine—fit in, keep up, or move on! Alternatively, they have treated older adults as fragile and singled them out for special, cautious treatment. Examples of how overcaution leads to failure, wasted time, and disinterest are seen in many a seniors' centre exercise program, where healthy seniors walk into class and then sit for most of the one-hour program doing gentle chair exercises.

Fortunately, recreational programming is now showing signs of becoming more sensitive to the diversity of older adult physical activity needs, paying attention to ethnic sensitivities and interests, and recognizing the inclination of men and women to select gender-preferred activities. While some co-ed activities such as forms of dancing, aquatic activities, and social skating have proved to be appealing to this population, programmers have learned that dancercize classes are filled almost exclusively with women, and weight rooms almost exclusively with men. Older men are scarce in community programs, not only because of their higher mortality rate in general but also because they tend to choose less leader-structured activities that can be done alone or in small groups (running, swimming lengths, slow-pitch baseball, and old-timer's hockey and golf).

Ideally, habitual physical activity patterns need to be re-established in middle age so that sport skills and functional fitness are not drastically lost. Strategies that run counter to the traditional view that fast-paced aerobic exercise is what is required to be fit may just add confusion to contemporary notions about being active. Probably a 'more is better, but a little is better than nothing' approach is warranted (Mummery 1995). As well, language is important. The 'dose-response' jargon of exercise physiologists may overmedicalize what should be, for most people, a playful, social, and active recreation experience.

Social support for older adult physical activity may be the one factor most likely to motivate older people to increase their involvement and it can be provided in a number of ways (O'Brien Cousins 1995b). Family members can praise (rather than criticize) older relatives for maintaining an active lifestyle. Active friends need to be given priority in late life. Physicians who are overly cautious about daily walking and mobility exercises and strength training several times a week can be replaced with those who view exercise promotion as primary prevention rather than a therapeutic option (Smith et al. 1992).

Older people need to be informed that it is sedentary living, not physically active living, that places them at risk of sudden death from heart attacks. The known risks of participation are so low that the standard advice to potential exercisers could arguably change to: 'Consult your physician if you are contemplating decreasing your physical activity.' We need to address financial incentives that support health care policies at the expense of health promotion since this sustains a dependency on professional care services rather than self-care initiatives. The only way to get a free fitness test in Canada is to have a heart attack! While a majority of seniors in Canada may be house-bound during the most trying weeks of winter and are unable or unwilling to pay for taxis to get to places where they could advance their health, they know that older people will get a free ambulance ride to the local hospital when they become sick.

Persuading the aging public about the benefits of physical activity through education and the media could require years of costly and sustained advocacy. Public efforts may be better spent on targeting motivated but subactive populations, and offering advice on how easy it can be for them to get started, where in their communities they can get help and companionship, and how they can ensure their personal enjoyment through self-paced involvement. While fearmongering is not a recommended strategy, we do know that older people are worried about dementia and Alzheimer's disease, as well as losing their ability to live independently. Linking physical activity to the cognitive benefits of delaying and preventing dementia, and linking active lifestyles to improved prospects for independent living to the last days of life may provide the kind of incentives needed to mobilize large numbers of older men and women.

Creating a Culture of Positive Aging

In *The Journey of Life*, Thomas Cole (1992) argues that we must find the will to imagine a more just and beautiful future for the elderly. He advises us to confront images and stereotypes from the past and use them to serve the dilemmas of the present, encouraging policy makers to imagine age not as a loss of youth and bodily decline but as a gain in strength and wisdom. Yet scientific management and exercise formulas too often accept the former view, relating it to elderly men and women as homogeneous groups rather than groups characterized by diversity in a multicultural society. It is by now abundantly clear to those interested in the process of aging and the meaning of old age that there is a danger to individual autonomy and existential integrity that lies in the homogenization and scientific management of old age, which paints the elderly with one broad brush. By framing the 'problems of aging' and therefore the solutions as technical and biological, the effects of non-medical issues such as poverty, isolation, loss of role and status, ethnicity, and, of course gender, are all too often ignored (Robertson 1990). Also often ignored are the day-to-day experiences of aging, which should play such a large role in policy development and support mechanisms. Far too often the voices of the elderly, who can best portray the realities of their everyday lives, are not included in exercise prescriptions and lifestyle policies designed for them.

Contrary to popular opinion, most older people are fit enough to enjoy full lives and many manage well despite handicaps. New studies of aging are beginning to probe the complex dynamics of 'successful aging'. Life span approaches and understandings of the social construction of aging and disability are being embraced with a much greater appreciation of the elderly individual and his or her personal experiences. Interactions between health and disease are being explored more carefully in examining multiple pathways to old age. Recent national and international initiatives in health promotion and population health have begun to reflect more fully the realization that the factors that influence the lifestyle practices of the elderly are multiple and interactive, deeply embedded within the social, economic, and physical environment. Ongoing attempts to re-evaluate how health is created and maintained have moved from the earlier focus on lifestyle and health risk behaviours to one that pays attention to the underlying social conditions and strategies that might enhance better opportunities. The new Canadian health promotion policy, *Strategies for Population Health: Investing in the Health of Canada* (1994), seeks comprehensive action across the full range of determinants of health and may promote a useful guide and support to a broader range of strategies for assisting the elderly to 'get on the move'.

In some respects, fiscal restraint and health care reform across Canada are acting in concert to force a reconceptualization of health and exercise promotion for aging adults. While negative outcomes are evident, there are hints of a silver lining at the organizational level. Chronic downsizing in the federal Fitness Directorate has limited the efforts of the Senior's Secretariat for Fitness in the Third Age, but also removed administrative impediments to new ways of thinking and creative project development among community volunteers. The Active Living Coordinating Center for Older Adults survives as the only national coordinating body for elderly sport and physical activity and, with limited funding from Health Canada (New Horizon's Partners in Aging) and the Fitness Directorate, it has successfully conducted a number of community studies and pilot projects. Community development initiatives at the grassroots level such as Operation ABLE (Aging Better with a Little Exercise) are enabling communities in Alberta to promote quality of life and functional independence of seniors through health-promoting active living. Facilitating links and partnerships among active living leaders, programmers, gerontologists and administrators, health care providers and the medical profession, such initiatives assist in preventing the medicalization of everyday active recreation and advocating a community-driven, non-clinical approach towards older adult physical activity. By working to match people to people, people to programs, and people to resources, their aim is to overturn the old saying that 'You've reached old age when all you exercise is caution!'

Notes

1. Many functional abilities are reduced with aging. Hypotrophy of muscle is accelerated after the age of sixty, and muscle fibre life is also reduced. The decrease in VO_2 max is about 10 per cent per decade from age twenty to sixty, though exercise training in the fifth and sixth decades of life may slow this decline. However, much more information is needed about the performance capabilities of the elderly, particularly strength and power (Bouchard et al. 1988).

2. The questionnaire/interview is the most common approach to assess elderly participation in physical activity, but memory bias plays an important role, as does the definition of physical activity, which may include activity at work or home, leisure
activity, and very strenuous sport activity (Buskirk cited in Bouchard et al. 1988;
Powell and Paffenbarger 1985).

3. If women die older (by about seven years than men), their greater mean age means
that they will experience more illness, especially chronic illness and disability, than
men. After age sixty-five they will be three times more likely to reside in nursing
homes and to die there. One in four women (as compared to one in seven men) will
end their lives in institutions.

4. Some Master's athletes do provide life span examples of the potential to be an active
athlete at both ends of the life spectrum. A good example is Isobel Bleasdale
Cunningham from Ajax, Ontario, who holds Canada's world record for the over-
seventy-five category in the 100-m sprint. In 1937 she was world record holder for the
80-yard indoor sprint. Fifty years intervened between young Isobel, the sprinter, and
older Isobel, the Master's athlete. She was a schoolteacher, mother of four children,
divorced, and remarried. She did not run again until her seventies.

References

ALCCOA (Active Living Coordinating Center for Older Adults) and Health Canada. 1997.
Fit for Your Life Study: Progressive Strength Training for Older Adults. Edmonton: University of Alberta.

Ames, K., M. Hager, L. Wilson, and L. Buckley. 1990. 'Our Bodies, Their Selves: The
Bias Against Women in Health Research'. *Newsweek* (17 December):160.

Arber, S., and J. Ginn. 1991. *Gender and Later Life: A Sociological Analysis of Resources and
Constraints*. London: Sage.

Banner, L.W. 1993. *In Full Flower: Aging Women, Power and Sexuality*. New York:
Vintage Books.

Beckett, K.C., and C. Davison. 1995. 'Lifecourse and Lifestyle: The Social and Cultural
Location of Health Behaviors'. *Social Science and Medicine* 40:629–38.

Blair, S.N., H.W. Koh., N.F. Gordon, and R.S. Paffenbarger, Jr. 1992. 'How Much
Physical Activity Is Good for Health?' *Annual Review of Public Health* 13:99–126.

Bouchard, C., R.J. Shephard, T. Stephens, J.R. Sutton, and B.D. McPherson, eds. 1988. *Exercise, Fitness and Health: A Consensus of Current Knowledge*. Champaign, IL: Human Kinetics.

Burger, H., J. Canavan, W. Ey, I. Johnston, and B. Drinkwater. 1996. *Drug Testing in Master's Sport: Implications for Women*. Canberra: International Task Force for Women Sport International, Australia.

Buskirk, E.R. 1988. 'Exercise, Fitness and Aging'. In *Exercise, Fitness and Health*, edited by C. Bouchard, R.J. Shephard, T. Stephens, J.R. Sutton, and B.D. McPherson, 687–95. Champaign, IL: Human Kinetics.

Callahan, J.C., ed. 1993. *Menopause: A Midlife Passage*. Bloomington: Indiana University Press.

Carpenter, C.L. 1987. 'Exercise and Menopause'. *Fitness Management* 3:20–1.

Chisholm, P. 1996. 'How Much Exercise Is Too Much?' *Maclean's* 109, no. 23:46–7.

Chrisler, J.C., J.W. Torrey, and M.M. Matthes. 1991. 'Brittle Bones and Sagging Breasts: Loss of Femininity and Loss of Sanity: The Media Describe the Menopause'. In *Proceedings of the 8th Conference of the Society for Menstrual Cycle Research*, 23–35. Salt Lake City: Society for Menstrual Cycle Research.

Cole, T.R. 1992. *The Journey of Life: A Cultural History of Aging in America*. Cambridge: Cambridge University Press.

Cunningham, D.A., P.A. Rechnitzer, J.H. Howard, and A.P. Donner. 1987. 'Exercise Training of Men at Retirement: A Clinical Trial'. *Journal of Gerontology* 42:17–23.

Currier, A.F. 1897. *The Menopause*. New York: D. Appleton.

Drevenstedt, J. 1976. 'Perceptions of Onsets of Young Adulthood, Middle Age and Old Age'. *Journal of Gerontology* 31:53–7.

Ernst, E. 1990. 'Jogging for a Healthy Heart and Worn-Out Hips'. *Journal of Internal Medicine* 278:295–7.

Featherstone, M. 1991. 'The Body in Consumer Culture'. In *The Body: Social Process and Cultural Theory*, edited by M. Featherstone, M. Hepworth, and B.S. Turner, 170–96. London: Sage.

_____, and A. Wernick, eds. 1995. *Images of Aging: Cultural Representations of Later Life*. London: Routledge.

Fiatarone, M.A., E.C. Marks, N.D. Ryan, C.N. Meredith, L.A. Lipsitz, and W.J. Evans. 1990. 'High Intensity Strength Training in Nonogenarians: Effects on Skeletal Muscle'. *Journal of American Medical Association* 263:3029–34.

_____, E.F. O'Neill, N.D. Ryan, K.M. Clements, G.R. Solares, M.E. Nelson, S.B. Roberts, J.J. Kehayias, L.A. Lipsitz, and W.J. Evans. 1994. 'Exercise Training and Nutritional Supplementation for Physical Frailty in Very Elderly People'. *The New England Journal of Medicine* 330:1769–75.

_____, E.F. O'Neill, J. Asher, D. Levine, and N.D. Ryan. 1996. *Fit for Your Life Exercise Program: Training Manual*. Boston: Hebrew Rehabilitation Center.

Friedan, B. 1993. *The Fountain of Age*. New York: Simon and Schuster.

Fries, J.F. 1989. 'The Compression of Morbidity: Near or Far?' *The Milbank Quarterly* 67:208–32.

_____, H. Harrington, R. Edwards, L.A. Kent, and N. Richardson. 1994. 'Randomized Controlled Trial of Cost Reductions from a Health Education Program: The California Public Employees' Retirement System (PERS) Study'. *American Journal of Health Promotion* 8:216–23.

Heart and Stroke Foundation. 1995. 'Physical Inactivity Is a Fourth Factor'. *Lifelines* 1, 2:1.

Heislein, D.M., B.A. Harris, and A. Jette. 1994. 'A Strength Training Study for Postmenopausal Women: A Pilot Study'. *Archives of Physical Medicine & Rehabilitation* 75:198–204.

Hicks, J.B. 1877. 'The Croonian Lectures on the Difference Between the Sexes in Regard to the Aspect and Treatment of Disease'. *British Medical Journal* 11:473–6.

Kamler, B., et al. 1995. 'Mirror Mirror on the Wall: Reflections on Aging'. *Australian Cultural History* 14:1–22.

Katz, S., L.G. Branch, M.H. Branson, J.A. Papsidero, B.C. Beck, and D.S. Greer. 1983. 'Active Life Expectancy'. *New England Journal of Medicine* 309:1218–23.

Keeler, E.B., et al. 1989. 'The External Costs of a Sedentary Lifestyle'. *American Journal of Public Health* 79, 8:975–81.

Khaw, H. 1990. 'Healthy Aging: A Population Approach'. *Geriatric Medicine* 21:39–44.

Kogan, N. 1979. 'A Study of Age Categorization'. *Journal of Gerontology* 34:358–67.

Lee, A. 1991. 'Women and Aerobic Exercise: Directions for Research Development'. *Annals of Behavioral Medicine* 13, no. 3:133–40.

Leng, K.W. 1996. 'On Menopause and Cyborgs: Or, Towards Feminist Cyborg Politics of Menopause'. *Body and Society* 2, no. 3:33–52.

Lipka, R.P. 1987. 'Women: Why Does Society Age Them Sooner?' *Contemporary Educational Psychology* 12:110–18.

Lock, M. 1993. *Encounters with Aging: Mythologies of Menopause in Japan and North America*. Berkeley: University of California Press.

Lupton, D. 1996. 'Constructing the Menopausal Body: The Discourses on Hormone Replacement Therapy'. *Body and Society* 2, no. 1:91–7.

McArthur, K. 1997. 'We're Retiring Sooner'. *The Globe and Mail* (12 June):1.

McCartney, N., A.L. Hicks, J. Martin, and C.E. Webber. 1996. 'A Longitudinal Trial of Weight Training in the Elderly: Continual Improvements in Year 2'. *Journal of Gerontology* 51A, B425–B433.

Macdonald, B., and C. Rich. 1995. *Look Me in the Eye: Old Women, Aging and Ageism*. San Francisco: Spinsters Inc.

MacIntyre, S., K. Hunt, and H. Sweeting. 1996. 'Gender Differences in Health: Are Things Really as Simple as They Seem?' *Social Science and Medicine* 42, no. 4:617–24.

MacNeill, M. 1995. 'Moving a Nation: The Social Marketing of Gender in Television and Print Campaigns by ParticipACTION'. Paper presented at the Annual conference of the North American Society for the Sociology of Sport, Sacramento, US.

McPherson, B.D. 1994. 'Sociocultural Perspectives on Aging and Physical Activity'. *Journal of Aging and Physical Activity* 2:329–53.

Markula, P. 1995. 'Firm But Shapely, Fit But Sexy, Strong But Thin: The Postmodern Aerobicizing Female Bodies'. *Sociology of Sport Journal* 44:424–53.

Martin, D., and M. Notelovitz. 1993. 'Effects of Aerobic Training on Bone Mineral Density of Postmenopausal Women'. *Journal of Bone and Mineral Research* 8, no. 8:931–6.

Minkler, M., and C. Estes, eds. 1991. *Critical Perspectives on Aging: The Political Economy of Growing Old*. New York: Baywood.

Mor-Barak, M.E., A.E. Scharlach, L. Birba, and J. Sokolov. 1992. 'Employment, Social Networks, and Health in the Retirement Years'. *International Journal of Aging & Human Development* 35, no. 2:145–59.

Mummery, K. 1995. 'The Case for Incorporating Physical Activity into One's Lifestyle'. *Research Update* 2:1.

Nelson, M.E., E.C. Fisher, F.A. Dilmanian, G.E. Dallal, and W.J. Evans. 1991. 'A 1-Year Walking Program and Increased Dietary Calcium in Postmenopausal Women: Effects on Bone'. *The American Journal of Clinical Nutrition* 53:1304–11.

Norland, J.A. 1994. *Profile of Canada's Seniors*. Statistics Canada. Scarborough: Prentice-Hall.

O'Brien Cousins, S. 1995a. 'Anticipated Exertion for Exercise Activities Among Women Over Age 70'. *Canadian Woman Studies* 15, no. 4:73–7.

_____. 1995b. 'Social Support for Exercise Among Elderly Women in Canada'. *Health Promotion International* 104, no. 4:273–82.

_____. 1997. 'Promoting Active Living and Health Eating Among Older Canadians'. In *Canada Health Action: Building on the Legacy, Volume 2: Determinants of Health for Seniors*, 144–76. Ottawa: Editions Multimondes, National Forum on Health.

_____. 1998. *Exercise, Aging and Health: Overcoming Barriers to an Active Old Age*. Washington, DC: Taylor and Francis.

_____, and P. Vertinsky. 1991. 'Unfit Survivors: Exercise as a Resource for Aging Women'. *The Gerontologist* 31, no. 3:347–57.

O'Brien Cousins, S., and A.C. Burgess. 1992. 'Perspectives on Older Adults in Sport and Physical Activity'. *Educational Gerontology* 18:461–81.

_____, and P.R. Conger. 1991. 'No Time to Look Back: Approaching the Finish Line of Life's Course'. *The International Journal of Aging and Human Development* 33:75–87.

_____, and W. Janzen. 1998. 'Older Adult Beliefs About Exercise'. In *Exercise, Aging and Health*, edited by S. O'Brien Cousins, 71–96. Washington, DC: Taylor and Francis.

_____, and N. Keating. 1995. 'Life Cycle Patterns of Physical Activity Among Sedentary and Active Older Women'. *Journal of Aging and Physical Activity* 3:340–59.

_____, and P. Vertinsky. 1995. 'Recapturing the Physical Activity Experiences of the Old: A Study of Three Women'. *Journal of Aging and Physical Activity* 3:146–62.

Paffenbarger, R.S., and I.M. Lee. 1996. 'Do Physical Activity and Physical Fitness Arrest Premature Mortality?' In *Exercise and Sport Science Reviews*, edited by J.O. Holloszy, 135–71. Baltimore: Williams and Williams.

Powell, K.E., and R.S. Paffenbarger, Jr. 1985. 'Workshop on Epidemiological Public Health Aspects of Physical Activity and Exercise: A Summary'. *Public Health Reports* 100:118–25.

Rippe, J.M., and A. Ward. 1992. 'Medicine, Exercise, Nutrition and Health: A Vision for the 90s'. *Medicine, Exercise, Nutrition and Health* 1:1–4.

Rips, J. 1993. 'Who Needs a Menopause Policy?' In *Menopause: A Midlife Passage*, edited by J.C. Callahan, 79–91. Bloomington: Indiana University.

Robertson, A. 1990. 'The Politics of Alzheimer's Disease: A Case Study in Apocalyptic Demography'. *International Journal of Health Services* 20:429–42.

Roebuck, J., and J. Slaughter. 1979. 'Ladies and Pensioners: Stereotypes and Public Policy Affecting Old Women in England, 1880–1940'. *Journal of Social History* 13:105–14.

Russell, S. 1997. *Active Living Among Older Canadians: Trends and Directions for Action*. Ottawa: Canadian Fitness and Lifestyle Research Institute Report.

Schaberg, G. J.E. Ballard, B.C. McKeown, and S.A. Zinkgraf. 1990. 'Body Composition Alterations Consequent to an Exercise Program for Pre and Postmenopausal Women'. *The Journal of Sports Medicine & Physical Fitness* 30:426–33.

Shephard, R.J. 1987. *Economic Benefits of Enhanced Fitness*. Champaign, IL: Human Kinetics.

_____. 1994. 'Demography of Health-Related Fitness Levels Within and Between Populations'. In *Physical Activity, Fitness and Health*, edited by C. Bouchard, R. Shephard, and T. Stephens, 239–56. Champaign, IL: Human Kinetics.

Smith, L.W., T.L. Patterson, and I. Grant. 1992. 'Work, Retirement and Activity: Coping Challenges for the Elderly'. In *Handbook of Social Development: A Lifespan Perspective*, edited by V.B. Van Hasselt and M. Herson, 475–502. New York: Plenum Press.

Smith-Rosenberg, C. 1985. *Disorderly Conduct: Visions of Gender in Victorian America*. New York: Alfred A. Knopf.

Spirduso, W.W. 1995. *The Physical Dimensions of Aging*. Champaign, IL: Human Kinetics.

_____, and P.G. MacRae. 1991. 'Physical Exercise and the Quality of Life in the Frail Elderly'. In *The Concept and Measurement of Quality of Life in the Frail Elderly*, edited by J.E. Birren, J.E. Lubben, J.C. Rowe, and D.E. Deutchman, 226–55. New York: Academic Press.

Stephens, T.L., and C.L. Craig, eds. 1990. *The Well-Being of Canadians: Highlights of the 1988 Campbell's Survey*. Ottawa: Canadian Fitness and Lifestyle Research Institute.

Stillman, R.J., T.G. Lohman, M.H. Slaughter, and B.H. Massey. 1986. 'Physical Activity and Bone Mineral Content in Women Aged 30–85 Years'. *Medicine and Science in Sports Exercise* 18, no. 5:576–80.

US Department of Health and Human Services. 1996. *Physical Activity and Health: A Report of the Surgeon General*. Atlanta: US Department of Health and Human Services, Center for Disease Control and Prevention, National Center for Chronic Disease Prevention and Health Promotion.
Vertinsky, P.A. 1994. *The Eternally Wounded Woman: Women, Doctors and Exercise in the Late Nineteenth Century*. Urbana: University of Illinois Press.

_____. 1995. 'Stereotypes of Aging Women and Exercise: An Historical Perspective'. *Journal of Aging and Physical Activity* 3:223–37.

Wilbur, J., A. Dan, C. Hedricks, and K. Holm. 1990. 'The Relationship Among Menopausal Status, Menopausal Symptoms, and Physical Activity in Midlife Women'. *Family and Community Health* (November):67–78.

Wolfgang, V., and H. Pongratz. 1988. 'Retirement and the Lifestyles of Older Women'. *Aging and Society* 8:63–84.

Chapter 8

Doing Race, Doing Gender:

First Nations, 'Sport', and Gender Relations[1]

Victoria Paraschak

Gender relations are embedded in the cultural practices of all societies. These relations (re)produce a distinctiveness between men and women,[2] which often translates into differences in power.[3] Gender relations also (re)produce hierarchies among men or among women based on characteristics such as race, class, age, physical ability, and sexual orientation.[4] Over time, these socially constructed gender relations become 'naturalized'—most individuals accept them as appropriate and necessary for the effective operation of their society.

For First Nations athletes, too, participating in physical activities (re)creates a naturalized understanding about what it means to be male or female in their society. In doing sport, they are also 'doing gender', although the process may be different depending on whether the sport is organized in terms of Native or Euroamerican interests.[5] When these athletes participate in physical activities controlled by Euroamericans, they may encounter a Euroamerican understanding of maleness and femaleness that does not align with Native understandings. Inevitably, race[6] becomes a defining aspect of their athletic experience, and Native athletes end up 'doing race' as well as 'doing gender'. These different contexts help shape the ways in which First Nations men and women view themselves and how they are viewed by others in North America. In order to explore the complexity of gender relations for First Nations peoples in sport, this chapter examines four different intersections of racial and gender relations.

The first intersection, race embedded within gender relations, examines the reproduction of Native racial identity in gendered sport practices under Native control. Intragender racial hierarchies, the second intersection, looks at situations where race is a hierarchical social marker within male and female sport practices, hierarchies that tend to marginalize non-mainstream participants. Explicitly symbolic race/gender relations comprise the third intersection. In these instances, Native organizers and participants consciously set out to make their sport practices 'Native', which affects the gendered nature of those practices. Finally, this chapter explores race/gender relations in the sporting practices of Native people that symbolize the 'Other' to non-Natives. In such cases, racial identity and gender relations for Native participants are constructed in a manner that reproduces non-Native stereotypes about Native Americans.

These intersections, as I call them, represent the outcome of my exploration of the processes by which Native peoples come to know about and/or reproduce racialized gender identities in Canada. They are neither fixed nor exhaustive but may shift and change across time according to different social and political circumstances.

Race Embedded within Gender Relations

Particular racial and gender identities come to seem natural and normal through participation in daily life. Often people's awareness of their race does not consciously shape their gender relations, even though the gender relations that result clearly have a definable racial character. As we will see, in the First Nations sporting context, gender relations are often played out in conjunction with racial identities.

Sport and games are an ongoing, important aspect of Native cultural life. Overviews of First Nations' sport and games identify the importance of these activities for ceremonial purposes, for their physical conditioning, and for their enjoyment (Churchill et al. 1979; Culin [1907] 1992; Oxendine 1988; Zeman 1988). Accounts of involvement in lacrosse (Vennum 1994), running (Nabokov 1981), and traditional games festivals (Heine 1995; Paraschak 1997) primarily document male participation, although articles on Native females in sport (Cheska 1974; Craig 1973; Paraschak 1990, 1995, 1996a; Smith 1993) also provide some historical evidence of Native women's love of games such as double ball, a traditional but now largely ignored Native team sport played almost exclusively by women. In double ball, two balls were joined by a thong, and sticks were used to advance them towards a goal. Teams could range in size from six to 100 players per side, and the style of play was vigorous (Oxendine 1988). Native women have also been active and successful in a variety of contemporary sports including basketball, softball, track, rodeo, cross-country skiing, and lacrosse.

Although both Native men and women play sport, there has often been a gender imbalance in the recognition of their accomplishments (Paraschak 1996a). For example, in the first twenty-three years of the Canadian Tom Longboat Award (given to outstanding Native athletes), there was only one female recipient. Also, only one of fifty-seven inductees into the American Indian Hall of Fame was female in the first thirteen years of its existence from 1972 to 1985. In sum, while sport has been an important aspect in the lives of both Native men and women, the value placed on their involvement has tended to privilege male over female accomplishments. Three specific case-studies discussed below further illustrate the relationship between gender and sport in First Nations communities.

Tlingit Culture

In his examination of the role of gambling games in the social construction of gender in Tlingit culture during the mid-nineteenth century, Heine (1991:346–7) explained why 'women in traditional Tlingit society engaged in competitive games distinctly less frequently than did men . . . [especially in] betting and gambling games'. Fundamentally, he suggested, the gender division of labour meant that while men had most of the day to be idle, often spending it on gaming,

> . . . women had to work considerably longer to fulfil their culturally defined domestic and economic obligations. . . . Because relatively smaller amounts of leisure time were available to women, their opportunities to engage in games were subject to greater restrictions (Heine 1991:347–8).

Beyond these simple time constraints, Heine (1991) also reported on cultural practices that effectively excluded women from their games. For example, part of the process of involvement for men entailed participating in purification rituals that were supposed to improve their luck. Women rarely participated in these rituals. What is more, women were considered particularly impure during menstruation, which was perceived to make them unfit for sport and games. These factors—the gender division of labour and cultural practices based on gender—'acted as a constraint on women's opportunities to engage in those games that included gambling and betting' (Heine 1991:349).

Such gambling games, often enjoyed by Native adults, usually resulted in an exchange of wealth. For example, in hand-guessing games such as *la-hall*, opponents sat across from each other, with the wagered stakes between them. The guesser attempted to identify the hand in which his opponent held the unmarked (versus the marked) stick, losing his wager if he was incorrect (Oxendine 1988). Significantly, though, the personal property changing hands (such as rifles or tobacco), signifying the wealth and status of each player, was owned by men, not women. Tradeable items produced by women, such as baskets, mats, and clothing, were not used in gambling. Consequently, as Heine (1991:351) explains, '[b]ecause items to be wagered in these [gambling] games were owned by the men almost exclusively, women did not participate'. The games, then, gave men opportunities to symbolically express (and attain) their rank, social status, personal identity, and prestige. And while women often had a measure of control over economic capital (i.e., materials traded to obtain other needed products), it was symbolic capital (to which women had little access) that produced honour and prestige in a gender hierarchy. Patterns of participation in

gambling games thus provided a site for (re)construction of masculine dominance in traditional Tlingit culture (Heine 1991).

Inuit Culture

In another study, Collings and Condon (1996) examined the construction of Inuit
male self-esteem through involvement in hockey on Holman Island in the
Northwest Territories. These authors outlined several ways in which Inuit life
had been transformed over the past twenty years, and how participation in
hockey had become associated with status and achievement:

> In a community where there are limited opportunities for young males to attain
> high status (either in the old status hierarchy of hunting/fishing/trapping or the
> new status hierarchy of high paying employment), playing hockey well and being
> on a winning team contribute much to a young man's sense of identity and self-
> worth (Collings and Condon 1996:256).

Moreover, in a world where Natives fell short of Whites in other areas of life
(such as education and employment), Inuit male teenagers took pride in their
athletic abilities. They 'gain much satisfaction from the knowledge that in the
area of basketball and volleyball [and hockey], they compete on the same level
as their white counterparts' (O'Neil cited in Collings and Condon 1996:258).

As with White players (Young, White, and McTeer 1994), injured hockey
players often received special attention from other players and spectators.
Injuries, and their occasional dramatization, sometimes provided an excuse for
failure, and sometimes enhanced a sense of achievement for players who had
been able to play with and overcome pain (Collings and Condon 1996).

Condon (1995) also looked at the changes in recreation patterns for Inuit
youth more generally. He noted that while both male and female adolescent
athletes had become more competitive in their approach towards sport over time,
gender differences had persisted:

> Although females are considerably more verbal during sports play than they were
> just ten years ago, males tend to be much more boisterous and competitive. They
> are also much more likely to engage in verbal and physical confrontations than
> females, who tend to display more sportsmanlike conduct. Just as in the South,
> women's sports do not attract the crowds that usually attend men's sporting events.
> . . . Thus, although some women may be excellent athletes, they rarely receive the
> recognition that is showered upon male hockey players, even mediocre ones . . .
> females [also] seem to outgrow their sports involvement earlier than males . . .
> game involvement . . . is easily outgrown as adult responsibilities are assumed
> (Condon 1995:58–9).

Condon (1995) argued that competitive sport also provided a place for Inuit youth—both male and female—to display prowess and attractiveness to the opposite sex, for example by 'showing off' or wearing tight-fitting athletic clothing. As he explained, 'In this respect, the significance of sports to sexuality and courtship are not much different in Holman than in southern society' (Condon 1995:65).

Iroquois Culture

In earlier work (Paraschak 1990, 1996a) I focused specifically on the sport experiences of Iroquois women of the Six Nations reserve in southwestern Ontario, who have traditionally structured their social life on matrilineal principles. Through a content analysis of sport coverage in the community newspaper, I documented Native women's involvement from 1968 to 1980 both as participants and as organizers. These women were active in a wide variety of sports in both Euroamerican and all-Indian contexts: '[they] participated in an expansive sport system which included Reserve leagues, organized leagues off the Reserve, and national and international tournaments' (Paraschak 1990:70). In a later article, I (Paraschak 1996a) profiled five multisport women who demonstrated continuing athletic skill and/or involvement at an élite sport level well into their adult years. My findings indicated ongoing interest and success in sport by many Native women on the Six Nations reserve.

Intragender Racial Hierarchies

Race is sometimes used as a marker of difference between participants in an activity. For example, accounts by Native professional hockey players, such as Ted Nolan and Stan Jonathan, suggest that they experienced racism or conditional acceptance. Nolan was initially treated like an outsider by his teammates after he joined the hockey system, and Jonathan endured racist comments directed at him by spectators (*The Sports Network* 1991). It is thus possible that individual and institutionalized acts of racism within sport help to construct hierarchies between groups of males and females. Media accounts of Native athletes often emphasize their race, establishing for First Nations participants that they are Native first, and that their race differentiates them from others of the same gender in that sport.

In much of North American sport, maleness is evaluated on a continuum, with the most physical, and/or most violent, and/or least artistic sport considered those that best represent masculinity. For instance, football and ice hockey are considered highly 'masculine', while sports such as figure skating and diving are viewed as less 'masculine'. Male football and hockey players, therefore, have their masculinity reinforced through their participation more so than male figure skaters and divers. There is, however, also a pecking order of masculinity *within* each sport. For example, inferences that physical abilities are more 'natural' for athletes of colour than for White athletes reinforce a particular and racist view of masculinity. In such cases, athletes of colour might on the one hand be valued positively for their physical skills, but on the other hand not given the respect accorded to White male athletes who are considered physically talented, and also intelligent and more hard-working. That First Nations athletes have been marginalized in these ways can be seen in media accounts of successful Native athletes such as Tom Longboat, an Iroquoian long-distance runner from the early 1900s. On this issue, Kidd (1983) documents and debunks racist critiques levelled at Longboat in the newspapers, which criticized his training techniques even as they praised his 'natural' athletic talents.

An intramale hierarchy based on styles of play has also been identified in Inuit hockey. Collings and Condon (1996) noted a common claim among White southerners in the North—that hockey was a universal [i.e., non-racial] activity:

> [Hockey] brings people together in friendly, managed competition . . . hockey is a universal language, easily spoken by all involved, regardless of race or culture. . . . This attitude is frequently expressed by white southerners who work in the Arctic, and the main objective of many of these recreationally minded people is to encourage people to play sports and to teach them the proper, [non-racial] Canadian way of doing so (Collings and Condon 1996:257).

Collings and Condon (1996) went on to show, however, that non-Inuit who played hockey in the Holman league frequently complained about the Inuit style of play:

> [Southerners] frequently complain that Holman Inuit do not have well-developed skills and do not use teamwork. . . . The game is often violent in a manner unfamiliar to these outsiders. . . . A former [White] recreation coordinator once complained that the problem with the way Inuit play hockey was that they 'weren't real men.' They relied on hitting people from behind and skating away (what Holman players call 'bothering') instead of dropping the gloves and fighting it out on the ice. According to Inuit informants, this same recreation coordinator was famous for chasing those players he perceived were taking cheap shots at him from behind (Collings and Condon 1996:257).

This Inuit style of play fits with traditional Native methods of violent expression, which rarely involve face-to-face confrontation. Non-Inuit players, however, adhere to different norms 'in which the players drop their gloves and seek to pulverize each other with their fists in a face-to-face encounter' (Collings and Condon 1996:257), which is perceived to be more 'manly'. In doing so, non-Inuit players create a hierarchy of masculine behaviours that emphasizes confrontational and aggressive masculinity (Gillet, White, and Young 1996).

Interestingly, Inuit athletes construct different norms of masculinity. Collings and Condon (1996) noted that many of their Inuit informants insisted that: "'Inuit skate faster than non-Inuit." This suggests an alternate mechanism by which some young people can define themselves as Inuit. Not only do Inuit hunt and fish . . . they skate faster and shoot harder than the non-Inuit who play against them' (Collings and Condon 1996:261). This alternative hierarchy of masculinity, in which Native male athletes see themselves as being more athletically talented than White athletes, aligns with the previously mentioned societal assumption that Black athletes are more gifted in some sports than Whites (Hoberman 1997).

Of course, the characterization of the behaviour of First Nations men in sport as 'less civilized' has historical precedent. The traditional Native sport of *tewaarathon*, or lacrosse, was reconfigured in a more 'civilized' direction in 1869 by W. George Beers, who created the first standardized set of rules for the game:

> The present game, improved and reduced to rule by the whites, employs the greatest combination of physical and mental activity white men can sustain in recreation. And is as much superior to the original [Indian game] as civilization is to barbarism, baseball to its old English parent of rounders, or a pretty Canadian girl to any uncultivated squaw (Beers cited in Vennum 1994:265).

This statement by W. George Beers, the White 'father' credited by many (c.f., Vellathotham and Jones 1974) with introducing the sport of lacrosse, is permeated by hierarchical race and gender meanings. This imbalance of race and gender power was further cemented in 1880 when Native (male) athletes, as a race, were banned from amateur lacrosse, ostensibly because many Native athletes were being paid—a class issue—and because their style of play was considered quite violent—a race issue (Metcalfe 1976; Vennum 1994). Thus, through institutionalized racism a hierarchy was established among male athletes of different races in lacrosse.

Evidence of a racial hierarchy in women's sport is more difficult to find, in part because there has been so little written on Native women in sport. However, historical evidence points to differential treatment of Native women rodeo competitors at the turn of the century. At that time, rodeo cowgirls were part of a culture that celebrated athleticism, skill, competitiveness, and grit as appropriate female traits (LeCompte 1993). While LeCompte found no record of participation by African-American women or Chicanas in the rodeo, in some rodeos prior to the Second World War there were special events for Native Americans, including races for 'Squaws'. In order to compete, both male and female Native competitors sometimes had to camp on the rodeo ground and provide 'Native entertainment'.

Only a few of these competitors went on to compete in mainstream rodeo, although 'several females, including Emma Blackfox, Good Elk, and Princess Redbird, [did move] beyond the special events to succeed in standard competition' (LeCompte 1993:3). Today, rodeos no longer include special 'Indian' events. Native athletes formed their own rodeo circuit in the 1970s, and as LeCompte (1993) noted, today some of their top competitors, such as Shelly Bird-Matthews, 1990 barrel racing champion at the Indian National Rodeo Finals, progress to the National Finals Rodeo. For example, in 1991 Bird-Matthews was 'a rookie qualifier for the barrel racing finals at the National Finals Rodeo, the world's richest rodeo' (LeCompte 1993:3). In sum, while a racial hierarchy among female rodeo competitors did exist during the early years of rodeo, there is some anecdotal evidence that opportunities for rodeo competitions have expanded in recent years.

Explicitly Symbolic Race/Gender Relations

When cultural practices lie within the control of Native individuals, activities are sometimes set up to emphasize their racial uniqueness in relation to mainstream activities. This (re)production of a desired racial identity has particular notions of gender embedded within it. Ceremonial dances, powwows, and traditional games and sports (such as lacrosse) are prominent in symbolic declarations of a distinctive racial identity for First Nations peoples (Deloria 1993).

For example, in the Native newspaper *Windspeaker*, an article about the upcoming North American Indigenous Games included a photograph of two young Native children (a boy and a girl), dressed in traditional clothes and with their faces painted, holding a cheque from a Royal Bank representative (Hayes 1996). Another article on the Games included a photograph of Aboriginal adults in traditional dress arriving in an 'Aboriginal ocean-going canoe' (Barnsley 1997:4)—even though the sixteen events in the North American Indigenous Games were all contemporary, mainstream sports. Thus, the images selected by the newspaper depicted an explicitly Native racial identity.

Lacrosse has also been used as a vehicle for the expression of racial uniqueness. In the early 1970s the Iroquois formed their own league for box lacrosse, and it was from this organization that the impetus came in 1983 to form a national Iroquois team, including players from all six Iroquois nations. In 1990 the Iroquois Nationals competed in the Lacrosse World Games, using their own Haudenosaunee passports (George-Kanentiio 1995). This was the first time they had been accepted for international competition in more than a century (Vennum 1994). There are now national Iroquois teams for women and juniors as well as men. Oren Lyons, one of the principal figures of the Iroquois Nationals, sees this team as a highly visible expression of sovereignty, being:

... the first completely Indian sports team to achieve full national recognition by other countries ... [he advocates] for the retention of native traditions while promoting activities which strengthen Indian political rights ... sovereignty ... is a people acting upon their principles and undertaking collective actions which make for distinctions (George-Kanentiio 1995:94).

The photograph that accompanied this text in *Akwesasne Notes* showed Lyons in traditional dress holding a lacrosse stick, with his hand on the shoulder of a younger male Native lacrosse player dressed in modern equipment and his Iroquois Nationals jersey. The message was clear: the racial identity and racial distinctiveness of both male individuals had been consciously and explicitly constructed for the reader.

A similar construction of racial identity is evident in accounts of powwows (Paraschak 1996b). Native athletes, both male and female, speak about their experience of dancing as something that is *beyond* sport. Amos Keye, head judge at the Grand River Champion of Champions powwow, explains:

When executing your dance and it's coming together—your outfit, your feet, the music—the euphoria just carries you through the song. . . . When you become euphoric you become oblivious to the pain so you have more stamina and can dance 4 to 5 minutes in the sun with 40 to 50 pounds of stuff in 40 degree weather. . . . You demonstrate to the Creator how proud you are in your body—you demonstrate that you are well and thankful for the breath of life in you (cited in Green 1997:2).

Powwows are clearly delineated by gender. While powwows were initially held by male warrior society members, today's events include men, women, and children, although males and females compete in separate events. Gender relations are reflected in the style of their dance. Women were originally only involved in a supportive dance role, exhibiting a style that was very modest. A more vigorous male style of dance, and male dominance in powwow organizations, reflected broader male leadership among Northern Plains tribal cultures. However, in keeping with other changes in gender relations over time, women have won expanded roles at powwows, and increased the vigour of some of their dance events (in particular the very active Fancy Dances, including the Shawl and Jingle Dress Dances) (Huenemann 1992; Kavanagh 1992; Paraschak 1996b).

Race/Gender Relations Symbolic of the 'Other'

Euroamericans come to know who they are, in part, by knowing how they differ from the 'Other'—that is, people from other cultures. Depictions of otherness are usually stereotypical and framed within a Euroamerican context.[7] For example, stereotypes of Natives are widespread in the entertainment industry. Berkhofer (1979), among others, has identified the images of Native Americans in film, photographs, literature, and the popular media, where they are often portrayed as 'lacking history, disappearing, culturally static, childlike, silent, and part of the natural world. Different nations/tribes of Native Americans are invisible and go unrecognized as the image almost always portrayed is that of the "generic American Indian"' (Davis 1993:14). Native athletes have also been portrayed stereotypically as belonging to a distinct, exotic, inferior race who could not be civilized.

Representations of First Nations peoples in popular culture have thus been shaped by their role as the exotic 'Other' in North American life. In sport, this process began early. When Native lacrosse players went on tour to England in 1876 and 1883, and participated in exhibition matches in the United States (e.g., in Chicago in 1895), they were often displayed as a spectacle (Morrow 1982; Vennum 1994). Their lacrosse skills, while impressive, were insufficient to warrant their inclusion—they had to appear 'Indian' as well. Predominantly non-Native crowds were attracted to seeing:

> . . . a genuine, primitive, violent sport. And to make certain that the Indian players fit European expectations, tour promoters invariably saw that they wore feathered headdresses, moccasins, and other stereotypical costuming for the game. Frequently the players had to perform double duty by concluding their entertainment with a 'war dance' (Vennum 1994:268).

While there was an attempt, through these tours, to increase interest in playing lacrosse, 'not only were Indians the best players to demonstrate the game but they were an attraction in themselves . . . a curiosity' (Vennum 1994:267). These tours represented male Native lacrosse players as savages in much the same way that they were portrayed in Wild West shows or theatrical plays at that time.

A form of 'civilized' masculinity was thus being constructed, largely by parodying Native 'savages' against White 'amateurs'. Although race was privileged over gender as a marker of difference for these athletes, images of gender were being reproduced at the same time through notions of racialized masculinity.

This practice continues in a similar form today. In Alberta the Wild Horse Show and Buffalo Chase concludes 'as five young Indian warriors, riding bareback, sporting war paint and clad in fur and buckskin, drive eight young buffalo down the hillside and into a rodeo ring' (Albrecht 1997:B3). The idea for this show was stimulated by tourists' desire to see live animals in action at the nearby Head-Smashed-In Buffalo Jump. The show, a virtual fabrication, reproduces imagery of a savage Native masculinity.

The Euroamerican stereotypification of Indians as mascots at sport events also has a long history. In 1867 the first White lacrosse team in the United States called itself the 'Mohawk Lacrosse Club' (Vennum 1994). Since then, there has been a plethora of Indian mascots used throughout the sport world, and the issue has become hotly contested (Coakley 1998). For example, Davis (1993) challenged racialized masculinities connected with Indian mascots, arguing that they provided a particular version of American masculinity that was founded on Western mythology:

> The stereotype typically associated with the mascots is that of bloodthirsty savage. Native Americans are stereotyped as wild, aggressive, violent, brave, stoic, and as having a fighting spirit, traits commonly valued in athletics. . . . The myth of Native Americans as aggressors is particularly offensive because it distorts the historical reality of the white invasion of Native American lands and the conquering of people on these lands (Davis 1993:12).

Davis pointed out how the stereotypes connected with mascots reflected differences in power of Natives and Whites. It was Euroamericans who decided how Indian mascots would be depicted. The diversity of Native American cultures was ignored, and the meanings inherent in their cultural practices (such as drumming, dancing, singing, and the use of religious symbols) were misrepresented and trivialized.

Mascots also continue to project stereotyped images specifically of historical Native men, since mascots of Native women do not exist. Davis pointed out that Indian mascots were linked to masculinity, and that they were rarely connected to women's teams. Thus, 'Indian' inferred male Indian, along with qualities such as aggression and violence. White settlers were seen as the civilizers, meting out legitimate violence in order to tame primitive savages and bring democracy and freedom to the West (Davis 1993). White masculinity supposedly entailed a civilized form of violence, justified by provocation from uncivilized, dangerous Natives.

Kimmel (1987:237) explained that American aggression and violence was distinctive: 'not like a bully, seeking a confrontation, but rather in response to provocation'. He also argued that many of the common characteristics of the American social character, such as aggression, are the defining features of compulsive masculinity, 'a masculinity that must always prove itself and that is always in doubt' (Kimmel 1987:237). Thus, historical Native stereotypes have been used to justify policies that have attempted to discriminate against Native Americans and their cultures.

By contrast, Kimmel (1987:238) identified the (usually White) cowboy as a central American cultural hero—'the embodiment of the American spirit'. Embedded in the imagery of Indian mascots was this 'cowboy' version of Euroamerican masculinity, which was aligned with conceptions of hegemonic masculinity (Davis 1993).[8] Thus, the maintenance of racialized masculinities (Native versus Euroamerican) helped perpetuate the cowboy masculinity still valued by many American males. As Davis (1993:17) puts it, 'Native Americans were only viewed as 'positive' symbols of a proud fighting spirit after they were conquered, and only after large scale resistance to White control was eliminated'. In order for Euroamerican masculinity to be seen as strong, their foes (the conquered Indians) must be seen as having been equally strong.

Conclusion

This historical examination of First Nations peoples in sport illuminates various intersecting relationships between racial identity and gender relations over time. In situations where Native peoples have been in control of sport, race has sometimes been unexamined but embedded nevertheless within gender relations. At other times, Native participants have set out to emphasize a distinctive racial identity, thus (re)producing explicitly symbolic race/gender relations. Once control over sport is shifted into non-Native hands, however, racial hierarchies that marginalize Native athletes have often been constructed. In addition, select stereotypic images of Native peoples are often (re)produced in sport, which symbolize Natives as the 'Other' within mainstream society.

In terms of gender relations among Native peoples, some accounts (Cheska 1974; Craig 1973; Paraschak 1990, 1995, 1996a) suggest that there has been an acceptance of female involvement as indicated by evidence of active female involvement and interest. However, other accounts (Collings and Condon 1996; Condon 1995; Heine 1991) suggest that sport and traditional activities were historically more popular and accessible to men, and that in contemporary society, Native men have been more able than women to gain self-esteem and acceptance through their sporting prowess. These trends support the position that Native sport, like Euroamerican sport, retains patriarchal underpinnings.

First Nations sport culture does, however, reflect ongoing shifts in gender relations between Native and non-Native communities, and within Native communities. It also indicates, in some instances, a choice on the part of Native participants to use sport in an explicitly symbolic way in order to galvanize a particular, preferred First Nations' racial identity.

While athletes competing in all-Native environments (re)produce gender relations specific to their culture, Native men and women often encounter racism as an integral part of their experience in mainstream sport. Historically, a racial hierarchy was constructed, with 'civilized' (i.e., non-Native) forms of gender behaviour as the preferred choice. Native behaviour was monitored and reshaped, even eliminated in order to realign it with mainstream, non-Native values. Acceptable forms of behaviour were clarified, in part, by contrasting them against stereotyped 'uncivilized' behaviours of Native peoples.

In sum, power relations in the lives of the First Nations peoples are complex. Gender processes and identities commonly involve racial identities, and often are framed by the colonial relations of power between Natives and Euroamericans.

Thus, when we look at the power of Native peoples to define sport for themselves and to gain access to societal resources in the pursuit of such possibilities, we certainly need to compare opportunities for Native peoples relative to those for non-Natives, but we also need to compare how sport has been structured within and between Native communities themselves. Only by conducting such a multilayered analysis does the full complexity of gender processes that touch Native communities and sports become clear.

Notes

1. The Eurocentric conception of 'sport' limits an understanding of the role of gender relations in the construction and reproduction of physical cultural practices, which may be perceived by some as sport, recreation, leisure, 'traditional games', entertainment, and/or religious practices. Therefore, I will use this term in its widest interpretation.

2. Lorber (1993) explores, for example, how gender ideology constructs biological dichotomies to justify 'naturalized' male-female differences. She thus challenges the argument that innate biological male-female differences lead to necessarily different and unequal gender roles in society.

3. Power, as used in this chapter, includes the capacity to (1) structure and institutionalize sport in preferred ways, (2) establish select sport traditions, and (3) define the range of 'legitimate' practices and meanings associated with dominant sport patterns (Gruneau 1988). Richard Dyer notes that 'Power in contemporary society habitually passes itself off as embodied in the normal as opposed to the superior' (cited in hooks 1995:36). See *Ethos* 25, no. 1 (e.g., Stoler 1997) for several papers addressing the relationship between race as a category of power and race as a category of mind.

4. For example, Frankenberg (1993) examines racialized constructions of masculinity and femininity in her book, *White Women, Race Matters: The Social Construction of Whiteness*. hooks (1995) identifies the relational nature of race and class, noting that privileged Blacks avoid discussing class and instead emphasize race alone as the system of domination, thus failing to note the ways that class power mediates the degree of racist exploitation that occurs. Messner (1990) looks specifically at masculinities in sport, which are differentially shaped by social class and race.

5. West and Zimmerman (1991:24) talk about 'doing gender'. The process involves creating differences between males and females, then using those differences 'to reinforce the "essentialness" of gender' in standardized social occasions such as sporting events. There is thus an ongoing construction of gender relations through the 'doing' of cultural practices.

6. I use the term 'race' here as a socially constructed marker of difference, based on perceived visual differences in skin colour between individuals.

7. hooks (1995:38) identifies the stereotype as one form of representation, which is 'a projection on to the Other that makes them less threatening'.

8. If the settling of the West helped to define Euroamerican manhood, and sport has replaced the frontier as a site where masculinity can be preserved, then it seems feasible that Western frontier symbolism would be carried through into sport (see Davis 1993).

References

Albrecht, C. 1997. 'Buffalo Roam, and Run Again'. *The Windsor Star* (13 September):B3.

Barnsley, P. 1997. 'BC Prepares to Host '97 Indigenous Games'. *Windspeaker* (June):4.

Berkhofer, R. 1979. *The White Man's Indian*. New York: Vintage Books.

Cheska, A. 1974. 'Ball Game Participation of North American Indian Women'. *Proceedings from Third Canadian Symposium on History of Sport and Physical Education*, 1–32. Halifax: Dalhousie University.

Churchill, W., N. Hill, Jr, and M.J. Barlow. 1979. 'An Historical Overview of Twentieth Century Native American Athletes'. *The Indian Historian* 12:22–32.

Coakley, J. 1998. *Sport in Society: Issues and Controversies*, 6th edn. New York: Irwin McGraw-Hill.

Collings, P., and R. Condon. 1996. 'Blood on the Ice: Status, Self-Esteem, and Ritual Injury Among Inuit Hockey Players'. *Human Organization* 55:253–62.

Condon, R. 1995. 'The Rise of the Leisure Class: Adolescence and Recreational Acculturation in the Canadian Arctic'. *Ethos* 23:47–68.

Craig, S. 1973. 'Indian Sportswomen'. *The Sportswoman* 1:10–13.

Culin, S. [1907] 1992. *Games of the North American Indians*. Lincoln: University of Nebraska Press.

Davis, L. 1993. 'Protest Against the Use of Native American Mascots: A Challenge to Traditional American Identity'. *Journal of Sport and Social Issues* 17:9–22.

Deloria, P. 1993. 'Being a Twentieth-Century Indian'. In *The Native Americans: An Illustrated History*, edited by E. Ballantine and I. Ballantine, 386–405. Atlanta: Turner Publishing.

Frankenberg, R. 1993. *The Social Construction of Whiteness: White Women, Race Matters*. Minneapolis: University of Minnesota Press.

George-Kanentiio, D. 1995. 'The Iroquois Nationals: Creating a Sports Revolution for American Indians'. *Akwesasne Notes* 1:95.

Gillet, J., P. White, and K. Young. 1996. 'The Prime Minister of Saturday Night: Don Cherry, the CBC, and the Cultural Production of Intolerance'. In *Seeing Ourselves: Media Power and Policy in Canada*, edited by H. Holmes and D. Taras, 59–72. Toronto: Harcourt Brace.

Green, S. 1997. 'Powwow Preparations'. *Tekawennake* 23:1–2.

Gruneau, R. 1988. 'Modernization or Hegemony: Two Views on Sport and Social Development'. In *Not Just a Game: Essays in Canadian Sport Sociology*, edited by J. Harvey and H. Cantelon, 9–32. Ottawa: University of Ottawa Press.

Hayes, R. 1996. 'Games Sign Corporate Sponsors: But the 1997 Indigenous Games Funding Is Still Far from Settled'. *Windspeaker* (December):16.

Heine, M. 1991. 'The Symbolic Capital of Honor: Gambling Games and the Social Construction of Gender in Tlingit Indian Culture'. *Play & Culture* 4:346–58.

————. 1995. 'Gwich'in Tsii'in: A History of Gwich'in Athapaskan Games'. Ph.D. dissertation, University of Alberta.

Hoberman, J. 1997. *Darwin's Athletes: How Sport Has Damaged Black America and Preserved the Myth of Race*. Boston: Houghton Mifflin.

hooks, b. 1995. *Killing Rage: Ending Racism*. New York: Henry Holt and Company.

Huenemann, L. 1992. 'Northern Plains Dance'. In *Native American Dance: Ceremonies and Social Traditions*, edited by C. Heth, 125–47. Washington, DC: National Museum of the American Indian, Smithsonian Institution.

Kavanagh, T. 1992. 'Southern Plains Dance: Tradition and Dynamism'. In *Native American Dance: Ceremonies and Social Traditions*, edited by C. Heth, 105–23. Washington, DC: National Museum of the American Indian, Smithsonian Institution.

Kidd, B. 1983. 'In Defense of Tom Longboat'. *Canadian Journal of History of Sport* XIV:34–63.

Kimmel, M. 1987. 'The Cult of Masculinity: American Social Character and the Legacy of the Cowboy'. In *Beyond Patriarchy: Essays by Men on Pleasure, Power, and Change*, edited by M. Kaufman, 235–49. Toronto: Oxford University Press.

LeCompte, M. 1993. *Cowgirls of the Rodeo: Pioneer Professional Athletes*. Chicago: University of Illinois Press.

Lorber, J. 1993. 'Believing Is Seeing: Biology as Ideology'. *Gender and Society* 7:568–81.

Messner, M. 1990. 'Masculinities and Athletic Careers: Bonding and Status Differences'. In *Sport, Men and the Gender Order: Critical Feminist Perspectives*, edited by M. Messner and D. Sabo, 97–108. Champaign, IL: Human Kinetics.

Metcalfe, A. 1976. 'Sport and Athletics: A Case Study of Lacrosse in Canada, 1840–1889'. *Journal of Sport History* 3:1–19.

Morrow, D. 1982. 'The Canadian Image Abroad: The Great Lacrosse Tours of 1876 and 1883'. *Proceedings of the Fifth Canadian Symposium on the History of Sport and Physical Education*, 11–23. Toronto: University of Toronto.

Nabokov, P. 1981. *Indian Running: Native American History and Tradition*. Santa Fe: Ancient City Press.

Oxendine, J. 1988. *American Indian Sports Heritage*. Champaign, IL: Human Kinetics.

Paraschak, V. 1990. 'Organized Sport for Native Females on the Six Nations Reserve, Ontario from 1968–1980: A Comparison of Dominant and Emergent Sport Systems'. *Canadian Journal of History of Sport* XXI:70–80.

_____. 1995. 'Invisible But Not Absent: Aboriginal Women in Sport and Recreation'. *Canadian Women's Studies* 15:71–2.

_____. 1996a. 'An Examination of Sport for Aboriginal Females on the Six Nations Reserve, Ontario, from 1968 to 1980'. In *Women of the First Nations: Power, Wisdom and Strength*, edited by C. Miller and P. Chuchryk, 83–96. Winnipeg: University of Manitoba Press.

_____. 1996b. 'Racialized Spaces: Cultural Regulation, Aboriginal Agency and Powwows'. *Avante* 2:7–18.

_____. 1997. 'Variations in Race Relations: Sporting Events for Native Peoples in Canada'. *Sociology of Sport Journal* 14:1–21.

Smith, G. 1993. 'A Woman of the People'. *Sports Illustrated* (1 March):54–64.

Stoler, A.L. 1997. 'On Political and Psychological Essentialisms'. *Ethos* 25:101–6.

The Sports Network. 1991. 'For the Love of the Game: A White Man's Game?'

Vellathottam, T., and K. Jones. 1974. 'Highlights in the Development of Canadian Lacrosse to 1931'. *Canadian Journal of History of Sport and Physical Education* III:31–47.

Vennum, T. 1994. *American Indian Lacrosse: Little Brother of War*. Washington, DC: Smithsonian Institution Press.

West, C., and D. Zimmerman. 1991. 'Doing Gender'. In *The Social Construction of Gender*, edited by J. Lorber and S. Farrell, 13–37. Newbury Park, CA: Sage.

Young, K., P. White, and W. McTeer. 1994. 'Body Talk: Male Athletes Reflect on Sport, Injury, and Pain'. *Sociology of Sport Journal* 11:175–94.

Zeman, B. 1988. *To Run with Longboat: Twelve Stories of Indian Athletes in Canada*. Edmonton: GMS Ventures Inc.

Chapter 9

Women, Sport, and Sexualities:

Breaking the Silences

Helen Jefferson Lenskyj

An understanding of sexuality issues is central to any analysis of gender and sport. Sport, perhaps more than other human activities that take place in the public realm, compels us to consider the physical body and in doing so we inevitably observe both the biological sex of that body (male or female) and its socially constructed gender identity (masculine or feminine). Gender identities are not, however, viewed or evaluated equally. In a society where the 'sexploitation' of female bodies is an everyday occurrence in the media, advertising, and entertainment industries, female athletes' bodies are also routinely subjected to inappropriate sexualization and objectification, while male athletes are evaluated primarily in terms of their sporting ability. In this chapter, the social construction of gender identity in and through contemporary sporting practices will be examined, with particular attention to lesbian invisibility in sport.

Gender, Sport, and Sexualities

In the Canadian sporting context, as in most Western countries, there is a close fit between the ideal male/masculine body and that of the male athlete. Consider the physical and social characteristics of that national icon of Canadian manhood, the NHL player: tall, strong, muscular, White, middle class, and heterosexual. This approved brand of masculinity, which has been termed 'hegemonic masculinity' (Connell 1987), both reflects and reinforces prevailing ideologies and social systems.

It is against the standard of hegemonic masculinity that most Canadian boys and men are measured and, in many cases, found lacking. For example, it is not uncommon for parents or teachers of a non-conforming ('sissy') boy to encourage (or even force) him to take up a team or combat sport 'for his own good'. With this masculinizing function so central to Canadian sport, it is easy to see why girls and women continue to be treated as outsiders and intruders. If, according to this line of thinking, sport makes boys into (heterosexual) men, what, then, does it do to girls?

Although many Canadian girls and women now have greater access to sport in schools and communities, many kinds of sporting activities are still viewed as inappropriate for girls and women, primarily because they are perceived to 'masculinize'. As well as developing the physical attributes of hegemonic masculinity (such as strength, endurance, and muscularity), sport is believed to promote so-called masculine personality traits such as risk taking, dominance, and aggression. Sport has the potential to change women's minds as well as women's bodies and, if this were allowed, it could be argued that the entire balance of power between the sexes could be in jeopardy (Lenskyj 1986).

The concept of 'emphasized femininity' (Connell 1987)—for example, the Barbie doll image—helps to explain how societal expectations concerning approved female behaviour and presentation of self are reproduced and reinforced. In this process, an emphasis on secondary sex differences helps to reinforce male dominance, female subordination, and conventional expressions of heterosexuality. It is no coincidence that a woman shaped like Barbie would not be a very successful participant in most current sporting events. Nor is it a coincidence that many of the changes that take place in the adolescent male's body during puberty—increased muscular strength and lean body mass, for example—enhance his athletic performance, while the changes in the adolescent female's body—the development of breasts and hips, and increased body fat— are likely to impede her performance in many sports.

However, although the types of sports that are most highly regarded and rewarded in North America today generally require the approved 'masculine' body, it is also possible to imagine a world of sport based on alternative values and attributes such as grace, coordination, flexibility, and aesthetic appeal—a sporting arena where women and children and people of all body types and levels of ability were welcomed. Certainly, dramatic changes in society, specifically in power relations based on gender, social class, race/ethnicity, and sexuality differences, would need to occur before this inclusive vision of sporting practices could be implemented. An important first step towards this goal is to uncover the hidden or taken-for-granted ways in which sport is used to promote hegemonic masculinity and emphasized femininity both in the sport context and in the wider Canadian society.

The 'Isms' in Sport

Female sport has long suffered from the destructive impact of several related forces, the most significant being sexism, homophobia, and heterosexism. These can be defined briefly as follows. Sexism refers to unfair and prejudiced treatment of women, both at the individual and the institutional level. In sport, the exclusion of females has commonly been achieved by invoking the 'female frailty' myth—that is, the notion that anatomy and physiology make the female body weak and injury-prone, and hence unsuited to most sporting activities (Lenskyj 1986). Homophobia signifies an irrational fear or hatred of lesbians and gay men, manifested in harassment and even physical or sexual violence. Heterosexism refers to social systems in which heterosexuality is rewarded and reinforced as the only normal, natural and/or appropriate expression of human sexuality. Other kinds of prejudice can interact with these 'isms' to limit women's equal access to sport, the most serious being 'classism' and racism evident in the policies and practices of sport organizations and the wider society.

Because of the long-standing popular view that women who play 'men's sports' are sexually suspect, sportswomen of all sexual orientations may be targets of homophobic harassment. Hence, many lesbians in sport are understandably secretive about their sexual orientation, while heterosexual women may disassociate themselves from their lesbian teammates. As a result of this 'chilly climate', solidarity among women in sport is eroded. When rifts occur within women's sport organizations, as they frequently do, they reduce the effectiveness of advocacy work aimed at improving the status of women in sport (Lenskyj 1990).

Only in the last few years have sport leaders begun systematically to address the problem of harassment and violence experienced by girls and women in sport contexts. It is interesting to note how the recent disclosures of sexual abuse suffered by young *male* hockey players galvanized the Canadian sporting community, the media, and the public. Several highly publicized cases involved young men who, as adolescents, had been sexually abused by male coaches or hockey arena employees. Decades of harassment and sexual violation of girls and women in sport have, however, failed to evoke similar levels of organizational or emotional response. Even when several young women disclosed their experiences of sexual abuse by their male coaches on CBC television in 1993, national and provincial sport organizations did not respond by developing system-wide policies and procedures.

It is ironic that the intense public response to the hockey scandals was prompted by homophobia and heterosexism: in the 'wholesome' world of (male) hockey, according to this line of reasoning, one would not expect to find men who were sexually attracted to adolescent boys. Conversely, the relative tolerance in some sport circles towards male coaches who prey on young female athletes reflects a heterosexist view of 'normal' male sexual expression (Lenskyj 1992).

Gender and Sexuality in Sport Research

In the 1960s and 1970s sport researchers began to take issues of gender and sexuality into account, although their work generally failed to challenge hegemonic masculinity and emphasized femininity. In 1965 Metheny developed a sport typology with some implicit messages about sexuality. For example, she found that sport involving the use of heavy objects or body contact exceeded the boundaries of middle-class White femininity, which required handling only light objects and involved physical separation (e.g., a net in tennis) between opponents. Most team, contact, and combat sport did not meet these requirements.

In a similar vein, sport scholars of the 1970s identified what they termed the 'apologetic' in women's sport—the practice of devoting time and energy to gender-appropriate modes of self-presentation in dress, hairstyles, and general 'ladylike' deportment (Felshin 1974). This phenomenon was largely a response to the public and media obsession with female athletes' physical appearance and marital and family status, exemplified by headlines that stressed the 'housewife' status of Olympic medal winners. The possibility that sportswomen's 'apologetic' behaviour might be a reasonable response to the climate of heterosexism and homophobia in sport was rarely articulated.

At the same time, most sport psychologists were preoccupied with the presumed 'role conflict' that sportswomen must experience because of the alleged incompatibility between 'femininity' and athletic competence (for critiques, see Allison 1991; Hall 1981). 'Femininity' and 'masculinity' were initially treated as polar opposites, and even when bipolar scales were introduced and androgyny was held up as the new standard of desirable sex-role adjustment, sportswomen continued to be theorized as 'problems'. It became clear that 'feminine' in sex role/sport socialization studies was a codeword for heterosexual. Within this tradition, many sex-role researchers set out to demonstrate that sportswomen, particularly those in traditionally male sports or male-dominated occupations (coaches and administrators for example), ranked low on femininity scales, or high on masculinity and androgyny scales. They persisted in their efforts as late as the 1990s, thus entrenching the very stereotypes that more progressive researchers were attempting to dispel.

As well as being heterosexist, this way of thinking indicates some confusion between the concepts of sex differentiation (male/female), sex-role orientation (masculine/feminine/androgynous), and sexual orientation (homosexual/bisexual/heterosexual). Sex differentiation is based on genetic, morphological, hormonal, and social criteria. There is no necessary correlation between morphological or hormonal factors and sexual orientation, and research on the possible genetic roots of sexual orientation remains inconclusive. The use of social criteria in sex differentiation and sex-role orientation is by definition imprecise, since social definitions of sex-appropriate behaviour vary according to specific historical and social-cultural contexts. What is seen as appropriate behaviour for women in one culture—for example, decorating one's body—may be viewed as a masculine activity in another. Turning to sport examples, in baseball, spitting may be more commonly associated with male than female players (and therefore considered inappropriate for 'feminine' women). However, if the context were marathon running, spitting would probably have no particular gender association.

It is an erroneous and circular argument to claim that heterosexual women are more feminine in their sex-role orientation than lesbians, since culturally specific (North American) definitions of 'femininity' are largely based on the appearance and behaviour of heterosexual women, and connotations of 'femininity' are closely linked to notions of heterosexual identity and attractiveness. An individual's conformity or non-conformity to prevailing definitions of appropriate sex-role behaviour is a poor predictor of sexual orientation. In the sport context, this means that a woman's self-presentation and style in softball, for example, might be perceived as rendering her less 'feminine' than her counterpart in figure skating. Such superficial perceptions reveal little about sexual orientation and much about the social construction of the 'feminine' woman. Equally important, they are indicative of the value placed on the appearance of heterosexual femininity in female sport; as long as sportswomen *appear* heterosexual, the status quo can be maintained.

Breaking the Silence about Sport and Sexuality

By the 1980s and early 1990s, the advocacy efforts of the women's movements and the lesbian/gay rights movements were having some positive influence on opening up discussion about sexuality issues in sport. Recognition that lesbians do play sport and that homophobia is a pervasive problem was becoming evident in the mainstream sport studies literature.

It is encouraging to note that in the last decade many feminist sport scholars have begun to examine the ways in which female sexualities are constructed and constrained by homophobia and heterosexism. They have documented how girls and women in sport experience pressure from family, peers, coaches, and the media to present themselves as unequivocally heterosexual in appearance and behaviour to avoid the 'lesbian label'. Thus, valuable time and energy are wasted in misguided efforts to present female sport and sportwomen as 'feminine' while open or outspoken lesbians are accused of damaging the reputation of their sport (see, for example, Burroughs et al. 1995; Fusco 1992; Krane 1996; Rogers 1995). The 'divide and rule' tactics of homophobic sport leaders and media effectively deepen the rifts between lesbian and non-lesbian athletes and, lacking political solidarity, sportswomen have little hope of challenging the male monopoly on sport resources. General discussions of homophobic attitudes and practices are also appearing more frequently in sport scholarship—see, for example, Etue and Williams (1996) on Canadian women's ice hockey, Scraton (1992) on British secondary school physical education, and Hargreaves (1994) and Kane and Greendorfer (1994) on representations of sexuality in female sport. A special issue of *Women in Sport and Physical Activity Journal* (Fall 1997) is the first of its kind to devote a special issue to lesbians in sport (Lenskyj 1997).

Focus on Lesbians in Sport

One of the most significant histories of sexuality and sport in the United States is Susan Cahn's *Coming on Strong* (1993). Her interviews with women growing up and coming out as lesbian from the 1930s to the 1950s and her analysis of the impact of conservative popular opinion of female physical education and sport provide a comprehensive picture of the uneasy relationship between lesbians and sport. My own book, *Out of Bounds: Women, Sport and Sexuality* (1986), examined similar trends in physical education, the medical establishment, and the media from 1890 to the 1980s, with a particular focus on Canada.

It has been shown that in some scenarios sport has provided a haven for women who prefer a homosocial environment, ostensibly free from pressure to behave and present oneself in a conventionally heterosexual manner. In these cases, sport was well known by lesbians as a relatively safe place and a possible contact point. When same-sex relationships were not only socially stigmatized but also prohibited by law, it was important for women to develop safe alternatives to gay bars as places to meet other lesbians. At the same time, growing public, media, and commercial interest in women's sport threatened the safety of lesbian athletes. The 'femininity' (and hence, the heterosexuality) of all female athletes came under scrutiny and the economic survival of female sport came to rely in large part on an appropriately 'feminine' image (Cahn 1993; Lenskyj 1986).

A lesbian sport anthology edited by Susan Fox Rogers (1995) provides further insights into the pervasive problem of homophobia, including a compelling account by Mariah Burton Nelson of her experiences while coming out as a lesbian in women's professional basketball. Nelson explains how, in the 1980s, an earlier version of this article had been purchased twice—by *Ms* magazine and *Women's Sports*—but had never appeared in print because of publishers' fears that advertisers would withdraw their accounts from magazines that mentioned lesbians (Nelson 1994). Her anecdote amply illustrates the obstacles to lesbian visibility in the 1980s. As one of the few sportswomen who was prepared to risk disclosing her lesbian identity, Nelson was denied the right to do so by publishers concerned about losing advertising dollars.

In a parallel Canadian example, national volleyball coach Betty Baxter, in a 1984 interview for CBC television, stated that she believed she had been fired from her position because she was lesbian. However, the power of her decision to come out as a lesbian on national television was significantly diluted by CBC editors, who used the interviewer's voice to dub over Betty's own telling of her story.

Nelson (1991) also grappled with other kinds of contradictions in the lives of lesbian professional athletes in her earlier book, *Are We Winning Yet?* Her study included interviews with lesbian professional golfers, who revealed how their fears of losing sponsorship dollars and popularity with their heterosexual fans resulted, paradoxically, in their resentment of openly lesbian fans and secrecy and shame about their own lesbian identities.

While it is tempting to conclude from these examples that economic forces lie behind lesbian (in)visibility in sport, other evidence reveals that the issue is more complex. A college coach who identified herself as lesbian (but only in her 'private life') was among the most homophobic of the women interviewed in Rogers's anthology. Apparently believing the 'mannish lesbian' or the 'third sex' myth, this coach stated:

> People feel they [lesbian players] have an unfair advantage in terms of their physical abilities and they think they intimidate other players . . . too many lesbians in women's sports make for a lot of problems that create bad teams and bad team playing and have an overall detrimental effect on the sports themselves (Brownworth 1994:82ff.).

I have cited her statement in full in order to point to the barriers to social change in female sport, and to the inadequacies of the lesbian/heterosexual dichotomy for understanding the dynamics of homophobia. Although she is lesbian herself, this coach's statement reveals internalized homophobia: not only in her self-hatred, self-denial, and the splitting of her private and public lives but also in her resentment and hostility towards other lesbians, especially those who are open about their sexuality. Until the sport climate is more lesbian-positive, it is understandable that some lesbians will develop coping strategies that may work in the short term, but that in the long term are detrimental both to themselves and to women's sport. As an Olympic coach interviewed by Brownworth suggested in expressing her concerns about the cycle of discrimination,

> I would love to be able to come out and have every lesbian in sports come out. I think that if that happened, there would be a lot less of this kind of underhanded and subtle discrimination. But stereotypes are hard to break down. I wouldn't know how you'd even begin to go about it (Brownworth 1994:86).

This vicious circle of invisibility and homophobia in female sport needs to be interrupted on a number of levels, both individual and institutional, before social change can be effected. To this end, coalitions of lesbian and heterosexual women in sport are needed to add strength and numbers to these interventions. For example, harassment policies should specifically include homophobic harassment; employment policies should identify sexual orientation as prohibited grounds for discrimination in hiring and promotion; and health benefits plans should include same-sex as well as opposite-sex partners. It should become routine for same-sex as well as opposite-sex partners to attend sport-related social gatherings, and representations of lesbians should be included in promotional materials such as sport posters and videos, which currently reflect heterosexist assumptions. Such everyday acts would make sport a more comfortable and welcoming place for women of all sexual orientations.

Physical Education

Pressure to conceal one's lesbian identity is particularly acute for women who work in physical education with children. The homophobic myth that lesbians and gay men are pedophiles still holds sway despite ample evidence that the vast majority of pedophiles are heterosexually identified men. Even lesbians who work in postsecondary physical education or athletic departments face some of the same pressures because they work in an instructional capacity with adolescents and young adults. Gondola and Fitzpatrick (1985) and Griffin (1989) are among the early physical educators who challenged homophobia in these contexts. Others have also focused on the experiences of lesbians and gay men in education—Khayatt (1992) being one of the few Canadian examples—and some of these have examined the specific challenges confronting lesbian physical education teachers (Clarke 1993; Harbeck 1992; Woods and Harbeck 1992). Like other lesbians in sport, many lesbian PE teachers feared homophobic harassment or loss of their jobs if they disclosed their sexuality. Consequently, they often used the strategy of 'passing' as heterosexual and distanced themselves from students and colleagues and from political issues relating to homosexuality and lesbianism. As one of the participants in Woods and Harbeck's study stated, 'I'm trying to keep it [my lesbian life] very separate from my teaching' (Woods and Harbeck 1992:149). At the same time, others took advantage of the less formal dress code in PE, which makes the act of 'passing' somewhat easier. Despite school environments that were 'deeply enveloped in homophobia and heterosexism' (Woods and Harbeck 1992:160), a minority of teachers actively confronted the issues and supported lesbian/gay students. One teacher, for example, challenged students every time they used the word 'gay' as a put-down (Woods and Harbeck 1992).

Because homophobia and heterosexism have a negative impact not only on lesbians but on all physical educators, male and female, heterosexual and homosexual, Woods and Harbeck propose collective action on the part of the entire profession to deal with the fear and isolation experienced by lesbian and gay colleagues. It is therefore encouraging to see that some North American physical education organizations have led the way by putting homophobia on their conference agendas (Griffin 1989; Griffin and Genasci 1990; Sabo 1987). However, as Bouchier (1997) has documented in her analysis of lesbian sport history, there is still significant opposition to open discussion of these issues in some PE circles.

Community Sport

Of the various team sports organized at the local community level, softball has long represented a safe place for women to meet and socialize with other lesbians. The relatively recent development of lesbian softball leagues in many Canadian cities continues this tradition, but with added political impact because of their open identification as a lesbian (or lesbian-positive) space. Such leagues, which are organized along feminist principles of inclusiveness regarding sporting skills and physical ability, as well as ethnicities and socio-economic status, constitute a significant challenge to mainstream female sport (Birrell and Richter 1987). Toronto's Notso Amazon Softball League is a good example of this development (Lenskyj 1994).

Although there is evidence of progress at the community level with lesbian and/or gay softball leagues flourishing in many North American cities, positive media representations are more difficult to find. A disappointing example is the 1995 Canadian National Film Board production titled *Baseball Girls*, which documents historical and contemporary developments in the sport. While the film's celebration of women's baseball and softball is welcome, it is unfortunate that its characterizion of the players reinforces decades of lesbian invisibility and silencing. Not only is there no spoken recognition that baseball is a sport practised by women of all sexualities but excessive attention is paid to the heterosexuality of some of the women portrayed. Largely irrelevant topics such as players' images of the 'ideal' man, their marriage plans, and their sexual interest in the male umpire were emphasized in the filmmakers' apparent attempt to establish the heterosexual credentials of all involved. Market forces cannot be blamed entirely for this emphasis, since the National Film Board is subsidized by the federal government and has in the past portrayed open lesbians. One can perhaps conclude that the world of sport was considered too homophobic to permit lesbian softball players to come out on film.

Conclusion

Although the links between gender, sexuality, and sport are increasingly being addressed in the critical sport literature, relatively little has been written about lesbians' actual experiences. For many of the lesbians on the front lines of women's sport, the barriers posed by heterosexism and homophobia often seem insurmountable. These women fear harassment, violence, ostracism, and job loss if their identities become known. Additionally, their peers may blame them for giving women's sport 'a bad name' and driving away potential sponsors and allies.

At the same time, there are signs of progressive social change: provincial and federal legislation names sexual orientation as prohibited grounds for discrimination; anti-discrimination policies exist in universities, school boards, and workplaces across Canada; harassment policies have been developed by national and provincial sport organizations; and there are growing levels of public consciousness and discussion about sexuality. Canadian courts have ruled that employers have a legal as well as moral responsibility to ensure an harassment-free workplace and, in sport, this means that coaches, physical educators, and sport administrators ignore problems of sexism, heterosexism, and homophobia at their own peril.

In the wake of allegations of abuse in ice hockey early in 1997, provincial ministries of sport and recreation in both Ontario and British Columbia announced harassment prevention programs and in Ottawa, a group of over thirty national sport organizations and government bodies began developing national harassment prevention strategies. Although one is unlikely to find explicit mention of homophobic harassment of lesbians in these government initiatives, at least the groundwork has been laid in terms of policies and procedures for dealing with individual or systemic discrimination on the grounds of sexual preference.

References

Allison, M. 1991. 'Role Conflict and the Female Athlete: Preoccupation with Little Grounding'. *Journal of Applied Sport Psychology* 3:49–60.

Baseball Girls. 1995. L. Siegel, narrator, writer, and director. S. Basmajian, producer. National Film Board of Canada.

Birrell, S., and D. Richter. 1987. 'Is a Diamond Forever? Feminist Transformations of Sport'. *Women's Studies International Forum* 10:369–79.

Bouchier, N. 1997. 'Odd Girls on the Playing Field: The History of Lesbians and Social Stigma in Sport'. Paper presented at the University College Symposium on Sport and Society, University of Toronto.

Brownworth, V. 1994. 'The Competitive Closet'. In *Sports Dykes*, edited by S.F. Rogers, 75–86. New York: St Martin's Press.

Burroughs, A., L. Seebohm, and L. Ashburn. 1995. '"Add Sex and Stir": Homophobic Coverage of Women's Cricket in Australia'. *Journal of Sport and Social Issues* 19:266–84.

Cahn, S. 1993. *Coming on Strong: Gender and Sexuality in Twentieth Century Women's Sport*. New York: Free Press.

Clarke, G. 1993. 'Towards an Understanding of the Lives and Lifestyles of Lesbian Physical Education Teachers'. Paper presented to the North American Society for the Sociology of Sport Conference, Ottawa.

Connell, R.W. 1987. *Gender and Power*. Stanford: Stanford University Press.

Etue, E., and M. Williams. 1996. *On the Edge: Women Making Hockey History*. Toronto: Women's Press.

Felshin, J. 1974. 'The Dialectics of Women and Sport'. In *The American Woman in Sport*, edited by E. Gerber, J. Felshin, P. Berlin, and W. Wyrick, 179–210. Reading, MA: Addison-Wesley.

Fusco, C. 1992. 'Lesbians and Locker Rooms: The Subjective Experiences of Lesbians in Sport'. Paper presented to the North American Society for the Sociology of Sport Conference, Ottawa.

Gondola, J., and T. Fitzpatrick. 1985. 'Homophobia in Girls' Sport: "Names" That Can Hurt Us . . . All of Us'. *Equal Play* (Spring/Summer):18–19.

Griffin, P. 1984. 'How to Identity Homophobia in Women's Athletic Programs'. Paper presented to the New Agenda for Women in Sport Regional Conference, Philadelphia.

_____. 1989. 'Homophobia in Physical Education'. *Canadian Association for Health, Physical Education and Recreation Journal* 55:27–31.

_____, and J. Genasci. 1990. 'Addressing Homophobia in Physical Education: Responsibilities for Teachers and Researchers'. In *Sport, Men and the Gender Order: Critical Feminist Perspectives*, edited by M. Messner and D. Sabo, 211–21. Champaign, IL: Human Kinetics.

Hall, M.A. 1981. 'Sport, Sex Roles and Sexual Identity'. Paper #1. Ottawa: Canadian Research Institute for the Advancement of Women.

Harbeck, K., ed. 1992. *Coming Out of the Classroom Closet*. New York: Harrington Park Press.

Hargreaves, J. 1994. *Sporting Females*. London: Routledge.

Kane, M.J., and S. Greendorfer. 1994. 'The Media's Role in Accommodating and Resisting Stereotyped Images of Women in Sport'. In *Women, Media and Sport*, edited by P. Creedon, 28–44. Thousand Oaks, CA: Sage.

Khayatt, M. 1992. *Lesbian Teachers: An Invisible Presence*. New York: State University of New York Press.

Krane, V. 1996. 'Lesbians in Sport: Towards Acknowledgement, Understanding and Theory'. *Journal of Sport and Exercise Psychology* 18:237–46.

Lenskyj, H. 1986. *Out of Bounds: Women, Sport and Sexuality*. Toronto: Women's Press.

_____. 1990. 'Combating Homophobia in Sport and Physical Education: Academic and Professional Responsibilities'. *Sociology of Sport Journal* 8:61–9.

_____. 1992. 'Unsafe at Home Base: Women's Experiences of Sexual Harassment in University Sport and Physical Education'. *Women in Sport and Physical Activity Journal* 1:19–33.

_____. 1994. 'Sexuality and Femininity in Sport Contexts: Issues and Alternatives'. *Journal of Sport and Social Issues* 18:356–76.

_____. 1997. 'No Fear? Lesbians in Sport and Physical Education'. *Women in Sport and Physical Activity Journal* 6:7–22.
Metheny, E. 1965. *Connotations of Movement in Sport and Dance*. Reading, MA: Addison-Wesley.

Nelson, M.B. 1991. *Are We Winning Yet?* New York: Random House.

_____. 1994. *Paid to Play a Game*. In *Sports Dykes*, edited by S.F. Rogers, 87–94. New York: St Martin's Press.

Rogers, S.F., ed. 1995. *Sports Dykes*. New York: St Martin's Press.

Sabo, D. 1987. 'Opening the Closet Door: Some Political Implications of Doing Controversial Research'. Paper presented to the American Association for Health, Physical Education, Recreation and Dance Conference, Las Vegas.

Scraton, S. 1992. *Shaping Up to Womanhood*. Buckingham, UK: Open University Press.

Woods, S., and K. Harbeck. 1992. 'Living in Two Worlds: The Identity Management Strategies Used by Lesbian Physical Educators'. In *Coming Out of the Classroom Closet*, edited by K. Harbeck, 141–65. New York: Harrington Park Press.

Chapter 10

Fear and Trembling:

Homophobia in Men's Sport

Brian Pronger

Men's sport is typically seen as an expression of macho heterosexual identity, yet it also has an important homoerotic dimension. The physical contact of sport, the life of the locker-room, and the masculine cult of muscular, fit, and healthy bodies play to men's homoerotic sensibilities—sensibilities that express for them their deepest sense of who they are and their place in the world. For others, however, the homoerotic play of sport poses a terrible threat: it threatens their sense of who they are; it threatens their values; it threatens their feelings about how the world ought to be. Often quite unconsciously, they tend to deny or repress the homoerotic elements of sport, but these men who wouldn't call themselves gay also enjoy the 'masculinity' of sport. In fact, it may be the masculine promise of sport that appeals to them most, keeping them in front of the television set for hours at a time, carried away by the fantasy of men running around a playing field, chasing balls and other men. In high school and college the powerful allure of masculinity also induces many boys and young men to participate in contact sports like hockey and football. At least in part, they go through all of that so they can come close to the masculine mystique. But most of them will draw the line when the desire for masculinity becomes *explicitly* homoerotic. They will react with fear, a fear frequently laced with hostility.

Why is it that sport makes some men tremble with happy erotic anticipation and others quiver with hateful erotic fear? What I will suggest in this chapter is that deep in the structure of the gender order and of men's sport itself is a powerful homoerotic theme. It is a theme everybody knows about intuitively or perhaps even secretly, but, because of its immensely threatening (indeed subversive) significance, most prefer to deny it. At the centre of a world that is supposed to symbolize and celebrate masculinity, and which in fact is supposed to endow men with a powerful sense of heterosexual masculinity, is a fascinating homosexual paradox.[1]

At least in youth and for many people throughout life, the experience of homosexual desire goes hand in hand with hiding it. What is so fearful about homosexuality that boys with unrequited or fulfilled homosexual desires feel that they should conceal it? Is it just ignorance of another way of life or is it a deep sense of the significance of homosexuality that makes people afraid?

In order to understand homophobia, we must first appreciate both what is potentially fearful about homosexuality and how homosexuality differs from heterosexuality. Is it the simple physical fact that one involves sexual activity between males and females and the other between males, or is there a deeper distinction? Some men and boys who engage in homosexual behaviour find it to be a more or less simple physical sexual release. It might be a substitute for heterosexual sex, or an experiment with homosexuality that ultimately fails to resonate with the erotic needs of the experimenter—homosexuality emerges for them as inauthentic. Others, however, find homosexual activity to be harmonious, a true realization of their erotic aspirations. Evidently, the different experiences of hetero- and homosexuality are more than matters of objective physical facts about the combinations of male and female genitalia—the more important issue involves the *meaning* one finds in one's sexuality and that of others.

If homosexuality were simply a variation of a common sexual urge, merely a matter of preference or personal taste, as is often maintained (at least in 'liberal' circles), there would be less concern about it in our culture. The reason why homosexuality is a controversial issue in our society is because it undermines the *myth of gender*, a myth upon which all our human relations are based. By giving more power and prestige to half the members of our society (men) and denying the same to the other half (women), this myth determines in many respects the way people live. It permeates not only the most important institutions of our society such as religion, medicine, law, history, the arts, and sport, but it is also deeply, perhaps indelibly, imprinted on the psyche of every human being in our culture. The myth of gender has also been responsible for many centuries of subjugation, oppression, and exploitation. Homosexuality, although it by no means relinquishes the myth, subverts it. As I will explain below, homosexuality is a violation of masculinity in our culture.

Sexual Mythology[2]

There has been considerable scholarly debate over the last fifteen years about the nature of sexuality (DeCecco and Elia 1993; Stein 1992). At the core of this debate is the issue of whether sexuality is a phenomenon common to all humans of every culture and time (known as the essentialist position), or whether it is historically and culturally contingent (the social constructionist position). Considering the widely documented variability in sexualities over time and between cultures, most historians, sociologists, anthropologists, and philosophers now study sex within a social constructionist framework. In that framework, understanding homophobia requires an appreciation of the cultural context in which it takes place.

One of the most influential historians of sexuality is Michel Foucault (1980, 1985), who argued that sex has become a pivot for the organization and control of life in the modern world. Foucault contends that sexuality, rather than being (from the Victorian era to the present) the object of repression, has become increasingly central to human affairs to the extent that much of life has been organized around sex in the second half of the twentieth century. People now tend to take their sexuality very seriously as a primary source of identity, insight, and self-realization that sets a range of social boundaries; it determines their acceptability as human beings, their cultural status, the legality of their familial relationships, the character of their intimacies, and the patterns of their consumption. Foucault points out that these constructions of personal life are pivotal in forming the social order. He calls this the 'biopower'; society is ordered and controlled not so much through the repression of sexual desire but by the active production of ways of life that restrict desire. People become what society wants them to be, actively pursuing ways of life that serve larger political and economic interests. For instance, taken-for-granted ideas of what are 'normal' and 'abnormal' sexualities encourage people to pursue certain erotic experiences and avoid others.

In the nineteenth century, sexuality was centred on the extended, patriarchal, and heterosexually ordered family. This dominant social organization of desire formed a disciplined social order that contributed to the larger political and economic imperatives, which required a self-controlled population to serve the needs of an emerging patriarchal consumer capitalism. In this way exotic desire becomes a tool for social order. People pursue erotic experiences with their bodies in ways that serve the social order, so they will pursue erotic relations in accordance with the social orders of gender, race, and class. For example, there are White middle-class men who are willing to pursue erotic relations only with White middle-class women, thus reproducing in their own erotic lives social structures of race, class, gender, and heterosexism.[3]

An erotic experience is an event that unites ideas, emotions, cultural discourses, and bodily experience in such a way that these all become incarnate in individual physical lives. Eros, of course, includes genital sexual expression, but it is not limited to such expression. Dancing, for instance, can be an erotic activity. Sport can also be erotic—a mode of bodily expression, of the desire to move and make contact with our fellow human beings. The gendered organization of sport, therefore, is significant in an erotic way.

Erotic experiences take on physical, concrete forms. Consider, for example, the experience of just thinking about a scene you find sexually exciting. Now compare that to the experience of masturbating to the same imagined scene. The masturbation experience is more intense, more involving, more actual. In this way, Eros is our ability to experience with our bodies the less tangible worlds of ideas and emotions. This might be clearer if you think of our erotic capacity metaphorically as a musical instrument. On the violin, for instance, you can play a vast spectrum of music. Your choice of music and interpretation of it will be an expression of yourself by way of the musical traditions of our culture. In a similar way, our erotic ability is the facility to express ourselves through our bodies in the context of cultural traditions. Since it is sex or gender that obviously decides the difference between a homosexual and heterosexual encounter, it is to gender that I will turn my attention. This doesn't mean that gender is the only erotic dimension, but because gender is so pervasive and has over thousands of years become implicit in Western ways of being human, it is an inescapable element of our erotic experience.

There is an important distinction between sex and gender. Sex is a physiological distinction that is drawn between male and female, whereas gender is a cultural distinction dividing power between men, women, boys, and girls. Gender polarizes the sexes, giving them mythic significance and status. Roland Barthes (1957) points out that myths are cultural forms that make socially constructed realities seem 'natural' and apolitical, as though they were beyond the power of human agency or control. Anthropology, however, has taught us that what is considered 'natural' varies enormously between cultures. When something is called 'natural', there is often a sense that it is the product not of our social, political realities but of 'nature', which is considered a force greater than ourselves. Barthes argues that to say something is 'natural' is to make a judgement. What is meant when we say that a phenomenon is 'natural' is that it fits a political view of the world—a view that is the product of tradition. The gender myth makes the traditional division of power in our culture between males and females seem natural, ahistorical, universal, and necessarily the way things must be.

The gender myth involves three related axes: physical sex (male/female), sociocultural status (man/woman), and signs of gender (masculine/feminine). *Physical sex* characteristics are a matter of being male or female, that is, having the X or Y chromosome and the biological tendencies related to it: male or female genitalia and secondary sex characteristics. *Sociocultural status* is what it means to be a man or a woman in our culture. The gender order in Western culture is hierarchical and divided into two; men are considered superior to women. This is seen as the birthright of men and exists independently of any individual merit. Being a man automatically places one on the dominant side of this mythic power relationship.

The *signs of gender* are gestures such as different body comportments, clothing customs, and hairstyles, as well as complex behaviours such as 'being a football player'. These gestures indicate the forcefulness or the significance that one's gender is supposed to take. Also within the myth of gender, masculine and feminine body parts, such as clitorises and penises, become cultural signs of the hierarchy of gender: 'cunts' and 'cocks'. The mythic division of gender power is both created and expressed in the complex relationship between the symbols of masculinity and femininity and the use of them by men and women. This process intensifies or diminishes the dominance or submissiveness associated with the sociocultural status of being a man or a women.

In our culture, gender is a kind of prison. It is difficult to think about another person without thinking of his or her gender. For example, if you meet a person briefly, you may well forget almost everything about him or her. It is very unlikely, however, that you will forget whether it was a man or a woman. Almost everyone is aware of the gender of the person with whom he or she is having sex. It's difficult to conceive of sexual relations in which gender would have no place in the experience. Because gender is fundamentally a matter of power, knowing a person's gender is essentially a matter of knowing his or her status within the gender order (Wittig 1992). This way of knowing emerges from one's earliest indoctrination in gender, a process that has been thousands of years in the making and which affects our thinking about ourselves and our relation to others. Our earliest cultural experience of ourselves and others has been mediated by the language of gender power. And so the erotic appeal of soft breasts or hard pectoral muscles, a clitoris or a penis is the appeal of embodied feminine or masculine *symbols of power*. As long as masculine or feminine bodies have erotic allure, the power of gender myth will play a role in erotic experience.

Rather than eroticizing the *difference* between men and women (which is the erotic incarnation of the mythic *power* of men over women), homosexuality eroticizes gender *affinity*. At its most basic level, homosexuality is the eroticization of the fundamentally equal power of men. Now, this doesn't mean that men in homosexual relations are in *every* way equal—we all know of sexual scenes in which one partner may have considerable power over the other—but at the basic level of gender, there is equality. What is crucial here, though, is that because homosexuality eroticizes *affinity*, it is an erotic violation of manhood. It undermines the mythic power of men. By focusing on affinity rather than difference, homosexuality gnaws at masculinity, weakening the gender order. But because masculinity is also at the heart of homoerotic desire, homosexuality is essentially a *paradox* in the myth of gender. This paradoxical sabotage of masculinity is the source of homophobia, especially in sport where the production of heterosexual masculinity is crucial.

Heteroeroticism is *orthodox* eroticization because it is the incarnation of the myth of gender difference. Homoeroticism, on the other hand, is the *paradoxical* erotic incarnation of gender affinity within the myth of gender power. The word 'paradox' means something contrary to received opinion. According to the *Oxford English Dictionary*, the Greek prefix 'para' means 'alongside, past or beyond'. Thus, homosexuality is paradoxical because it exists alongside the received tradition of gender. By eroticizing *affinity*, homosexuality undermines the erotic essence of the gender myth, which is the eroticization of the patriarchal difference of power between men and women. Homosexuality is also a paradox because homoerotic desire both reveres and violates masculinity.

Homophobia is often understood by liberals as an irrational fear of homosexuality. The liberal position is that homo- and heterosexuality are essentially the same and it is only ignorance that makes people perceive the former as threatening. In that framework, those who understand homosexuality, who have a rational appreciation of it, have nothing to fear. I propose the opposite. What I suggest is that because homosexuality undermines the social construction of gender power, homophobia is not an *irrational* fear. It is in fact a *rational* fear— of the disruption of the myth of gender. As an aversion to the sabotage of masculinity, homophobia is part of the structure of orthodoxy that helps preserve the myth of masculine power. Of course, only those who are committed to perpetuating the myth of gender power are fearful of the disruptive potential of homosexuality. For those who would like to see these myths eroded, homosexuality is not threatening; it is a welcome contributor to the political process through which the social construction of gender is challenged.

Homophobia in Sport

Sport is a traditional theatre for the playing out of myths. The ancient Greek Olympic Games were religious celebrations in which the central myths of Hellenic culture were dramatized. In our contemporary culture, sport is an expression of the myth of orthodox masculinity. In general, but also with some exceptions, the most 'masculine' sports (for example, boxing, North American football, and ice hockey) tend to be the most violent. Less masculine sports are those in which struggle rather than violence is a dominant characteristic; the athlete struggles with his opponents and/or himself without perpetrating violence. Such sports would include tennis, swimming, and track. The least masculine sports are those where success is determined by the combination of skill and aesthetic expression: figure skating, diving, and gymnastics. These aesthetic sports are generally considered the least masculine because they involve the lowest degree of person-to-person aggression. As many studies have shown, a connection between masculinity, aggression, violence, and sport is well established in North American culture.

In sum, sport practice is, in large part, an important expression of orthodox masculinity. Because homosexuality is a departure from sexual orthodoxy, homosexual athletes tend to be feared, mistrusted, and stigmatized. They are perceived as 'letting down the team' by sabotaging the types of masculinity that sport tends to celebrate. This homosexual emasculation of sport has essentially two thrusts: (1) the subversion of the masculine identity that is associated with being 'sporty', and (2) the homoerotic potential that lurks in the homosocial context of the sport itself. I will now address each of these in turn.

Subversion of 'Sporty' Masculine Identity

Participation in the more masculine sports confers on men and boys the mantle of a masculine identity. Participation in sport gives males both the sense of power derived from being able to move and take up space in aggressive and domi-neering ways (Whitson 1994; Whitson and MacIntosh 1990), and also bestows the mythic aura of a masculine identity. A man or a boy who plays a sport like football is seen as capable not only of *performing* masculine manoeuvres, such as physically and psychically overpowering his opponents, but is also understood to *be* masculine.

The capacity to behave in masculine ways is also interpreted as a sign of something deeper. A masculine performance is commonly understood to emanate from a masculine identity, even though the relationship between masculine sporting participation and masculine identity is actually circular. For instance, anyone who plays football must be masculine; and playing football helps to make one masculine. In this way, participation in masculine sport both confirms and confers masculine identity. However, achieving masculine identity through sport is fraught with anxieties (Connell 1990; Kidd 1987; Messner 1992; Messner and Sabo 1994). As I have suggested elsewhere, this anxiety comes from an awareness that the myth of masculinity is fragile (Pronger 1992). Consequently, men and boys must work hard to preserve the myth of their masculine identity, performing rituals and constructing cultural practices that serve to constantly reproduce it. Those who are most concerned about the repli-cation of the myth of masculinity carefully engage in gender-specific perfor-mances (Butler 1990). They wear only those clothes, move in only those ways, engage in only those pleasures, and associate with only those kinds of people that reinforce the myth of masculinity—at least in public. They also tend not to cross-dress, flap their wrists and mince their walk, or pursue homosexual company.

Because heterosexuality is the orthodox sexual expression of masculinity, it forms an important part of the masculine identity. Talk of heterosexual 'conquest' is commonplace in locker-room banter and other aspects of the social environ-ment of sport. There is a pervasive expectation, the 'assumption of heterosexual-ity' (sometimes called 'heterosexism'), that the vast majority of male athletes are heterosexual. This is particularly the case in masculine team sport where male bonding is stressed. Because the homosexual paradox undermines orthodox mas-culinity, any homosexual presence in masculine sport would threaten the credi-bility of sport as a confirmation of a masculine identity. Homosexual men and boys, therefore, are not welcome in the vast majority of sport settings.

Homophobia helps to keep the myth of masculinity in sport 'pure'. Verbal insults like 'fag', 'pansy', and 'sissy' still commonly directed by coaches and team-mates at athletes who are not 'doing' masculinity sufficiently well effectively discourage homosexual men and boys from participating in sport. Similarly, the pervasiveness of anti-gay jokes reinforces the general impression that homosex-uality is not welcome.

Of course, if there was a visible and significant presence of gay men and boys in sport, it would limit sport's capacity to confer orthodox masculine identity. An overt gay presence would suggest that sport is not effective in conferring orthodox sexuality. However, because of heterosexism and homophobia, men and boys with homosexual proclivities generally avoid macho team sports. For example, almost all of the men I interviewed for *The Arena of Masculinity* said that they would have been ostracized, if not violently abused, if they had participated in masculine team sports as openly homosexual, which likely accounts for the almost total absence of openly gay men in masculine sports. While over the last twenty years homosexuality has taken a higher profile in popular mainstream culture—in films, on television, in popular music, and fashion—in men's sport it has remained anathema. More than twenty years ago, NFL player David Kopay publicly declared his homosexuality. Since then, no other high-profile male athletes have followed suit while continuing their athletic career.

Homophobia operates in a significantly different fashion in the 'less masculine' sports where there is often a considerable gay presence. Because social conformity is not usually as integral to individual sports as it is to team sports, individual sport can be more hospitable environments for gay boys and men. It is therefore easier for homosexual athletes to have a gay identity in these sports. Nevertheless, almost all athletes at the more highly competitive level, regardless of their sport, keep their homosexuality a secret as long as they are competing. At the recreational and community level of sport, it is often easier for gay-identified men and boys to participate in individual rather than team sports. The aesthetic sports—such as diving, gymnastics, and figure skating, where there is a greater presence of declared gay men—are relatively hospitable, although that does not mean that these sports are not in many ways homophobic. Homosexuality remains an open secret in these sports. And while there are many gay men in them, very few high-profile athletes feel safe publicly declaring their homosexuality because of a fear of homophobic blacklisting. Consequently, even sports such as figure skating remain at least ostensibly 'straight'. The well-known Canadian figure skater Brian Orser exemplified this kind of homophobia in his recent attempt to block publicity of a palimony suit launched by his former lover.

Together, homophobia and heterosexism keep the myth of masculinity alive in sport. The seeming absence of homosexual athletes contributes to the idea that sport is a vehicle for the reproduction of orthodox masculine identity. But the important qualifying word here is 'seeming'. Over the last century, homosexually inclined men and boys have learned to conceal their paradoxical masculinity in order to survive. Homosexual men and boys who like the athleticism of masculine sports, despite its homophobia, as well as some who find erotic pleasure in the seeming orthodoxy of masculine sport, are able to participate by 'passing as straight'. Masculinity is a performance of gender available to almost anyone willing to go to the trouble. This leaves the 'true' (orthodox or paradoxical) identity of men who perform the masculine rites of sport open to question.

The Homoerotic Potential of Sport

The social constructionist position from which I am writing does not maintain that people do not have essential homosexual or heterosexual identities that emanate from some 'natural' sexual core. Rather, sexuality is understood as the product of a complex social, cultural, and psychic governance that Foucault has called 'biopower'. Sexuality is an historically contingent socio-cultural phenomenon that orders human desire. In this way sexuality is much like language. For example, those of us raised with English as our mother tongue tend to think that our thoughts in that language are 'natural'. They are, however, profoundly shaped by the history and traditions of that language. Similarly, the seeming naturalness of one's sexual desire is produced within the history and tradition of sexual culture. One of the ways that sexuality has been organized in recent history is along the axis of normal and deviant where deviance is regarded as prohibited territory. I and others (Butler 1990; Wittig 1992) have suggested that 'normal' sexuality is fulfilled in the orthodoxy of heterosexuality. Homosexuality deviates from this normality. Homophobia is the structurally functional fear that promotes an aversion to intermale sexual relations, thus preserving hetrosexual orthodoxy. It is an especially important fear in traditional, all-male environments that celebrate and further the aspirations of patriarchy—such as the military, the police, and men's sport. Interestingly, while the military and the police have both recently become more inclusive of women, sport remains impervious to the larger liberal transformations of gender and continues to be almost entirely segregated along the lines of gender. Men's sport is still a predominantly homosocial environment, a fact that many people have trouble accepting.

Sport is a profoundly erotic cultural form. Earlier I argued that Eros is our ability to realize through our bodies the less tangible worlds of culture, ideas, and emotions. Sport is erotic because it is a way of producing meaning in and through the body. Some of that meaning is transcendent. For example, the profound and spiritually uplifting experience in sport that is sometimes called 'flow' or being in 'the zone' is one of the more powerful and authentic erotic possibilities of sport. In another sense, though, *men's* sport is also erotic because it affords men the opportunity to produce through their bodies the myth of masculinity. Like many other patriarchal institutions, sport has mostly been designed to include men and exclude women. Unlike business, academia, and many other traditionally male-dominated venues, however, sport explicitly involves the body. Indeed, the body is at the very centre of sport. Men pit themselves against other men using their own bodies, the bodies of their teammates and of their opponents to produce the feeling of masculinity. Many sporting men take significant pleasure in that cult of embodied masculinity. For the most part, they will not allow women to participate with them—it would undermine the exclusive masculinity of the experience. In this way the exclusivity of men's sport, ironically enough, has an important homoerotic element.

Sport offers men the opportunity to eroticize masculinity, but still maintain their orthodox status. Orthodoxy is preserved by homophobic rules that limit intermale eroticism. Take, for example, the fact that nakedness and body contact are integral to the culture of men's sport. Men's locker-rooms and showers are typically designed in a way that maximizes the possibilities for displaying and observing the naked body. By contrast, women's locker-rooms are usually designed so that women can have privacy while changing and showering. Men's facilities seldom, if ever, have private cubicles for showering and changing. It is normal for men to walk around the locker-room with their genitals exposed; frequently the towel is carried around the neck rather than wrapped around the waist, modestly covering the genitals and buttocks. The body is very much on display and looking at bodies is the norm. However, orthodoxy is preserved in the midst of all of this by unwritten rules about conduct: one must never show sexual excitement by having an erection; masturbation is forbidden; one's gaze should be surreptitious; one should not allow one's hands to linger too lovingly or too long on one's own body; and there should be no physical contact with the naked men by whom one is surrounded.

In contact sports there are both official rules that govern appropriate forms of contact and unofficial rules that determine 'normal' and 'deviant' forms of contact. In the latter category it is acceptable to slap fellow players on the butt and to give them enthusiastic hugs in victorious moments, but it is unacceptable to allow a slap to become a lingering caress or to give a loving, reassuring hug in moments of defeat. In boxing it is 'normal' for competitors to hit each other's bodies, to draw blood, to feel each other's sweat, and even to knock their opponents unconscious. It is 'deviant', however, to kiss, to lick, to caress, or to provoke orgasms. In rugby it is 'normal' to put one's arms around the waists of other men, to shove one's head between the hips of others, to push and grasp at bodies. It is 'deviant', however, to continue holding players for long after the play, to stroke them, to playfully bite them or to touch their genital regions. These unofficial but strictly observed rules have an important function. They prevent the homoeroticism of sport from sliding into the dangerous area of the paradox. These rules are homophobic, though, because they define the pleasures of the homoerotic paradox as deviant and unacceptable. They limit the bodily pleasures of the homosocial/erotic environment of sport to dynamics that maintain orthodoxy and cast homosexuality in a negative light.

The tension between the homoeroticism and homophobia of sport often deters homosexual boys and men from participating. They fear that they will not be able to negotiate the enticements to homoerotic contact, which are laced with fear of the same. For other men and boys, on the other hand, the often fine line between normal and deviant homoeroticism in sport affords them the opportunity to engage in a homoerotic culture without losing their orthodox status. This can be a conscious or unconscious manoeuvre.

Gay Community Sport

The heterosexism and homophobia of most sport milieux make them uncomfortable for gay men and boys who have accepted homosexuality as an integral and legitimate part of their lives. One of the products of the gay liberation movement has been the creation of specifically gay sport organizations. Gay athletic clubs, which can be found in major cities in Europe, Australia, New Zealand, North America, and parts of South America and Africa, constitute an important part of gay community life. The objectives of gay sports groups is essentially twofold: to promote social interaction, and to provide athletic opportunities for people who share a way of life. The number and variety of gay community sport clubs is extensive, although space affords only a brief sampling of this significant facet of gay culture here. In many places the largest gay organizations are sport clubs. There are 'outing clubs' associated with the International Gay and Lesbian Outdoor Organization. These have names like the 'Out and Out Club' and organize activities such as camping jamborees, bicycle tours, cross-country and downhill skiing, hiking, canoeing, parachuting, and white-water rafting. Included in the list of organized gay community sports are groups such as Spokes, a cycling club in Vancouver; Gruppo Pesce, a swimming group in Milan; Paris Lutte Amateur Groupe, a wrestling club in Paris; and the Penguins, a San Francisco hockey team.

There are also many gay sport governing bodies. For instance, the North American Gay Amateur Athletic Alliance is a non-profit organization dedicated to promoting amateur softball for all people, but with a special emphasis on gay participation. As with similar bodies in other sports, it establishes uniform playing rules and regulations. Other governing bodies include the International Gay Bowling Association, the International Gay and Lesbian Aquatics Association, and the International Gay and Lesbian Hockey Association.

The ideological significance of gay sport is noteworthy. Over the last fifteen years or so, there has been a shift in focus in gay culture from the dynamics of oppression and liberation to an emphasis on gay pride. An important expression of gay pride can be found in sport. In many cities the most important annual gay event is Pride Day, which often includes athletic events such as 10-km runs and swim meets. The most prestigious international gay pride event is the Gay Games. An international festival of athletic competition and the arts, the Gay Games were launched in 1982 and are held quadrennially as a celebration of the international gay community. The first and second Games were held in San Francisco, the third in Vancouver, the fourth in New York, and the fifth in Amsterdam. The Games are overseen by the Federation of Gay Games, based in San Francisco.

The Games were founded by a physician and former Olympic decathalete, Tom Waddell, and organized by a mostly volunteer group called San Francisco Arts and Athletics. The 1982 Games involved 1,300 male and female athletes in sixteen sports. At the 1994 Games in New York 10,870 athletes participated in more than thirty sports, with 55,000 spectators at the closing ceremonies. Like the ancient games of Olympia, the athletic competitions of the Gay Games are complemented by festivals of the arts. In her opening address to the 1986 Games, novelist Rita Mae Brown highlighted the meaning of the Games. 'These games are not just a celebration of skill; they are a celebration of who we are and what we have become—a celebration of the best in us.'

Tom Waddell said that the Games were 'conceived as a new idea in the meaning of sport based on inclusion rather than exclusion'. Anyone is welcome to compete regardless of race, sex, age, nationality, sexual orientation, religion, or athletic ability. In keeping with the Master's movement in sport, athletes compete with each other in their own age group. To date, there have been no minimum qualifying standards in any of the events. Many of the sports are officially sanctioned by their respective national Master's organizations. Athletes participate not as representatives of their respective countries but as individuals on behalf of cities and towns.

Conclusion

Sport plays an important role in the reproduction of orthodox masculinity, both by affirming and conferring a masculine identity and by affording men the opportunity to eroticize masculinity in ways that are not threatening. Structural homophobia and heterosexism make that possible. Men's and boys' sports are promoted and celebrated for their socializing of males into orthodox masculinity. The homophobia that keeps men's sport orthodox and thus productive of patriarchal gender difference is not just a fear of the mere presence of gay men in sport. It is also a subconscious fear that the decidedly homosocial world of men's sport will appear or become overtly homoerotic. Nevertheless, the masculine significance of sport and the athletic body bears a secret mingling of the orthodox and paradoxical interpretations of the gender myth. It is that secret which is both alluring and fearful to men who are attracted to the myth of gender as it is reproduced in the masculinizing culture of sport.

Notes

1. Because there are significant differences in the construction of homophobia in men's and women's sport, I will focus on *male* homosexuality. Another chapter in this anthology deals with homophobia in women's sport. This chapter draws upon and synthesizes work I have published in *The Arena of Masculinity: Sports, Homosexuality and the Meaning of Sex*, as well as in *The Encyclopaedia of Homosexuality* (forthcoming).

2. The following is a précis of the theory of sexuality I discuss in my book, *The Arena of Masculinity: Sports, Homosexuality and the Meaning of Sex*.

3. While Foucault himself does not talk about gender in the context of biopolitics, his theory does not preclude it (Bartky 1988; Bordo 1989; Diamond and Quinby 1988; Halperin 1995; Lydon 1988; Martin 1988; Sawicki 1988).

References

Barthes, R. 1957. *Mythologies*. London: Paladin.

Bartky, S. 1988. 'Foucault, Femininity, and the Modernization of Patriarchal Power'. In *Feminism and Foucault: Reflections on Resistance*, edited by I. Diamond and L. Quinby, 61–86. Boston: Northeastern University Press.

Bordo, S. 1989. 'The Body and the Reproduction of Femininity: A Feminist Appropriation of Foucault'. In *Gender/Body/Knowledge*, edited by S. Bordo, 13–33. New Brunswick, NJ: Rutgers University Press.

Butler, J. 1990. *Gender Trouble: Feminism and the Subversion of Identity*. New York: Routledge.

Connell, R. 1990. 'An Iron Man: The Body and Some Contradictions of Hegemonic Masculinity'. In *Sport, Men and the Gender Order: Critical Feminist Perspectives*, edited by M. Messner and D. Sabo, 83–96. Champaign, IL: Human Kinetics.

DeCecco, J., and J. Elia, eds. 1993. *If You Seduce a Straight Person, Can You Make Them Gay? Issues in Biological Essentialism Versus Social Constructionism in Gay and Lesbian Identities*. New York: Harrington Park Press.

Diamond, I., and L. Quinby, eds. 1988. *Feminism and Foucault: Reflections on Resistance*. Boston: Northeastern University Press.

Foucault, M. 1980. *The History of Sexuality: Volume I: An Introduction*. New York: Vintage.

_____. 1985. *The Uses of Pleasure: The History of Sexuality*. New York: Vintage.

Halperin, D. 1995. *Saint Foucault: Towards a Gay Hagiography*. New York: Oxford University Press.

Kidd, B. 1987. 'Sports and Masculinity'. In *Beyond Patriarchy: Essays by Men on Masculinity*, edited by M. Kaufman, 250–65. Toronto: Oxford University Press.

Lydon, M. 1988. 'Foucault and Feminism: A Romance of Many Dimensions'. In *Feminism and Foucault: Reflections on Resistance*, edited by I. Diamond and L. Quinby, 135–48. Boston: Northeastern University Press.

Martin, B. 1988. 'Feminism, Criticism and Foucault'. In *Feminism and Foucault: Reflections on Resistance*, edited by I. Diamond and L. Quinby, 3–20. Boston: Northeastern University Press.

Messner, M. 1992. *Power at Play*. Boston: Beacon.

———, and D. Sabo, eds. 1990. *Sport, Men and the Gender Order: Critical Feminist Perspectives*. Champaign, IL: Human Kinetics.

———, and D. Sabo. 1994. *Sex, Violence and Power in Sports: Rethinking Masculinity*. Freedom, CA: Crossing Press.

Pronger, B. 1990. *The Arena of Masculinity: Sports, Homosexuality and the Meaning of Sex*. New York: St Martin's Press.

———. 1992. *The Arena of Masculinity: Sports, Homosexuality and the Meaning of Sex*. Toronto: University of Toronto Press.

———. Forthcoming. 'Gay Games'. In *The Encyclopedia of Homosexuality*, 2nd edn, edited by G. Haggerty. New York: Guland.

Sawicki, J. 1988. 'Identity Politics and Sexual Freedom: Foucault and Feminism'. In *Feminism and Foucault: Reflections on Resistance*, edited by I. Diamond and L. Quinby. Boston: Northeastern University Press.

———. 1991. *Disciplining Foucault: Feminism, Power and the Body*. New York: Routledge.

Stein, E. 1992. *Forms of Desire: Sexual Orientation and the Social Constructionist Controversy*. New York: Routledge.

Whitson, D. 1990. 'Sport in the Social Construction of Masculinity'. In *Sport, Men and the Gender Order: Critical Feminist Perspectives*, edited by M. Messner and D. Sabo, 19–30. Champaign, IL: Human Kinetics.

———. 1994. 'The Embodiment of Gender: Discipline, Domination, and Empowerment'. In *Women, Sport, and Culture*, edited by S. Birrell and C. Cole, 353–72. Champaign, IL: Human Kinetics.

———, and D. MacIntosh. 1990. 'The Scientization of Physical Education: Discourses of Performance'. *Quest* 42:40–51.

Wittig, M. 1992. *The Straight Mind and Other Essays*. Boston: Beacon.

Woods, G. 1987. *Articulate Flesh: Male Homoeroticism and Modern Poetry*. New Haven: Yale University Press.

Chapter 11

Gender and Organizational Power in Canadian Sport

Jim McKay

The gender inequalities documented in the other chapters of this book are particularly evident in managerial positions in sport: only seven of the ninety-four members of the powerful International Olympic Committee are women; only six of the 174 national Olympic associations in the world have women presidents; and only about 25 per cent of national sport organizations (NSOs) in Canada have women in senior management positions (Hall 1995; Hall et al. 1989). Moreover, female managers tend to be concentrated in so-called 'soft' areas (e.g., affirmative action, youth sport, people with disabilities, women's events, human resources, and public relations), whereas male managers generally dominate the 'hard' sectors (e.g., finance, marketing, policy planning, talent identification, sport science, élite sport, Olympic sport, and men's events). In order to address these sorts of gender imbalances, Sport Canada (SC), the agency responsible for the national funding and planning of amateur sport, has implemented affirmative action (AA) programs for women in sport. This chapter addresses the extent to which AA initiatives can bring about more equitable gender relations in sport. The findings reported here are taken from a larger, comparative analysis in which I analysed the effectiveness of AA policies for women in sport by the Australian, Canadian, and New Zealand governments (McKay 1997).

Methods and Theory

In 1992 and 1993 I conducted in-depth interviews with seven men and eight women who were current or former managers in SC, and two women managers and four women members of the Canadian Association for the Advancement of Women and Sport (CAAWS), the leading sportswomen's advocacy group in Canada. The questionnaire used for the interviews was adapted from standardized instruments used in previous studies of barriers to women coaches and managers

(Hall et al. 1989; White and Brackenridge 1985; White et al. 1991) and the hurdles faced by women in the Canadian public service (Ministry of Supply and Services 1991). The interviews probed beyond distributional and categorical issues, though, focusing also on the intersubjective and relational aspects of gender in organizations (Hall 1996). Consequently, I followed the lead of other research that foregrounded men's and women's 'voices' in order to provide in-depth analyses of the meanings respondents assigned to their everyday experiences of organizational life (Freeman 1990; Hall 1993; Pringle 1988; Roper 1994; Williams 1995).

As it turned out, male respondents were much less talkative than women about perceived barriers to advancement, AA policy, prejudice, and discrimination. They were also less responsive to open-ended questions during interviews. Consequently, less in-depth information was elicited from them on these topics as will be evident from the following findings. Because this study examined the perceptions of men and women occupying powerful managerial positions in Canadian sport, the topic was extremely sensitive—threatening, perhaps, to an existing male-dominated power structure. For this reason, and to maintain confidentiality, respondents have been given pseudonyms.

The gendered dynamics of sporting organizations reported here were informed conceptually by Connell's (1987) social constructionist approach to gender relations and identities. Connell suggests that we need to examine how articulations between the macrolevel *gender order* and microlevel *gender regimes* (e.g., religion, sport, work, the state, the media, family life) are underpinned by the entwined structures of *labour*, *power*, and *cathexis*. Broadly speaking, labour refers to the organization of work-related responsibilities, power to implicit and overt modes of social control, and cathexis to patterns of sexuality.

Structures of Labour: What We Know From the Literature

In industrialized countries, the vertical and horizontal segregation of work organizations is particularly evident in the high ratio of women in occupations with relatively low levels of authority, prestige, and remuneration, as well as women's disproportionate contribution to unpaid domestic labour and caregiving. These gendered divisions are especially pronounced in managerial occupations. Only about 5 per cent of women (mostly from Anglo backgrounds) are senior managers and most are concentrated in 'pink ghettos' (e.g., AA, public relations, human resources) that are stereotyped as 'women's work' (Fagenson 1993; Powell 1993; Tanton 1994). Liff and Wajcmen (1995:90–1) cite a major British study on women managers that begins by stating that, 'a visitor from Mars could be forgiven for thinking that management jobs have been specifically designed for men married to full-time wives and mothers who shoulder the burden of family life'. According to Antal and Izraeli (1993:63), 'probably the single most important hurdle for women in management in all industrial-ized countries is the persistent stereotype that associates management with being male'.

These gendered hierarchies are readily evident in Canadian management. A 1991 survey found that the percentages of women in senior management posi-tions in the top 250 Canadian companies were as follows: industrial (6.1 per cent), Crown corporations (5.6 per cent), financial services (7.9 per cent), insur-ance (14.2 per cent), and other (5.9 per cent) (Allan 1991). A comprehensive study of the Canadian public service reported that only 12 per cent of its senior managers were women (Ministry of Supply and Services 1991).

Findings: Perceptions of Equity

When I asked women why there were so few women in decision-making posi-tions at Sport Canada, almost all identified either the particularly masculine ambience of sport and/or the strength of men's networks. Meredith claimed that women were excluded by the male-dominated mentoring mechanisms that operate in organizations:

> It seems to me that men's 'comfort zone' only extends to other men. I see men 'cloning' other men all the time around here, but they just don't seem to be comfortable doing it with the women.
>
> *Q:* What do you mean by 'cloning'?
>
> *A:* A kind of informal process—the boys giving one another tips on what the political lie of the land is, providing them with contacts, how to come across to the powers-that-be around here and with [NSOs], a kind of apprenticeship.
>
> *Q:* And there is no equivalent for women?
>
> *A:* Well, most of this stuff goes on in places where we don't fit in—bars, locker rooms, the golf course—so there's virtually no opportunity to access those networks. I think the women around here are very supportive of one another, but it's more like a survival strategy, not something that really helps you move up the ladder.

By contrast, when I asked men why there were so few women in decision-making positions, only one pointed to the importance of predominantly male networks. The other men generally attributed women's underrepresentation to 'tradition', 'society', 'natural' sexual differences, or as the normal outcome of meritocratic competition. In these ways, structures of labour were clearly inter-preted differently by the men and women I spoke to. While the women were quick to identify the exclusionary and discriminatory potential of these struc-tures, men, who after all had benefited from them as a gender class, typically invoked familiar rationalizations for men's success in the workplace.

Findings: Work and Family Responsibilities

As noted, men were much less talkative than women about prejudice and discrimination. When men were asked how often they thought about gender-related issues, most indicated that they did so very rarely. Child care, travel, prolonged working hours, and domestic responsibilities had relatively little impact on married men's careers. Like married women, though, married men often mentioned problems fulfilling both their work and family responsibilities. However, most married men were able to compartmentalize their work and family duties by giving priority to the former. Whereas married men could put paid work ahead of domestic responsibilities, most married women felt forced to balance both spheres even when they had considerate partners. According to Sylvia:

> I think one of the massive hurdles is that we also have to do the second shift. Now, my husband is just great—I couldn't ask for a more supportive guy. But his boss expects him to be there from eight until six. I also work crazy hours, but when it comes to the crunch, I'm the one who generally has to chauffeur the kids around to school, hockey practice, the music lessons, and do the shopping, etc. So guess whose career gets put on hold most of the time?

Women described this 'time-bind' syndrome (Hochschild 1997) with phrases like 'struggle', 'walking a tightrope', 'double bind', 'panic', 'frantic', and 'chaotic', whereas most men alluded to it more matter-of-factly. Regardless of their marital status, nearly all men had continuous career paths, as did unmarried women without children. However, marriage, childbirth, a partner's change in employment, or domestic responsibilities had disrupted the careers of all of the married women. Most women were generally unhappy and distressed about their organization's inflexible work schedule. Two men also expressed displeasure about their work arrangements. As Matt suggested:

> It's a totally insane environment. You've got to make sure you're here early and don't leave before 6 p.m.—that's definitely not kosher. You've also got to come in on the weekends, at least for a while, just to be seen to be around. I just feel that things are measured more by the quantity than the quality of what you do. I'm not saying that our stuff is second-rate, but I could do the same amount of work in 10 or 12 hours over four days and then maybe able to spend some time with the kids.

Most women discerned that powerful male networks, in combination with SC's insensitivity to women's family obligations, severely hindered their own career prospects. A variety of related metaphors were used to describe these perceived constraints: 'glass ceilings', 'brick walls', 'hoops', 'blockages', 'hurdles', 'ghettos', 'on the outside looking in', 'passing the ball but never having it passed back', and 'being kept in the dark'.

Structures of Power: What We Know From the Literature

Men control most sites of organized coercion and surveillance in society (e.g., the police, military, judiciary) and perpetrate most of the violence against both women and other men. Men, most of whom are friends or relatives of their victims, perpetrate the vast majority of sexual assaults against women. Thus, it is absolutely crucial to view sexual assault and harassment not as the random acts of psychopathic individuals but as the 'normal' behavior of men who accept aggression, intimidation, and violence as an appropriate and necessary aspect of their relationships with women.

This 'iron fist' is complemented by an ideological 'velvet glove' that 'persuades' both men and women that the ascendancy of men's values, interests, and privileges is both natural and legitimate. Connell uses the concepts *hegemonic masculinity* and *emphasized femininity* to describe this form of cultural power. The former term refers to the 'culturally idealized form of masculine character', which associates masculinity with 'toughness and competitiveness', the 'subordination of women', and 'the marginalization of gay men' (Connell 1990:83, 94). Emphasized femininity is defined by women's accommodation of 'the interests and desires of men' and 'women's compliance with this subordination', while other forms of femininity 'are defined by complex strategic combinations of resistance and co-operation' (Connell 1987:183–4).

Findings: Sexual Harassment

None of the men but most of the women indicated that they either had been sexually harassed or witnessed sexual harassment of other women. For instance, Liz related the events surrounding a friend who applied unsuccessfully for a position with an NSO:

> Her husband happened to be talking with somebody on the hiring committee who had loose lips and said that the reason she didn't get the job was because [a senior manager not on the selection committee] vetoed it. She was very distraught because this particular guy had made some advances towards her a year or so previously and she had rejected them. She felt it was purely based on that, because this guy has a reputation of being a sexual harasser.

Women also complained that men often made jokes of a sexual nature that were, in fact, intimidating. As will be seen in the following section, these different perceptions of language were linked to contrasting styles of management between men and women.

Finding: Conflicting Styles of Management

According to Chase (1988), professional women have to contend with negative stereotypes about women in general. Chase suggests that professional women try to avoid being typecast by setting exceedingly high standards. This places them in a contradictory situation: they must perform extraordinarily well by male standards, but in a manner that does not threaten men's stereotypes about 'appropriate' feminine behaviour; they need to be tough without being 'macho'; they have to take risks but also be consistently outstanding; they have to be ambitious but not expect equal treatment; and they must assume responsibility but follow others' advice. Morrison et al. (1987:60) liken this situation to that of a diving contest: 'the dives performed by women must have a higher degree of difficulty, yet the judges do not follow the customary procedure of factoring the difficulty into the score they give'. Thus, it is not surprising that most women remarked that their consultative styles conflicted with men's adversarial tactics. According to Gisela:

> My bottom line is that everything is negotiable and the best way to deal with confrontations is by talking things through. That's why I am so often on the outer with some of the macho guys I have to deal with. I mean, some of their behaviour is absolutely appalling!
>
> Q: What's your response in that sort of situation?
>
> A: Well, I try to remain calm and civil. I don't mind a bit of creative conflict, but I'll be damned if I'll demean myself by sinking to their level—I couldn't look at myself in the mirror. I don't buy that 'boys will be boys' line; it just condones a type of bully-boy behavior that society is better off without.

Since most men believed that sporting organizations functioned on the principle of equal opportunity, they generally denied that they wielded power over women. However, virtually all women perceived that men were generally unwilling to recognize power differences. Consequently, women reported devoting considerable time and energy to resisting their subordinate status: 'I find it exhausting just holding the line sometimes. The guys around here are a pretty good bunch overall, but there still is always that edge—the banter, the barbs, the innuendo that equity programs means that women are getting special treatment—I wish!' (Liz). Yet none of the women wanted to become 'like men'—that is, to be defeminized—and were critical of senior women who did not use their positions to assist other women. But in identifying themselves as *professional* women who wanted to be judged solely on merit, most women distanced themselves from lesbianism and/or feminist practices that were outside a conventional liberal mode:

> I'm not a feminist in so far as fairness is really what's most important to me, that in the end it's the best person for the job. I think some of the real feminists come

across very aggressively and don't do our cause any good in the eyes of the male[s], because it makes them very defensive. When they feel that their position is being threatened, it just makes the next part of the progress a little bit more difficult (Margaret).

Probably the most telling indicator of women's subordinate status was that although some individual female managers held powerful positions, this usually entailed supervising other women in peripheral areas. Unlike men, women seldom had collective power, especially *over* men.

Structures of Cathexis: What We Know From the Literature

Cathexis is defined as 'sexual social relationships' that 'are organized around one person's emotional attachments to another' (Connell 1987:111–12). The dominant pattern of desire in capitalist societies is based on binary, hierarchical sexual difference and heterosexual partnership. Yet Connell stresses that cathectic attachments are not fully explained by sexual difference because heterosexual women are sexualized to an extent that heterosexual men are not. In his words, 'the erotic reciprocity in hegemonic heterosexuality is based on unequal exchange' (Connell 1987:113). In this respect, Connell emphasizes that hegemonic heterosexuality is replete with internal tensions, interweaves uneasily with homosexuality, is constantly challenged, and has to be continually defended and reasserted.

Findings: Techniques of Self-Presentation

None of the men reported monitoring their bodily practices or personal appearance. However, many women commented that in order to be taken seriously, they regulated their everyday appearance in accordance with heterosexual taboos:

> I really like pastels but never wear them because you don't want to be seen as a 'girl'. You never wear anything low-cut or see-through—that'd be seen as too sleazy. Anything frilly or lacy is out, because you don't want to look like a bimbo. So you have to power dress if you want to be taken seriously—the 10-inch shoulder pads, the digital briefcase, the mobile phone [laughs] (Kylie).

Such strategies of self-presentation were intertwined with the dilemma mentioned earlier of balancing professional and feminine identities. In the case of dress, most women engaged in 'desexualizing' practices for two main reasons. First, they wanted to avoid having their professionalism discredited by innuendoes about 'flaunting' their sexuality or 'sleeping their way to the top'—tactics that both men and women were alleged to have used to undermine ambitious women. Second, they wanted to avoid any association with lesbianism.

Findings: Homophobia

Given the regime of heterosexism embedded in the structures of labour and power described earlier, it is not surprising that homosexuality had a deviant status. Some men and women indicated that although they were 'comfortable' with gays and lesbians, their coworkers, bosses, clients, and the general public were not: 'There's a notion that some sports are dominated by lesbians, so the question that gets asked is: 'How involved should [our organization] be in this and that sport?' There's some folks that don't want their young girls being involved with the gays in the sport movement' (Frank).

Many women reported that because they played sport or were working in a traditionally male domain, they either had witnessed or been subjected to lesbian-baiting. Women who openly declared that they were feminists felt that heterosexual women's fear of being labelled lesbians and the conservative politics of sportswomen made it difficult to forge solidarity:

> The problem with women in sport is that they don't understand what mainstream feminism is about—its diversity and understanding that I may be a lesbian and you're a heterosexual, but we should get that out front, talk about it, and get on with getting on. It's no good hiding these differences. Women in sport are so conservative because they've bought right into the high-performance model. They're cut off from grassroots recreation and grassroots feminism. Mainstream feminists see that what's going down in sport as the same as what's happening in other areas. But there also are the mainstream feminists who really don't see much point in dealing with sport, because it isn't as important as abortion, reproduction, and so on. So sport tends to get colonized by fairly apolitical types of sportswomen . . . they identify first with being in sport and being a woman second (Cherie).

Dealing with heterosexist attitudes and behaviour towards lesbians was just one of the many contentious issues that managers had to confront in implementing AA programs.

'Doing' Affirmative Action

An important issue surrounding the implementation of AA is the everyday meanings that people attach to it. In this section, I analyse some of the contradictory and conflicting ways in which AA was defined and deployed by male and female managers.

One man was opposed to AA because he believed that his organization was already based on the principle of equal opportunity. Most men were in favour of AA provided it did not threaten the principle of merit. Another man was sympathetic because his partner had experienced difficulty in returning to work, and two others stated that they had become supporters of AA as a result of vicariously experiencing discrimination through their partners or daughters. Tom was supportive of AA because of the nurturing qualities that he thought women brought to sport:

> We need to get more women because of that caregiving aspect they bring. It's been my experience with [NSOs] that the needs of youngsters seem to be addressed more by women. Like at last weekend's soccer tournament, the mothers were the first to embrace the youngsters off the field and cool them down. The fathers are more stand-offish and macho.

Ian supported AA because he thought it had long-term pay-offs in human resource management:

> I'd say that, all things being equal, I'd take the woman on. Even if I was just a little concerned that the woman might be marginally less skillful, I'd take her on because it's an investment. Having a flat management structure here means that there's no room for promotion, so I have to ensure that people here have got the ability to go on to something better when they leave. NSOs would never wear quotas, so I change them by a philosophy of encouragement and subversion. I don't know how professional that is, but that's how I have to do it. Quotas only cause more antagonism by virtue of being seen as compulsory—strong arm tactics by 'Big Brother'.

However, all of these men also saw AA as 'a women's issue'—an 'add women and stir' situation. AA was perceived as something that men did *to* or *for* women rather than a process that involved adjustments for both sexes. Most women expressed ambivalence about AA, believing that it was undesirable but required given that so many men were insensitive to gender inequalities. Not surprisingly, most of the more strident supporters of AA were AA managers themselves and/or were involved in various sportswomen's advocacy organizations. In most cases, their strong endorsement of AA stemmed from direct contact with a feminist or a feminist organization that had politicized them. These women saw AA as a progressive step in the larger project of reconfiguring sport in ways that valued women's experiences.

Nearly all AA managers reported an array of contradictory emotions associated with their work: idealism, pragmatism, disillusionment, demoralization, beleagueredness, and burn-out. Every manager said that AA could not be 'sold' on its own merits and had to be tied to some kind of 'carrot' or 'stick':

I sell equity to men based on a very bottom-line business model because that's the argument I hear from them all the time. My response is, 'Okay, let's look at this from a financial perspective. There's a lot of things you can do about equity that don't cost you a cent, and there's a lot of things that if you're real serious about them can make a you a lot of money by making your sport more attractive to 52 per cent of the population. Smart marketers do it. The National Rifle Association in the United States is on a major marketing drive with products preying on women's fear of violence to tap into that market share [grimaces]. So why don't we tap into that huge pool of women too?' So my argument from the monetary side is that it's just good management. It's also the law, so if you're not equitable you're opening yourself up to some legal challenges, which could cost you a whole lot of money. So I tell them that they can do some things for free, they can make some money, and if they don't do it they can find themselves dishing out a lot of dough to lawyers (Monica).

Ingrid stated that managing AA was a case of 'the three Us: undervalued, undermined, and underpaid', and that she needed to be pragmatic in her strategies:

Ideally, you want people to pursue [AA] because they have internalized it as a core value and their attitudes have changed. However, I am satisfied if they simply change their behaviour in order that sport is more accessible for girls and women. Hopefully, their attitudes may change afterwards. I've tried for years to change attitudes and not met with much success. So I've said, 'Fine, we're out of the attitude changing business, I want you to change your behaviour and here's how you can do it. What I want you to do differently as a coach is change your behaviour in such and such a way.' That's going to keep me satisfied for now. Granted, it isn't as powerful as the attitude shift, but short of generational change, I don't know how I change somebody's attitudes who hasn't bought into the core values of equity.

Alison articulated a common complaint that inadequate funding and failure to impose sanctions on NSOs that did not meet regulations sent a contradictory message both internally and externally:

Money talks, so if [the government] comes out and says, 'Okay, we really want more women coaches and we're prepared to fund it properly,' then people are going to take notice. What I have to fight against is the [government] saying that it wants to increase women's participation, but not giving me the money to do it. That sends out the wrong signals [to NSOs]. So when I go out there to talk to them about their gender equity plans, they just laugh at me and say, 'Why doesn't the [government] put its money where its mouth is?'

Like most AA managers, Tanya felt weary from continuously having to 'put out fires':

I worked really hard to get homophobia on the agenda, just to let parents know that they don't have to worry about their daughters being molested by lesbians when they play sport. Then the media got a hold of our policy statement and said we were running an all-lesbian organization at the taxpayers' expense. It's a touchy subject at the best of times without having to deal with that kind of shit.

These and similar experiences led Roxanne to despair over the slow pace of change: 'Some things have obviously changed for the better, but I honestly believe that we've just scratched the surface because most sports are still dominated by men. Now we're getting this backlash just because a few scraps have been tossed our way.'

So far I have analysed gendered structures of labour, power, and cathexis in sporting organizations. With respect to labour, most women felt that men were unaware of how women might be disadvantaged by lack of adequate child care, inflexible working hours, and masculine biases in recruiting, interviewing, hiring, training, and promotion. In terms of power, most women indicated that they either had been harassed or witnessed the harassment of other women. Women also objected to men's verbal styles and did not want to be defeminized by emulating men's combative managerial practices. However, they also wanted to be judged on merit, and so distanced themselves from being associated with lesbianism and any feminist practices that were not within a liberal framework. Homosexuality had a transgressive status and homophobia was common.

Conclusion: One Cheer for Affirmative Action

Those who believe that AA in Canada's sport administration has led to more equitable relationships between men and women will be disappointed by the results of this study. Although caution must be exercised in drawing generalizations from small samples in two organizations, these findings corroborate the broader picture painted by Hall et al.'s (1989) earlier survey of gender hierarchies in Canadian NSOs and similar studies conducted in other countries (see, for example, Cameron 1996; Fasting and Sisjord 1986; Knoppers 1992; Raivio 1986; West and Brackenridge 1990; White and Brackenridge 1985). They are also congruent with the results of the Australian and New Zealand segments of my larger study.

The findings also lend weight to Whitson and Macintosh's (1990) study of policy-making processes in NSOs in Canada. Whitson and Macintosh reported that most managers perceived barriers to women's participation to lie outside of sport and that AA policies impeded the development of élite performance. Despite some moves by SC, Whitson and Macintosh concluded that meagre financial and moral commitments to AA gave executives of NSOs a justification for also assigning a low priority to it:

. . . the federal government's emphasis on high-performance sport, and its preoccupation with institutionalizing a performance support system capable of
preparing elite Canadian athletes to compete successfully in international sport,
have undercut the pursuit of equity-related objectives (Whitson and Macintosh
1990:27–8).

Moreover, there is little evidence that the post-Mulroney era has brought
either substantial increases in Canadian women's economic or political power
(Bacchi 1996; Maroney and Luxton 1997). Sporting organizations have been and
are still affected by the 'corporate push' in Canadian society (Whitson and
Gruneau 1997). Processes of rationalization and commodification have shifted
federal policies away from a broad concern with both recreational and high-
performance sport to a narrow focus on the latter (Berrett 1993; Harvey et al.
1995; Kidd 1995). SC's pressure for organizations to embrace the principles of
corporate managerialism has meant that nearly all NSOs now have CEOs and
managers for advertising, marketing, and public relations, and are highly dependent on either the private and/or state sector for support. As Kikulius et al. (1992)
argue, NSOs have gone from being kitchen table operations to being managed
from the boardroom or executive office. In 1994 the manager of SC's Women's
Program resigned and the Policy, Planning, and Evaluation Unit subsumed her
responsibilities. As this chapter was being written, a new manager of the
Women's Program had still not been appointed.

As it is currently framed, it is likely that AA will have limited success in facilitating more equitable gender relations. Even if it were possible to increase the
number of women in sporting organizations, it will not necessarily change their
essentially masculine cultures and the stresses that women experience in working
within them (McKenna 1997). If an organization recruits more women but
retains AA policies that are based on sameness rather than differences, it is
unlikely that there will be much impact on what Cockburn (1991:219) calls the
'white male heterosexual and largely ablebodied ruling monoculture'.

According to Hall (1994), the evolution of CAAWS is another example of the
schizoid political predicament faced by other women's sport organizations she
has studied in Australia, Canada, the United Kingdom, and the United States—
whether to promote *sport for women* or *women in sport*: 'The former denotes a
more radical feminist perspective in the sense that CAAWS is a women's organization that promotes its aims through sport; the latter represents a distinctly
liberal approach which seeks to improve the lot of women already in sport
through a sports organization for women' (Hall 1994:54). Hall argues that the
combined effects of a male domination of sport, the traditionally conservative
political views of sportswomen, and pressure from the state have depoliticized
CAAWS's activities and gradually moved it towards a liberal-feminist orientation.
Founded by a small group of activists in 1981, CAAWS was supported by SC's
Women's Program until 1984 when it began receiving most of its funds from the

Secretary of State Women's Program. However, in 1990 the Secretary of State withdrew its support and CAAWS was relocated to the Sport, Fitness, and Administration Centre in Ottawa. This shift made it more difficult for CAAWS to be at arm's length from SC. Hall claims that, despite some of CAAWS's lesbian-positive and anti-homophobic initiatives, attempts to keep these and other mainstream feminist issues (e.g., sexual harassment, violence against women, the politics of difference) on the agenda have encountered resistance both within and outside the organization. Furthermore, there has been a tendency for women's sporting organizations to emulate the hierarchical aspects of bureaucratic organizations as professional experts skilled in marketing, business administration, and management supplant grassroots volunteers. Hall et al. (1989:42) predicted that AA issues would be co-opted by the rational bureaucratic culture and masculine discourses that dominate sporting organizations:

> From a radical feminist perspective . . . the problem of change for the betterment of women (and men) is how to create change so that the values of people in power are not necessarily the values of a fundamentally homogeneous group of specifically white, middle-aged men of privilege. If women who are imitation men are placed in these positions, fundamental change will not occur (Hall et al. 1989:42).

On the basis of the findings of this and other studies, it is possible to make a number of recommendations. Some of the steps that are necessary for achieving more equitable relationships between men and women in sport are:

- Enshrining a zero-tolerance policy towards sexism and sexual violence in sport. This involves requiring male administrators, coaches, and athletes to complete violence-prevention programs, and enshrining recommendations and checklists that administrators, coaches, and athletes can use to be proactive towards sexual harassment (Katz 1995; Lenskyj 1992; Parrot et al. 1994).
- Framing AA in ways that question men's privileges and exclusionary practices rather than women's 'disadvantage' or 'underrepresentation' (Bacchi 1996; Burton 1991).
- Eradicating the ways in which sport contributes to impoverished ideals of masculinity by glorifying misogyny and violence (Messner and Sabo 1994).
- Changing the androcentric and homophobic cultures of sporting organizations (Griffin 1992; Lenskyj 1991).
- Adopting the practices of successful feminist organizations in order to specify strategies for dismantling the institutional barriers that systematically favour men and disadvantage women. This includes providing affordable, quality child care; reducing working hours; establishing equitable *pro rata* benefits for casual workers; strict rather than cosmetic enforcement of AA legislation; and shifting from a rationality of the market to a rationality of care (Yeatman 1994).

- Getting issues of men, masculinity, sexuality, sexual harassment, and leadership on AA agendas, especially in management training programs (Hearn, 1992, 1994; Maier 1992; Simmons 1989).
- Linking these internal organizational issues with pro-feminist, gay-affirmative, male-positive movements among men, as well as forging strategic alliances with women, people with disabilities, and people of colour. This entails privileged men encouraging other privileged men to empathize with the struggle of devalued and excluded groups to demonstrate that the politics of equality and the politics of difference are compatible rather than opposing principles (Bell et al. 1993).

It would be a retrograde step to dismiss AA programs in the federal sport structure because they do not cater to the 'needs of all women'. As Connell (1990:536) notes, AA initiatives provide some leverage for some women even if they are not connected with 'a more radical form of engagement with the state'. For instance, many of the programs and publications of CAAWS and SC have presented alternatives for women, albeit for a restricted audience. Nevertheless, the assimilation of AA into the masculine model of sport and the corporate managerial regime that pervades sport and the public and private sectors means that the state is complicit in a process by which 'malestream' sport is doing more to change women than women are to change sport.

Note

I would like to thank the State University of New York Press for allowing me to reproduce material that appeared in J. McKay, *Managing Gender: Affirmative Action and Organizational Power in Australian, Canadian, and New Zealand Sport* (Albany: State University of New York Press, 1997).

References

Allan, J. 1991. 'When Women Set the Rules'. *Canadian Business* 64:40–3.

Antal, A., and D. Izraeli. 1993. 'A Global Comparison of Women in Management: Women Managers in Their Homeland and as Expatriates'. In *Women in Management*, edited by E. Fagenson, 52–96. London: Sage.

Bacchi, C. 1996. *The Politics of Affirmative Action*. Thousand Oaks, CA: Sage.

Bell, E., T. Denton, and S. Nkomo. 1993. 'Women of Color in Management: Toward an Inclusive Analysis'. In *Women in Management*, edited by E. Fagenson, 105–30. London: Sage.

Berrett, T. 1993. 'The Sponsorship of Amateur Sport: Government, National Sport Organization, and Corporate Perspectives'. *Loisir et Société/Society and Leisure* 16:323–46.

Bluckert, P. 1989. 'Courage and Spark: Discovering New Meanings and Expressions of Leadership by Men'. *Equal Opportunities International* 8:21–4.

Burton, C. 1991. *The Promise and the Price: The Struggle for Equal Opportunity in Women's Employment*. Sydney: Allen & Unwin.

Cameron, J. 1996. *Trail Blazers: Women Who Manage New Zealand Sport*. Christchurch: Sport Inclined.

Chase, S. 1988. 'Making Sense of "The Woman Who Becomes a Man"'. In *Gender and Discourse: The Power of Talk*, edited by A. Todd and S. Fisher, 275–95. Norwood: Albex.

Cockburn, C. 1991. *In the Way of Women: Men's Resistance to Sex Equality in Organizations*. London: Macmillan.

Connell, R. 1987. *Gender and Power*. Sydney: Allen & Unwin.

_____. 1990. 'The State, Gender and Sexual Politics: Theory and Appraisal'. *Theory and Society* 19:507–44.

Fagenson, E., ed. 1993. *Women in Management*. London: Sage.

Fasting, K., and M. Sisjord. 1986. 'Gender, Verbal Behaviour and Power in Sports Organisations'. *Scandinavian Journal of Sports Science* 8:81–5.

Freeman, S. 1990. *Managing Lives: Corporate Women and Social Change*. Amherst: University of Massachusetts Press.

Griffin, P. 1992. 'Changing the Game: Homophobia, Sexism, and Lesbians in Sport'. *Quest* 44:251–65.

Hall, E. 1993. 'Waitering/Waitressing: Engendering the Work of Table Servers'. *Gender & Society* 7:329–46.

Hall, M.A. 1994. 'Women's Sport Advocacy Organizations: Comparing Feminist Activism in Sport'. *Journal of Comparative Physical Education and Sport* 16:50–9.

_____. 1995. 'Women in Sport: From Liberal Activism to Radical Cultural Struggle'. In *Changing Methods: Feminists Transforming Practice,* edited by L. Code and S. Burt. Toronto: Broadview Press.

_____. 1996. *Feminism and Sporting Bodies: Essays in Theory and Practice*. Champaign, IL: Human Kinetics.

_____, D. Cullen, and T. Slack. 1989. 'Organizational Elites Recreating Themselves: The Gender Structure of National Sports Organizations'. *Quest* 41:28–45.

Harvey, J., L. Thibault, and G. Rail. 1995. 'Neo-corporatism: The Political Management System in Canadian Amateur Sport and Fitness'. *Journal of Sport and Social Issues* 19:249–65.

Hearn, J. 1992. 'Changing Men and Changing Managements: A Review of Issues and Actions'. *Women in Management Review* 7:3–8.

_____. 1994. 'Changing Men and Changing Managements: Social Change, Social Research and Social Action'. In *Women and Management: Current Research Issues*, edited by M. Davidson and C. Cooper. London: Paul Chapman.

Hochschild, A. 1997. *The Time Bind: When Work Becomes Home and Home Becomes Work*. New York: Metropolitan Books.

Katz, J. 1995. 'Reconstructing Masculinity in the Locker Room: The Mentors in Violence Project'. *Harvard Educational Review* 65:163–74.

Kidd, B. 1995. 'Inequality in Sport, the Corporation, and the State: An Agenda for Social Scientists'. *Journal of Sport and Social Issues* 19:232–48.

Kikulius, L., T. Slack, and B. Hinings. 1992. 'Institutionally Specific Design Archetypes: A Framework for Understanding Change in National Sport Organizations'. *International Review for the Sociology of Sport* 27:343–69.

Knoppers, A. 1992. 'Explaining Male Dominance and Sex Segregation in Coaching: Three Approaches'. *Quest* 44:210–27.

Lenskyj, H. 1991. 'Combating Homophobia in Sport and Physical Education'. *Sociology of Sport Journal* 8:61–9.

_____. 1992. 'Sexual Harassment: Female Athletes' Experiences and Coaches Responsibilities'. *Science Periodical on Research and Technology in Sport* 12:1–5.

Liff, S., and J. Wajcman. 1995. '"Sameness" and "Difference" Revisited: Which Way Forward for Equal Opportunity Initiatives?' *Journal of Management Studies* 33:79–84.

McKay, J. 1997. *Managing Gender: Affirmative Action and Organizational Power in Australian, Canadian, and New Zealand Sport*. Albany: State University of New York Press.

McKenna, E. 1997. *When Work Doesn't Work Anymore*. New York: Hodder & Stoughton.

Maier, M. 1992. 'Evolving Paradigms of Management in Organizations: A Gendered Analysis'. *Journal of Management Studies* 4:29–42.

Maroney, H., and M. Luxton. 1997. 'Gender at Work: Canadian Feminist Political Economy Since 1988'. In *Understanding Canada: Building on the New Canadian Political Economy*, edited by W. Clement, 85–117. Montréal and Kingston: McGill-Queen's University Press.

Messner, M., and D. Sabo, eds. 1994. *Sex, Violence and Power in Sports: Rethinking Masculinity*. Freedom, CA: The Crossing Press.

Ministry of Supply & Services. 1991. *Beneath the Veneer: The Report of the Task Force on Barriers to Women in the Public Service*. Ottawa: Canadian Government Publishing Service.

Morrison, A., R. White, and E. Van Velsor. 1987. *Breaking the Glass Ceiling*. New York: Addison-Wesley.

Parrot, A., N. Cummings, T. Marchell, and J. Hofher. 1994. 'A Rape Awareness and Prevention Model for Male Athletes'. *Journal of American College Health* 42:179–84.

Powell, G. 1993. *Women and Men in Management*, 2nd edn. London: Sage.

Pringle, R. 1988. *Secretaries Talk: Sexuality, Power and Work*. Sydney, Allen & Unwin.

Raivio, M.R. 1986. 'The Life and Careers of Women in Leading Positions in Finnish Sports Organisations'. In *Sport, Culture, Society: International Perspectives*, edited by J. Mangan and R. Small, 270–8. London: E. & F. Spon.

Roper, M. 1994. *The British Organizational Man Since 1945*. Oxford: Oxford University Press.

Simmons, M. 1989. 'Creating a New Men's Leadership: Developing a Theory and Practice'. *Equal Opportunities International* 8:16–20.

Tanton, M., ed. 1994. *Women in Management: A Developing Presence*. London: Routledge.

West, A., and C. Brackenridge. 1990. *Wot! No Women Sports Coaches? A Report on the Issues Relating to Women's Lives as Sports Coaches in the United Kingdom: 1989/1990*. Sheffield, UK: Sheffield City Polytechnic, PAVIC Publications.

_____, and C. Brackenridge. 1985. 'Who Rules Sport? Gender Divisions in the Power Structure of British Sports Organisations from 1960'. *International Review for the Sociology of Sport* 20:96–107.

_____, R. Mayglothing, and C. Carr. 1991. *The Dedicated Few—the Social World of Women Coaches in Britain in the 1990s.* Chichester, UK: West Sussex Institute of Higher Education, Centre for the Study and Promotion of Sport and Recreation for Women and Girls.

Whitson, D., and R. Gruneau. 1997. 'The (Real) Integrated Circus: Political Economy, Popular Culture, and "Major League" Sport'. In *Understanding Canada: Building on the New Canadian Political Economy*, edited by W. Clement, 359–85. Montréal and Kingston: McGill-Queen's University Press.

_____, and D. Macintosh. 1990. 'Equity vs. High Performance in Canadian Amateur Sport'. *Canadian Association for Health, Physical Education and Recreation Journal* (May/June):27–30.

Williams, C. 1995. *Still a Man's World: Men Who Do Women's Work*. Berkeley: University of California Press.

Yeatman, A. 1994. 'Women and the State'. In *Contemporary Australian Feminism*, edited by K. Hughes, 177–97. Melbourne: Longman Cheshire.

Chapter 12

Social Marketing, Gender, and the Science of Fitness:

A Case-Study of ParticipACTION Campaigns

Margaret MacNeill

ParticipACTION is a communications agency that straddles the private and public health fitness sectors in Canada. Founded in 1971, the central goal of ParticipACTION is to 'redefine what it means to be Canadian' by: (1) fostering a national self-image of Canadians as responsible, active citizens who keep fit to be healthy, and (2) promoting Canada internationally as a nation of vibrant and healthy people (ParticipACTION 1991a). Patriotic tag lines such as 'Let's get Canada moving again' (ParticipACTION 1973), 'ParticipACTION salutes Russ Berrett—60 goals—another great moment in Canadian sport' (1976), and musical jingles such as 'Way to go Canada!' (1989) have frequently anchored public service announcements (PSAs).

In this chapter a critical feminist media studies approach is employed to examine gendered differences in images of active and 'unfit' people in ParticipACTION's public awareness campaigns promoting fitness and sporting pastimes. As we will see, the embodiment of gender is never stagnant. For example, ParticipACTION's extremely narrow focus in the 1970s on enhancing the cardiovascular health of middle-class, White Anglo-Saxon males widened in the 1980s to include other types of people. Women participated in aerobic fitness and dancing in ParticipACTION's public service announcements in the early 1980s. It took approximately fifteen years from the inaugural 1971 campaign for female spokespeople to be introduced as fitness authority figures. Other alternative images of fit Canadians as women and men with disabilities, children, seniors, and people from a diversity of ethnocultural backgrounds broke through ParticipACTION's visual barrier in the mid-1980s. However, while ParticipACTION's visions of the 'typically' fit and sedentary Canadian have significantly broadened over the last three decades, media depictions of male and female activity role models have remained fairly conservative.

Two central arguments are presented in this chapter. First, ParticipACTION's media representations have remained steadfastly middle class and heterosexist in their depictions of gendered bodies and lifestyles since the agency's debut. Second, meanings attached to the word 'fit' are produced using particular languages of science (*scientificity*) that privilege both physiological measurements of fitness and health, and behavioural solutions to the 'problem' of sedentary living. In addressing these arguments, this chapter will also discuss (1) the formal techniques of social marketing employed by ParticipACTION, (2) ideologies of healthism and the reproduction of a neoconservative moral imperative of self-responsibility, (3) the contradictions between the political economy of public health goals and 'blaming the individual victim' for his or her poor level of health, and (4) the emphasis on gender difference.

Gender and Feminist Cultural Studies

Using a feminist cultural studies approach, this chapter draws upon the work of Ann Hall (1990:226) to assume that gender means a set of power relations in which 'men, as a social group, have more power over women than women have over them; they are not fixed, rather they are subject to historical change and they can be transformed'. Thus, gender can refer to both the cultural production of a range of femininities and masculinities in physical culture, *and* to the insti-tutionalized relationships of power between men and women. With regard to the latter conception of gender, the institutions of professional sport and the Olympic Games, for example, are primarily governed by males who provide fewer events and rewards to women.

Promoting a feminist cultural studies approach, Hall (1993:54–5) advocates that gender studies should be pursued in a manner that is historically grounded, sensitive to other demographic differences (e.g., ethnicity), and that melds research about gender with initiatives for political change. This approach is particularly useful for deconstructing media campaigns like ParticipACTION's because it 'unpacks' gendered and other assumptions.

Media representations of gender are often representative of rather complex power relations of gender in our society. While gender is popularly understood as a dichotomy, in fact many genders exist. Multiple forms of masculinities and fem-ininities are constructed by the athletes participating within sporting and fitness organizations and by media. Differences in 'appropriate' attire between men and women, for example, illustrate the diversity of genders negotiated in the sphere of sport. Historically, white tennis shorts versus tennis skirts have clearly sepa-rated men and women in the professional ranks due to strict rules that originated in Victorian private club traditions. However, these gendered markers can and have been challenged and reconstituted. Many sport journalists and tennis fans were initially shocked in the 1920s when Suzanne Lenglen shortened her skirt to the knees to play at Wimbledon. Likewise, when Andre Agassi arrived on the men's professional circuit with long, bleached blond hair and wearing torn grunge shorts under his tennis whites in the 1980s, his image received a great deal of public scrutiny. Currently, observations of public tennis courts in any municipality in Canada during the summer will likely reveal players with a wide array of body types wearing clothes that disregard tennis traditions, including women and men in track pants or black biker shorts, and women donning baseball caps rather than traditional visors. Thus, there is a continuum of many masculinities and femininities for both athletes and media to draw upon to construct gender.

Gender can also be variably marked by social background factors like age, ethnicity, sexual orientation, and class. For example, media images of African-American NBA player Dennis Rodman's frequent gender-morphing contrast with the staid images of fitness leader Hal Johnson on ParticipACTION's 'Body Break' spots for over the past fifteen years. Rodman's surly body politic conveys a rebellious gender-blending masculinity. 'The Worm', as he has been nicknamed by the sport media, frequently challenges the race and gendered markers on his body by changing the jewellery pierced into his tattooed skin, by changing his hair colour weekly, and by cross-dressing.

Canadian Hal Johnson, on the other hand, has changed little during his tenure with ParticipACTION. During the 1980s and early 1990s he appeared with Joanne McLeod as a spokesperson for ParticipACTION in 'Body Break' PSAs. In the early PSAs Johnson was consistently presented as an impeccably groomed instructor conservatively silhouetted in a track suit. This, combined with his easygoing style of instruction, conveyed a conservative middle-class masculinity that de-emphasized the ethnocultural markers of his mixed heritage. His image condensed markers like race, gender, and age in an attempt to attract particular segments of the population.

Health Promotion and the Social Marketing of Physical Activity

Health promotion and communication messages *appear* to be apolitical, but are actually intensely political. For example, dominant themes in the social marketing of fitness in Canada have tended to emphasize self-responsibility for physical and emotional health. However, sociocultural barriers to participation in physical activity—such as poverty, racism, violence, and lack of accessible recreational opportunities—have been relatively ignored. Rather, behaviourist frameworks for public health education (stressing information exchange, attitude shifts, motivation, and behaviour modification) and physiological formulas for fitness (e.g., The 'F.I.T.T. Formula' for achieving fitness, requiring attention to frequency, intensity, time, and type of activity) have dominated ParticipACTION. These individualist approaches to social marketing have made inequitable power structures in Canada invisible.

A formal strategy of communication planning called social marketing emerged in the health promotion field in the 1970s (Lefebvre 1992). This method has always been steeped in the strategies of commercial marketing (e.g., planning advertising campaigns around the '4 Ps' of marketing: price, product, promotion, and market placement) (Lefebvre and Flora 1988). Kotler and Zaltman coined the phrase 'social marketing' in 1971 to demonstrate that communication campaigns could be designed to enhance the *acceptability* of social ideas by informing, persuading, and reminding target audiences of particular ideas. Behavioural science tenets of this *information processing theory* assume that audience members will acquire (1) the *awareness of risk* of inactivity and the related consequences of ill health, (2) develop *attitudes of personal concern* about the risks of sedentary lifestyles, (3) develop an *intent to change* to become more physically active, and (4) *adopt* active lifestyles. In privileging this approach to health promotion, ParticipACTION has always assumed that the simple exchange of health information with audience members at the right place and time would produce healthier bodies and a healthier population.

As suggested earlier, the broader political-economic and cultural environments of inequity are ignored in such simplistic models of information exchange and interpretation. They assume that fitness advice is absorbed and acted upon by Canadians in the way intended by the health promoters. Motivational information is assumed to be sufficient to move large sections of the population to initiate a lifestyle change. However, there is little evidence that the social marketing of fitness prescriptions and motivational slogans alone are effective. In order for health promotion campaigns to achieve greater success, a combination of education, public policy about health and social justice, improvements in services and opportunities for active recreation, and community support to address gender equity must be pursued together with the ParticipACTION-style public service announcements.

The Science of Selling Fitness and the Fitness of Science

Check your pulse. If it's over 75 per minute your heart needs your help. Fitness. In your heart you know it's right. Participaction: the Canadian movement for personal fitness (ParticipACTION 1977).

Contrary to conventional wisdom, the medical/scientific bodies of knowledge informing the health promotion field are not objective—they are cultural formations. Consequently, health promotion, as a formal discipline of study and profession, has achieved what Michel Foucault (1970) calls '*scientificity*'. In other words, physiological advice about fitness has become institutionalized. Advice about achieving regular bouts of physical activity at minimum intensity levels to promote healthy hearts, or medical lists of risk factors for cardiovascular disease (such as sedentary lifestyles, tobacco consumption, etc.) serve to reinforce narrow cultural codes of 'fit' and 'unfit' bodies.

The scholarly field of medical knowledge informing health promotion is part of a web of power that identifies epidemiological pathologies in individual citizens and tends to present the nation with individualist solutions. The dominant medical ideology of health promotion offers fitness as a *prescriptive* dose of preventive medicine. Health promotion thereby becomes a larger project of social construction that (1) attempts to gain consent to particular definitions of healthy lifestyles, (2) reproduces professional structures of power that narrowly measure health and epidemiological pathology (such as through morbidity rates), and (3) decides which segments of a national population are worthy of attention by the health care and health promotion system.

Scientificity and Gender

An important sociocultural question to ask about scientificity is, 'Who's health is important?' As a proponent of scientificity, early ParticipACTION initiatives tended to promote a male heterosexist vision of individual and family health within an emphatically middle-class vision of recreation. While the importance of women's health was ignored in the 1970s, the health of women and families became a focus in the 1980s. For example, the 'Re-Generations' print campaign in the 1980s promoted better nutrition and activity as a route to weight loss for individual women and families without considering the broader implications of reinforcing the stereotypes of feminine beauty as requiring slimness:

> Jennifer, Sarah and Maisie. Three generations of one family with a common goal. Getting fit.
>
> It started as a group effort to help young Jennifer overcome a weight problem. But it didn't end that way. Because fitness is catching. As Jennifer's programme began to show results, mother and grandmother joined in. Today all three are enjoying the rewards of keeping fit through better eating habits and a little exercise. It's the regeneration of the three generations.
>
> One very healthy family portrait that illustrates just how easy it is to make fitness a part of everyday living.
>
> Jennifer, Sarah and Maisie. Ready set and fit for a lifetime of living (ParticipACTION 1980s Copykit).

The notion that fitness can be employed to address body weight 'problems' has historically been associated more with females than males in ParticipACTION campaigns.

Dominant images of women in ParticipACTION initiatives have shifted significantly over time, beginning with ParticipACTION advertisements of the nagging housewife in the 1975 television campaign 'Nostalgia', to the dancer/aerobic participant in 1983 spot 'Do it', to the 1990 image of the female expert in 'Body Break' office fitness campaigns. Male imagery has been more consistent but still variable in health promotions by ParticipACTION. In the 1970s males were typically depicted in public service announcements as Caucasian, middle-aged sportsmen and professional working men. In the 1980s and early 1990s males were also constructed as young fitness experts and musical stars with active lifestyles representing a variety of ethnocultural communities who make 'appropriate' nutritional choices (such as singer Billy Newton Davis, who is depicted in the 'Vitality' series riding his bike and later enjoying a bowl of pasta).

ParticipACTION messages are indeed political in that they involve the exchange of health information between the government and the population. These messages incorporate ideologies of *healthism*, which are particular systems of beliefs that present fitness and other 'health' enhancing activities as a moral obligation (Crawford 1980; White, Young, and Gillett 1995). In ParticipACTION's PSAs, as we now see, the obligation has historically included the surveillance of gender.

Prescribing Fitness and the Surveillance of Gender

ParticipACTION's focus has shifted from a narrow physiological notion of 'fitness' in the 1970s and 1980s to the promotion of 'active healthy living' in the 1990s. Officially, ParticipACTION (1991a:3) employs a 'communications' approach that aims for 'creativity, a sense of humour, and balance' in order to tune Canadians into messages about 'quality of life'. Lifestyles and fitness programs are supposed to be projected as enjoyable in PSAs to get Canadians to 'buy in' to the campaign (ParticipACTION 1991a:3). Examples of media campaigns in the 1980s used to motivate Canadians into regular action included: 'Fitness is fun. Try some'; 'Walk a block a day'; 'Don't just think about it. Do it'; 'Make your move'; and 'The great outdoors: Canada—the world's largest fitness club' (ParticipACTION 1980s Copykit). ParticipACTION has shifted from overt techniques of instilling guilt about fitness levels in the 1970s (as later examples will demonstrate) to promoting simple slogans of encouragement and nutritional advice in such campaign series as 'Vitality': 'Grab on to the good times! Enjoy eating well and being active. Feel good about yourself' (ParticipACTION 1990s Copykit). The underlying intent promotes individual solutions to reduce illness and achieve wellness with one's own personal resources.

The gradual shift away from a prescriptive notion of 'fitness' and towards a concept of 'active living' has led to considerable debate within ParticipACTION and the scholarly field of exercise physiology. In promoting a less prescriptive approach to fitness in the 1990s, ParticipACTION has been criticized for 'aiming too low' by some lifestyle researchers (Stephens and Craig 1990). 'Walk a block today', and 'Do it your way, everyday' messages, for instance, are the types of active living messages that have been refuted as not being sufficient to motivate people to raise heart rates to a level of intensity and duration required to promote cardiovascular health (Stephens and Craig 1990). In an attempt to reassert traditional biophysiological authority to challenge active living policies and programs, recent consensus statements about the role of physical activity have been published to proclaim that physical benefits can be achieved from regular *moderate* physical activity (cf., Bouchard et al. 1993).

As suggested earlier, fitness 'principles' and other health messages that target individuals are value laden and morally prescriptive. While the shift away from an exercise physiology prescriptive approach has been partially redressed through the emergence of a more holistic set of *active living* campaigns in the 1990s, the onus continues to be on individual Canadians to get and keep fit.

In this regard, Crawford (1980) argues that an ideology of 'healthism' has become a dominant way of thinking in North America. Recently, White, Young, and Gillett (1995) elaborated on this ideology of healthism with reference to the 'morality' of exercise and other health-promoting behaviours:

> Whether it is through exercise, diet or stress management, the avoidance of disease through personal effort has become a dominant cultural motif. Consequently, self-control, personal resolve and deferment of gratification, all connected to traditionally bourgeois notions of 'clean living', are associated with personal redemption through the demonstration of 'moral character'. Crucially the ideology of healthism also tends to place responsibility for body vigilance solely on the individual, and deflects attention away from the social and cultural conditions which shape and constrain health (White, Young, and Gillett 1995:160).

The ideology of healthism is quietly woven into the fabric of recent social marketing campaigns addressing physical activity. Interviews with ParticipACTION personnel revealed that the promotion of the ideology of healthism was neither a conscious effort nor a conspiratorial mandate of the organization (Colbeck 1995; Costas 1995; Salmon 1995, 1997). Rather, the sense of self-responsibility they wish to cultivate in the population and their disregard for sociocultural barriers to regular physical activity (such as poverty, gender inequity, and racism in Canadian culture) are reflections of the long-term and unquestioned leadership of exercise physiologists in this agency. The daily work of graphic artists, corporate liaisons, and directors of communication at ParticipACTION have always been guided by the technical knowledge of an exercise physiologist (Salmon 1995).

The embodiment of a gendered morality in 'keep fit' messages has not been a concern for professional social marketers even though, as demonstrated earlier, the contested terrain of gender is political. Concerns for how fitness campaigns present bodies marked by gender (as well as class, race, etc.) and for how audience members interpret and employ these messages in constructing their beliefs about health have not been formally addressed by the ParticipACTION agency.

This inattention to gender is clearly evident in ParticipACTION's encouragement of *self-surveillance*. To apply Featherstone's (1983) arguments about body maintenance in consumer culture, ParticipACTION has demanded that Canadians be individually vigilant about health maintenance. 'Self-inflicted illness' is to be avoided in order to service the body for the purposes of work. This, combined with promises of cosmetic bodily improvements, build on the promotion of youthful and 'body beautiful' images in health promotion advertisements (Featherstone 1983). The 1983 public service announcement '*Do it*,' for example, clearly reproduced these themes. In this promotion, women were depicted engaging in a number of pursuits such as aerobic dancing, throwing a football in a bikini, skipping, and roller-skating. The visual framing of female bodies by ParticipACTION in television spots reinforces the construction of particular gendered bodies by suggesting women engage in traditional aesthetically pleasing activities or wear sexy outfits when playing non-traditional sports such as football.

The 'Make your move' series provides another example of how certain types of gender are produced in government health promotions. In one PSA, the outlines of two young female figure skaters lacing up their skates are anchored with:

> 'You've starting skating again?' . . . 'Yes, I'm working on a new figure' . . . Put winter on ice. Go to your neighbourhood rink. Catch up on old friends and meet new ones! Make your move (ParticipACTION 1990s Copykit).

The series encourages young women to change their bodies through activity. The word play around 'figure', melding the action of skating designs on ice and the aesthetically slim bodies of athletes in this traditional female sport, narrowly reproduces a notion of healthy femaleness focused on appearance.

The male audience is also primed on how to survey its lifestyle for bodywork required to enhance heterosexual appeal. Magazine advertisements in the same campaign series targeted males with sexual innuendos about 'making moves' on females. For example, male adolescents were promised they could win the attention of teenaged girls if they quit playing video games and became active. A teen complains, 'I wish I could go out with Sally.' His video game competitor replies, 'She is already out—cycling with Bobby.' The tag line anchoring this exchange is: 'The better you feel, the better you'll look. Eat right, be active . . . and you never know what might happen. *Make your move*' (ParticipACTION 1990s Copykit).

Media-promoted surveillance of the body in ParticipACTION PSAs has predominantly been guided by 'anthropometric scientificity' that categorizes bodies into slim, muscular, and obese somatotypes. Virtuousness is defined by a state of mesomorphy (the trim, muscular body). Russ Kisby, the long-term president of ParticipACTION, admits to being a 'disciple of somatotypes' (Steen 1995:E2). He believes social marketing should match body types with 'right' activity such as promoting swimming for overweight Canadians and running for the slim (Steen 1995:E2). In this way ParticipACTION has tended to oversimplify the association between body weight and health despite the trend in the Canadian health promotion field redefining health as a resource for living and not merely a state of being.

These dominant images have not gone without criticism. Challenges from feminist media critiques and critical medical researchers have successfully fostered a shift in campaigns away from promotions of dieting to promotions of nutrition and vigorous wellness. In 1986 the former Ministry of National Health and Welfare (now Health Canada) reached an official consensus that 'Vitality' would be the mainstay of health promotions in all agencies. 'Vitality' campaigns now advocate that individuals and families make better personal choices between food groups and change everyday behaviours. Health Canada's 'Vitality' campaign, originally written by ParticipACTION for Health Canada, stresses 'healthy good-looking bodies come in a variety of shapes and sizes' (Health Canada and ParticipACTION 1995:3). The campaign has attempted to promote what are now assumed by the federal government to be three key elements to health: (1) eating well, (2) being active, and (3) feeling good about oneself (Health Canada, and ParticipACTION 1995:3).

However, the legitimacy of scientificity has rarely been questioned or challenged. From the outset, 'Vitality' campaigns have employed a psychobehavioural framework to improve the mind, body, and spirit of the individual Canadian (Health Canada and ParticipACTION 1995). Strategies written into these campaigns include: (1) positive self-talk ('think positive thoughts'); (2) setting realistic goals and thinking realistically about self-image; (3) practising 'altruistic egoism' to reduce stress and enhance self-esteem (such as walking your 'elderly neighbour's dog', 'baking cookies for the church bazaar', or filling a 'shift at the food bank'); (4) observing physical and emotional triggers; and (5) engaging in 'internal jogging' or laughter (Health Canada and ParticipACTION 1995). These attempts to inform viewers and readers of 'simple, practical, day-to-day things they can do' and to motivate themselves and their families to action (ParticipACTION 1991a) have also served to promote sensitivity to self-surveillance. To understand more fully the gendering processes and rationale behind ParticipACTION's social marketing strategies, a broader examination of this marketing arm of the state is required.

'Blaming the Victim': Marketing Personal Responsibility

ParticipACTION emerged at a juncture in Canadian history when ways of thinking about population health were shifting from a curative disease model to a preventive disease/wellness model. The agency was created as a semiautonomous communication vehicle of the federal government in an era of deepening economic concerns. Low productivity rates (as measured by gross national product, employee attendance, and absentee rates) and rising health care costs motivated the federal government of Canada to employ physical activity as an instrument of the welfare system in the postwar era (Macintosh, Bedecki, and Franks 1987). *A New Perspective on the Health of Canadians* (also known as the Lalonde Report), for example, argued that Canadian citizens could make better lifestyle choices to reduce the economic burden that preventable diseases placed upon the health care system (Lalonde 1994). In this report, Marc Lalonde, the federal minister of the Department of Health and Welfare Canada at that time, argued that educating the population to move would be an effective tactic because a concern for 'increasing physical recreation has never been higher' (Lalonde 1974:5–6).

The Lalonde Report attempted to shift the burden of health care away from hospitals and from the state as a national 'insurance broker' (Lalonde 1974). The blame for poor health and the burden of care were placed on the shoulders of individual Canadians without acknowledging the many barriers to health such as poverty (Labonte 1994; Labonte and Penfold 1981; Vayda 1977). Individual Canadians with risk factors for preventable diseases became the focus of public service announcements. To reap the rewards of a healthy body, the government employed ParticipACTION to tell citizens that they must 'pull themselves up by their own boot straps'. Consequently, 'blaming the victims' for levels of disease and rising health care costs have mediated the promotion of 'lifestyle' (Ingham 1986).

Another government policy promoting self-responsibility for good health was Bill C-131, The Fitness and Amateur Sport Act (1961). This act was passed in 1961 to foster national unity by using high-performance athletics to promote mass participation in fitness activities and recreational sport. The promotion of fitness was ignored throughout the 1960s (Macintosh, Bedecki, and Franks 1987). To redress this oversight, the federal government decided a 'fresh approach' to activity promotion was needed to improve the health and fitness levels of the 'average Canadian' in the 1970s (ParticipACTION 1991a:2). This led to the creation of ParticipACTION.

Today, ParticipACTION staff frequently cite the costs of poor health to justify their continued government support, even though the effect of programs on activity rates and the health status of Canadians has not been documented. Until the early 1990s, ParticipACTION received $2 million per year in core funding from Fitness Canada (ParticipACTION 1991a). Since 1994, ParticipACTION has received $750,000 from the Fitness Directorate of Health Canada to produce PSAs (Salmon 1997). The costs of illness—such as direct medical care costs, low productivity rates of workers, and insurance claims from preventable injuries—continue to serve as justification for continued federal funding (Habib 1991).

However, many Canadians do not connect physical activity with general health. A Statistics Canada (1995) survey, for example, found that 62 per cent of the nation rate their health as excellent even though only 17 per cent of all Canadians are regularly active. The number of citizens who associate levels of physical fitness with health have therefore been exaggerated by ParticipACTION. Indeed, the recent growth in activity rates has been fostered only *in part* by public health promotions. Private clubs, fitness and sporting goods, exercise videos, workout magazines, and fitness services have also played a significant role in motivating the nation to action (MacNeill 1998).

In the 1970s ParticipACTION addressed only the need for men to get 'fit' and to find stress-reducing activities to avoid heart attacks and premature death. 'Technical' advice about the science of physical fitness was borrowed from exercise physiologists in Canadian universities to set minimum standards of regular physical activity (Salmon 1995).

The first campaign targeting men was broadcast on television during the half-time show of the 1973 Grey Cup Football Championship. Broadcasting time and production expertise were donated by both the private (CTV) and public (CBC) national networks, and by the Canadian Football League (CFL) to support this inaugural campaign. In a fifteen-second commercial, the average level of fitness of a thirty-year-old Canadian and a sixty-year-old Swede were compared. The inaugural advertisement depicted a Canadian and a Swedish jogger running down a path. A male commentator observed:

> These men are about evenly matched—that's because the average thirty year old Canadian is in about the same physical shape as the average sixty year old Swede. Run, walk, cycle—let's get Canada moving again (ParticipACTION 1973).

The 'Canadian versus Swede' advertisement (1973) appeared six times during half-time to serve as a direct wake-up call to Canadian males (ParticipACTION 1991a). It remains the most memorable campaign in the history of ParticipACTION, according to independent market research (Salmon 1997). The explicit intent of this PSA was to embarrass a nation of workers during their leisure time as they watched the CFL Grey Cup Championship on television.

The physiological comparison of fitness between 'average' citizens of two different nations has never been substantiated with research by ParticipACTION. ParticipACTION's PSAs in the 1970s did not provide advice about how to get fit, how to gain access to active opportunities, address the nature of urban living, calculate the costs of active recreation and sport participation, or provide advice about how to overcome gendered inequities in access to recreation. In another attempt to combine a 'fear' approach and physiological advice, a television spot called 'Motivation' depicted a middle-aged man scurrying to get out of his office (ParticipACTION 1974). Grabbing his gym bag and a racquet, the Caucasian actor happily closes his office door to reveal a 'Funeral Director' title on his door. The narrator concludes the public service announcement with 'Some people are more motivated than others' (ParticipACTION 1974).

While men were assumed to be *the working nation* at risk of illness in the 1970s campaigns, women's paid work and unpaid domestic labour were undervalued. Adult females made up less than half of the paid labour force at this time. In 1976 45.2 per cent of women and 77.6 per cent of men were considered part of the paid labour force (Statistics Canada 1986:Table 11). In the 1990s a gendered division of labour and a focus on the workplace continues. Today, men continue to be foregrounded as paid employees in the labour force who discover ways to overcome lifestyle obstacles by cycling in the 'Ride your bike to work—make your move' campaign televised by ParticipACTION in 1991. Women have been more likely to be portrayed pursuing light activities—such as walking, dancing, gardening, or engaged in domestic activities such as pushing baby strollers—as they do during the 1991 television campaign. Early ParticipACTION campaigns tended to neglect women's health, fitness levels, non-domestic roles, and work as fitness leaders. The introduction of the 'Body Break' series in the 1980s abruptly changed the image of females in ParticipACTION campaigns. This fitness promotion series, providing specific advice about to get fit and avoid injury, was a partnership between ParticipACTION and hired spokespeople (Joanne McLeod and Hal Johnson). It marked the introduction of a White woman and a Black man as fitness experts who address diverse audiences. This impetus for more inclusiveness of women, seniors, and people with disabilities in fitness representations came from a set of 'Blueprints for Action' mandated by Fitness Canada (Salmon 1997).

Current Social Marketing Strategies

The business strategy of ParticipACTION currently involves a three-pronged approach: gaining free media exposure as unpaid public service announcements, attracting corporate and government support for initiatives, and establishing local networks of effective communication and events (ParticipACTION 1991a). In 1991 ParticipACTION cited pollsters to promote their success: independent researchers had found that 84 per cent of Canadians were aware of the ParticipACTION agency, and that 95 per cent of the survey respondents believed that ParticipACTION campaigns were helping Canadians to become more physically active and aware of the health benefits of activity (ParticipACTION 1991a). Furthermore, ParticipACTION estimated it had attracted donations worth over $250 million in print media space and broadcast media time (Salmon 1997). Corporate logos and media signatures are now melded with ParticipACTION campaigns. Four million Canadians and 20 million people in other nations are enrolled in ParticipACTION events organized by schools and health departments. Promotions suggested by ParticipACTION have recently included Schneiders[R] Lifestyle[R] 'Sneaker Day' (1994) and Crownlife[R] 'Summer Active' events (1996).

Attaining an 89 per cent logo recognition rate among Canadians is taken by the agency to be their proudest measure of promotional success (ParticipACTION 1991a). A sense of familiarity with ParticipACTION's pinwheel icon has only been surpassed by widespread recognition of the McDonald's 'golden arches' and the 'swoosh' symbol of Nike. ParticipACTION's 'Do it' promotion in the 1980s has recently been recycled with Nike's famous 'Just do it' slogan in the 'Just do it daily for life campaign' promoted by the Canadian Association of Health, Physical Education, Recreation and Dance. But recognition of a fitness symbol does not necessarily translate into higher levels of physical activity.

Rhetoric about the 'social determinants of health', currently mediating public health policy, has failed to address sexism of activity promotions. Despite ignoring equity issues, ParticipACTION believes that it can help foster the broad base for health because 'our efforts will contribute significantly to strategies for improving health, containing health care costs, increasing productivity, ecological balance, sustainable development and generally improving the quality of life in Canada' (ParticipACTION 1991a).

In 1997 former Minister of Health David Dingwall requested promotions to link physical inactivity to the incidence of specific diseases such as diabetes, heart disease, and breast cancer. In response to this request, ParticipACTION now plans to shift away from a targeted 'social' approach of addressing different segments of the Canadian population and focus instead on specific 'disease-of-the-month' preventions (Salmon 1997). A resurgence of biomedical ideologies of healthism is expected and more gender-sensitive media interventions are not anticipated. ParticipACTION's social marketing plan does not include advocacy for equity.

Conclusions

ParticipACTION is located at a crossroads between public health promotion, consumer culture, and gender relations where discourses of self-responsibility, citizenry, and shifting notions of masculinity and femininity reside. Campaigns have historically made an intervention in the health promotion sector by putting the physiological and stress-reducing benefits of regular physical activity onto the public health agenda. Since the 1970s, the print and broadcast PSAs have regularly increased awareness of population fitness levels and have offered motivational tips to educate individuals about activity choices.

Research into the degree to which the agency has heightened awareness and whether campaigns have resulted in more activity have not been determined in research. The agency has neither engaged in political interventions to improve opportunities for disadvantaged segments of the population to be more active, nor has it challenged its own hegemonic promotions of narrow gender definitions. Public service announcements have tended to reproduce images of traditional gender relations and stereotypes.

How ParticipACTION promotions are interpreted by different segments of the Canadian population, particularly males and females, remains unquestioned in the agency's market research. Information on how audience members reject, incorporate, or transform public service announcements as a resource for constructing fit bodies and lifestyles needs to be gathered using research methods such as grounded focus group interviews with audience members or ethnographic field research.

A number of arguments have been presented in this case-study of gendered ParticipACTION campaigns. At a broad level, ParticipACTION is a social marketing agency of the federal government promoting an individualist responsibility for fitness and health. As a disease prevention and health promotion unit of Health Canada, it is likely that ParticipACTION will continue to advocate individual responsibility for fitness levels. The current postwelfare state continues to blame the victims of poor health without fully considering the gendered costs of living.

Two other arguments about media representations of fitness and health have been highlighted in this chapter. First, ParticipACTION's media role models have tended to be constructed in a manner that embodies middle-class and heterosexist visions of active, healthy living. Second, this agency's vision of 'fit' has been consistently mediated by physiological and behavioural forms of *scientificity*.

Overall, ParticipACTION's social marketing of fitness has failed to proactively remove structural constraints to greater involvement such as those experienced by less advantaged groups. ParticipACTION's promotion of active living is a passionate but officially 'apolitical' venture in health communication. Contrary to this official belief espoused by ParticipACTION, this chapter has shown that the very production and distribution of particular gendered images of fitness are profoundly political actions in our culture.

Note

The author gratefully acknowledges a grant from the Canadian Fitness and Lifestyle Research Institute for reseach on social marketing approaches used in part of this chapter.

References

Bouchard, C., R.J. Shephard, and T. Stephens, eds. 1993. *Physical Activity, Fitness and Health: Consensus Statement*. Champaign, IL: Human Kinetics.

Colbeck, N. 1995. Director of communications, director of community programs, ParticipACTION, personal interview, Toronto, 4 October.

Costas, C. 1995. Corporate communications, ParticipACTION, personal interview, Toronto, 20 September.

Crawford, R. 1980. 'Healthism and the Medicalization of Everyday Life'. *International Journal of Health Services* 10:365–88.

Featherstone, M. 1983. 'The Body in Consumer Culture'. *Theory, Culture and Society* 1:18–33.

Foucault, M. 1970. *The Archaeology of Knowledge*. London: Tavistock.

Habib, M. 1991. 'ParticipACTION Still Vital at Age 20'. *The Toronto Star* (29 November):F2.

Hall, A. 1990. 'How Should We Theorize Gender in the Context of Sports?' In *Sport, Men and the Gender Order: Critical Feminist Perspectives*, edited by M. Messner and D. Sabo, 223–39. Champaign, IL: Human Kinetics.

_____. 1993. 'Gender and Sport in the 1990s: Feminism, Culture and Politics'. *Sport Science Review* 2:48–68.

Health Canada and ParticipACTION. 1995. 'Vitality: ParticipACTION Makes Perfect'. Print media insert. Ottawa: Health Canada.

Ingham, A. 1986. 'From Public Issue to Personal Trouble: Well-being and the Fiscal Crisis of the State'. *Sociology of Sport Journal* 2:43–54.

Kotler, P., and G. Zaltman. 1971. 'Social Marketing: An Approach to Planned Social Change'. *Journal of Marketing* 35:3–12.

Labonte, R. 1994. 'Death of a Program, Birth of a Metaphor: The Development of Health Promotion in Canada'. In *Health Promotion in Canada: Provincial, National and International Perspectives*, edited by A. Pederson, M. O'Neill, and I. Rootman, 72–90. Toronto: W.B. Saunders.

_____, and S. Penfold. 1981. 'Canadian Perspectives in Health Promotion: A Critique'. *Health Education* 19:4–9.

Lalonde, M. 1974. *A New Perspective on the Health of Canadians: A Working Document*, April. Ottawa: Health and Welfare Canada.

Lefebvre, R. 1992. 'Social Marketing and Health Promotion'. In *Health Promotion: Disciplines and Diversity*, edited by R. Bunton and G. MacDonald, 153–81. London: Routledge.

_____, and J. Flora. 1988. 'Social Marketing and Public Health Intervention'. *Health Education Quarterly* 15:299–315.

Macintosh, D., with T. Bedecki and C. Franks. 1987. *Sport and Politics in Canada*. Montréal: McGill-Queen's University Press.

MacNeill, M. 1998. 'Sex, Lies and Videotape: The Cultural and Political Economies of Celebrity Fitness Videos'. In *Sport and Postmodern Times: Culture, Gender, Sexuality, the Body and Sport*, edited by G. Rail and J. Harvey, 163–84. New York: State University of New York Press.

Ministry of Fitness and Amateur Sport. 1961. Fitness and Amateur Sport Act, Bill C-131, Chapter F-25. Ottawa: Queen's Printer.

ParticipACTION. 1973. 'Let's get Canada moving'. Tape of ParticipACTION PSA.

_____. 1974. 'Motivation'. Tape of ParticipACTION PSA.

_____. 1975. 'Nostalgia'. Tape of ParticipACTION PSA.

_____. 1976. 'Great moments in Canadian sport'. Tape of ParticipACTION PSA.

_____. 1977 'Check your pulse', magazine PSA in *Coaching Review*, back cover.

_____. 1980s. Copykit for print PSAs containing: 'Do it'; 'Fit is fun: Try some'; 'Make your move'; 'Re-generations'; 'The great outdoors'; 'Walk a block a day'.

_____. 1983. 'Do it'. Tape of ParticipACTION PSA.

_____. 1986. 'Vitality: ParticipACTION makes perfect'. Tape of ParticipACTION PSA.

_____. 1989. 'Way to go Canada'. Tape of ParticipACTION PSA.

_____. 1990. 'Body Break'.

_____. 1990s. Copykit for print PSAs containing: 'Just do it daily for life'; 'Make your move series'; 'Vitality: Grab on to the good times'.

_____. 1991a. 'Background Notes on ParticipACTION: A Guide to Potential Sponsors'. Toronto: ParticipACTION.

_____. 1991b. 'Ride your bike to work'. Tape of ParticipACTION PSA.

Salmon, A. 1995. National technical director, ParticipACTION, personal interview, Toronto, 4 October.

_____. 1997. National technical director, ParticipACTION, telephone interview, Toronto, 30 April.

Statistics Canada. 1986. *The Labour Force*. Catalogue no. 71–001. Ottawa: Supply and Services Canada.

_____. 1995. *National Population Health Survey*. Ottawa: Ministry of Supply and Services.

Steen, B. 1995. 'One, Two, Hold That Stretch: Enticing People to Get Fit Is Russ Kisby's Mission at ParticipACTION'. *The Toronto Star* (11 June):E1–E2.

Stephens, T., and C. Craig. 1990. *The Well-being of Canadians: Highlighting the 1988 Campbell's Survey*. Ottawa: The Canadian Lifestyle and Fitness Research Institute.

Vayda, E. 1977. 'Preventative Programs and the Political Process'. *Modern Medicine in Canada* 32:260–4.

White, P., K. Young, and J. Gillett. 1995. 'Bodywork as a Moral Imperative: Some Critical Notes on Health and Fitness'. *Society and Leisure* 18:159–82.

Chapter 13

'Cool Pose' Incorporated:
The Marketing of Black Masculinity in Canadian NBA Coverage

Brian Wilson

Some African-American males have channeled their creative energies into the construction of a symbolic universe. Denied access to mainstream avenues of success, they have created their own voice. Unique patterns of speech, walk, and demeanor express the *cool pose*. This strategic style allows the black male to tip society's imbalanced scales in his favour. Coolness means poise under pressure and the ability to maintain detachment, even during tense encounters. Being cool invigorates a life that would otherwise be degrading and empty. . . . Cool pose brings a dynamic vitality into the black male's everyday encounters, transforming the mundane into the sublime and making the routine spectacular.

—R. Majors and J. Billson, *Cool Pose*

. . . subcultures, and many of the activities that take place within them, represent 'symbolic violations of the social order' that provoke censure from the dominant culture. One example of censure is the *incorporation* of the subcultural style by popular culture industries.

—S. Baron, 'Resistance and Its Consequences'

In the face of widespread oppression, institutionalized racism, and limited opportunity, many Black males empower themselves with a 'cool pose'.[1] Sport, particularly basketball, are sites where young Black males symbolically oppose the dominant White group and create identity by developing both a flamboyant on-court language (now popularly known as 'trash talking') and a repertoire of spectacular 'playground' moves and high-flying dunks. For celebrity Black professional athletes like Shaquille O'Neal and the now-retired Michael Jordan, this distinct form of masculinity is asserted on a televised, transnational stage.

Although the 'cool pose' is but one of many coping strategies and masculine identities adopted by Black males, it is the most spectacular and assertive. Yet the symbolic power gained by Black males who use this strategy should not be mistaken for real power in Canadian society. For this reason, the 'cool pose' has been described as a 'marginalized masculinity' to show the relationship between the masculine identities of dominant (White male) groups and subordinate ethnic groups. Black male sport stars, who are exemplars of masculine toughness for Black and White men, are still representatives of a marginalized group because 'the fame and wealth of individual stars has no trickle-down effect; it does not yield social authority to black men generally' (Connell 1995:81).

Despite the marginalized status of the 'cool pose', sport marketers (as well as rap/hip hop music promoters and movie directors like Spike Lee) have, in recent years, recognized, reformulated, and expanded the appeal of this form of Black masculinity for a mass audience. For example, the National Basketball Association (NBA) and corporations such as Nike, McDonald's, and Coca-Cola regularly feature Black athletes (either celebrity athletes or fictional 'playground' athletes) in advertising campaigns emphasizing Black masculine athleticism, style, creativity, and aggression—the 'cool pose'. In essence, behaviours and attitudes that were previously symbols of Black male identity and resistance have now been appropriated and incorporated by big business.

There are ongoing debates surrounding the extent to which corporations exploit and stereotype Black male culture. In the United States these issues have received attention both in the popular media and in scholarly research. With the widespread marketing of the 'cool pose,' there follows logically a need to understand these issues as they relate to other cultures. Andrews et al. (1996) have done some preliminary work in this area by examining how the mass promotion of Michael Jordan, the premier NBA celebrity, and his assertive and empowered Black masculinity is received in Britain, New Zealand, and Poland. Their research was intended to gain insight into how American-based marketing of Black male culture has been integrated into the popular advertising and popular culture of other countries, and to understand the meanings that the Black male athlete and inner-city culture have for audiences in these countries. The goal of this chapter is to understand these processes in the Canadian context and to address issues related to the power of advertising, racial stereotyping, and masculine cultures. This is an important step if we consider the recent expansion of the NBA into Toronto and Vancouver and the subsequent increase in Canadians' exposure to NBA and basketball-related marketing. Furthermore, Canada's susceptibility to American-based marketing practices requires examination considering Canada's unique ethnic/racial population mix and its geographic positioning as a neighbour of the United States.

The structure of this chapter is as follows. First, the evolution of and issues surrounding the marketing of Black masculinity and basketball are discussed in relation to the marketing history of the NBA. Second, the media analysis method used in this chapter is explained with reference to deconstruction techniques that are often used in studies of advertising. Third, the use of 'cool pose' as a coping mechanism for Black males is explored within the racial context of Canada.

Finally, a brief case-study is presented of Black athlete portrayals in commercial advertising during Toronto Raptors telecasts, and evidence is provided of the ways that the 'cool pose' has been marketed in Canada. Overall, this chapter argues that the marketing techniques used by some commercial sponsors of NBA games potentially create or reinforce stereotypical perceptions of Black males for Canadian audiences, while at the same time eroding the symbolic (albeit limited) meaning of the 'cool pose' for the identities of some Black Canadian males.

Marketing Black Masculinity and Basketball: A Brief History

> Basketball is an especially complex and contradictory social space because it simultaneously privileges and commodifies a stigmatized black aesthetic, a style of play associated with the racially-coded inner city (Cole and Denny 1994:129).

The marketing of Black masculinity as it relates to the evolution of modern professional basketball has proceeded through three highly integrated periods up to the present.

Period 1: The (Unsuccessful) Marketing of Inner-City Culture

The NBA and its short-lived rival league, the American Basketball Association (ABA), failed to effectively package Black masculine culture in the 1970s and early 1980s. According to Cole and Denny (1994:129), the failure of the league(s) and their sponsors to garner marketing support or substantial audiences was due in part to the game's explicit association 'with an urban black masculinity coded as threatening through the number of African-American players in the league, their expressive style of play and a lifestyle depicted by the media . . . through endemic cocaine use'. Although the 'cool pose' of the time was not altogether different from today—with expressive player nicknames like the 'Iceman', 'Dr J', 'Silk', and 'Chocolate Thunder', along with a distinct style of play characterized by grace, 'hang time', and power—urban Black culture was generally not appealing to audiences in the United States or elsewhere.

Period 2: Magic, Larry, 'Air' Jordan . . . and Inner-City Culture

The NBA and associated advertisers, particularly athletic-apparel companies like Nike and Converse, changed their approach to promoting the game and its players in the mid-1980s. As McDonald (1996:348) argues, the NBA distanced itself from the 'racist associations' that linked 'the predominantly Black athletic labour force with an "undisciplined" style of play and the stigma of drug abuse'. By promoting professional basketball 'as an appealing cultural event complete with stylized play and extraordinary larger-than-life personalities', new meanings were associated with Black masculinity in an effort to court White middle-class audiences (McDonald 1996:348). For example, the rivalry between Black superstar Magic Johnson and White superstar Larry Bird was marketed in such a way that Johnson became the 'embodiment of an acceptable, *non-threatening* [emphasis added] face of (Black) masculinity' (Cole and Denny 1994:129)—a masculinity associated with 'exceptional skill, hard work, dedication, and determination' (McDonald 1996:348). Similarly, Magic was successfully promoted as both a sport hero and AIDS hero after announcing that he had tested positive for HIV in 1991 (King 1993).

Positive, unthreatening images of Michael Jordan also emerged during his inaugural NBA season in 1984–5. Although the earliest marketing initiatives surrounding Jordan focused on the 'playground' values of 'hang time' and physical prowess, it became clear to corporate image makers that if Jordan were to become an 'All-American' phenomenon, 'they could not afford to explicitly associate him with the threatening aspects of black American existence' (Andrews 1996:137). This realization initiated a mass-marketing scheme that eventually brought Jordan to celebrity icon status. Andrews (1996:139) argues that this promotional strategy made the NBA 'accessible to the White American population who had previously been turned off, and turned away by the game's overtly black demeanor'.

Despite the apparent simplicity of this emergent trend, the marketing of Black masculinity during this period was contradictory and complex. Although athletes such as Magic Johnson, and later on Michael Jordan, were portrayed in ways that deflected attention from the threatening aspects of their 'Blackness', the marketing of traditional, stereotypical forms of Black masculinity was still common. Advertisements made explicit and intentional links with an inner-city toughness and intimidation known as 'attitude' (Lull 1995:77). This ineffective marketing practice in the 1970s was coming in vogue for companies trying to reach Black audiences who identify with inner-city 'attitude' and White youth who were adopting Black styles. Wonsek (1992) describes how these menacing images were used in Nike and Reebok commercials shown during 1988 National Collegiate Athletic Association men's basketball tournament coverage:

> The Nike commercials featured a couple of athletic and powerful looking black males in the foreground emerging from a New York subway station wearing athletic warm-up clothes, and, of course, Nike athletic shoes. The image is overwhelming and somewhat threatening, feeding the stereotype that one black youth constitutes a gang to be feared by law-abiding citizens. The Reebok commercials also capitalized on their portrayal of black males playing basketball in city playgrounds. . . . Insidious in these athletic apparel commercials was the use of 'street talk' by black males. . . . For example, in the Reebok commercial, one black character related the story of a particular street legend: 'You talk about playground legends—He come down the court. . .'. The Nike commercial accentuated its already threatening visual image with the addition of this type of language: as the

young men emerged from the subway station, a voice-over announced: 'Ya gonna learn a lesson about intimidation' (Wonsek 1992:456–7).

The use of 'inner-city' images such as these was common for athletic-apparel companies at this time and, as we shall see, this continued into the 1990s.

Period 3: The 'Disneyfied' NBA, the 'All-American' Michael Jordan . . . and Inner-City Culture

By the 1990s, the NBA's (and commissioner David Stern's) choice to align its marketing scheme with that of Disney, 'the corporate exemplar of wholesome entertainment', allowed the league and its players to become globalized commodities, thus realizing the goals set by advertisers in the second period (McDonald 1996:349). Michael Jordan's popularity reached almost unprecedented heights as he became one of the most celebrated athletes and individuals (Black or not) on the planet. By positioning Jordan as an attractive, talented, reliable, trustworthy, conservative family man in commercials for sponsors such as Hanes underwear, a nearly impeccable image was fostered. This is an example of what Andrews (1996:139) considers the 'most pertinent of Jordan's "exceptional qualities"', that is, his 'understated racial identity, as opposed to his superlative basketball displays'. However, this is not to say that Jordan has been disconnected from a Black masculine athletic identity—only the threatening aspects of this identity. For example, the 'cool' notion of 'hang time' is still central to his positioning in many commercials (as in a recent Gatorade commercial where Jordan is shown jumping to a basketball hoop that appears to be hundreds of feet in the air), while the highlight reels of his amazing on-court feats have always been fused to his mass-mediated identity.

As in the second marketing period, the marketing schemes surrounding Jordan and other 'good guy' Blacks such as Grant Hill, 'Penny' Hardaway, and David Robinson were contradicted by the widespread use of 'attitude advertising'. In some 'attitude' commercials, like the Nike and Reebok ones mentioned earlier, fictional playground Black athletes were used to market the culture of the inner city. Other 'attitude' commercials took a different approach, featuring celebrity 'antihero(s)' (Andrews 1996:141) like Charles Barkley. In Barkley's case, Nike highlighted his reputation as a skilled, aggressive, outspoken basketball player (who is known to bully opponents and insult teammates and coaches) and as a flamboyant off-court personality (known for dating celebrity Madonna and fighting in public). According to Lull (1995:77) (and admitted by Nike), it was these parts of Barkley's personality, 'the raging, irresponsible, egomaniacal brute—that Nike exploit[ed] to sell shoes'. For example,

In his earliest commercial slot [for Nike], a black and white commercial inspired by the musical *Hell's-a-Poppin'*, Barkley was initially surrounded by a group of journalists and photographers, one of which he ends up punching. The ensuing newspaper headline predictably reads 'Charles-a-Poppin.' Even in the renowned Barkley versus Godzilla commercial, the humorous nature of the narrative cannot detract from the fact that Barkley is being portrayed as little more than an overtly physical and aggressive, almost animal-like individual. Likewise, in the recent 'Barkley of Seville' commercial, which in lampooning the excesses of operatic expression, still has Charles killing the referee (Andrews 1996:141).

Although Barkley's commercialized persona has softened over the years, these techniques are still commonly associated with other 'bad' athletes, such as the infamous Dennis Rodman (who promoted Converse products) and outspoken rookie Alan Iverson (Reebok).

Paradoxes and Contradictions

The latter two periods, while distinct in the extent to which some celebrity Black athletes shed their explicit associations with the inner city, are characterized by relatively polarized depictions of Black masculinity. On the one hand, Michael Jordan and other 'good Blacks' (Wenner 1995) represent a Black masculinity that, while associated with 'cool pose' basketball attributes such as 'hang time', physicality, and expressive basketball moves, are not threatening or brash. On the other hand, sport marketers (and particularly athletic-apparel companies) have also appealed to audiences by marketing 'attitude' to youth who might see shoes and apparel as a statement about their masculine identities (Hickey 1990; Lull 1995:77).

Deconstructing Black Masculinity in Advertising

Early advertising usually state[d] its message explicitly through the medium of written text . . . but starting in the mid-1920s visual representation became most common, and the relationship between the text and visual image became complementary—that is, the text explained the visual. In the postwar period, and especially since the early 1960s, the functions of text moved away from explaining the visual and toward a more cryptic form, in which text appeared as a kind of 'key' to the visual. . . . In all, the effect was to make the commercial message more ambiguous; a 'reading' of it depended on relating elements of the ad's internal structure to each other, as well as drawing in references from the external world (Leiss, Kline, and Jhally 1990:199)

To critically assess recent debates about the potentially negative consequences of commercials featuring Black male athletes and inner-city 'cool' culture, it is crucial to understand how meanings are embedded in television commercials. As

Leiss, Kline, and Jhally (1990) explain, television commercials and other forms of contemporary advertising are comprised of a strategically constructed system of signs that is meant to generate implicit meanings for the viewer/consumer. Signs are anything that have meaning, like gestures (e.g., a 'knowing' wink), objects (e.g., a 'romantic' rose), or locations (e.g., Wall Street's association with stock trading). The study of signs and sign associations is called semiology (Barthes 1973; De Saussure 1966). Semiologists who analyse media texts (such as television commercials) separate the sign into two components: the signifier and the signified. The material vehicle of meaning (such as a rose) is the signifier; the signified is the actual meaning (the rose means romantic). Signs can have different meanings for different people, depending on one's acquired knowledge and cultural experiences, although there is believed to be a 'preferred' or dominant reading that most people will have (Hall 1980).

When decoding advertisements, the semiologist attempts to link the objects of the ad (such as the rose) to the cultural knowledge of the audience (an audience that would understand the relationship between a rose and romance). More than looking at individual objects, decoding requires an understanding of the ways these objects work together to create a story or message. If the semiologist is not adequately aware of the audience's cultural knowledge (or referent system), then an accurate decoding cannot take place. In saying this, it is important to note that the meanings of advertisements are not self-evident, as Leiss, Kline, and Jhally suggest:

> The semiological approach . . . suggests that the meaning of an ad does not float on the surface, just waiting to be internalized by the viewer, but is built up out of the ways that different signs are organized and related to each other, both within the ad and through external references to the wider belief systems. More specifically, for advertising to create meaning, the reader or the viewer has to do some 'work' (Leiss, Kline, and Jhally 1990:201–2).

For semiologists who understand the relevant cultural meanings of sport-related advertising and relevant race issues, potential interpretations and consequences of commercials featuring Black athletes can be examined.

Athletic-apparel commercials provide excellent examples of how signs can be organized to create meanings and how these meanings can be decoded. Consider an athletic-apparel commercial that shows young Black males playing basketball on a playground against a backdrop of run-down buildings covered with graffiti. Likely associations might include: (1) that the setting is inner-city America, possibly New York or Chicago, known hotbeds for African-American basketball players; (2) that the area is poverty stricken and dangerous, characteristics generally associated (particularly in the media) with graffiti, groups of young Black males, and inner-city America; and (3) an assumption that the young Black males are 'naturally' superior basketball players (a common belief based on the high percentage of African-American athletes in professional sport), whose style includes fancy moves, slam-dunks, and trash talking—popular associations with the city game (and the mass-marketed 'cool pose'). A decoding would be completed when these overt and subtle meanings were organized into the story of an inner-city basketball game.

Many of the following critiques focus on the assumptions that are uncovered in these kinds of semiotic analyses. Certainly the interpretations and related issues expressed here are not relevant to every audience. If a person or group does not watch basketball, or is from a culture where these (stereotypical) understandings of Black athletes are not common knowledge, then interpretations of the commercial would not match those mentioned earlier. However, it is also clear that the mass media reinforce 'natural', 'common-sense', and 'taken-for-granted' perceptions about the real world for many audience groups (Hall 1985). The central issues and related critiques surrounding Black athlete media portrayals in Canadian popular culture are outlined below.

The Exploitation of Black Masculine Culture

Advertisers, and in particular those who market athletic apparel, have in many cases rearticulated and exploited Black male culture in commercial advertising. They have taken the oppositional and resistant potential of the 'cool pose' and repackaged it as a commodity for consumption by a variety of audiences, ranging from 'inner city black boys to suburban white girls who high-five and call each other "homegirls"' (Lull 1995:78). In some cases, this widespread appropriation of Black style leaves Black teens angry and somewhat disempowered (Baines 1997; Wilson and Sparks 1996).

Another highly publicized controversy surrounds the extent to which athletic-apparel companies using 'attitude' and celebrity athlete-based marketing strategies have redefined 'cool' in ways that stimulate demand for expensive athletic apparel (see Wilson and Sparks 1996). This is particularly disturbing considering the recent reports of 'black on black' violence over athletic apparel and youth gang identification with athletic apparel (Dyson 1993:70; Telander 1990:37). Similar concerns exist about the vulnerability of youth 'as the audience with the greatest gullibility and the least amount of money', and as a group who 'think they can achieve their dreams by putting out good money' (Buchignani 1990:A4). Still other critics suggest that the media success of the celebrity Black athlete in commercial advertising reinforces the myth that social mobility through sport is broadly attainable for Black youth (Wenner 1994; see Leonard 1996 for a discussion of the considerable odds faced by African-American youth who attempt to secure basketball scholarships and make the NBA).

Wonsek (1992:457) argues that because Blacks are overrepresented in stereotypical roles such as inner-city athlete and, by association, as gang members and criminals, audiences are led to believe that Blacks are '"naturally" inferior, "naturally" threatening and "naturally" athletic'. Even the visibility of celebrity athletes as product spokespersons is considered by some to be limiting for Blacks because it emphasizes the Black's positioning as 'athlete only' and trivializes the achievements of Blacks in non-sport roles and careers (Wonsek 1992; York 1991). Although there is limited research showing how youth audiences actually respond to commercials that feature Black athletes, the subject of Black media portrayals and issues surrounding the power of television to influence audiences require consideration (Wilson and Sparks 1996). This mediated ideology of 'natural athleticism' (see Davis 1990 and Carlston 1986 for responses to these spurious claims) is reflected in the distribution of athletes across playing positions in major league sports, where Blacks have historically been overrepresented in playing positions 'defined as requiring speed, quickness, and quick physical reactions' (outfielders, wide receivers) and underrepresented (compared to Whites) in positions requiring 'leadership, decision-making skills, and dependability' (pitcher, quarterback) (Coakley 1990:216). Although basketball has become an exception to these trends because of 'recent changes in ideas about the skills and characteristics needed to play various positions' (Coakley 1990:216), stereotypes and prejudices perpetuated by some coaches and scouts, combined with the low percentage of Blacks in management positions and stereotypical media portrayals, are in part a result of and support for many taken-for-granted assumptions about the Black male athlete.

The Apolitical Black Athlete

There are also criticisms of the contemporary celebrity Black athlete's silence on social issues. In the 1960s and 1970s the African-American athlete and Black masculinity were synonymous with political resistance. Athletes like John Carlos and Tommie Smith, who raised their black-gloved fists above their heads in a Black power salute on the medal podium during the 1968 Olympic Games, and outspoken activist/boxer Muhammad Ali, used their celebrity status as a means to express a 'rebellious masculinity' (hooks 1994). This stance contrasts with those taken by many of today's celebrity Black athletes such as Michael Jordan. McDonald (1996) illuminates the comparison of Ali and Jordan:

> Ali and Jordan exemplify distinctions between two divergent eras: where Ali embodied the pride of Black resolve in the 1960s, the commodification of Michael Jordan in the 1980s and 1990s is a sign of increasingly reactionary times. While also commodified, Ali was among a group of African American athletes who helped publicize issues like economic stratification and racial segregation (McDonald 1996:348).

Similarly, Dyson (1993:70) argues that today's celebrity Black athletes appear unwilling to take responsibility for the negative consequences of sneaker companies' exploitation of Black masculine cultural expressions, classifying the athletes' (re)actions as 'ineffectual' and 'defensive'. Although these athletes' dispositions are viewed by many as a sign of the times dominated by conservative politics, according to Andrews (1996), the commodified celebrity Black athlete exists within a racist ideology that says it's okay to be Black, but not 'too Black':

> Many in the white population are gracious enough to accept, even adulate, African-Americans, but only if they do not explicitly assert their blackness: If you're black, you are not expected to harp on it, if you do then you are, to use the racist vernacular, a 'jumped up nigger'. African Americans are tolerated, even valorized, if they abdicate their race, and are seen to successfully assimilate into the practices, value system, and identity, of white America (Andrews: 1996:140).

This is consistent with the view that the media support a 'politics of comfort', where the images of Blacks in certain contexts are non-threatening attempts to de-emphasize racial differences/problems ('enlightened' racism) to maintain White audiences (McKay 1995).

Locating the American Black Athlete in the Canadian Racial and Ethnic Context

While these issues have particular significance for American audiences, portrayals of (American) Blacks are also central to Canadian professional basketball coverage. However, this is not to say that these portrayals have the same impacts on Canadian audiences as they would on American audiences, or that these audiences interpret these portrayals in similar ways. On the contrary, it is necessary to understand how widely distributed American-based culture is modified by the local Canadian context (Appadurai 1990; Lash and Urry 1994; Lull 1995).

Research has shown that there are fewer educational and economic opportunities for visible minorities in Canada compared to those of European descent (Agocs and Boyd 1993; Boyd 1992; Satzewich and Li 1987). Evidence of unequal treatment, systemic discrimination, and failure to accommodate diversity have been well documented in studies of occupations (Agocs and Boyd 1993; Boyd 1992; Collinson et al. 1990; Fernandez 1988; Henry and Ginzberg 1993). Ethnographic research on the experiences of those of Black and Caribbean origin in Toronto revealed perceived racial discrimination in, among other areas, employment, education, and the justice system (Henry 1994).

However, this evidence of direct discriminatory practices and institutional and structural disadvantages for Blacks in Canada (see also Cannon 1995), while incisive, still contrasts with an American system that is characterized by widespread segregation and racial violence (cf., Connell 1995; Dyson 1995; Omi 1989; Omi and Winant 1994). For example, the Canadian Blacks in Henry's (1994) study had found an economic niche for themselves in either wage labour or self-employment—findings that contrast with the overwhelming poverty and unemployment characterizing the Black underclass in the United States.

'Cool Pose' in Canada

Evidence suggests that the 'cool pose' is also a symbolic expression of resistance against discrimination for Black Canadian youth. Ethnographic research in an inner-city Toronto school conducted by Solomon (1992) showed 'Black' forms of symbolic resistance to be asserted by two groups of Black youth, the 'jocks' and the 'rastas'. The groups had distinct patterns of dress, hairstyle, communication, and demeanour that acted as race-based resistance against the expectations of their high school—expectations that these youth considered to be insensitive to their distinct racial background and experiences. For these youth, sport was also a primary means of achieving a race-based identity and a sense of manliness. Solomon draws on Willis's (British) model to suggest that sport allowed them to preserve 'a degree of machoism from the real and imputed degradation of their conditions' (Willis 1976:153). In other research on youth audiences and youth style, Wilson and Sparks (1996:417) found that a group of middle-class Black males in Toronto 'distinguished their own Black style and "dress code" from that of White adolescents', and, moreover, 'appeared to define their masculine identities somewhat through fashion, emphasizing the social pressures to wear [celebrity athlete-endorsed apparel]'. While Solomon's and Wilson and Sparks's findings cannot be directly paralleled to the 'cool pose' of inner-city America because of Canada's distinct racial context, there is still a symbolic resistance against systemic and structural racism.

The Marketing of Black Masculinity in Canada: An Examination of Commercial Advertising During Toronto Raptors Television Coverage

Although NBA basketball has been available to Canadian audiences for years through cable television from the United States, the coverage has expanded dramatically since the Toronto Raptors and Vancouver Grizzlies began to play in 1995. In this section, examples of the marketing of Black masculinity in television commercials shown during Canadian-based Toronto Raptors broadcasts on the Canadian Television Network (a national broadcaster) and the New VR (a local, southern Ontario station) will be examined. Preferred meanings associated with these commercials are identified and conceptual issues surrounding the impacts of Black athlete portrayals on Canadian audiences are assessed.

Findings

There has been a clear trend among major sponsors of Toronto Raptors broadcasts to use images of Black male culture in their commercial advertisements. While some commercials have simply featured Black athlete spokespersons, making only implicit references to their playing ability or playing style, or showing actual highlights of the players' on-court performances, other commercials made definitive associations with 'cool pose' features such as 'hang time', flashy on-court moves, street language, aggression, intimidation, and inner-city basketball. Below I discuss four ads shown regularly during Raptors broadcasts that demonstrate some of these themes as they were used in commercials. The first two were shown during Raptors games over the 1996–7 season and are examples of companies attempting to associate their product with athletics and Black culture. The second two ads, both shown during the 1995–6 season, are athletic-apparel commercials that emphasize their already well-established associations with athletics and Black culture. Although I have separated athletic-apparel commercials to highlight the positioning of this commercial genre, which has a history of exploiting Black culture, this is an artificial separation. To understand the larger meaning and impacts of these portrayals, it is necessary to be attentive to the various ways that Black culture is transmitted in news reports, magazine articles, print advertising, television sitcoms, and in movies. The various media sources together 'naturalize' these messages for audiences.

In this analysis, I have provided a snapshot of the ways that Black masculinity has been constructed in Canadian commercial advertising during basketball game coverage, and show how these commercials are located in a media culture where portrayals of Black athletes tend to reinforce common-sense beliefs about the 'dangerous' (Kellner 1996; Lule 1995), 'naturally athletic', 'intellectually inferior' (Sailes 1993) Black male. Although I have provided only one reading of these commercials, this reading highlights the potentially negative consequences of media portrayals of the Black athlete.

Black Masculinity, Flights, and Cell Phones

Commercial advertisements for Air Canada and Bell Mobility (Cellular phones) used fictional portrayals of Black athletes within the context of inner-city basketball. In the Air Canada commercial, a young Black man with a shaved head is shown against a shadowy background. Because of the darkness, the viewer cannot see the eyes of the man and the setting is unknown. Through the darkness, the man is then shown dribbling a basketball, spinning and deking towards a basketball hoop with chain mesh. A deep male background voice is heard saying, 'When they said expansion, we were there' (referring to the expansion of the NBA to include the Toronto Raptors). The scene then flashes to another Black man who, by his appearance (wearing headphones, a one-piece work-suit, and holding two orange flashlights, one in each hand) is supposed to be an airport runway guide. The background voice then says, 'Because this is our kind of movement', followed by 'Because once you got possession . . . it's all your sky.' The runway guide then points his flashlights as if to say, 'Take off', as the basketball player jumps into the air. The player is shown flying through the air (in slow motion) towards the basketball hoop, his legs climbing through the air as he holds the ball high above his head. When the player reaches the hoop, he aggressively slam-dunks the basketball with two hands and hangs onto the rim. The player is then shown at a distance, revealing to the viewer that the basketball hoop is actually mounted on the back fin of an airplane that has a Canadian maple leaf symbol and the Air Canada logo painted on the side. The background voice then says, 'Air Canada, a major sponsor of the Raptors, flying with the best.' The commercial ends with the runway guide crossing his flashlights as if to say 'successful take-off' and the words 'Air Canada, flying with the best' appear on the screen against a black backdrop.

The second commercial, one for Bell Mobility, opens with a Black male bouncing a basketball and standing against a backdrop of a rundown, graffiti-covered brick wall. Standing beside the player is what appears to be an 'alien'—a person wearing a loose, silver-coloured suit that covers the entire body and head. A background voice is then heard counting down 'Three, two, one.' When the countdown ends, the player then launches into the air, apparently aided by the special powers of the alien. The scene then flashes to the basketball player, who is flying straight up to the sky, out of an inner-city setting that includes a fence with graffiti, rundown buildings, and a smokestack. The scene then moves to a close-up of the player's outstretched body, flying into space and holding the basketball. The player is yelling—the yelling is similar to the sound made by some basketball players during aggressive 'in-your-face' slam-dunks and blocked shots. The words 'Serious Airtime' are then flashed across the screen, referring to the basketball player's ability to stay in the air and to the amount of telephone airtime that people can have if they subscribe to Bell Mobility's telephone systems. The basketball player is then shown levitating above the clouds, having escaped the earth's gravity. The words 'Bell Mobility' are then floated across the screen to conclude the commercial.

In these commercials, images of Blackness were evident in the references to flight, aggression, power, grace, threat, and poverty. The exaggerated flight motif used in all commercials played on the valued ability (associated with ghetto basketball culture) to perform 'ceiling-climbing, high-flying, gravity-defying' dunks (associated most closely with legendary leapers Julius 'Dr J' Erving and Michael 'Air' Jordan) (Majors 1990:112). The two-handed 'power dunk', followed by the rim-hanging (in the Air Canada commercial), played on popular basketball imagery surrounding renowned 'power dunkers', such as Darryl 'Chocolate Thunder' Dawkins, Shaquille 'Shaq' O'Neal, and Shawn 'The Rain Man' Kemp. McDonald (1996:352) characterizes these kinds of exaggerated flights as 'the merging of technology with ideology', a merger that reifies notions of African Americans as naturally athletic, as 'born to dunk'. McDonald (1996) also argues that the media's emphasis on the Black athlete's aggressive demeanour, menacing presence, and apparent ability to 'defy gravity' are degrading and limiting:

These associations are rooted in the racist assumptions that Black men are 'closer to nature' than White man and from Victorian notions that Africans have a different genetic makeup from their more genteel and intellectual European counterparts. Rooted in allegedly natural differences, these ideologies have helped to restrict Black men to certain occupational niches such as sports, music, and entertainment (McDonald 1996:353).

The use of darkness and shadows, particularly in the Air Canada commercial, appear to 'accent the stark quality of the "hood"' (Lull 1995:76) and effectively 'sell the ghetto' to a viewer fascinated with the Black inner city. Other images, including the chain mesh and the graffiti (both commonly associated with the ghetto playground), as well as the brief image of rundown buildings, reinforce this theme. Even the language and voices of both commercials are borrowed from popular racial imagery. For example, the use of street talk laden with poor grammar (e.g., the line 'once you got possession' from the Air Canada commercial) potentially 'reinforces perceived differences between blacks and whites' (Wonsek 1992:457). Considering the racial context of Canada that implicitly and explicitly supports stereotypical ideologies surrounding race, it seems likely that some audiences might infer from these images, as Wonsek (1992:457) suggests, that 'blacks are "naturally" inferior [both intellectually and morally], "naturally" threatening and "naturally" athletic'.

Similarly, the high representation of Black athletes in commercials for many of the Raptors' major sponsors over the last two seasons (including ads for Gatorade, Reebok, Starter, Topps playing cards, Nike, Foot Locker, Sears, Bell Canada, and Air Canada) supports a trend whereby the mediated Black is 'athlete only'. This builds on more extensive research that has shown that Blacks in commercial advertising tend to be vastly overrepresented in the role of 'athlete' (Wilson 1995; Wonsek 1992). While it makes some sense that Black athletes (fictional and real) would be used to promote products during basketball games dominated by Black athletes, these portrayals exist in an overall media context where Blacks are consistently overrepresented as athletes, entertainers and criminals, and underrepresented (or non-existent) in all other areas (Corea 1990; Greenberg and Brand 1994; Real 1989). On this basis, it is not unreasonable to suggest that viewers harbouring stereotypical preconceptions about Blacks would have at least tentative grounds to believe that Blacks are not (able) participants in other areas of Canadian society.

Black Masculinity and Sneakers[2]

In a Reebok commercial shown during the 1995–6 season, NBA star Glenn Robinson is shown in a gym, talking about the different moves that he can use to beat his opponent. While he speaks, clips of Robinson performing these moves in NBA games are flashed on the screen. The commercial ends with Robinson saying that he is 'not hot-doggin' (meaning 'showing off' his moves on the court), 'I'm just marking my territory.' Following Robinson's last statement, a gate that looks like a playground gate is shown slamming shut. The gate has the Reebok slogan 'This is my planet' on it, painted on a metal sign. All clips of Robinson talking in this commercial are shown in black and white.

A Nike commercial, also shown during the 1995–6 season, featured renowned NBA 'trash talker' Gary Payton. Payton is shown wearing a blindfold while outplaying an opponent in a dark gym. Once the game is over, Payton takes off the blindfold and pushes his opponent away from him. There is no talking or music in this commercial—only the sound of sneakers, the bouncing ball, and the breathing of the players. The commercial ends with the Nike 'swoosh' logo shown against a dark background with the ominous, steady sound of the basketball bouncing.

More so than the depictions in the Air Canada and Bell commercials, these ads made explicit links with gangs ('I'm just marking my territory'), inner-city culture (the playground gate), intimidation, and violence. Both Payton and Robinson were shown to be intolerant of and aggressive towards those who threaten 'what's theirs'. Both were positioned in ominous settings that empha-sized the menace and threat associated with the ghetto. These links with the negative, stereotypical aspects of Black masculine culture are inseparable from the related (if not explicit) associations with African-American basketball players. These promotional techniques, intended to fashion threatening identi-ties for products spokespersons and product, are consistent with those used by other apparel companies (like those discussed in the previous section), which have marketed misbehaviour and aggression along with playing style. In essence, these companies are attempting to 'take the speed and power of the [basketball] court and distill it and concentrate it into a message that misbehaviour or intim-idation are true badges of manhood—and the route to victory' (Christie 1995:A12).

Overall, these commercials draw on popular racist stereotypes about Black culture while commodifying the symbolically resistant 'cool pose' to market products. Although not all Canadian audiences will make the intended associa-tions identified in this semiotic analysis, these are relevant interpretations consid-ering recent evidence about Black males' perceptions of racism and non-Black youths' 'raced' interpretations of Black television portrayals (Wilson 1995; Wilson and Sparks forthcoming).

Discussion and Conclusions

Clearly, the promotion of Black culture is widespread in the context of televised basketball in Canada. Black masculine culture pervades the advertising portrayals explained here and in other areas of professional basketball promotion, such as weekly youth-oriented shows like 'NBA Dunk Street', which highlight many of the spectacular aspects of the game for young Canadian audiences. Other media analyses of player profiles and newspaper coverage also consistently reinforce the themes identified earlier (see Wilson 1997).

The (potential) consequences of the commodification of Black culture and the Black athlete in Canada for Black youth are complex. While there is some evidence to suggest that Canadian Black males are unhappy that White males ('wiggers') are co-opting their symbols of resistance (Baines 1997; Wilson and Sparks 1996), there does not appear to be a decline in product demand among Black males. In fact, young Black male style still requires and values athletic apparel promoted by celebrity Black athletes. It is also important to consider Majors's (1990) argument that sport (and the 'cool pose' in general), while symbolically empowering in the short term, is actually inhibiting for Black males who have focused their efforts on sport, an avenue with extremely limited opportunities for social mobility. In other words, while suburban White youth sometimes pretend to be Black as part of negotiating their adolescent identities, inner-city Canadian Black youths' 'pursuance of sport, combined with other acts of resistance in which they engage increases their prospects for assuming low-paying, insecure jobs when they leave school' (Tanner 1996, drawing on Solomon 1992). Baines (1997) explains the irony of 'Black' style for youth:

> A black kid dressing and being 'black' is a suspect; a white kid dressing and acting 'black' is just rebelling. What makes one kid cool makes another a criminal. Wiggers like to act black, but they have the luxury of being able to escape the role by simply shedding their clothes (Baines 1997:80).

The marketing of the 'cool pose', while reinforcing these sport-related values and narrowing the aspirations of these Canadian youth, also contributes to the stereotyping of Black males more broadly. These portrayals reinforce negative stereotypes that support a society that continues to limit Blacks in education and employment and discriminate against them in the justice system. While Nike and other companies argue that they have intentionally used commercial messages to publicize social issues such as race (including a recent commercial featuring golf star Tiger Woods, who says 'There are still courses in the U.S. that I am not allowed to play because of the colour of my skin'), this position is in some ways contradictory. In her discussion of a Nike cause-related advertising campaign that focused on inner-city youth's access to sport, Cole (1996) has argued that these commercials provide overly simplistic solutions to the complex problem of racial inequality in ways that blame young Black males for the ills of the inner city and for their own marginalized status.

It is also apparent that the 'cool pose' and other forms of masculine resistance generally exclude women. For example, during Black protests surrounding the 1968 Mexico Olympics, an event best remembered in Black history for the medal podium protest by Tommie Smith and John Carlos, Black women were not involved (Moore 1991). Although Majors and Billson (1992) acknowledge that Black women, on occasion, use their own 'cool' behaviours to help counter the effects of racism and social oppression, these forms of resistance are located in a popular media context where Black women have also been portrayed in complex and often degrading ways—as 'sign(s) of sexual experience' (hooks 1995:29), victims of various forms of abuse, or as courageous leaders of fatherless homes. Again, any actual power that might be derived from this female 'coolness' is overshadowed, diluted, or ignored. However, with the mass marketing of the 'cool' female in recent campaigns during the Women's National Basketball Association's first season, these messages should be further investigated.

On this basis, there is a need to examine and highlight the potentially negative impacts of Black media portrayals and to work through education to develop more critical media skills as part of a struggle against taken-for-granted understandings. Towards this end, there is a need to consider how actual (as opposed to assumed) audiences interpret media portrayals, so that semiotic analyses of race portrayals can more adequately contribute to understandings about the impacts of the media texts on viewer opinions and perceptions (Bobo 1995; Bodroghkozy 1995; Hunt 1997; Jhally and Lewis 1992; Wilson and Sparks 1996). Finally, there is a need to consider the burden of responsibility for media producers, advertisers, and celebrity athletes, as well as audiences, who are involved in the exploitive and irresponsible commodification of Black male culture. Although media literacy initiatives and critical media research are important steps to inform audiences, more proactive (and less defensive) stances by advertisers and celebrity Black athlete spokespersons would be crucial advances.

Certainly, these comments and recommendations are only preliminary attempts to better understand issues of race, class, gender, and youth that exist in media industries and other Canadian institutions. However, given the pervasiveness of mass-marketed NBA products (and Black athletes) within Canadian popular culture, professional basketball is a primary site where these issues can be considered on a local, national, and global scale.

Notes

1. I use the term 'Black' in this chapter to refer to individuals of African or Caribbean descent. The meaning of 'Black' in Canada refers most often to those of Caribbean descent, who make up approximately 450,000 people in Canada (Economic Council of Canada 1991; Statistics Canada 1992). I use the term African American in only a few instances when emphasizing one's *American* background, or when using another author's preferred terminology. Also, in this chapter the term 'Black masculinity' refers to the 'cool pose' coping strategy.

2. The following commercials were also analysed as part of a larger study focused on the 'raced' portrayals of Black athletes in Toronto and elsewhere in Canada across various mediums and genres, including newspaper sports sections, television commercials, cause-related commercial messages, and basketball player profiles (see Wilson 1997).

References

Agocs, C., and M. Boyd. 1993. 'The Canadian Ethnic Mosaic Recast for the 1990's'. In *Social Inequality in Canada*, edited by J. Curtis, E. Grabb, and N. Guppy, 330–52. Scarborough: Prentice-Hall.

Andrews, D. 1996. 'The Fact(s) of Michael Jordan's Blackness: Excavating a Floating Racial Signifier'. *Sociology of Sport Journal* 13, no. 3:125–58.

_____, B. Carrington, Z. Mazur, and S. Jackson. 1996. 'Jordanscapes: A Preliminary Analysis of the Global Popular'. *Sociology of Sport Journal* 13, no. 4:428–57.

Appadurai, A. 1990. 'Disjuncture and Difference in the Global Cultural Economy'. In *Global Culture: Nationalism, Globalization and Modernity*, edited by M. Featherstone, 295–310. London: Sage.

Baines, A. 1997. 'Black Like Me'. *Toronto Life* (January):78–81.

Baron, S. 1989. 'Resistance and Its Consequences: The Street Culture of Punks'. *Youth & Society* 21, no. 2:207–37.

Barthes, R. 1973. *Mythologies*. London: Paladin.

Bobo, J. 1995. 'The Color Purple: Black Women as Cultural Readers'. In *Gender, Race and Class in the Media*, edited by G. Dines and J. Humez, 52–60. Thousand Oaks, CA: Sage.

Bodroghkozy, A. 1995. '"Is This What You Meant by Color TV?": Race, Gender, and Contested Meanings in NBC's Julia'. In *Gender, Race and Class in the Media*, edited by G. Dines and J. Humez, 413–23. Thousand Oaks, CA: Sage.

Boyd, M. 1992. 'Gender, Visible Minority, and Immigrant Earnings Inequality: Reassessing an Employment Equity Premise'. In *Deconstructing a Nation: Immigration, Multiculturalism and Racism in 90s Canada*, edited by V. Satzewich, 279–321. Halifax: Fernwood Publishing.

Buchignani, W. 1990. 'Big Name Footwear Has Parents Running Scared'. *Montreal Gazette* (28 October):A1, A4.

Cannon, M. 1995. *The Invisible Empire: Racism in Canada*. Toronto: Random House.

Carlston, D. 1986. 'An Environmental Explanation for Race Differences in Basketball Performance'. In *Fractured Focus: Sport as a Reflection of Society*, edited by R. Lapchick, 87–110. Toronto: Lexington Books.

Christie, J. 1995. 'Bad Behavior Can Prove Profitable'. *The Globe and Mail* (13 February):A12.

Coakley, J. 1990. *Sport in Society: Issues and Controversies*. Toronto: Times Mirror/Mosby College Publishing.

Cole, C. 1996. 'American Jordan: P.L.A.Y., Consensus, and Punishment'. *Sociology of Sport Journal* 13, no. 4:366–97.

_____, and H. Denny. 1994. 'Visualizing Deviance in Post-Reagan America: Magic Johnson, AIDS, and the Promiscuous World of Professional Sport'. *Critical Sociology* 20, no. 3:123–47.

Collinson, D., D. Knights, and M. Collinson. 1990. *Managing to Discriminate*. London: Routledge, Chapman and Hall.

Connell, R. 1995. *Masculinities*. Berkeley: University of California Press.

Corea, A. 1990. 'Racism and the American Way of Media'. In *Questioning the Media*, edited by J. Downing, A. Mohammadi, and A. Sreberny-Mohammadi, 255–66. Newbury Park, CA: Sage.

Davis, L. 1990. 'The Articulation of Difference: White Preoccupation with the Question of Racially Linked Genetic Differences Among Athletes'. *Sociology of Sport Journal* 7, no. 2:179–87.

De Saussure, F. 1966. *Course in General Linguistics*. New York: McGraw-Hill.

Dyson, M. 1993. 'Be Like Mike? Michael Jordan and the Pedagogy of Desire'. *Cultural Studies* 7, no. 1:64–72.

_____. 1995. *Making Malcolm*. New York: Oxford University Press.

Economic Council of Canada. 1991. *New Faces in the Crowd*. EC22–171/1991E. Ottawa: Economic Council of Canada.

Fernandez, J. 1988. *Racism and Sexism in Corporate Life*. Englewood Cliffs: Prentice-Hall.

Greenberg, B., and J. Brand. 1994. 'Minorities and the Mass Media: 1970's to 1990's'. In *Media Effects: Advances in Theory and Research*, edited by J. Bryant and D. Zillman, 273–314. Hillsdale, NJ: Erlbaum Associates.

Hall, S. 1980. 'Encoding/Decoding'. In *Culture, Media, Language: Working Papers in Cultural Studies 1972–79*, edited by S. Hall, D. Hobson, A. Lowe, and P. Willis, 128–39. London: Hutchison.

_____. 1985. 'Signification, Representation, Ideology: Althusser and Post-structuralist Debates'. *Critical Studies in Mass Communication* 2, no. 2:91–114.

Henry, F. 1994. *The Caribbean Diaspora in Toronto: Learning to Live with Racism*. Toronto: University of Toronto Press.

_____, and E. Ginzberg. 1990. 'Racial Discrimination in Employment'. In *Images of Canada*, edited by J. Curtis and L. Tepperman, 302–9. Toronto: Prentice-Hall.

Hickey, P. 1990. 'If the Shoe Fits'. *Montreal Gazette* (28 October):A3.

hooks, b. 1994. 'Feminism Inside: Toward a Body Politic'. In *Black Male: Representation of Masculinity in Contemporary Art*, edited by T. Golden, 127–40. New York: Whitney Museum of American Art.

_____. 1995. 'Madonna: Plantation Mistress or Soul Sister'. In *Gender, Race and Class in the Media*, edited by G. Dines and J. Humez, 28–32. Thousand Oaks, CA: Sage.

Hunt, D. 1997. *Screening the Los Angeles 'Riots': Race, Seeing and Resistance*. New York: Cambridge University Press.

Jhally, S., and J. Lewis. 1992. *Enlightened Racism: The Cosby Show, Audiences, and the Myth of the American Dream*. Boulder: Westview Press.

Kellner, D. 1996. 'Sports, Media Culture, and Race—Some Reflections on Michael Jordan'. *Sociology of Sport Journal* 13, no. 4:458–68.

King, S. 1993. 'The Politics of the Body and the Body Politic: Magic Johnson and the Ideology of AIDS'. *Sociology of Sport Journal* 10, no. 3:270–85.

Lash, S., and J. Urry. 1994. *Economies of Signs and Space*. London: Sage.

Leiss, W., S. Kline, and S. Jhally. 1990. *Social Communication in Advertising: Persons, Products and Images of Well-being*. Scarborough: Nelson Canada.

Leonard, W. 1996. 'The Odds of Transiting from One Level of Sport Participation to Another'. *Sociology of Sport Journal* 13, no. 3:288–99.

Lule, J. 1995. 'The Rape of Mike Tyson: Race, the Press and Symbolic Types'. *Critical Studies in Mass Communication* 12:176–95.

Lull, J. 1995. *Media, Communication, Culture*. New York: Columbia University Press.

McDonald, M. 1996. 'Michael Jordan's Family Values: Marketing, Meaning, and Post-Reagan America'. *Sociology of Sport Journal* 13, no. 4:344–65.

McKay, J. 1995. '"Just Do It": Corporate Sports Slogans and the Political Economy of Enlightened Racism'. *Discourse: Studies in the Cultural Politics of Education* 16, no. 2:191–201.

Majors, R. 1990. 'Cool Pose: Black Masculinity and Sports'. In *Sport, Men and the Gender Order: Critical Feminist Perspectives*, edited by M. Messner and D. Sabo, 109–14. Champaign, IL: Human Kinetics.

_____, and J. Billson. 1992. *Cool Pose: The Dilemmas of Black Manhood*. New York: Lexington Books.

Moore, K. 1991. 'The Eye of the Storm'. *Sports Illustrated* 12:62–73.

Omi, M. 1989. 'In Living Colour: Race and American Culture'. In *Cultural Politics in Contemporary America*, edited by I. Angus and S. Jhally, 111–12. New York: Routledge.

_____, and H. Winant. 1994. *Racial Formation in the United States: From the 1960's to the 1990's*, 2nd edn. New York: Routledge.

Real, M. 1989. *Super Media: A Cultural Studies Approach*. Newbury Park, CA: Sage.

Sailes, G. 1993. 'An Investigation of Campus Stereotypes: The Myth of Black Athletic Superiority and the Dumb Jock Stereotype'. *Sociology of Sport Journal* 10:88–97.

Satzewich, V., and P. Li. 1987. 'Immigrant Labour in Canada: The Cost and Benefit of Ethnic Origin in the Job Market'. *Canadian Journal of Sociology* 12, no. 3:229–41.

Solomon, P. 1992. *Black Resistance in High School: Forging a Separatist Culture*. Albany: State University of New York Press.

Statistics Canada. 1992. *Viewing 1990 Culture Statistics*. Ottawa: Statistics Canada.

Tanner, J. 1996. *Teenage Troubles: Youth and Deviance in Canada*. Toronto: Nelson Canada.

Telander, R. 1990. 'Senseless'. *Sports Illustrated* (14 May):36–8, 43–4, 46, 49.

Wenner, L. 1994. 'The Dream Team, Communicative Dirt, and the Marketing of Synergy: USA Basketball and Cross-merchandising in Television Commercials'. *Journal of Sport and Social Issues* 18, no. 1:27–47.

_____. 1995. 'The Good, the Bad and the Ugly: Race, Sport, and the Public Eye'. *Journal of Sport and Social Issues* 19, no. 3:227–31.

Willis, P. 1976. *Profane Culture*. London: Chatto and Windus.

Wilson, B. 1995. 'Audience Reactions to the Portrayal of Blacks in Athletic Apparel'. MA thesis, University of British Columbia.

_____. 1997. '"Good Blacks and Bad Blacks": Media Constructions of African-American Athletes in Canadian Basketball'. *International Review for the Sociology of Sport* 32, no. 2:177–89.

_____, and R. Sparks. 1996.'"It's Gotta Be the Shoes": Youth, Race, and Sneaker Commercials'. *Sociology of Sport Journal* 13, no. 4:398–427.

_____, and R. Sparks. Forthcoming. 'Impacts of Black Athlete Media Portrayals on Canadian Youth'. *Canadian Journal of Communication*.

Wonsek, P. 1992. 'College Basketball on Television: A Study of Racism in the Media'. *Media, Culture and Society* 14:449–61.

York, S., producer. 1991. 'Selling the Dream', television broadcast. Washington, DC: Smithsonian Institution.

Chapter 14

Physical Activity in the Lives of Women with Disabilities

Jennifer Hoyle and Philip White

> Different kinds of bodies give us different raw materials for artfully constructing our view-points of life.
> —D.H. Johnson, *Body: Recovering Our Sensual Wisdom*

The first author of this chapter is a non-disabled mother of two teenagers (ages nineteen and fourteen) with physical and developmental disabilities. Her life as a parent and active caregiver has shown her that, as a woman living in a male-dominated world, she shares experiences with people with disabilities. First, being a woman makes her much more vulnerable to discrimination, harassment, and violence—an experience that has, in retrospect, affected some of her parenting decisions when helping her children live within mainstream society. Second, in terms of the issue of disability, she was initially socialized into an acceptance of traditional medical practices that constructed her children's limitations only in negative terms. Subsequently, she has realized that, from her children's perspective, being 'different' is simply part of their life experience. They have never known otherwise.

Her gendered experiences and the prevalent definition of the non-disabled body as the 'general' case and the disabled body as 'other' have also affected how she and her children have experienced sport and physical activity. Put simply, her family has been adversely affected by exclusionary forces rooted in both gender and disability discrimination. To overcome limited opportunities connected both to gender and disability, it has been necessary to seek out physical education professionals who are willing to move beyond conventional definitions of sport and who are able to creatively provide physical activity opportunities for those with disabilities. Part of their challenge has been to innovatively make sport and physical activity more inclusive and flexible enough to involve and meet the needs of different types of bodies.

The purpose of this chapter is to report on the role of physical activity in the lives of women with disabilities, and to approach an understanding of issues that need addressing in order to cater to the needs of women with disabilities. The chapter is informed both by the first-hand experience of a mother who has struggled, often through trial and error, to involve her children in physical activity, and by feminist theorizing on the lived reality of women with disabilities. Theories of feminism, it will be argued, both help undermine the usefulness of the term 'disability' and also help clarify how public policy can better address concerns surrounding women's health.

Feminism and Disability

Before the relatively recent emergence of a literature exploring the lived experiences of people with disabilities (see Blackford 1993; Fine and Asch 1988; Hillyer 1993; Morris 1989, 1993; Wendell 1989, 1993), disability had predominantly been conceptualized only in negative terms. The disabled person was defined as different, problematic, a passive victim of a 'personal tragedy'. More recently, research has challenged this view, asserting that the experiences of disabled people themselves have been overlooked. This progressive body of work has placed the *experience* of disability at its core, in much the same way that feminist-inspired research has focused on women's interpretations of their own lives. In what follows, the potential of feminist theory for developing a clearer understanding of the social construction of disability will be addressed.

Traditional views of disability have tended to construct a fixed dichotomy of ability/disability, defining the former as positive and the latter as negative. Aside from being overly simplistic, the imagery of 'disadvantage' associated with disability has many consequences, many of which define the disabled person as 'other' or 'passive victim'. Largely overlooked is the fact that rather than being a fixed category, disability is often experienced as a fluid and shifting set of life conditions (Shildrick and Price 1996).

In the absence of representation through the voices of people with disabilities, stereotyping has resulted in demeaning images of them, images that have become deeply ingrained in social institutions and practices (Bickenbach 1993). In light of this, feminist theory complements disability research in terms of the advances it has made in bringing the voices of oppressed groups to the fore (Jaggar 1983; Tong 1989). Specifically, challenges to previously dominant views of disability and alternative interpretations of the social world have emerged.

One such interpretation is the acknowledgement that women and people with disabilities do not necessarily view their experiences in negative terms. As Hillyer (1993:15) suggests, people with disabilities are well aware of their limitations and the negative attributes associated with the 'losses that cannot be repaired'. *Both* the strengths and weaknesses of these losses become part of their reality. For example, when asked about her disabled baseball teammates, one of the daughters of the first author of this paper argued that rather than being disabled, 'they were merely different'.

While these theoretical developments can help us better understand the experiences of disabled people, there is reason to be cautious in adopting an 'add disability and stir' approach in applying feminist theory to the study of disability issues. For example, as Morris (1993) and Cassidy et al. (1995) have suggested, feminist research itself has yet to incorporate the subjective experiences of women with disabilities and has tended to focus on the experiences of non-disabled women. That is to say, boundaries between the disabled and the non-disabled have rarely been examined, resulting in the silencing of embodied experiences of disabled women.

Sport and Disabilities

Research on sport and gender has emphasized how powerful groups in society exercise a disproportionate amount of influence on how sport is played (DePauw 1994, 1997; Theberge 1985). For example, while women have made many inroads into the world of sport, it is still a predominantly gendered activity that reflects values and interests traditionally associated with men and masculinity (Birrell and Richter 1987; Hall 1984). Thus, a great deal of sport in Canada emphasizes winning (more than the experience of participation) and encourages ways of playing that are risky and require high levels of commitment (Birrell and Richter 1987). Consequently, sport tends to celebrate physical ableness and conventional (forceful) versions of masculinity, thus legitimizing the idea of the universality of a non-disabled social order (DePauw 1994). Having said this, there are also those who propose alternatives to male domination, promoting instead sports that are 'process oriented, collective, supportive and inclusive' (Birrell and Richter 1987:408), attributes that are often devalued in and by mainstream sport.

For disabled people, dominant sport values have a constraining effect on participation for several reasons. First, and most obviously, people with disabilities have fewer opportunities to be involved in recreational programs; these programs are simply less available. Second, programs that are available tend to segregate the disabled from the non-disabled and rarely meet the needs of people with disabilities who would like to be more 'integrated'. Third, rather than focusing on providing opportunities for enjoyable recreation, funding is often channelled towards therapeutic programs aimed at helping individuals with disabilities to become more self-reliant and less dependent on social services (Crawford 1989).

Segregated sport for the disabled is organized in a variety of ways. Some sport is organized around the dominant sport model, emphasizing competitiveness, hierarchy, and winning (Hall et al. 1991). An example of this would be the Paralympic Games in which international athletes with varied physical disabilities compete against each other in a range of sporting activities. For athletes with physical disabilities, these Games are comparable to the conventional Olympic Games. Other approaches coexist in some ways with the dominant model, but are also modified. For example, the Paralympic Games also use a classification system for type of disability that has been developed to enhance opportunity for sport participation and to create an environment that is more equitable for all involved (Blake 1992; Sherrill 1993). The Games involve several classifications based on varying degrees of strength and functional ability, under which people with, for example, cerebral palsy (CP) can compete.

While classification systems allow for the recognition and inclusion of different types of limitations, they are often fiercely debated. For instance, the classification system used for the 1992 Paralympic Games resulted in the exclusion of some athletes who might otherwise have participated. The system classified athletes according to their functional ability with regard to a specific sport rather than according to disability grouping so that any athlete, regardless of disability 'type', could take part in a sport if they had the functional ability to do so (Blake 1992). The change resulted in a shift towards higher standards of competition, to the promotion and acceptance of athletes with disabilities as 'serious' athletes, and to the increased inclusion of athletes with disabilities into sport for non-disabled people (Blake 1992). The effect of the changes was to reduce the number of winners per event and increase the significance of medals awarded to athletes. Many athletes who were unable to achieve the necessary standards because of their fixed physical limitations were excluded. As is evident from this example, there are conflicting visions within the world of sport for people with disabilities. In brief, the growing popularity and commercial appeal of the Paralympics does not necessarily serve well the interests of other athletes with disabilities whose goals are less competitive.

In many ways, segregated games perpetuate negative stereotypes. As Nixon (1984:68) has argued, in order to challenge such stereotypes, people with disabilities need to interact with non-disabled people in 'informal interpersonal' ways within social institutions such as sport. In such contexts, disabled athletes contradict and debunk negative attributes implied by stereotypes. However, although this process may help some disabled athletes become more legitimate in relation to the dominant 'abled' sport culture, it can be alienating for others. Consequently, athletes with limited abilities are marginalized by those who have overcome their disabilities and have managed to fit into mainstream sport (Hillyer 1993).

Research on the physical activity experiences of women with disabilities is scarce. That which does exist tends to examine the type of physical activities that women with disabilities participate in, the constraints to involvement they contend with, and how being a woman with a physical disability in society marginalizes them not only as women but as people with disabilities too. While this may in part be true, emphasizing an individual's disadvantaged position tends to inhibit creative change and deflects attention from positive experiences.

One way to approach an understanding of this issue is to posit that a person experiences the world through her body and, consequently, it is through this 'living body' that the meaning of the world is revealed (Merleau-Ponty 1962). The 'living body' is experienced on a continual biological basis in an immediate and fundamental way, and is thought about or rationalized in the mind. Our body, both unconsciously and consciously, reacts both to the environment and to itself (Van den Berg 1972).

How the body is perceived by others determines to some extent how it is lived in and cared for. Clearly, disabled and non-disabled bodies are evaluated differently by different people, but feelings about one's body are not only explained by the norms, expectations, and responses of others. They are also influenced by subjective physical experiences of the body.

Inability, through disability, to carry out prescribed physical movement necessitates either modification of the techniques needed for the activity or the modification of personal movements in order to take part in the activity. Innovation of this kind is often empowering and indeed the experience of disability can give a perspective on movement that cannot be appreciated by those who have only the experience of non-disabled practices. As will be suggested below, people with disabilities are aware of both the limitations and also the uniqueness of their bodies while living within a culture that idealizes performative body types and actions.

Methodology

This study is based on data collected by the first author as part of her Master's thesis (Hoyle 1996). To explore the experiences of women with disabilities, she collected and analysed oral histories. The strength of this method is that the history is written from the narrator's perspective and places her in the biographical context within which she lives. In this way, one can examine how women with disabilities are affected by their environment and how they in turn affect their physical and social environments.

Data were collected from a small sample of nine women, three each with congenital, acquired, and progressive disabilities. An acquired disability (such as spinal cord injury) is one that an individual acquires after living for a period of time as a non-disabled person. A congenital disability (such as cerebral palsy or spina bifida) is one with which a person is born. Progressive disabilities (such as multiple sclerosis or muscular dystrophy) involve moving from a non-disabled state to a disabled state over a period of time. It was important to have women from each of these categories of disability participate in the study in order to gain insight into their differing standpoints.

The term 'conversation' was preferred over 'interview' as it gave a more personal, relaxed, and less power-imbalanced connotation to the meeting between the researcher and narrator. In order to probe the experiences of the women, it was more important for the researcher to listen to their stories expressed in their own unique ways rather than to set a fixed schedule for the interviews. Flexibility also allowed the narrators to direct the flow of information as much as the researcher, a dynamic that does not occur using a more structured approach.

The few fixed prompts made by the researcher were associated with demographics (i.e., age, residence, marital status, employment status, and how the respondents defined their disability and leisure). The respondents were also asked to talk about what leisure meant to them, and about their leisure experiences over time. Their responses triggered further conversation on areas of interest and some questions of clarification from the researcher.

Of course, given the subject matter, flexibility in the data collection process was also important for practical reasons. The physical abilities of the respondents determined the location and type of conversation and/or how the information was relayed to the researcher. For example, most conversations took place in the women's homes as transportation was a problem for them. One woman who had difficulty relaying verbal information typed out her own oral history.

The respondents ranged in age from twenty-five to forty-nine. Two were married and living with their partners. Four of the remaining women had been married and were now divorced. Over half of the women had some postsecondary education. At the time of the conversations, eight of the women were unemployed. Over half of the women received a disability pension from the Ontario provincial government. Four of the women lived in supportive living units (SLU) provided by the March of Dimes, which provided them with attendant care. Two women lived in accessible units in cooperative housing, one woman lived in her own home, another lived with her parents, and one woman rented her own apartment.

Women with Disabilities Talk about Their Bodies and Physical Activity

In Western society, some body types are idealized more than others and women are positioned against an inaccessible body ideal more so than men (Wendell 1989, 1993). Value is placed particularly on the youthful, thin, sensual body—an emphasis that can hinder both non-disabled and disabled women from identifying with and living comfortably in their bodies (Shilling 1993:3). In this context, the experience of female disablement 'may be seen as the further marginalization of the already marginal' (Shildrick and Price 1996:101). The women in the study, though, experienced both their material bodies and the social responses to their bodies. When forced to live as females with disabilities within a society that places high values on health and beauty (from a non-disabled orientation), their experiences of their bodies provide a unique understanding of the world.

Under the weight of body ideals, women with disabilities are often viewed as 'defective, unattractive, and unable to manage their own bodies' (Cassidy et al. 1995:55). Like non-disabled women, disabled women are objectified, but in a unique way. As Malec (1993:22) has suggested, a woman with a disability is objectified twice; her disability defines her as an 'object of curiosity', but her femaleness also defines her as a sexual object.

Debbie is a twenty-five-year-old university student working on a degree in recreation. She has cerebral palsy that affects her balance and coordination, and explained how her disability, gender, and sexuality interact:

> It [disability] is central to my whole body image, but it is not the only thing. It is something that I am constantly reminded of and something that makes me a little uneasy in social situations . . . you know, you'll see this really good-looking person, and you say to yourself 'Wow. I wonder if they know they're so good looking.' And then in that split second you'll say, 'Oh they'd never be interested in me.'

Debbie's perception of her own attractiveness to others grows out of a learned negative body image of herself based both upon her sex and her disability.

Similarly, Annette, a forty-nine-year-old woman with multiple sclerosis, also expressed concerns about the effects of her disability on her perceived attractiveness. Annette lived alone and independently in her apartment with the help of full-time attendant care. With limited mobility in her arms and legs, she talked of how her disability affected her perceived role as a woman. Referring to the impact of disability on dating, she said: 'I think men do not like women to have disabilities. They'd rather have a "normal" woman because they want . . . to be cared for.' In other words, Annette felt that her physical limitations made her less attractive to men because she would find it difficult to fulfil the traditional female role of 'nurturer'.

Many of the women made a clear distinction between the actual functional ability of their bodies and stereotyped perceptions about physical impairment, arguing that the latter tend to objectify the body. Forty-three-year-old Ada, for example, emphasized the importance of personalizing the disabled condition:

> It doesn't matter what disease you have, it's whether you can lift your arm [that's important]. And in arthritis, maybe some people can lift their arms and some can't. It's just a label for a disease . . . And you might function differently at different times too. And people with cerebral palsy, there's a broad range of functionality.

The experience of living in a disabled body, though, was not only viewed negatively. As Wendell (1993) has argued, by accepting the suffering body, new thoughts and experiences develop that can acknowledge the sensations of the body while not being ruled by them. The experiences of the conscious mind and the unconscious body are sometimes connected when limitations of the body are accepted.

Debbie argued that the experience of a body limited by physical and cultural factors had created a deeper understanding of her personal philosophy of the purpose in life:

> To a certain extent it hurts that people can be so superficial not to be able to look beyond the shell. Really, your body is just a way for you to transport you around the earth. After you pass onto the next life, your body is not going to be all that important. Who you are, what you mean, how you treat other people, that's going to be a hell of a lot more important than if your body is beautiful or defective or whatever.

This kind of awareness of the body's limitations and sensations, coupled with the reflective qualities of the mind, suggest that some women with disabilities may have experiential knowledge unavailable to many people in the mainstream non-disabled culture. They may, for instance, be better equipped to go beyond the dominant cultural conceptions of the female and non-disabled body with regard to physical activity.

A moving example of how the mind is used to transcend physical limitations was revealed by Carol. At forty-three, Carol lives with her husband and has been diagnosed as having a form of muscular dystrophy called Friedreich's ataxia which creates, among other things, poor muscle coordination. In her case, Carol had developed the ability to use her mind to participate in the leisure forms unavailable to her body:

> I love to dance but I can't. I do it in my mind. I've never told anybody about that. I'm afraid people would think I'm nuts. I'm always dancing in my head. All kinds of dances like tap dancing, not ballet, I love jazz. . . . I skate and walk sometimes in my mind. Everything that I can't do [physically], I do it in my mind.

Carol's experiences and strategies highlight how traditional types of sport and physical activity can be alienating for those who cannot approximate an acceptable level of performance. People who move in physically different ways tend to be marginalized. For example, in dominant physical or sport culture, practice routines and drills employed in teaching physical skills are often relatively mechanistic. When they become ritualized, alternative ways of moving become stigmatized.

As already argued, the development of classification systems in games like the Paralympics is itself a reflection of traditional sport values because these systems are premised on dominant notions of competition, establishing winners, and mechanistic definitions of sport performance. For some, this can be intimidating.

Debbie suggested that her problem with classification systems is that they are defined so broadly that they exclude the differing functional abilities in each classification. She explained: 'I could be running against someone who was a "CP 6" but much more capable of doing those things than I was.' 'CP 6' refers to any person with cerebral palsy who is affected by fluctuating muscle tone, is able to walk without assistive devices, and has moderate to severe involvement of three or four limbs, creating poor balance and coordination (Sherrill 1993:629). This can include a wide range of functioning ability. Consequently, classification systems are problematic because the emphasis on competition can be alienating for people who are classified together but have less functional abilities than others within their grouping.

Similarly, Debbie's involvement in sport was also marred by the lack of alternatives to the competitive model. Jaded by her experiences, she felt forced to reframe her objective in physical activities: 'Any sport that I do is a hobby. Any competing that I do is a hobby because I've finally come to the point in my life where I can say that I am striving for *my* personal best, not the person beside me, not the person in front of me.' Thus, Debbie's goals were reoriented to relate more to herself than to others or to some objective standard that seemed inevitably to make her feel badly about her physical ability.

The Desire for Physical Activity

Despite intense frustration over limited opportunities, many of the women expressed desire to be more physically active. Their needs varied, however. For Debbie, being physically active had a positive impact on her impairments: 'I deal with various medical things every day like migraine headaches and muscle spasms, stiffness, and soreness. Imagine how much worse it would be if I wasn't constantly moving around.' Ada, who has fibromyalgia, which creates muscle weakness, pain, and fatigue in her joints and muscles, suggested that activities that did not fight gravity had a twofold positive effect: they provided easy physical exercise as well as the ability to be more independent in physical activity. As she explained:

> . . . there have been times when I've been weak. I couldn't even move, so somebody would do a range of motion for me. That's not very satisfactory. I really need to do it myself and swimming for me is a way to do it. . . . It's kind of like an anti-gravity work-out. You're not working against gravity, which makes it difficult.

Clearly, swimming allowed Ada to move freely and independently while providing her with the exercise she needed.

For Ada, some activities were easier than others. For example, she referred to canoeing as an activity that was conducive to her physical needs: 'It's really quite a smooth motion, like swimming or bicycling, and you can rest when you want.' Renatta, a twenty-five-year-old woman with cerebral palsy, referred to the therapeutic qualities of swimming: 'I love the pool. I love the water. It's very therapeutic and it's very relieving.' The specific needs related to the impairment of both of these women required them to rest frequently, to take time to move the body and move it slowly. In this respect, the type of activity they participated in was a more practical matter than is usually the case for non-disabled people.

The opportunity to be socially active was also key for most of the women. For example, Ada took part in a canoe trip that involved collaboration between an organization that serviced people with disabilities and one that traditionally serviced non-disabled people: 'It wasn't a special camp. . . . It was an integrated disabled and non-disabled canoe trip organized through the March of Dimes and Canadian Wilderness Trips.' This trip provided an opportunity for Ada to be an active participant with the other disabled and non-disabled people. In this integrated setting, and as she was unable to help out with the more physical tasks involved in canoeing (such as lifting), she creatively established an area of contribution to the whole: 'I couldn't do a lot of lifting, but what I could do, like, I knew the stars. . . . You've gotta dig sometimes for your talents.' In brief, this integrated setting allowed Ada the crucial freedom to participate in her own way rather than focusing on what she was unable to do. Clearly, the net effect is both to move towards more positive images of people with disabilities and to enhance the individual self-worth of the participant.

Adapting to the Challenges of Physical Activity

Not surprisingly, many of the women who participated in this study learned much about their bodies and physical activity through a process of trial and error. Since both their gender and their disability limited opportunities to participate, the women had to use their own initiative to find ways to do what they wanted. In the process, they learned not only about their disabilities but also their capabilities. In this light, Johnson (1992) promotes what he calls a 'technology of authenticity', which encourages people to develop their own sense of authority and their own way of carrying out a task. A 'technology of authenticity' would also encourage people to become more aware of muscles used in the movement associated with an activity and to explore the personal range of motions needed in order to carry out a specific activity successfully.

By increasing body awareness in this way, individuals learn to move and enjoy their bodies in ways that are dictated by inner awareness rather than being externally directed. On the one hand, there may be a socially acceptable, taken-for-granted way of doing a particular activity. On the other hand, since we all have differing functional abilities, it may be easier to perform that activity in different ways according to differing abilities. In fact, developing body awareness in this way reconnects the body and mind so that the learning of movement is physically rather than socially based. For example, Ada (again, a fibromyalgia sufferer) described how her desire to paddle a canoe was realized despite her physical limitation through the use of mechanical devices: 'I got knee pads and I got this thing to go around my waist to support me, and a neck brace. And wrist brace. You should see me canoe. I look like I'm wearing armour. But that's what I need in order to be able to paddle.' Ada's account also points to how humour is often adopted in disabled culture to make the day-to-day difficulties of disability more bearable.

Sometimes living in a disabled body requires becoming more familiar with the potential of the body than might otherwise be the case. For example, Debbie described how movement education helped her become more aware of what she could do with her body. This, in turn, gave her new insight into the specific physical abilities of the body: 'It helped me to discover my body, why I move in certain ways and why I do other things.' Physical limitations mean that the mind and the body have to work together in different ways. For example, Debbie used imagery in a basketball game situation in order to feel safe: 'I imagine that there is something that prevents other players from touching me. It's not that I don't like to be touched, but I need that space for assurance that they are not going to knock me right on my can.' Here, the awareness of how quickly and smoothly her body moves and the actions required by the formal game itself forces Debbie to respect the needs of both the body and the mind in order to play the game.

All of the women described how they carried out physical activities differently than non-disabled people as a result of their physical impairments. For example, forty-eight-year-old Ann had a heart condition and the limited use of one leg only. She had to play table tennis on that leg and knew what was required so as not to overexert herself:

> If I take a spritz of nitrogen before I start, then I can play a couple of games before I get into any problem at all. I don't have any balance, mind you. . . . I'd get the chair the right distance from the table and I would warn everybody I'd be playing with, 'Please don't be nasty and serve way back here' . . . But I can stand hanging onto the table . . .

In Ann's case, a combination of respect for her limitations, space and equipment needs, and the understanding of teammates made her desire to be physically active a reality.

Clearly, adaptation was a central theme in the physical activity experiences of these women. For example, as a forty-one-year-old woman who had a bruised spinal cord affecting her ability to use her arms and legs, Louise incorporated her adaptability and her sense of humour: 'If I want to do something I think "There's got to be a way I can do this" and "What do I have to do to do it?" . . . I never had this inventive mind before my disability.' Although the necessity of adaptation was a *given* for these women, it was their desire that forced them to implement their creativity in practical ways.

In sum, the women often adapted to their disabilities through heightened awareness of their functional abilities. In other words, through their experience of physical limitations, they became aware of their functional abilities and learned how to adaptively use and move their body parts accordingly.

Discussion

Physical differences between people create the liberating possibility of moving and experiencing the body in various and exciting ways. This can be a problem if there is an assumption of 'normal' ways to move the body. For example, in dominant sport models the body is given prescribed ways to move in order to perform specific athletic skills. One can find the 'correct' ways to execute a basketball jump shot in hundreds of coaching manuals. In such models, the body becomes an object that is subject to specified actions, rules, and regulations. Here the body is used more often as a means to an end rather than as a source of knowledge in and of itself. When movement norms become socially accepted and ingrained, the physical movements of people with disabilities become stigmatized as separate from, even deviant in, the rest of society. So long as disablement in physical activity is seen as 'other' or as a fixed category, the boundaries between the disabled and the non-disabled are left undisturbed. As we have shown in this chapter, feminist theory can help unwrap the ways in which the body is constructed and maintained as disabled.

The findings of this small study suggest that many women with disabilities want to be more physically active and that, despite functional limitations, they often find a way to increase their involvement. Gender, although a significant factor in the lives of these women, did not have as big an impact on them as their disability, though many had internalized social norms associated with both the female and the non-disabled body. For example, some expressed concern about their physical appearance because this marked them as different from other women. They were acutely aware of living in bodies that did not meet the social standards associated with health and beauty. As they were conscious of cultural norms associated with gender (such as female body image), their concerns were more intensely expressed.

The respondents were also concerned that stereotypes about their disabilities often worked insidiously in such a way that non-disabled people commonly underestimate their actual abilities and physical potential. This is one reason why people with disabilities like to be active in integrated settings that provide opportunities for them to debunk negative stereotypes. Such opportunities also contest fixed dichomoties of disabled/non-disabled that reinforce boundaries between sameness and difference.

Since functional ability was often variable for these women, adaptation was a constant feature in their lives. Modes of adaptation include alternative ways of thinking about physical activity, sometimes involving the use of imagination, and sometimes the reorientation of activity goals to meet personal rather than social expectations. In fact, physical limitations forced some of the women to make connections between their mind and body, which created new levels of physical and spiritual awareness. They took pleasure in finding new ways of carrying out desired activities through a process of trial and error. They went beyond the taken for granted into areas of transformation and personal discovery. It is this adaptive response, the construction of an alternative identity and a resistance to existing norms, that was uncovered by the use of qualitative methods and feminist theory in this study. As unique individuals, the women we talked to often refused to 'perform' their disability (Shildrick and Price 1996), to give in to the 'othering' process.

We are aware that this study has only begun to scratch the surface in terms of sport, gender, and disability. On one level, larger studies employing representative samples are needed to better understand broader concerns around sport, gender, and disability. On another level, much more in-depth research regarding the meaning of the physical body for women and men with disabilities should be conducted. In particular, before appropriate programming and policy can be initiated, a better understanding of the needs of men and women with different kinds of disabilities and different social backgrounds is required.

This research also indicated that physical activity for women with disabilities has an important social function. Further comparative research conducted with other groups of women and other social groups could investigate whether or not this need is more prevalent among women with disabilities than among other participant groups. Such information could be helpful in policy development regarding sport and recreation. Finally, the first author hopes that her personal journey of exploration, reflection, and active response to her children's needs will help inform progressive and inclusive recreation models that attract and value people with and without disabilities.

Note

We would like to acknowledge that partial funding for this project came from the McMaster Research Centre for the Promotion of Women's Health.

References

Bickenbach, J.E. 1993. *Physical Disability and Social Policy*. Toronto: University of Toronto Press.

Birrell, S., and D. Richter. 1987. 'Is a Diamond Forever? Feminist Transformation of Sport'. *Women's Studies International Forum* 10:395–409.

Blackford, K. 1993. 'Feminizing the Multiple Sclerosis Society of Canada'. *Canadian Woman Studies* 13:124–8.

Blake, N. 1992. 'Integrated Classification in Elite Disabled Sport'. *Disability Today* 1:26–7.

Cassidy, B., R. Lord, and N. Mandell. 1995. 'Silenced and Forgotten Women: Race, Poverty, and Disability'. In *Feminist Issues: Race, Class and Sexuality*, edited by Nancy Mandell, 32–66. Scarborough: Prentice-Hall.

Crawford, C. 1989. 'A View from the Sidelines: Disability, Poverty and Recreation in Canada'. *Journal of Leisurability* 16:3–19.

DePauw, K. 1994. 'A Feminist Perspective on Sports and Sports Organizations for Persons with Disabilities'. In *The Outlook: Vista '93*, edited by R.D. Steadward, E.R. Nelson, and G.D. Wheeler, 467–77. Jasper, AB: Rick Hansen Centre.

_____. 1997. 'The (In)visibility of Disability: Cultural Contexts and "Sporting Bodies"'. *Quest* 49:416–30.

Fine, M., and A. Asch. 1988. 'Disability Beyond Stigma: Social Interaction, Discrimination, and Activism'. *Journal of Social Issues* 44:3–21.

Hall, A., T. Slack, G. Smith, and D. Whitson. 1991. *Sport in Canadian Society*. Toronto: McClelland & Stewart.

Hall, M.A. 1984. 'Towards a Feminist Analysis of Gender Inequality in Sport'. In *Sport and the Sociological Imagination*, edited by N. Theberge and P. Donnelly, 82–103. Fort Worth: Texas Christian University Press.

Hillyer, B. 1993. *Feminism and Disability*. Norman: University of Oklahoma Press.

Hoyle, J. 1996. 'Leisure and Women with Disabilities: New Directions in Subjective Experience'. MA thesis, McMaster University.

Jaggar, A. 1983. *Feminist Politics and Human Nature*. Totowa, NJ: Rowman and Allanheld.

Johnson, D.H. 1992. *Body: Recovering Our Sensual Wisdom*. Berkeley: North Atlantic Books.

Malec, C. 1993. 'The Double Objectification'. *Canadian Woman Studies* 13:22–3.

Merleau-Ponty, M. 1962. *Phenomenology of Perception*, translated by Colin Smith. New York: The Humanities Press.

Morris, J. 1989. *Price Against Prejudice: Transforming Attitudes to Disability*. Philadelphia: New Society Publishers.

_____. 1993. 'Feminism and Disability'. *Feminist Review* 43:57–70.

Nixon, H.L. 1984. 'Handicapism and Sport: New Directions for Sport Sociology Research'. In *Sport and the Sociological Imagination*, edited by N. Theberge and P. Donnelly, 162–76. Fort Worth: Texas Christian University Press.

Sherrill, C. 1993. *Adapted Physical Activity, Recreation and Sport: Crossdisciplinary and Lifespan*. Dubuque, IA: W.C.B. Brown & Benchmark Publishers.

Shildrick, M., and J. Price. 1996. 'Breaking the Boundaries of the Broken Body'. *Body and Society* 2:93–113.

Shilling, C. 1993. *The Body and Social Theory*. London: Sage.

Theberge, N. 1985. 'Toward a Feminist Alternative to Sport as a Male Preserve'. *Quest* 37:193–202.

Tong, R. 1989. *Feminist Thought*. Cambridge, MA: Polity Press.

Van den Berg, J.H. 1972. *A Different Existence*. Pittsburgh: Duquesne University Press.

Wendell, S. 1989. 'Towards a Feminist Theory of Disability'. *Hypatia* 4:104–24.

_____. 1993. 'Feminism, Disability and Transcendence of the Body'. *Canadian Woman Studies* 13:116–22.

Chapter 15

Sport-Related Hazing:

An Inquiry into Male and Female Involvement

Jamie Bryshun and Kevin Young

Introduction: Gender, Power, and Identity in Sport

In North American sport, a 'rookie' is an athlete who is participating with a team for the first time. The use of this term seems to apply regardless of gender, age, or athletic experience. An athlete may be labelled a rookie several times, including each time she or he joins a new team. Rookies progress to veteran status once they complete their first season. As this chapter will demonstrate, the process through which rookies gain acceptance as team members is both similar in terms of gender, but also different in type and degree.

In many societies and cultures around the world, veteran members of social groups require new or potential members to demonstrate their commitment to the group. When neophytes are introduced to the new group or reach a particular age or status, they are often exposed to some form of ritualized initiation or 'hazing', which, though sometimes physically or psychologically painful, serves to consolidate their new identities (Driessen 1983–4:125–31; Sanday 1990:33–40). As a largely symbolic interactionist literature (cf., Meltzer et al. 1975; Strauss 1967; Stryker 1967) has shown, potential inductees are expected to form new 'selves' that are associated with membership and that eventually produce a new social position and rank for themselves within the group. Such a process often takes place in sport.

The values, attitudes, knowledge, and behaviours that a specific sports team upholds are produced and reproduced through ritualized initiations. The internal hierarchy of a team gives veterans power over rookies and creates a desire on the part of newcomers for acceptance and full membership status. As Sabo (1987:2) writes, socialization encourages initiates to think in hierarchical terms and to 'positively value [rather] than reject status differences'. Throughout sport-related rituals, veterans 'test' rookies and evaluate whether they have sufficiently adopted behaviours and beliefs required for membership. When neophytes resist, their resistance often provokes physical and psychological punishment. In general, but with exceptions, it is likely that the rookie athlete is ultimately faced with a choice: acceptance and internalization of the standards set out by the veterans, or rejection and eventual ostracism from the team.[1]

Feminist and other approaches have consistently shown that sport predominantly operates as a male-defined and male-dominated institution (Bryson 1983; Hall 1993; Hargreaves 1990; Kimmel and Messner 1990; Sabo 1987). As such, traditional male sport subcultures tend to place a considerable amount of pressure upon initiates to conform to 'masculinist' values and beliefs. Specifically, the identities neophyte athletes are pressured to assume coincide with values emphasizing such things as performance based on physical dominance, winning at all costs, and disdain for practices considered 'unmasculine' or feminine. As Sabo (1987) notes:

> In sport, boys are taught to define themselves as members of the 'team'. . . . They learn to identify 'up' (with coaches, first-teamers, and superstars) and not 'down' (with women, third-teamers, losers and quitters)(brackets in original, Sabo 1987:4).

In order to tap the formation of masculine identity in sport, it is important to research how social processes such as sport-related hazing are experienced by male athletes during different phases of membership. However, while such research may tell us a great deal about sport and notions of 'masculinity' and 'masculine identity', it reveals very little about female involvement and 'feminine' identity in sport. Thus, in order to understand how females are socialized into sport, it is also critical to explore sport subcultures populated by girls and women. Some preliminary research, for example, has shown that as more females have begun to participate in sports traditionally closed off to them, their orientations and incentives have become more closely aligned with traditionally 'masculine' sports worlds (Young and White 1995). On the other hand, it is also likely that socialization processes for female athletes differ from those of their male counterparts in such ways that identity formation within female sport does not reinforce 'masculine' traits but rather expresses a quite separate female presence and 'feminine' identity within sport subcultures (Young 1997; Young and White 1995).

At present, the information on sport-related hazing remains sketchy because so few studies have addressed the issue in any systematic way. This is especially true with respect to the involvement of females. Thus, with a focus on the involvement of both male and female athletes, this study begins to probe the extent, nature, and meanings of hazing in sport subcultures in Canada.

Hazing Practices in Historical and Social Context

There is an abundance of anthropological and historical literature on initiation practices based on case-studies, many of which illustrate the use of rituals to socialize young boys into manhood and set them apart from uninitiated peers and females (cf., Morinis 1985; Rosman and Rubel 1981; Toohey and Swann 1985). This literature shows, for example, that the Zuni tribe of New Mexico whipped boys to 'toughen them up' (Rosman and Rubel 1981:78–81), and that the Nandi tribe of East Africa publicly circumcized young boys to prepare them for sexual maturity and to inculcate in them the 'masculine' qualities of courage and pain endurance (Toohey and Swann 1985:330).

The emergence of more modern societies and what Elias (1978) would call 'civilizing processes' may have changed the forms that social group initiations take, but they have not eliminated initiations or their meanings altogether. In fact, whether it is the 'hell night' imposed upon freshmen students by their older peers in seventeenth-century France (Nuwer 1990:117), the nineteenth-century English public school system of 'fagging' where 'the right [was] exercised by the older boy to make the younger boy do what he likes' (Nuwer 1990:117), or the development of fraternity hazings in late nineteenth-century American schools and universities (Nuwer 1990:119), it is clear that many of the traditional social dimensions of hazing (i.e., the enforced formation of a new identity through often abusive rituals in a setting of unequal power relations) have been retained. Both the contemporary existence and gendered underpinnings of hazing can be illustrated by briefly reviewing what we know of the phenomenon in educational, military, and sport settings.

Educational Settings

Hazing has been a recurrent problem for officials in contemporary North American high schools. As early as 1905, for example, a thirteen-year-old boy from Lima, Ohio, died of pneumonia after 'being "hazed" by a number of schoolmates who . . . stuffed snow into his clothing' (Nuwer 1990:251). In 1924 two female Brooklyn high school students had Greek letters burned onto their foreheads and crosses drawn on their backs. According to Nuwer (1990:189, 194–6), the nationwide high school organization, National Future Farmers of America, has consistently hazed its new members. For example, at Loris High School in South Carolina, admission has apparently involved crawling under an electrified cattle fence while naked and wet, and at Cissna Park High School in Shabbona, Illinois, neophytes' hands were forcibly dipped in paint.

As troubling as hazing rituals have been for high school officials, they have posed an even greater problem in colleges and universities. As the following cases show, initiation activities have consistently occurred in university settings across North America and occasionally have had catastrophic consequences:

1984:   During 'Frosh Week', a male University of Saskatchewan student was found dead at the bottom of a seven-storey elevator shaft with his body covered with whipping cream and fire extinguisher fluid (Nuwer 1990:250).

1986:   At Carleton University, McMaster University, and the University of Toronto, freshmen endured practices such as coerced alcohol consumption, being pounded by fruits and vegetables, and being jammed into a 'sweatbox' with up to 160 other freshmen (Nuwer 1990:250).

1994:   A twenty-five-year-old male student died after being physically beaten during a fraternity initiation at Southeast Missouri State University (*Macleans* 30 January 1995:19).

Military Settings

Accounts of hazings in the military are also legion. The following are recent select cases that were reported in the media. They all involved clearly abusive initiation practices, but to our knowledge there is no reliable way of judging their representativeness:

1992:   An amateur video of the Canadian Airborne Regiment conducting hazing rituals at the Petawawa base, Ontario, showed drunken recruits being forced by colleagues to eat faeces, vomit, and urine-soaked bread, conduct simulated sex acts, as well as have their heads shaved and undergo shock-testing during a beer-drinking party (*Calgary Herald* 14 February 1995:A5; *Macleans* 30 January 1995:15, 16 October 1995:31).

1996:   Eleven officer cadets were charged with abusing another cadet in a hazing ritual at a training course at Canadian Forces Base Gagetown. One cadet was taped to a chair while his face was covered with toothpaste, shoe polish, foot powder, shampoo, camouflage paint, ink, and shaving cream. His underwear was torn off and sunscreen applied to his genitals. A plastic bag was placed over his head for a short time. The cadet was later hauled into a shower and exposed to alternating blasts of hot and cold water (*The Globe and Mail* 23 March 1996:A7).

1997:   A videotape of United States Marines conducting hazing rituals in North Carolina showed initiates screaming in pain while pins of achievement were smashed into their chests by veteran Marines in an initiation rite called 'blood winging' or 'gold winging' (*Calgary Herald* 1 February 1997:A2; *Calgary Sun* 1 February 1997:8).

Sport Settings

Our knowledge of the extent of hazing in sport is limited. There is no credible evidence from which to predict either the types of sport groups that consistently condone ritualized hazings or the frequency of sport-related hazing. With some exceptions, most of the data that do exist seem restricted to heavy contact, male-dominated team sports. For example, ethnographic studies conducted by Thomson (1976), Young (1983, 1988), and Donnelly and Young (1988, 1999) show that neophyte male rugby players have traditionally been hazed by veteran players through tasks often associated with heavy alcohol consumption, nudity, and violence. The postgame celebration is the traditional setting where rookie players are expected to consume large amounts of alcohol prior to being forced to complete initiation tasks. Young's (1983:129–31) study of male rugby players in southern Ontario in the early 1980s indicated that veteran players often displayed a 'take it or leave it' attitude to rookies. One case involved veterans coercing inebriated rookies into completing hazing rituals such as stripping naked, shaving their head hair and eyebrows, eating live goldfish, and carrying marshmallows coated with heat liniment between their naked buttocks—all conducted under the watchful eye of veterans who chanted sexually explicit songs and sprayed beer over the rookies.

Though the sociological study of hazing is far more limited, the media have reported hazing in ice hockey:

1988:   The Kent State University men's hockey team was suspended for one year following an incident in which five rookie players were given mohawk haircuts, had their pubic hair shaved, and were asked to drink a mixture of rum and beer. One player was hospitalized (Nuwer 1990:258).

1994:   Four members of a male hockey team in Chatham, Ontario, reported that they were forced to masturbate publicly. Thirteen people were charged with over 100 sexual offences in the case (*Macleans* 30 January 1995:17).

1994:   Rookie members of the Lethbridge Hurricanes of the Western Hockey League (WHL) were reported to have had their eyebrows shaved and were forced to compete against each other in events where, for example, marshmallows were inserted between their buttocks, and hockey pucks were thrown by veterans into buckets tied to their penises (*Lethbridge Herald* 18 March 1995:A4, C1).

1996:   Three University of Guelph students were cut from the men's Gryphons hockey team for refusing to participate in an initiation party in the team dressing room. The event allegedly involved drinking through funnels and games that included nude players eating faeces-contaminated marshmallows ('The Fifth Estate' 29 October 1997; *The Toronto Sun* 28 February 1996:5).

Further information on hazing in hockey is provided by Oliver (1990), who compiled observations while travelling with the Saskatoon Blades of the WHL during the 1989 season. In addition to accounts of hazing rituals, including a game called 'Red Rover' in which two naked rookies conduct a 'tug-o-war' while their penises are tied together, Oliver's study is important in illustrating that hazing can be an ongoing process that extends beyond the confines of the institutionalized 'Rookie Night' setting. Finally, the autobiographies and biographies of professional athletes are also potential sources of information on hazing in hockey. In one of the most famous cases, hockey superstar Wayne Gretzky speaks of having shaving cream rubbed in his hair, his eyebrows shaved, and his shoes stolen during his rookie season with the Edmonton Oilers (Gretzky and Reilly 1990:44, 50; Oliver 1990:51).

Not surprisingly, given its notorious culture of machismo (Courson 1991; Meggyesy 1971; Shaw 1972), hazing is also rumoured to be prevalent in football. There are reports of freshmen being forced to wear their helmets on buses in hot summer weather (*Calgary Herald* 30 August 1996:D2), being made to bite off the heads of live chickens in order to 'prove' their toughness to veterans (*Macleans* 30 January 1995:17), and being coerced to participate in abusive off-field 'games'. In one called 'The Gauntlet', for example, newcomers were physically beaten by veteran players, hosed down, and thrown in mud (Nuwer 1990:257–8). However, much of this type of information is anecdotal and of questionable reliability.

It is clear, then, that hazing rituals in a number of social settings are both historically grounded and retain significance. The social dynamics and power relations acted out in these rituals are complex, and the participation of new members (and possibly veterans) in them may be voluntary, involuntary, or both. But, more important, there is also evidence—at least for the three social institutions described here—that complicity in hazing events by officials and people in positions of authority often lends some structural legitimacy to hazing. For example, in the Canadian Airborne Regiment case, Major-General Brian Vernon, head of the Army in Ontario, was relieved of his duties in February 1995 after he prepared a report for Chief of Defence Staff, General John de Chastelain, which rationalized the hazing as 'innocuous'. Vernon stood by his report and later claimed in an interview that 'the tape shows nothing more than soldiers blowing off steam . . . a celebration after an arduous field-training exercise' and that 'the total effect is one of the male bonding which is essential for teamwork and cohesion in fighting units' (*Calgary Herald* 14 February 1995:A5). Similarly, following the University of Guelph hockey incident, which severely fragmented the team, the coach of the team condoned the hazing: 'The bottom line is [that there are] two kinds of hazing rituals. One is the degrading, damaging type, the other is fun and enjoyable. This was the fun and enjoyable type. . . . They're naked together every day. They shower together' ('The Fifth Estate' 29 October 1997; *The Toronto Sun* 28 February 1996:5). The assumptions and orientations contained in these rationalizations hint strongly at the gendered trappings of hazing in all male settings.

A Note on Method

This study is based on a convenience sample (Fowler 1993:11–16) of members of sports teams based in three western Canadian cities. Random sampling techniques were not used, but we did attempt to cover a range (of types and levels) of sports. The sample was selected from amateur and professional teams competing in eight contact sports (football, basketball, soccer, ice hockey, field hockey, rugby, water polo, wrestling) and three non-contact sports (volleyball, swimming, synchronized swimming).

Individual athletes (including roughly equal samples of both females and males, and rookies and veterans) were approached and asked to voluntarily participate in semistructured interviews. Because the literature suggests that social groups participating in hazing practices (such as those found in educational and military settings) have traditionally involved single-sex memberships, co-ed teams were not approached. In total, thirty athletes were interviewed between October 1996 and February 1997. The length of the interviews ranged from thirty-five minutes to ninety minutes; the average length was just under one hour. Sixteen respondents were male and fourteen were female; all were White. Seventeen competed in contact sports, and thirteen competed in non-contact sports. Eighteen were veteran athletes (with more than three seasons of experience in their current sport) and twelve were rookies. Seventeen were actively competing at the time of the interview, and thirteen were former athletes. The underlying purpose of the interviews was to tap personal experiences with hazing, and meanings attached to rookie/veteran statuses as well as the hazing process itself.

The Hazing Process

The Timing and Location of Hazing

Once the interviews began, it quickly became evident that hazing practices occurred routinely but in varying degrees across the sample. While there was clear evidence of continuous socialization into new sport-related identities, most teams hazed initiates during the by-now institutionalized event—Rookie Night. For all of the sports studied, the hazing process usually began soon after pre-season try-outs were finished and team rosters had been finalized. With the exception of football's so-called 'Rookie Show', athletes consistently termed their respective initiation event 'Rookie Night'.

We found no obvious attempt by veteran players to conceal the inevitability of some sort of initiation event for incoming players. Senior members communicated to their junior teammates, either verbally or, for example, by posting a notice in the locker-room, the date of their initiation, often well in advance. Some senior players on a variety of teams even went so far as to post a list of 'props' that the rookies needed to bring to their initiation event. Scare tactics were very much a part of this pre-event advertising. Male swimmers, for example, were required to bring an extra pair of underwear, condoms, and a beer glass. It turned out, as rookie swimmer Quinton explained, that only the glass was actually used throughout the night: 'I think they [the veterans] were just trying to scare us by not telling us what we needed those things for.'

Veterans tended to schedule Rookie Night on a weekend evening relatively early in their respective athletic seasons. Ursula, a female veteran volleyball player, rationalized such scheduling in terms of enhancing group solidarity: 'We try to do it at the beginning of the season in hopes that this gathering will ease tensions or [help rookies] make friends.' Some teams relied on group tradition when scheduling their particular event. Professional and amateur football players, for example, always held their Rookie Show on the last day of training camp. Likewise, and as Loren explained, men's basketball players initiated 'on the first Friday after the team has been [set] . . . right after prac- tice'. Both the men's and women's rugby teams initiated following the team's first game. Men's soccer and hockey teams conducted initiations 'on the first road trip' (Dave), while the women's soccer team 'always do it on a night when there's a cabaret' (Tanya).

More disparate than the timing of Rookie Night, the hazing of rookie athletes took place in a variety, and sometimes a combination, of locations. 'Private shows', which enabled veterans to control who witnessed the initiation activities, were conducted behind closed doors in settings such as the team's dressing room, the home of a veteran player, the team bus, or a hotel room. Public hazing enabled non-members to observe the activities. University cabarets (held both on and off campus) and local bars appeared to be the most common venues for public initiations by varsity teams, but other hazing activi- ties occurred in places such as parking lots, local bars/pubs, and shopping malls. It was evident that these public venues were deliberately selected by veteran members to single out and embarrass the rookies as they performed their required tasks.

Hazing Activities and 'Games'

The following accounts summarize the various hazing activities reported by the respondents.[2] They are classified according to sport, but in no particular order, and with both male and female athlete involvement represented wherever applicable.

Soccer
The men's amateur soccer team first initiated its rookies during a road trip at a hotel using a series of contests and tasks that players called the 'Rookie Olympics'. The evening began with all the rookies placing Twinkies under their armpits and running relays in the hotel hallway, collecting socks placed at either end. The losers of the race 'had to collect all the Twinkies and take a bite out of them' (Dave). A subsequent event was held in the bathroom, as rookie Tom reported:

> A veteran had already taken a dump [defecated] in a bag and put it on top of the toilet. They [veterans] cut up some bananas and put them into the toilet and then told us that we have to reach into the toilet for a beer, pull it out and drink it. We did all of this blindfolded.

The intent of this 'game' was to fool each rookie into thinking that he was reaching into a toilet full of faeces. Veterans used these events to test exactly how much abuse rookies would accept before they refused to participate or, as they perceived it, the extent of the rookies' intensity and commitment to the team.

Other events required rookies to sit in a hot-tub filled with ice and cold water for one minute. Those who failed were forced to consume more alcohol and repeat the ice treatment. At an event held at the annual 'Rookie Buy Night', the rookies were forced to go to a public bar wearing women's clothing. The word 'Rookie' was printed on their faces with a black marker, and they were expected to pay for drinks consumed by veteran players.

The women's soccer team followed similar hazing patterns. Their first road trip was replete with practical jokes that included putting ice and granola in the rookies' hotel beds. The team's Rookie Night, held several weeks later, began with initiation 'games' in the dressing room. Rookies had to eat peanut butter off the floor without using of their hands. Losers were forced to place a dollop of peanut butter under their armpits and keep it there for the rest of the night. As an indication of the implicitly heterosexist underpinnings of many of these sports hazings, the peanut butter could only be removed if a male stranger licked it off. The women's team also held what it called 'The Pickle Race', which involved rookies racing against one another down a hallway with pickles inserted into their (clothed) buttocks. The overall loser of the race was punished by having to eat her own pickle.

Other events for the female rookies included a so-called 'Kangaroo Court' in which rookies were forcibly blindfolded, 'charged' with various 'offences', and 'sentenced' to consume unpleasant tasting drinks. They were also forced to wear outrageous clothing in public and participate in a game called 'Scavenger Hunt', played at a team cabaret, which involved searching for condoms, soliciting financial donations, and having male hockey players sign their flesh.

Ice Hockey

Male hockey players had an abundance of initiation stories to tell, most involving coercive and closely policed rituals. Although the data on hockey hazings came from four male players who had been members of over eight different teams in five different leagues, their stories were surprisingly similar. For example, all of them recalled being involved in an event known in hockey circles as the 'The Holocaust', an activity that usually occurred on the team bus while travelling to or from a game:

The rookies would strip down and we would turn on the hot water in the bathroom. We would take all of their clothes and tie them up in balls, wrap them up in hockey tape and throw them in [the bathroom]. The rookies would be in there with all the lights off and they would all have to put their [own] clothes on and come out, and they would have a time limit (Vince).

One hockey team implemented a slightly different version of 'The Holocaust'. Instead of throwing the clothes into the washroom with the rookies, the veterans threw them out of the bus and into a ditch. In veteran Tim's account: 'They [the rookies] would have to go out there and get them, change and come back . . . oh yeah, it's cold. January or February.'

There were additional events that involved all of the hockey initiates. For example, when they arrived at a player's home for Rookie Night, one group of rookies was forced to strip naked. A veteran player dressed as a doctor and, in Steve's account, 'he'd have surgical gloves on and we [veterans] would put a circular weight with a hole in the middle over the rookies' dicks and shave around it'.

All of the male hockey players also recalled playing the so-called 'Gong Show' at least once during their careers. Similar to events that take place in other sport subcultures, the object of the game is for the rookies to humour the veterans by doing 'whatever it takes'. Predictably, the Gong Show is often an opportunity for vulgarity and excess. For instance, in Vince's words, one rookie 'placed a piece of paper on the floor in front of him and shit on the paper, in front of all the veterans'. Another rookie tied a bucket to his penis with a hockey skate lace. The bucket was then hung over a hockey stick that rested across the backs of two chairs. The apparent objective was for the veterans to slowly throw pucks into the bucket, pulling on the rookie's penis, until the rookie, in obvious discomfort, could appease his veteran teammates.

Other hockey hazings involved forcing novices to consume bizarre alcoholic beverages until they vomited, swim naked in a freezing lake in winter (the 'Lake Run'), and have obscenities printed on their bodies by veterans. While the female ice hockey players reported several ongoing 'socializing' tasks set for rookies, perhaps more so than any other sport in the sample, male hockey players reported an abundance of initiations that tended to involve nudity, physical punishments, and excessive amounts of alcohol consumption.

Wrestling
According to a five-year veteran, the men's wrestling team in the sample had consistently held a 'Rookie Buy Night' at a local bar as part of its annual initiation events. Although some of the same rules applied to the wrestling rookies as to the soccer rookies (i.e., each rookie had to buy each veteran a drink), the wrestlers changed the structure of this game so that rookies also had to *steal* beer

for the senior players. This version of the game became preferable for veterans, he noted, because 'The whole idea is that everyone is trying to be as deviant as possible.'

Wrestling veterans would often 'set the tone for the [Rookie] night', according to Neil, by challenging teammates (veterans and rookies alike in this case) to beer-drinking contests. In a further demonstration of machismo, veteran wrestlers would also dare the rookies to approach women with whom they were not acquainted in the bar:

> All throughout the night, the vets would just pick a girl in the bar and lay out the guidelines for a rookie . . . Like, "I dare you to go up to that girl and get her to buy you a drink," or "I dare you to go up to that girl and ask her if you can sit on her lap" . . . Stuff like that, just to see if the guys would do it. Once again if there isn't a rookie that is willing to do it, a veteran might go up and do it instead, so as just to show-up the rookie. . . . Sometimes it gets pretty outrageous and the women get really pissed-off at us. Many rookies have been told-off or slapped. All the veterans want them to do is try, right? It's almost as if they [veterans] would rather see somebody get slapped than succeed in doing their task (Neil).

Initiation for male wrestlers differed from various other teams' rookie initiations in that rather than simply observing events, wrestling veterans actively participated in them. Also wrestlers held their initiations in public settings only. Unlike the hockey players in the sample, male wrestlers did not physically harass rookies throughout their initiation events, but rather relied on heavy alcohol consumption and the harassment of female strangers as main activities in their initiations.

Volleyball

As part of their hazing activities, the women's volleyball team met at a veteran player's home prior to taking 'dressed-up' rookies to a men's volleyball game so that they could be seen 'getting hazed' by other fans in the stadium. At this game, and in Shawna's words: 'We [rookies] would have to do individual acts in front of the crowd, a solo cheer, or drink more.' Then, as Shawna explained, the rookies were taken to a cabaret where they were required to flirtatiously approach 'guys and ask them to buy us drinks'.

For the female volleyball players, alcohol was the main feature of the activities. Ursula recalled her initiation into a different volleyball team the year before:

> Last year when I was 'rookied' they had this whole agenda where you had to do a shot and run around and do this little circuit [race]—the idea was to get everyone to puke that night or just get totally hammered . . . the majority of the people [rookies] were knocked out by ten o'clock.

Following a men's volleyball game, female initiations during the most recent season progressed to a local bar and again involved excessive alcohol consumption. In Shawna's words: 'Then they [veterans] took us to the bar and from then on people had to go home early. It was messy. Yeah, people [rookies] were puking.'

A veteran male volleyball player recalled his days with a Canadian varsity volleyball team as less eventful compared to what he knew of events on the current men's team:

> We didn't really do that much back then. My last year was about the only time I can remember having a party. That's because we went to my cabin and had a Rookie Night out there. . . . We just had games, relays in the snow, played one-on-one [basketball], that's about it. Not any initiation stuff (Curtis).

Curtis's response is a clear example of the normalizing strategies that athletes often use to describe their initiation experiences. Although these athletes' accounts seem to trivialize the potential seriousness of the hazing process, the data suggest that coercive hazing events are common features of the membership process on many male and female sports teams.

Field Hockey

Female field hockey players also dressed up rookie players. In this case, rookies were required to don outdated women's clothing and consume alcohol while preparing to attend a cabaret. As veteran Tamara explained:

> [The veterans] brought alcohol and clothing. Everyone was drinking. We dressed them [the rookies] up in just gross polyester dresses and someone had brought some make-up. Most of them got 'rookie' painted on their forehead. One girl got a wig put on her. All of them had really bad make-up put on them.

As the team arrived at the cabaret, the field hockey rookies were

> . . . paired off with one or two veterans and given a Scavenger Hunt list. They were told that they had to go and find these things . . . condoms, a t-shirt, and drinks that they get somebody else to buy and [then] give them to the vets (Tamara).

Although alcohol clearly played a part in field hockey initiation 'games', Tamara felt that it was monitored closely: 'Nobody got sick or anything. We weren't pushing them to drink and get sick.' Despite Tamara's recollection, rookie Debbie remembered the events differently:

> All the time we had to drink gross stuff, I don't even know what it was. . . . We [rookies] had to shoot drinks together. We did that a couple of times. Some of the

girls were almost gagging. I think it's worse when you don't even know what you are drinking.

Debbie's initiation experiences were similar to those of many other rookie respondents in the sample who had to consume alcoholic or non-alcoholic 'shots' and dress up in unfashionable clothing. The Scavenger Hunt game played in this case was similar to the version played by the female soccer rookies, who also searched for specific items while they attended a cabaret.

Rugby

The male and female rugby players proved to be unique in the sense that they were members of teams that both practised *and* socialized together. Although neither the men's nor women's teams consistently used a formal term such as Rookie Night to describe their initiating activities, they did segregate their newest players and haze them after one of their first games of the season. Since the women's team was somewhat incorporated into the men's, predictably there were very similar initiation practices held by both squads. Specifically, initiations were exclusive to the post-game 'get-togethers' as Henry, a veteran male player, reported:

We don't really do much for initiations. We make sure that when the rookies do come out with us [veterans] after a game, they guzzle some beer. We usually make them race against one another. That's it. Just some drinking.

Tina, a veteran player on the women's team, indicated similar drinking rituals for female rookies, but added:

Rookies are a little scarce for us [on the women's team] because we are such a new sport for women. It is really hard for us to recruit new players. Last year we only had one new player so we couldn't really have a drinking race—we just made sure that she came out with us and had some shots [alcohol]. She always came out anyways.

It appeared that the post-game gatherings were the only arena for rugby initiations; there were no other reports of initiations outside of these few drinking activities.

Although the initiations reported by both male and female rugby players in the sample did not coincide with the rigorous events that have traditionally been linked with the sport (Donnelly and Young 1988; Thomson 1976; Young 1983), rookie initiations did take place for the rookie athletes in the sample, though perhaps in a less aggressive manner. Male and female players socialized both on and off the field together and in a similar fashion. Like wrestling, rugby initiations were confined to the public sphere and involved various games and tests of fortitude in the context of expected/enforced alcohol consumption.

Basketball

One men's basketball team's initiation event actually began during the day, as a former player described:

> We dress up all the rookies as women and they have to go to school wearing all that shit—make-up and everything. . . . They have rookie written on them some-where, they are either [wearing] a sign or [have it written] right on their face (Loren).

Similar to the women's soccer team's cabaret game of soliciting financial dona-tions, the men's basketball Rookies' Day consisted of players collecting as much money as possible from fellow students and professors in order to cover the costs of their event.

The evening's events started off with the rookies stripping down to one piece of clothing. In Loren's words: 'whichever piece they wanted, so basically their underwear. There was tons of booze, and the rookies couldn't sit on the chairs or couches. They had to sit on the floor.' The rookies then had to participate in a game, which required them to roll two dice. The total number that was rolled corresponded with a task that the rookie had to perform. Loren explained:

> One was called 'Find the Ball'. We waited until four guys rolled this one, it was like a seven or something. Once four guys rolled it they were told that there was a basketball hidden somewhere in the bleachers and they had to find it—the guy who found it didn't have to drink. . . . So they stripped naked and were sent into the gym where the women's team was practising. . . . Of course, there's no ball. So they eventually come back.

Another task was called 'The String and Pen'. Here, the rookie had to tie a marker to his penis with a short string and go to the library. Loren explained the purpose of this activity: 'They [the rookies] had to go out and get a girl to write her name and phone number onto his chest with this pen'. As the game unfolded, the remainder of the membership congregated in the dressing room to socialize and drink.

According to the veteran Loren, after all of the games were completed, 'The Annual Naked Run' occurred:

> This is the big tradition every year at D____. All the boys are boozed by this time and we get a half-ton truck and put all the rookies in the back [wearing] just a towel and their running shoes. They are dropped off all around the campus and they have to run back to the room.

Once the rookies found their way back to the dressing room, they were required to perform a skit as part of 'The Gong Show'. As Loren noted, rookies were 'told ahead of time to prepare something. They might sing a song or something. The worst skit is punished by drinking'. When asked if it was common to punish the 'losers' by making them drink more, the veteran replied, 'Yeah, otherwise the guys won't try as hard.'

Traditionally, the men's basketball Rookie Night has concluded at a local bar, but on the most recent occasion:

> That didn't quite work this year though. . . . Three out of the four rookies didn't make it and were passed-out or sick in the team room. . . . One was in the shower, one on the toilet and one on the floor. . . . It was ugly, man (Loren).

Unlike veterans Tamara (field hockey) and Ursula (volleyball) who felt that past initiations had been more demanding and punitive, Loren described his team's Rookie Night as one of the harshest since he joined the team.

Swimming

The rookie female swimmers were subjected to two separate evenings of initiation activities. On the first occasion, the rookies had to sell kisses at a local bar. In Mary's words: 'We had to walk around and sell them for a dollar each, but the veterans collected all of the money.' Predictably, the night's events also centred on a number of alcohol-related tasks, which, for at least one rookie, actually helped mediate the intimidation of her 'duties': 'It was way easier if we did [drink].' The players also had to attend a varsity football game with their faces painted with various colors and 'do cheers and be really loud'.

The second rookie night started at a veteran swimmer's house: 'One girl had to dress up in a bathrobe, weird dresses and stuff. They [the veterans] all had these stupid things that we had to do too—like pick your nose and eat it' (Mary). Before the team went to a cabaret, the rookies had to run around the neighbourhood, searching for items on a Scavenger Hunt list. One rookie explained: 'Every item you didn't get you got punished for it. I got everything and I still had to do stuff. It didn't matter' (Mary). The punishment for the rookies was having to wear 'more bad clothing or make-up' to the dance. Evidently, no alcohol was consumed at the house, which was a rare occurrence compared to previous swimming initiations. According to Liz, she and the other veteran swimmers decided to 'tame' their rookie initiations this year 'because last year a rookie got really sick from having to do [alcoholic] shots and they had to rush her to the hospital to get her stomach pumped'.

The men's swim team also met at a veteran's house for its Rookie Night event. There, the rookies had to play the role of 'servant' to the veteran players throughout the party, and were challenged to numerous drinking games: 'We would have to try and beat a veteran in guzzling a beer or doing like three shots in a row. . . . This went on throughout the night. I don't think any of us [the rookies] beat them [the veterans]' (Quinton). Quinton indicated that considerable amounts of alcohol were consumed by all the members for over seven hours of activities.

Synchronized Swimming

Unlike some of the other sports sampled, there appeared to be very little tradition in the initiation experiences of synchronized swimmers. However, all of the (female) swimmers indicated that they had either witnessed or participated in some form of initiation events while they were competing. One former swimmer, who competed and coached for over fifteen years, recalled how she and her teammates used to initiate novices while she was a veteran:

> I was right in there when it came to initiating. We weren't too crazy . . . not like football or hockey players, that's for sure. For our Rookie Night all we did is make the rookies jump off of the 10-m diving board. . . . Some of them had never done it before and were terrified, others did it, no problem. That's all we did, no booze or anything else. We were pretty tame back then, actually (Tracy).

Ingrid, another synchronized swimming veteran and current participant, explained how her team held its Rookie Night on its first road trip:

> All of the girls were in one of the hotel rooms and we [veterans] dressed all of the rookies up with funny make-up and hair styles. Then we made them go across the street to the store [together] and buy us chips, drinks, whatever the veterans wanted. . . . Some of us were drinking, but alcohol wasn't really an issue.

Ingrid also explained how initiations on her team were strictly limited to isolated events: 'something that happened on only one night and never happened after that'. She recalled her own initiation when she and other rookie swimmers on her team were required to drink shots of alcohol at a local bar. According to Ingrid, the veterans designated the evening as a Rookie Night, but there were no serious or excessive initiation activities: 'I don't even know if you can call it an initiation. . . . We didn't really have to do anything bad. The veterans even paid for it.'

Water Polo

A water polo player encountered hazing while he competed with several different teams at the varsity and national level. Steve, a veteran still actively involved in the sport, interpreted his hazing experiences in the following way:

> Very painful, to put it lightly. It's just a matter of time before everyone [the rookies] gets it. The big game is you never know when. The veterans constantly have you on the edge of your seat. It's almost like you just want it to happen so you can get it over with. The vets sometimes try to attempt it and then pull back. They are always threatening to do it. Some guys get it right at the beginning of the

season, others get it later, which I think is the worst because then you are constantly threatened by the vets. It is almost prolonged too long sometimes.

The specific initiation event that Steve was referring to is known in water polo circles as 'The Ginch Pull':

> The vets, whenever they do decide to get you, hold you down and pull your ginch [underwear] up your ass as high as it will go, of course it is pulling everything else up too—your testicles most importantly. There's no way you can get out of it once they have you 'cause it's you against about six or ten of them. Sometimes other rookies will jump in and try to save the guy who is getting initiated. Then the whole thing turns into a brawl and eventually nothing else happens. The rookies just get the shit kicked out of them and then they don't do it [interrupt] again (Steve).

The water polo teams for which Steve competed did not refer to these and other events as Rookie Night. Rookie initiation for the water polo players in this sample solely involved the completion of 'The Ginch Pull'. This, according to Steve, has traditionally occurred in hotel rooms and dressing rooms.

Football
By comparison, football players in the sample reported that initiation took place through very structured events. A former varsity and professional football player experienced only small variations throughout his initiations on several teams. All occurred during the pre-season:

> [During] my rookie year . . . we had to sing at lunch time. I had to do a vet's laundry. Take it home with me every day and clean it for him. Rookie Show was the last night of training camp. . . . We had to do skits. Skits are usually when they [the rookies] make fun of veterans (Scott).

Although the rookies were being humiliated in front of their teammates and coaches, one interesting aspect of the skits was that the rookies were able to poke fun at the veteran players, an opportunity that seemed unique to the football subculture.

Other events during varsity football Rookie Shows included relay races involving naked players, as Scott explained:

> The rookies had to go buck [strip naked] and we had olive races between the rookies. There's a chunk of ice at one end of the field and you have a bunch of olives sitting on top of it. Rookies have to sit down and pick one up with their ass and run across [the field] and put it down on the other side. You can't touch the olives with your hands or else you have to start again. The first one to move three olives wins

the race. The problem is that the ice is so damn cold on your ass, it is really hard to pick them up. Making them stay in your ass while you're running is another thing.

The professional teams for whom Scott played also had their rookies perform skits during alcohol-laden team lunches and dinners. He explained what the football players called 'The Gong Show': 'Every lunch time somebody [a rookie] was singing or performing some sort of skit. They would either get a thumbs-up or thumbs-down from the veterans.' Scott recalled the rookies having to clean the veterans' plates and bring them food during these team meals. Reports of aggressive football hazings collected during this study certainly coincide with information on initiation events conducted by football players on other teams across North America. Worth noting here is the uniqueness of football's Rookie Show and how it is exclusively set in the private domain (dressing room).

Interpretation and Future Research

Despite increasing social disapproval and closer policing of hazing, it continues to play a key role in sport. Hazings have created national scandals in the Canadian military as well as in Canadian ice hockey. Respondents willingly and often uncritically disclosed details on hazing in their respective sports. Perhaps surprisingly, none of the respondents reported being a member of a team that enforced codes of silence regarding team initiations. All of the athletes in the study, representing sport participants in three western Canadian cities, reported that they had experienced some form of hazing at least once in their athletic careers; many had been hazed several times.

The study suggests that hazing is linked both to gender socialization and sport socialization. Male and female veteran athletes support aggressive and domineering methods in initiating rookie teammates. In many sports, physical and emotional fortitude are valued qualities for successful socialization and for becoming a recognized member of the team and subculture more generally. During the initiation process, rookie athletes who resisted masculinist symbols and ideologies were sometimes labelled by the veteran members as weak and unwilling to 'take one for the team'.

On the surface it appeared as though both men and women athletes tended to exemplify these traditionally 'masculinist' traits during their initiations. Upon further investigation, there were subtle differences between the genders. Specifically, there were signs that women did not adhere as rigidly as their male counterparts to forms of aggression, dominance, and punishment in their initiations. The women's soccer team's 'Kangaroo Court' (held in a candlelit room), the women's volleyball and field hockey ceremonies (which involved head hair being sprayed, as opposed to the shaving of men's hockey rookies), and the overall absence of nudity hint at a somewhat more restrained version of hazing practices among women athletes in this traditionally male-defined arena, but there were exceptions. We found at least one case (volleyball) where coercive hazing rituals were pursued far more aggressively by the female players than by their male counterparts. It remains unclear how we may interpret these differences in terms of gender. In general, however, the articulation of power, status, and identity issues was clear in the hazing rituals of both male and female players.

The hazing incidents described in this study demonstrate consistent attempts by established members of sports teams to embarrass or humiliate the neophytes in front of the broader membership and, in some cases, outsiders. The objective, it seems, is to test the individual's fortitude and commitment to the team. Incidents such as the 'Lake Run' (men's hockey), the 'toilet game' (men's soccer), or dressing up various rookie players before going to a public dance or bar were all attempts by veterans to gauge the rookies' dedication. Interestingly, the data revealed that while some rookies were clearly anxious about being initiated, these often daunting and publicly embarrassing events were met with generally favourable rookie reactions.

Responses such as these suggest that players think outsiders tend to view hazing as a 'tolerable deviance' (Stebbins 1988:3–4), and that 'insiders' achieve a certain status by being hazed publicly. Even rituals involving the harassment of women, such as those of the men's basketball and wrestling teams, did not appear to cause discomfort among outsiders. Similarly, and supporting the heterosexist underpinnings of many sport-related hazings, the female soccer and volleyball rookies, who were required to approach male strangers at a dance and ask them to buy drinks or lick off the peanut butter that had been smeared in their armpits, did not elicit any negative social reactions.

The power process between rookies and veterans enables veterans to arouse fear and anxiety in the younger players (as with the synchronized swimmers who were forced to jump off a 10-m diving board, and the rookies who had their pubic hair shaved by men's hockey veterans). Many of these daunting and degrading initiation events served as rites of passage, which fulfilled a dual purpose—they helped rookies establish a new identity within the membership, while the veterans also benefited by having their dominant position within the team reinforced.

The data also suggest that hazing practices range from harmless high jinks and games to more serious cases involving physically dangerous or illegal activities. It is important not to trivialize the fact that many hazing incidents involve physically risky and even life-threatening activities that are understandably of concern to authorities, school administrators, and parents. For example, both the female swimmer who had to get her stomach pumped after being coerced into consuming excessive amounts of alcohol and the numerous other rookies who were forced to drink so much that they vomited could have conceivably died from alcohol poisoning. Yet, in what seems to be an illustration of what Sykes and Matza (1989) have called 'techniques of neutralization', both rookie and veteran athletes appeared to consistently downplay or normalize the often excessive, risky, or illegal hazing process.

As with the broader process of socialization itself, hazing is often a changeable and continuous activity. The data, which demonstrate the fundamentally ongoing character of identity formation and construction, call into question the view that Rookie Night signifies the beginning and end of ritualized hazings and the expression of hierarchical power between teammates; indeed, most subjects indicated that their team continued to operate hierarchically throughout the season. Rather than being limited to one or two specific initiation events, hazing often appears to last throughout the sporting season, albeit in different guises.

All of the respondents in the sample disclosed incidents in which rookie players had to perform certain tasks for the team during their rookie season, which supports the case for the *continuous* construction and confirmation of athletic identity in sports subcultures (Donnelly and Young 1988). Sometimes veteran players forced rookies to complete certain tasks and at other times, according to one veteran hockey player, 'You just do it. It's part of your job as a rookie. It is just assumed by everyone that the rookies pick up the pucks after practice. No questions asked' (Tim). In addition to such things as collecting equipment after practice, rookies were also required to clean the dressing room, carry extra baggage on road trips, and cook meals for the team. Also, rookies were often physically isolated from their veteran teammates during team meals, on the plane and bus during trips to games out of town, in the dressing room, as well as in hotel rooms. These findings confirm those of Young, White, and McTeer (1994), who found various examples of 'degradation ceremonies' for injured athletes. As in the present study, these practices were as common to the women's teams as they were to the men's.

The data also suggest an association between the nature of certain sports and the type of hazing. The more violent and physical the game, the more aggressive or even abusive the hazing seems to be. Athletes who competed in physical contact sports (particularly ice hockey, rugby, football, field hockey, and wrestling) tended to report more abusive hazing involving physical punishments than members of non-contact sports teams (such as volleyball, swimming, and synchronized swimming). Among others, these incidents included hockey's 'The Holocaust' and 'The Gong Show', football's rookie relays, and basketball's 'The String and Pen'. Alcohol was central in hazing events of contact sports teams (for instance, wrestling's 'Rookie Buy Night', as well as field hockey, ice hockey, and rugby's drinking contests). Alcohol tended to be less central in the hazing events of non-contact sports.

However, this apparent association between physicality in sport and excessive physicality in hazing is not clear-cut. Indeed, there were significant contradictions and paradoxes within both the contact and non-contact sport groups. The women's ice hockey team, for example, did not report overtly aggressive or abusive initiation practices that one might expect given the aggressive character of their sport. This was in sharp contrast to their male hockey counterparts whose Rookie Nights included many daunting tasks, physical punishments, and heavy use of alcohol. Instead, among women, more subtle socialization techniques were implemented throughout the season. In contrast, synchronized swimmers in the study reported separate incidents of being forced to consume shots of alcohol before jumping off an intimidating 10-m diving board. Clearly, the relationship between the character of the sport in question and the character of hazing events requires further study.

Given its obviously lengthy history and its presence in a variety of contemporary social settings, hazing remains curiously understudied. In the area of sport, the phenomenon is relatively untapped, which seems especially odd given the numerous scandals associated with sport over the years. Knowledge and policing of hazing in educational and military settings have increased lately, but information about hazing in sport appears to be lagging behind. And until very recently, we knew next to nothing about women's involvement in sport-related hazing.

While we have achieved our research goal in presenting here the first, albeit modest, study we know of uncovering systematic participation in hazing by Canadian female athletes, and while we now know unequivocally that male *and* female rookies may be hazed aggressively and abusively in the name of team solidarity and athlete identity, we are aware that the implications of hazing for gender processes in general remain unclear. Of course, we are hopeful that this important gap in our knowledge will be remedied by students of sport and gender in the near future.

Notes

1. The issue of whether hazing activities involve consent and voluntary participation or are more accurately described as involuntary and coercive has become a key one for social institutions such as schools and universities as well as the authorities. When conceived as degrading, abusive, and potentially dangerous practices rather than playful 'high jinks', hazing events clearly become a legal matter rather than simply a matter of in-group norms.

2. Space restrictions limit the detail offered in this section on hazing practices in each of these sports. For a more comprehensive account of these events, including more complete reactions from the players involved, see Bryshun (1997).

References

Bryshun, J. 1997. 'Hazing in Sport: An Exploratory Study of Veteran/Rookie Relations'. MA thesis, University of Calgary.

Bryson, L. 1983. 'Sport and the Oppression of Women'. *Australia and New Zealand Journal of Sociology* 19, no. 3:413–26.

Calgary Herald. 1995. '"Male Bonding" Antics Doom General'. (14 February):A2.

_____. 1996. 'High School Footballer Is Injured'. (30 August):D2.

_____. 1997. 'Brass Call Hazing Video Disgusting'. (1 February):A7.

Calgary Sun. 1997. 'Hazing Horror'. (1 February):8.

Courson, S. 1991. *False Glory*. Stamford, CT: Longmeadow.

Donnelly, P., and K. Young. 1988. 'The Construction and Confirmation of Identity in Sport Subcultures'. *Sociology of Sport Journal* 5:223–40.

_____, and K. Young. 1999. 'Rock Climbers and Rugby Players: Identity Construction and Confirmation'. In *Inside Sport*, edited by J. Coakley and P. Donnelly. New York: Routledge.

Driessen, H. 1983–4. 'Male Sociability and Rituals of Masculinity in Rural Andalusia'. *Anthropological Quarterly* 56–7:125–31.

Elias, N. 1978. *The History of Manners: The Civilizing Process*, vol. 1. New York: Pantheon.

'The Fifth Estate'. 1997. 29 October, Canadian Broadcasting Corporation.

Fowler, F.J. 1993. *Survey Research Methods*, 2nd edn. Newbury Park, CA: Sage.

The Globe and Mail. 1996. '11 Cadets Charged After Severe Hazing'. (29 October):A7.

Gretzky, W., and R. Reilly. 1990. *Gretzky: An Autobiography*. Toronto: HarperCollins.

Hall, A. 1993. 'Gender and Sport in the 1990s: Feminism, Culture and Politics'. *Sport Science Review* 2, no. 1:48–68.

Hargreaves, J. 1990. 'Gender on the Sports Agenda'. *International Review for the Sociology of Sport* 25, no. 4:287–305.

Kimmel, M.S., and M.A. Messner. 1990. *Men's Lives*. New York: Macmillan.

Lethbridge Herald. 1995. 'Of Hazing in Hockey'. (18 March):A4.

_____. 1995. 'Rites of Passage'. (18 March):C1.

Maclean's Magazine. 1995. 'Canada's Shame'. (30 January):14–18.

_____. 1995. 'Dubious Conduct'. (16 October):30–3.

Meggyesy, D. 1971. *Out of Their League*. Berkeley: Ramparts Press.

Meltzer, B.N., J.W. Petras, and L.T. Reynolds. 1975. *Symbolic Interactionism: Genesis, Varieties and Criticism*. London: Routledge and Kegan Paul.

Morinis, A. 1985. 'The Ritual Experience: Pain and the Transformation of Consciousness in Ordeals of Initiation'. *Ethos* 13, no. 4:150–73.

Nuwer, H. 1990. *Broken Pledges: The Deadly Rite of Hazing*. Marietta, GA: Longstreet Press.

Oliver, R. 1990. *The Making of Champions*. Markham, ON: Penguin.

Rosman, A., and P. Rubel. 1981. *The Tapestry of Culture*. Glenview, IL: Scott Foresman.

Sabo, D. 1987. 'Sport, Patriarchy and the Male Identity: New Questions About Men and Sport'. *Arena* 9, no. 2:1–30.

Shaw, D. 1972. *Meat on the Hoof*. New York: St Martin's Press.

Sanday, P.R. 1990. *Fraternity Gang Rape*. New York: New York University Press.

Stebbins, R. 1988. *Deviance: Tolerable Differences*. Toronto: McGraw-Hill Ryerson.

Strauss, A.L. 1967. 'Language and Identity'. In *Symbolic Interaction: A Reader in Social Psychology*, edited by J.G. Manis and B.N. Meltzer, 322–8. Boston: Allyn and Bacon.

Stryker, S. 1967. 'Role-Taking Accuracy and Adjustment'. In *Symbolic Interaction: A Reader in Social Psychology*, edited by J.G. Manis and B.N. Meltzer, 481–92. Boston: Allyn and Bacon.

Sykes, G., and D. Matza. 1989. 'Techniques of Neutralization: A Theory of Delinquency'. In *Deviant Behavior: A Text-Reader in the Sociology of Deviance*, edited by D. Kelly, 104–11. New York: St Martin's Press.

Thomson, R. 1976. 'Sport and Deviance: A Subcultural Analysis'. Ph.D. dissertation, University of Alberta.

Toohey, D.M., and C.P. Swann. 1985. 'A Comparative Study of North American Subcultures'. *Comparative Physical Education and Sport* 3:327–34.

The Toronto Sun. 1996. '"Sick" Ritual Hurts Guelph U. Hockey'. (28 February):5.

Young, K. 1983. 'The Subculture of Rugby Players: A Form of Resistance and Incorporation'. MA thesis, McMaster University.

_____. 1988. 'Performance, Control, and Public Image of Behavior in a Deviant Subculture: The Case of Rugby'. *Deviant Behavior* 9:275–93.

_____. 1993. 'Violence, Risk and Liability in Male Sports Culture'. *Sociology of Sport Journal* 10:373–96.

_____. 1997. 'Women, Sport, and Physicality: Preliminary Findings from a Canadian Study'. *International Review for the Sociology of Sport* 32:297–305.

_____, and P. White. 1995. 'Sport, Physical Danger, and Injury: The Experiences of Elite Women Athletes'. *Journal of Sport and Social Issues* 19:45–61.

_____, P. White, and W. McTeer. 1994. 'Body Talk: Male Athletes Reflect on Sport, Injury and Pain'. *Sociology of Sport Journal* 11:175–94.

Chapter 16

The Last Game?

Hockey and the Experience of Masculinity in Québec

Anouk Bélanger

In recent years, masculinity has become an extremely popular topic in social science research and popular psychology throughout the Western world. As part of this current interest, there has been considerable attention given to the concept of masculinity in the field of sport sociology (Connell 1987, 1990, 1995; Messner 1992; Pronger 1989, 1991). There is also a small, albeit growing, body of research on the links between sport, gender, and national identities (see Maguire 1996; Mangan 1996). However, this research on sport, gender, and nationalism remains marginal in the field as a whole. By contrast, I want to claim a more central place for the link between masculinity and nation in sociological writing on sport. In this chapter I use the specific historical context of Québec to explore these linkages as expressed in and through ice hockey. In doing so, I will address how the experience of history can be understood as an 'experience of identity' with clear gender implications.

I have chosen to focus my analysis on ice hockey because this sport has played a significant role in Québec's history and culture. At one level, of course, the Québécois' infatuation with hockey is nothing new or astonishing. Hockey has occupied a central cultural space across Canada since the beginning of the century. For example, Gruneau and Whitson comment on hockey's 'taken-for-granted' character in Canadian society:

> Hockey was the one thing in our youth that virtually all boys seemed to have in common—the stuff of everyday conversation, the regularly shared experience of after school and weekend play. . . . even people who dislike hockey have difficulty escaping its reach, its omnipresence in the media and in the everyday conversations that occur at the office, the playground, and the school (Gruneau and Whitson 1993:2).

But at another level, the roots of hockey seem to run even deeper in Québec society and culture than elsewhere in Canada, and extend into the Québécois' collective memory and imagination. One of the major reasons for this lies in the extent to which hockey has been understood *symbolically* in Québec as part of its national identity, and in hockey's participation in the construction of a specifically heterosexual, homophobic, and aggressive form of masculinity.

In order to analyse these issues in more detail, the chapter is organized into four sections: the first addresses the specificity of Québec's history; the second examines hockey and the question of cultural identity in Québec; the third section presents different perspectives on masculinity construction and sport; the fourth is a discussion of a short movie presented as a form of subversion to hockey's hegemonic masculinity. The conclusion pulls together a series of arguments around the interconnections between gender identity and national identity.

Some Historical Groundwork

It is impossible to do justice to the rich cultural history of Québec (or of any other province) in a few paragraphs. In order to lay a foundation for the argument of this chapter, it is necessary to provide some general historical groundwork because certain historical developments, particularly the way in which they have been *remembered* in Québec, deeply influence how the Québécois have understood themselves and others.

The defeat of the French on the Plains of Abraham in the fall of 1759—sometimes referred to as the 'Conquest'—has been mythologized in Québec as the defining moment when *les anglais* adopted the infinite Canadian wilderness. In the century after the 'Conquest', people of mostly British descent gradually adopted the appellation 'Canada' for themselves and created their other, 'French' Canada. In a time of great industrial expansion during the late nineteenth and early twentieth centuries, the majority of 'French Canadians' were concentrated in rural Québec, while some moved to industrial centres such as Montréal to sell their labour.

During that period, many Québécois came to view their society as one 'conquered, by-passed by the creative movement of history, one which served only as a labour force for productive structures set by others' (Schwartzwald 1991b:178). It was English Canadians who were the 'others' who set and controlled these 'productive structures', buying the labour of the Québécois who moved to industrial centres while the rest stayed in rural areas, often only to have their labour exploited in mines, mills, and farms they did not own. Finally, the so-called Quiet Revolution, a period of 'all-encompassing modernization' in the 1960s and 1970s, represented a time of growing nationalist sentiment and an increasing representation of French-speaking Canadians in government, the civil service, and higher education.

The Quiet Revolution in Québec was a very prolific time for anti-colonialist literature. Schwartzwald argues that the anti-colonialist discursive sphere developed in Québec during the 1960s and 1970s, 'although inspired by Sartre, Fanon, Memmi, Bercque, Guevara, Malcolm X and others, distinguished itself quickly' (Schwartzwald 1991b:177). Pierre Vallières's book, *White Niggers of America*, arguably became the best-known example of the Québécois' anti-colonialist genre. Vallières and other anti-colonialist writers of this period in Québec were attempting to construct a coherent national subjectivity to replace the fragmented subjectivity of the colonized. Also during this period, and as will be discussed later, hockey was 'pulled in' as one of the many cultural practices used to construct this national subjectivity.

The notion of the development of a 'national subject' through the anti-colonialist and nationalist discourses in Québec rests mainly on a particular image of 'us' and the 'other' (Schwartzwald 1991a). This image comprises a variety of dualities—heterosexuality/homosexuality, man/woman, French/English—that repeatedly intermingle. Schwartzwald (1991a) argues that a certain insecurity of the 'us' has led to a deeply rooted homophobic sexual tension in the culture. In Québec in the 1960s and 1970s this homophobic sexual anxiety accompanied the new nationalist project that wanted to break away from the 'conservative agrarian and clerically animated nationalism' of the past, 'a nationalist project that is progressive in its social objectives, and that situates itself within the universalizing discourse of all the great anti-colonial movements of the epoch in question' (Schwartzwald 1991b:179). As part of this anxiety, those regarded as enemies or 'sell-outs' to the cause of national revolution were the anglophone federalists who enjoyed economic power or the French élite associating with them, as opposed to the vast majority of Québécois whose main source of power lay in the one thing they truly owned—their physicality. As a result, the category of the 'other' in Québec was also *gendered*. To the active, virile, and 'authentic' Québec nationalist, the 'other' was the male federalist. The subject of this double-edged homophobic imaging was given the expression 'federast' in Schwartzwald's work (1991b), an expression playing on the words 'pederast' and 'federalist'.

It is important to mention that the nationalist's appropriation of vigorous physicality was more often metaphorical than literal. The nationalist discourse allied itself to the 'people', a cultural construction that carried with it a vulgarization of male working-class physicality. Similarly, the ideologized sense of masculinity in Québec on the nationalist side had to reconcile this metaphorical sense of physicality with the fact that many of the leaders of the national movement were 'intellectuals'. Still, as metaphor, the connections between 'nation' and a robust heterosexual masculinity were clear and provided a backdrop where different masculinities had to be articulated, positioned. In Québec a dominant masculinity linked to physicality and nationalism achieved a high degree of popular consensus. Along with this development, heterosexuality became a cultural 'requirement', and homoeroticism was pushed to the margins of social life. For the working-class Québécois especially, non-physically vigorous homosexual masculinities became symbolically linked to a specific type of man: the 'federalist'. This linkage between the discourses of masculinity and nationalism is not unusual in colonial societies. For example, Connell (1995:196) argues: 'In colonies, where conquered populations were not displaced or massacred but were made into a subordinated labour force on the spot—the gender consequences involved a reshaping of local cultures under the pressure of the colonizers'.

Hockey and the Question of Identity in Québec: The Campbell/Richard Episode

The historical and cultural analysis briefly introduced earlier focuses primarily on the man/woman duality and on the creation of a homophobic tension in Québec national culture. This notion of a metaduality of the 'us' and the 'other' in Québec's history can also be discussed from the perspective of the French/English duality. In this regard, it is interesting to see how the homophobic sexual tension described by Schwartzwald has pervaded ice hockey and interacted with an 'anglophobic' cultural tension. The representation of the 'other' as physically passive became, for many French Québécois, an opposition not only to their hegemonic masculinity but also a threat to their strong national identity. This nexus of tensions has been powerfully dramatized through hockey. One notable individual who embodied these tensions in Québec is former NHL President Clarence Campbell.

During the 1950s in Québec, *Le Canadien* was a team 'full of French-Canadian players, noted for a passionate style of play and fiercely supported by local fans' (Rutherford 1990:245). One of the star players for *Le Canadien* during this period was Maurice Richard, a player 'thought to boast the classic Gallic temperament: passionate, roistering, tough' (Rutherford 1990:251). When Clarence Campbell suspended Maurice Richard for violent play for a term including the end of the 1954–5 season *and* the Stanley Cup series (thus prohibiting Richard from accomplishing a goal-scoring record), Campbell became the symbolic 'other' both to Richard and to many Québécois. Richard represented the agrarian Québécois who had to sell his labour to an industry controlled and owned by anglophone Canadians. By contrast, Campbell came to represent the anglophone business owner who controlled most of Québec's economy during the postwar era, and in that sense was regarded as the 'other' in the construction of the national identity project. Richard's suspension provoked considerable controversy in the popular press and the now infamous 'Rocket Richard riots' in downtown Montréal.

This tension between Campbell and Richard was just one example of a symbolic battle on the ice between anglophones and francophones around a strong national identity and pride. As part of this symbolic battle, the insecurities and tensions of the national project were at play in a popular forum that allowed many Québécois to react and articulate their frustrations. It was a struggle in which, for many Québécois, the 'other' was not only the anglophone but the 'federast' described earlier. It is important to note here that there was something of a breach in these representations between the working class and many members of Québec's élite. This gap was characterized in the popular imagination by the lack of 'virility' (physical power) that was projected on the homosexual 'other'. On the federalist francophone élite of the 1950s and 1960s, Schwartzwald notes:

> These trained young men go on to become not the defenders of Québec indepen-
> dence, but true federasts like the fifis of Radio-Canada, the radio announcers on
> the French-language network with their European accents, or the tapette
> Trudeau, as the former Prime Minister and friend of Hertel's is referred to in the
> manifestos of the Front de Liberation du Québec (Schwartzwald 1991b:186).

During the period when the breach between the working class and the francophone élite was growing, the quest for symbols of masculine power became an increasingly important issue for many Québécois. This physical masculinity seemed to be one of the few ways for nationalist Québécois to empower themselves in front of the anglophones who, allied to certain branches of the clergy and the French bourgeoisie, were in control of the major social institutions and industries. It is particularly at this time that role models like Maurice Richard became important in embodying the very essence of Québécois identity and ethnic struggle. Richard in particular embodied the 'us' described by Schwartzwald, and the 'us' of a francophone/anglophone duality. On this point, Jean-Marie Pellerin, Maurice Richard's biographer, argues:

> After two centuries of frustration, the people of Québec had found a hero to
> avenge them of many humiliations. They had found a knight who, without any
> fear, would . . . engage in this symbolic battle in which are engaged francophones
> and anglophones on the ice. Maurice became their god (Pellerin 1971:72).

Hockey heroes like Maurice Richard became the embodiment of (physical) strength, power, and pride that came to fill the 'insecurity gap' of many male Québécois. In their long march to regain autonomy and a strong identity, the Québécois made cultural icons like Richard a springboard for hope. For example, Pellerin goes so far as to argue that Richard's career as a professional hockey player can be viewed as an encapsulation of Québec's history—of the struggle of the Québécois around pride and national identity. Pellerin's argument may be overstated, but there are certainly many instances where we are able to see the powerful influence of hockey (and the symbolic battles it dramatizes) on Québec's collective memory. The same can also be said of the capacity of hockey in other contexts to mirror the rivalries between Canadians and Americans (see Dryden 1983; Gruneau and Whitson 1993).

The Richard/Campbell episode goes beyond a conflict between two hockey personalities; it is best understood as an event that opens a window on the quest of the Québécois for a strong national identity. When Clarence Campbell suspended Richard in 1955, not only did the incident provoke the Rocket Richard riot, it also gave rise to a wave of nationalistic sentiment in the popular press. Examples of these reactions can be found in journals such as *Le Front Ouvrier*:

> The Richard Case: A racial issue! . . . Richard is the most amazing athlete of modern times and should be considered and respected as such. Unfortunately, he happens to be French-Canadian, and contrary to how we treat the English sport heroes, they have tried since his beginnings in the NHL to put a term on his reign as a monarch of hockey! . . . When will we have our share at the Canadian nation's banquet? When will we be free of those fanatics getting in the way of our emancipation in sports like in politics (cited in Pellerin 1971:93)!

Daily newspapers also responded to the incident, explaining the Richard riot in terms of nationalistic frustrations. The following quote from an article published in *Le Devoir* is illustrative:

> We killed my brother Richard. . . . French-Canadian nationalism seems to have found a refuge in hockey. The crowd manifesting its anger Thursday night was not solely animated by sport frustrations, but rather by the feeling of injustice against its hero. It was a frustrated mass of people protesting against their fate. This fate, Thursday night, had a name: Clarence Campbell, and he embodied all their real or imaginary adversaries (*Le Devoir* 21 March 1995).

My point is that hockey in Québec is a significant site for popular expression, and for that reason the clash between Campbell and Richard was readily interpreted from the standpoint of anti-colonialist and nationalist projects. Through hockey, and because of its unique history in Québec, many Québécois men were able to link a sense of masculine pride and physical vitality to a strong national pride and cultural identity. In other words, the game powerfully articulated an image of Québécois (and Canadian) manhood. The game also met the need for heroes in a country, Rutherford (1990:251–2) argues, that 'couldn't seem to find in its own past or present many people on whom to lavish worship'.

Hockey, the Thesis of the 'Surrogate Father' in Québec, and Research on Masculinities

As in Canada and North America more generally, the question of masculinity has gained increased attention in Québec over the last decade. Some commentators on this issue, notably pop-psychologist Guy Corneau, raise issues related to hockey and its apparent dramatization of identity struggles. Corneau is the 'father' of the men's movement 'made in Québec' or, as some people have called him, the Robert Bly of *La belle province*. Corneau first gained attention with his best-selling book, *Père manquent, fils manqué* (*Missing Father: Troubled Son*) (1989), which deals with what he believes is the decline of masculinity in Québec as a consequence of its colonial past. Corneau argues that this particular aspect of Québec's history is still deeply embedded in the Québécois male's insecure sense of self. Responses to this insecurity are not expressed through politics but through a therapeutic approach that Corneau based on 'the colonized complex'. Québécois males have systematically shrunk their historical past in order to project it onto their own current life experience. A lack of self-confidence, it is argued, is passed down from father to son, generating a fragile collective masculinity. In order to 'heal' this generalized fragile masculinity in Québec, Corneau proposes a set of values and ideas with which to reorient men's activities and reinforce their 'insecure' identities.

The premise behind Corneau's proposals is that it is only in distinctive masculine environments that Québécois 'sons' will be able to lose their gender insecurity. Contact with strong male role models, initiation rituals, and opportunities both to express aggression and to develop a certain intimacy (that would reinforce their heterosexual masculinity) are necessary conditions for building and sustaining a strong masculinity among young Québécois. In the absence of such 'masculine' environments, Corneau argues, young Québécois males will internalize an insecurity mainly concentrated in sexual identity. The purpose of providing homosocial male environments also makes sense according to Corneau (1989:108) because 'the strict division of the sexes has always prevailed historically in education, religion, sport, etc.' The need to express male aggression to reinforce masculinity is rooted in the belief that 'a man is not a man until he is in touch with his brute and savage energy' (Corneau 1989:129).

Corneau hypothesizes that hockey in Québec serves as a surrogate family to men and boys, and that teams fulfil a need to belong as Québécois males. What is important here is not to discuss whether hockey has helped reassert masculinity but to look at the extent to which the world of hockey represents the environment described earlier, and whether it reinforces certain models and values around gender identity. Hockey has undoubtedly acted as a place where males can receive gender training that supports the fragile process of masculinization. Gruneau and Whitson (1993) argue, for example, how Canadians' belief that hockey is important for making boys into men has been understood as 'common sense'. This shared belief in hockey as a training ground for a particular 'desired' masculinity helps explain resistance to challenges or threats to hockey's status as a homosocial world.

What makes hockey so aptly suited for linking masculinity with nationalism is the extent to which the sport has tended to operate as a predominantly homosocial environment. By the term 'homosocial environment' I mean a setting that is constructed by and for men and where women participate only at a symbolic level (Sedgewick 1985). A homosocial world such as hockey, where heterosexism and homophobia tend to dominate, requires women to support a particular type of masculinity (e.g., by participating as a man's partner and supporter). According to Bird (1996), homosociality

> ... promotes clear distinctions between men and women through segregation in social institutions ... homosocial interaction, among heterosexual men, contributes to the maintenance of hegemonic masculinity norms by supporting meanings associated with identities that fit hegemonic ideals while suppressing meanings associated with nonhegemonic masculinity identities (Bird 1996:121).

Gruneau and Whitson (1993) demonstrate how hockey has been developed almost exclusively by men for men and how 'in hockey, the existing gender order is made to appear natural, rather than something that has been socially and historically constructed and thereby open to change'. This underlines the importance of the 'natural appearance' of hockey's homosocial world and the difficulty of changing it. Hockey's 'natural order' in which women are clearly marginalized is expressed in the following quotation taken from the biography of French-Canadian hockey star Guy Lafleur in a section where the author discusses the expected 'social place' of Lafleur's wife:

> She knew that hockey was a terribly exclusive male world where women did not play any role, did not have any voice, or any authority. The 'hockey wives' often get less attention than the exciting and easy 'groupies'. But she had yet to discover that marrying a hockey player meant embracing a very excessive and totalitarian religion (Germain 1990:232).

In this context, the difficulty of highlighting the inequality of such 'naturalized' and 'necessary' relations is again exemplified by Lise Lafleur trying to explain these inequalities to her husband, who is caught up in the 'natural' aspect of hockey's homosociality:

> Lise: 'There is not one woman on the face of this earth that would accept such a situation. ... Try to imagine the reverse situation. Imagine a women's club on a road trip with their husbands gravitating around and always waiting for their match or drinking-session to be over. You men would all meet in the 'husband's room' and compare ties, cars, your kids' grades and golf handicaps ... with nothing else to do but to twiddle your thumbs during the game. ... there would always be groupies around your wives, dozens of handsome, elegant and available young men who would fancy them. And of course, your wives would find them attractive, would hand them autographs. ... Can you imagine? Can you imagine how the husbands would react?'

Guy: 'What can I say Lise? That's the way it is; that's hockey' (Germain 1990:234–5).

Lise Lafleur's comments, and Guy Lafleur's reaction to them, highlight the problematic naturalization of hockey's specific gender order. Within this 'natural' order a very specific definition of masculinity prevails.

The type of masculinity predominant in competitive sport in general and prevalent in ice hockey in particular is an aggressive heterosexual masculinity. According to Gruneau and Whitson (1993:191–2): 'Organized hockey developed as a distinctive masculine sub-culture, a game played almost exclusively by men and boys, and a game whose dominant practices and values have been those of a very specific model of aggressive masculinity'. This specific construction of a hegemonic masculinity in hockey has also been linked with anglophone expressions of Canadian national pride through hockey commentator Don Cherry. Cherry, a former player, coach, and now commentator for 'Hockey Night in Canada' (the oldest and most popular TV show in Canada), is a constant defender of a homophobic and aggressive masculinity as it is naturalized in hockey (Gillet, White, and Young 1996). Cherry's frequent and well-known diatribes against 'pinkos' and 'bleeding hearts' often make interconnections between nationality, political ideologies, and masculinity that also have parallels with the situation in Québec, although in Québec the connotations of non-robust physicality associated with effeminacy were at one point partly directed against the federalism that institutionally sustains the larger project of Canadian nationalism.

The literature on the construction of masculinity in sport is diverse. Most notably, this particular field of research has been significantly influenced by increasing involvement of female theorists who have questioned the 'natural order of sport' that defines the 'common sense' of hegemonic masculinity (Hall 1978, 1987; Hargreaves 1986). Although the work of feminist theorists in sport sociology has not been extensively focused on issues of masculinity *per se*, it has been influential recently. This trend is congruent with the broader field of social research emphasizing the institutional dimensions of masculinity.

Before further discussion of hockey in Québec, I would like to present briefly some of the perspectives on the construction of masculinity and sport in light of Corneau's approach to masculinity construction. Corneau's approach is similar in many ways to that of Robert Bly. The premise of Bly's most well-known book, *Iron John* (1990), is that men should celebrate their essential difference from women. Similar to Corneau's perspective, Bly emphasizes the necessity of initiation rites among men, and the important emotional damage wrought upon men by separation from their fathers. Further, both Bly and Corneau build their pop-psychological analyses on emotions rather than politics; they are working towards a *therapy* for masculinity as part of the 'mythopoetic men's movement'.

Some theorists, such as Raphaël (1988), though not normally associated with the therapeutic dimensions of Corneau and Bly, also believe in exclusive environments for men. Raphaël argues that because contemporary Western societies lack masculine rites of initiation found in tribal societies, sport is useful because it is one of the few places that offers young men a way of learning the masculine world of social values and norms. Sport also gives men a space where they may be completely separated from women, which is supposedly a necessary condition of their passage from boys to men and to the reinforcement of their masculinity.

The idea of the need for exclusive environments for men, and support for the initiation rites proposed by Corneau, Bly, Raphaël, and others, have been widely criticized. For example, the social theorist Pierre Bourdieu (1990:14) has argued, 'not only do they aim at installing a separation between the ones who went through it and the ones who did not, but also a separation between the ones who are socially worthy of undergoing such ritual and the ones who have been forever excluded: [e.g.] the women'.

Recent research on the construction of masculinity through sport has begun to account for the fact that there are a variety of masculinities and femininities in social life. These differing masculinities and femininities support the notion that there is no abstract masculine or feminine 'essence'; rather, gender identities arise out of the complex interactions *between* men and women (Messner and Sabo 1990). There is considerable research to suggest that the institution of sport has long played a key role in the construction and in the stabilization of certain types of masculinities and femininities. So entrenched is this process that, at the institutional level, sport is widely recognized as a fundamentally patriarchal institution that is male-organized, male-dominated, and male-oriented (Messner 1992).

However, Messner (1992:18) has also argued that it would be too simplistic to understand sport *only* as a patriarchal institution that reinforces the power of men over women. Although we tend to discuss and criticize hegemonic conceptions of masculinity, 'at any given historical moment, there are also competing masculinities, some hegemonic, some marginalized, some stigmatized. Hegemonic masculinity, the form dominant today, is defined in relation to various subordinated masculinities as well as in relation to femininities.' Used in this context, 'hegemonic' means the form of gender identity that manages to claim and sustain a leading position in social and cultural life. This does not imply a fixed set of rules and practices that are always the same everywhere. It is, in fact, always and everywhere socially and culturally constructed and always contestable. As Connell (1995) notes:

> At any given time, one form of masculinity rather than others is culturally exalted. Hegemonic masculinity can be defined as the configuration of gender practice which embodies the currently accepted answer to the problem of the legitimacy of patriarchy which guarantees the dominant position of men and subordination of women (Connell 1995:77).

As part of the idea of the *social construction* of gender identities, it is important to recognize that the role of sport in the construction and legitimization of a heterosexist and aggressive hegemonic masculinity and of homosocial environments has often displayed contradictory dimensions. For example, Pronger's (1989:3) research not only reveals the diversity of masculinities in sport, it also discusses the paradoxes of the representations of masculine forms in contemporary culture. Pronger reveals the paradox of a hegemonic heterosexist masculinity constructed in and through the institution of sport: 'Sport as a masculine genre presents some men with an archetypal mythic form for homoerotic desire: the sexy, muscular, masculine athlete. That desire is paradoxical, being at once a reverence for and violation of masculinity.'

Still, a relatively unified conception of hegemonic masculinity retains a strong command over 'common sense' among many men. The challenge is to understand how hegemonic masculinity is actually played out in the world of sport. It is also important to discuss in which ways those gender relations constructed in sport are connected to a broader social, cultural, historical, and national context. In the spirit of this challenge, I want to extend my earlier discussion of masculine and national identities to the context of hockey in Québec.

As mentioned earlier, it is important to keep in mind that the masculinities and femininities discussed here are not 'natural'—they are socially, politically, culturally, and institutionally constructed and reproduced. The notion of history is also crucial in the construction of specific forms of femininities and masculinities because, as Connell (1995:28) argues, 'definitions of masculinity are deeply enmeshed in the history of institutions and economic structures'. Other sport sociologists have also noted the importance of the institutional aspect of the construction of masculinities. For example, Gruneau and Whitson (1993) show how business and political interests have helped to construct the aggressive masculinity of professional hockey.

For scholars committed to gender equality, a major goal in the subfield of sport studies is to identify and promote forces that counterbalance or limit the production of hegemonic masculinity. The purpose of developing theories of masculinity is to make the analysis practical and constructive. Thus, Connell (1995:7) has argued that we 'need to go beyond scientific accounts and look at the practical base of masculinity . . . through which gender is done or accomplished in everyday life'. Connell also believes that practical bases of masculinity can be emancipatory as opposed to oppressive, or they may even be both at the same time. I believe this complexity is evident in hockey in Québec in the sense that it sometimes conveys elements that support aspects of Corneau's mythopoetic vision, but at other times conveys a set of values that progressive social movements are struggling to overcome. This kind of tension between values and models expressed in sport is particularly evident in the case of hockey in Québec. How do we explain that a cultural practice can be completely reactionary in one sense and yet still captivate the imagination and idolatry of a nation evolving in other ways?

Competing Masculinities in Hockey: A Case-Study—'The Last Game'

I also want to argue that representations of masculinity in hockey can be seen in a variety of ways that oscillate between emancipatory, controlling, subversive, and reactionary. One particular representation of masculinity in hockey can be seen as subversive, which, while involving traditional homosocial patterns, implicitly questions the prevailing gender order, not only in hockey but in Québec more generally. The representations I am referring to appear in the Canadian-made short movie 'The Last Game,' which parodies the traditions of hockey and its homosocial world.

As part of the Montréal Sextet produced for the city's 350th Anniversary, Michel Brault's 'The Last Game' constructs a representation of tensions within traditional models of gender relations and new social movements for which hockey sometimes provided a backdrop. 'The Last Game' tells the story of a couple in their sixties who decide, during a hockey game at the Montréal Forum, to get a divorce. They have been devoted hockey fans for the last twenty years. The couple's relationship demonstrates the exclusive character of the homosocial world of hockey. The male spectators participate 'by proxy' through an affective solidarity and identification with the game; the female spectators also participate, but in a different way. This movie shows the omnipresence of hockey in the everyday life of many Québécois and the importance of hockey as a powerful cultural form that provides a useful perspective on a number of important aspects of Québec culture.

In the film, hockey represents the values of the husband, values that the wife has occasion to criticize. The film demonstrates how, on the one hand, the gendered dynamics of the world of hockey have been internalized by many men. On the other hand, hockey also reflects women's struggles to reconcile their relationship with those men and their attempts to move ahead as active subjects rather than as objects. As Bourdieu (1990:7) has suggested, 'women enter the dialectic of [gender] distinction rather as objects than as subjects'. This is exactly what Madeleine, the wife in the divorcing couple, is seeking to be: her own subject, not a symbolic accessory to her husband's masculinity. After twenty years of hockey, Madeleine does not care to watch anymore. She has, as it were, had enough, and she wants to change the power dynamic of her marriage. Thus, during the second period of the game she gathers her courage and tells her husband Roger:

> I have decided I [am] not going to wash your clothes anymore. I won't do your dishes. I won't cook for you anymore. I won't clean, and most of all, I won't come to watch hockey with you every Saturday night. It took me a long time, but I have made up my mind. I don't want to sacrifice my life for yours anymore. I want to retire, I want to retire from marriage. This was my last game.

This scene reflects the reactionary potential of traditional models of gender relations, yet also demonstrates a paradoxical acceptance of naturalized models of gender relations in hockey.

Although this particular representation of gender relations focuses graphically on a hockey game at the Montréal Forum, it also captures the dynamic of residential life in Québec on Saturday nights. I refer here to the popular expressions 'Saturday night widow' or the 'hockey widow'. Until relatively recently, most Canadian homes had only one television set, which meant that on Saturday nights 'Hockey Night in Canada' ('La soirée du hockey') prevailed in thousands of households. Therefore, and in Rutherford's (1990:245) words, 'many of the women watching hockey were captive viewers compelled to view the game or suffer the fate of being a hockey "widow"'.

The difficulty of thinking beyond the dominant constructions of gender (especially for men who tend to benefit from those constructions) is highlighted by this example. 'The Last Game' dramatizes the limits of masculinity in the character of the husband, Roger. Madeleine, the wife, tries to address problems that are outside of Roger's 'common sense' understanding of gender, a process that exposes irreconcilable tensions, not only between the two characters but also between two differing sets of values. Roger's failure to recognize the boundaries of his own masculinity results in a complete failure to comprehend the basis of his wife's unhappiness. As a result, he immediately rejects her argument, understanding her concerns from his naturalized homosocial environment: 'You're sure it's not menopause causing your little crisis?' (Brault 1993).

In this regard, Bourdieu (1990) argues that it is not only women who are victims of power relations of gender. Men are also prisoners and victims, albeit in different ways (as White and Young discuss elsewhere in this book). Bourdieu (1990:21) writes: 'the dominant [man] is dominated but by his own domination' and asks why this point tends to be ignored by feminist critics. In the film, for example, Roger is ultimately the victim of his own incapacity to understand and empathize with his wife, but this does not change the fact that women are generally subordinate in gender power relations. Commenting on the complexities of the play of power in gender relations, Connell (1995) is less inclined than Bourdieu to emphasize that some men are only and always operating from a dominating gender position, and may even experience their own forms of domination. He writes: 'The number of men rigorously practising the hegemonic pattern in its entirety may be quite small. Yet the majority of men gain from its hegemony, since they benefit from the patriarchal dividend, the advantage men in general gain from the overall subordination of women' (Connell 1995:79).

What makes 'The Last Game' so socially relevant is that the gender relations portrayed in the film are widely and insidiously evident especially for a particular generation in Québec culture. Through our understanding of the film, and our earlier discussion of Guy and Lise Lafleur and the lives of Maurice and Lucille Richard, we can make connections with some of the ideas outlined at the beginning of this chapter. These examples reveal how the construction of masculinities relates to the construction of femininities. Gender identities also change with time and place, and although 'gender relations and identities merge in organized social relations, they may change at different rhythms, with resulting tensions in masculinity and femininity' (Connell 1995:29). The tension between Roger and Madeleine in 'The Last Game', or between Guy and Lise Lafleur, happens when the women begin to articulate their concerns and seek their autonomy by challenging the traditional values of their husbands' homosocial environment. There are, in sum, few places in Québec culture that express these 'traditional' masculine values more clearly than hockey. The fact that such 'traditional' masculine values have been connected at times to Québec's post-colonial aspirations for 'sovereignty' has given these values even greater strength.

Conclusion

Identities often have a powerful taken-for-granted character. They also typically have a *relational* character, which means that they are formed in connection with other identities. To understand how the processes of identity formation and reformation work, we need to explore the links between gender, symbolic processes, and social structures. In other words, 'To understand gender, we must constantly go beyond gender' (Connell 1995:76).

In this chapter I have used the specific context of Québec to look at some interconnections between national identity and masculine identity as expressed in and through ice hockey. I set out to show how the experience of history (of Québec, and of hockey) can become the experience of identities. Indeed, in Québec a hegemonic masculinity that has linked maleness to physicality and nationalism has over the years achieved a level of 'taken for grantedness'. The connections between nationhood and a robust heterosexual masculinity are quite clear and provide a backdrop where different masculinities have become organized and ordered. As this occurred, the potential for homoerotic pleasure was expelled from hegemonic conceptions of masculinity. Heterosexuality became a 'postcolonial' *requirement*, and homoeroticism was pushed to the margins of the nationalist project. In the popular imagination of the working-class Québécois especially, homosexual masculinities became symbolically linked to a specific type of man: the federast.

Especially before and around the time of the Quiet Revolution, the nationalist project in Québec was connected symbolically to a vigorous physicality associated with the 'authentic' working-class Québécois. This connection between nation and a robust heterosexual masculinity was articulated powerfully through the aggressive masculinity codes in ice hockey. Hockey in Québec was symbolically drawn into the anti-colonialist and nationalist projects of the postwar period. Through hockey and its unique history in Québec, some Québécois men were able to find the support of hegemonic masculinity an inspiration for a strong national pride and cultural identity. Through hockey heroes such as Maurice Richard and others, the game represented an image of Québécois manhood and compensated for the lack of national heroes elsewhere in Québec society.

However, in the aftermath of many social and cultural changes associated with the Quiet Revolution, ice hockey began to experience counterbalancing tensions with regard to gender identity. With the influence and the support of many social movements (such as the feminist and the gay rights movements), the traditional gender relations supported by the homosocial world of hockey showed signs of vulnerability. The example of Madeleine in the film 'The Last Game' shows how one Québec film-maker has attempted to dramatize contemporary tensions around gender relations that the homosocial world of hockey finds difficult to embrace. In this way, the film poses a broader question for social analysis: How do we frame the project of changing an historically arbitrary model of relations that has been naturalized and rendered invisible for many? How do we assure that the continuation of the capacity to think outside the institutionalized constraints prevailing in the established social practices, traditions, and popular beliefs will survive? I believe that the world of sport is an especially relevant site for posing and answering such questions.

References

Bird, S. 1996. 'Welcome to the Men's Club: Homosociality and the Maintenance of Hegemonic Masculinity'. *Gender & Society* 10:120–32.

Bly, R. 1990. *Iron John: A Book About Men*. Boston: Addison-Wesley.

Bourdieu, P. 1990. 'La domination masculine'. *Actes de la recherche en sciences sociales* 84:4–31.

Brault, M. 1993. *La dernière partie en Montréal vu par*. Montréal: Cinémaginaire-Montréal vu par Inc.-Atlantis Films Limited-National Film Board.

Connell, R. 1987. *Gender and Power*. Stanford: Stanford University Press.

_____. 1990. 'An Iron Man: The Body and Some Contradictions of Hegemonic Masculinity'. In *Sport, Men, and the Gender Order: Critical Feminist Perspectives*, edited by M. Messner and D. Sabo, 83–95. Champaign, IL: Human Kinetics.

_____. 1995. *Masculinities*. Berkeley: University of California Press.

Corneau, G. 1989. *Père manquant, fils manqué*. Montréal: Les Éditions de l'Homme.

Dryden, K. 1983. *The Game*. Toronto: Macmillan.

Germain, G. 1990. *Guy Lafleur: L'ombre et la lumière*. Montréal: Art Globa/Libre Expression.

Gillet, J., P. White, and K. Young. 1996. 'The Prime Minister of Saturday Night: Don Cherry, the CBC, and the Cultural Production of Intolerance'. In *Seeing Ourselves: Media Power and Policy in Canada* in H. Holmes and D. Taras, 59–72. Toronto: Harcourt Brace.

Gruneau, R., and D. Whitson. 1993. *Hockey Night in Canada: Sport, Identities and Cultural Politics*. Toronto: Garamond Press.

Hall, A. 1978. *Sport and Gender: A Feminist Perspective on the Sociology of Sport*. Sociology of Sport Monograph Series. Ottawa: Canadian Association of Health, Physical Education and Recreation.

_____, ed. 1987. 'The Gendering of Sport, Leisure, and Physical Education'. *Women's Studies International Forum* 10.

Hargreaves, J. 1986. 'Where's the Virtue? Where's the Grace? A Discussion of the Social Production of Gender Through Sport'. *Theory, Culture and Society* 3:109–21.

Maguire, J. 1996. 'Blade Runners: Canadian Migrants, Ice Hockey, and the Global Sports Process'. *Journal of Sport and Social Issues* 20:336–61.

Mangan, J., ed. 1996. *Tribal Identities*. London: Frank Cass & Co. Ltd.

Messner, M. 1992. *Power at Play: Sports and the Problem of Masculinity*. Boston: Beacon Press.

_____, and D. Sabo, eds. 1990. *Sport, Men, and the Gender Order: Critical Feminist Perspectives*. Champaign, IL: Human Kinetics.

Pellerin, J. 1971. *Maurice Richard: L'idole d'un peuple*. Montréal: Editions Trustar.

Pronger, B. 1989. *The Arena of Masculinity: Sports, Masculinity, and the Meaning of Sex*. Toronto: University of Toronto Press.

_____. 1991. 'Gay Jocks: A Phenomenology of Gay Men in Athletics'. In *Sport, Men, and the Gender Order: Critical Feminist Perspectives*, edited by M. Messner and D. Sabo, 141–52. Champaign, IL: Human Kinetics.

Raphaël, R. 1988. *The Men From the Boys: Rites of Passage in Male America*. Lincoln: University of Nebraska Press.

Rutherford, P. 1990. *When Television Was Young: Prime-Time Canada 1952–1967*. Toronto: University of Toronto Press.

Schwartzwald, R. 1991a. '(Homo)sexualité et problématique identitaire'. In *Fictions de l'identitaire au Québec*, edited by S. Simon, P. L'Hérault, R. Schwartzwald, and A. Nouss, 115–50. Montréal: XYZ Éditeur.

_____. 1991b. 'Fear of Federasty: Québec's Inverted Fictions'. In *Comparative American Identities: Race, Sex and Nationality in the Modern Text*, edited by H. Spillers, 175–95. New York: Routledge.

Sedgewick, E. 1985. *Between Men: English Literature and Male Homosocial Desire*. New York: Columbia University Press.

Vallières, P. 1971. *Nègres blancs d'Amérique*. Montréal: Editions Parti-Pris.

Afterword

In compiling this anthology, our objective was to demonstrate how sport plays an important role in the reproduction and transformation of social structures and social processes. While the various chapters demonstrate how relations of dominance and subordination tend to privilege men rather than women and straights rather than gays, they also underscore how the relationship between sport and gender is often complex, even paradoxical. For example, we see that although the world of sport is continually changing and subject to struggle, the balance of power continues to favour men and heterosexuals and marginalize women and gays. We also see, though, that the sports world is more equitable that it was only twenty years ago because women as well as some men (such as gay men and men of colour) have enjoyed limited success in their struggles to achieve greater parity. Many young women growing up in Canada face fewer barriers to sport involvement compared to their predecessors. The numbers of young women who have taken up rugby, soccer, rowing, ice hockey, and other sports in recent years would have been inconceivable not long ago. In testing the boundaries of what was previously considered 'inappropriate' sport for females, girls and women now explore new and empowering avenues of sporting experiences. However, such developments have not progressed in seamless, unhindered, and linear ways, and we are not advocating complacency. Typically, as many of the chapters attest, progress towards greater equity is invariably met with resistance. Much of women's sport involvement remains inhibited, marginalized, and subject to ridicule. This is also true of gays in sport.

As noted in the Preface, we were interested as editors to assemble a book that would be a unified whole. Fortunately, we were aided in this task by the contributors whose work predominantly focused on distributive research and relational issues. Although the chapters encompass a range of interdisciplinary approaches, the overarching organizing principle running through this collection—that gender is a central way in which sport is stratified—is illustrated in all kinds of relevant and illuminating ways. The chapters consistently emphasize that sport and gender relations can only be explored satisfactorily by placing the ideas of power and the social construction of meaning at the centre of the analysis. Power relations are pivotal to many of the chapters and help explain how subordinated groups in Canadian society are disadvantaged relative to dominant groups when it comes to participation in sport and physical activity. As the findings in the chapters on contemporary Canadian research show, gendered sporting practices are historically produced and reproduced over time in ways that tend to represent the interests of powerful groups in society—resulting in shifting patterns of inequality both between and within males and females.

Beyond the general overarching principle employed throughout the book, some other themes are also addressed. First, the articles point to the ways in which the relationship between sport and gender in Canada interfaces with other social factors such as sexuality, social class, race, age, disability, and heritage. As we suggested at the outset, the experiences of young, White, heterosexual, non-disabled sport participants are not the experiences of Canadians as a whole. By acknowledging diversity and purposely looking at sport and gender issues in terms of the lives of different types of Canadians, this book goes some way towards highlighting the range and complexities of sport in Canada. For example, the multiplicities of gender identities in sport in Canada lead to struggles over meanings attached to sport itself. Going back to our overarching principle, by looking at sport and gender in different contexts we are also able to document the diversity of relations of domination and subordination in Canada. Since Canadian society, just like other industrial societies, is stratified along a number of such dimensions, to examine gender alone would be to oversimplify the issue.

It is also evident from many of the chapters that masculinity and femininity are not singular concepts. When gender is conceptualized as involving a range of masculinities and femininities, the relationships between both sport and gender and sport and sexuality become clearer. As many of the contributions show, sport experiences in Canada are affected by power differences between men and men, and between women and women, as well as between women and men. At any given time or in different circumstances, some men and women may have power and influence over other men and women, which has consequences for how sport is organized, funded, and experienced. Consequently, this more multilayered approach to understanding gender uproots the myth that all men are more privileged in sport than all women, replacing it with the more accurate view that some groups of both women and men enjoy, more so than others, what Connell (1995:79) calls the 'dividends' of dominant gender relations.

In brief, the collection of readings shows that one is better able to investigate unequal gender relations and the oppression of women (and some men) if one understands the working of gender-related power and privilege. While gender is a complex and heterogeneous phenomenon replete with contradictions and paradoxes, and while there is a need to be sensitive to diversity among women and men, gender itself remains central to the construction of sport—and vice versa.

As a whole, we think that this book is helpful because it provides for the first time a medium for showcasing the breadth of Canadian scholarship on sport and gender. Although in many ways this book is only a beginning given the relative youth of the research area as a whole, this work takes a significant step forward by consistently focusing on *explaining* as well as *describing* how gender is 'played out' in sport. By emphasizing distributive and relational perspectives, the collection points to the potential of human agency for achieving progressive change in sport. Over and over, the contributors identify and illuminate the processes through which gender relations in sport are both reproduced and transformed.

We hope that this anthology will stimulate further research both by identifying the strengths of current scholarship as well as by the limitations of this anthology itself. With respect to limitations, a number of issues were not addressed here that are of profound importance. For example, since participation in sport and physical activity in the Canadian population remains quite low, which is clearly of concern to those who want to increase activity levels for the purposes of improving the health of the population, an obvious area of concern should be to research how gender affects experiences with sport and physical activity in the educational system and with children. Another area of future research attention might be to better recognize the multicultural nature of Canadian society and to study the sport experiences of different groups defined by race, ethnicity, and heritage in light of gender. Little is currently known about these types of relationships and interaction effects.

In sum, *Sport and Gender in Canada* represents both a step forward but also a reminder that we are only just beginning to scratch the surface of how sporting life is gendered. We look forward to the future growth of knowledge in this area, to the arrival on the scene of new scholars and new research, and the reactions of our students for whom this book has been assembled. We hope readers will find the book an accessible, enjoyable, and stimulating introduction to the complex and fascinating interaction between sport and gender in society.

Reference

Connell, R. 1995. *Masculinities*. Los Angeles: University of California Press.

Index